Matthew T. Dickerson, MA

ID0998593

MARRIAGE COUNSELING

A Christian Approach to Counseling Couples

Everett L. Worthington, Jr.

INTERVARSITY PRESS
DOWNERS GROVE, ILLINOIS 60515

© 1989 by Everett L. Worthington, Jr.

All rights reserved. No part of this book may be reproduced in any form without written permission from InterVarsity Press, P.O. Box 1400, Downers Grove, IL 60515.

InterVarsity Press is the book-publishing division of InterVarsity Christian Fellowship, a student movement active on campus at hundreds of universities, colleges and schools of nursing. For information about local and regional activities, write Public Relations Dept., InterVarsity Christian Fellowship, 6400 Schroeder Rd., P.O. Box 7895, Madison, WI 53707-7895.

Distributed in Canada through InterVarsity Press, 860 Denison St., Unit 3, Markham, Ontario L3R 4H1, Canada.

Unless otherwise noted, the Scripture quotations contained herein are from the Revised Standard Version of the Bible, copyrighted 1946, 1952, 1971 by the Division of Christian Education of the National Council of the Churches of Christ in the U.S.A. and are used by permission. All rights reserved. Verses marked TLB are taken from The Living Bible, copyright 1971 by Tyndale House Publishers, Wheaton, Ill. Used by permission.

Cover illustration: Roberta Polfus

ISBN 0-8308-1259-8

Printed in the United States of America ∞

Library of Congress Cataloging-in-Publication Data

Worthington, Everett L., 1946-
   Marriage counseling/by Everett L. Worthington, Jr.
      p.   cm.
   Bibliography: p.
   Includes index.
   ISBN 0-8308-1259-8
   1. Marriage counseling.   2. Pastoral counseling.   3. Marriage—
Religious aspects—Christianity.   I. Title.
BV4012.27.W67   1988
253.5—dc19
                                                        89-1697
                                                        CIP

| 18 | 17 | 16 | 15 | 14 | 13 | 12 | 11 | 10 | 9 | 8 | 7 | 6 | 5 | 4 | 3 | 2 | 1 |
| 99 | 98 | 97 | 96 | 95 | 94 | 93 | 92 | 91 | 90 | 89 | | | | | | | |

To: Christen, Jonathan, Becca and Katy Anna, our children, a special fruit of our marriage

"Children are a gift from God; they are his reward." Psalm 127:3 (LB)

List of Figures

List of Tables

Preface

I began counseling married couples in 1976, armed with two years' experience at individual counseling, substantial experience counseling small groups, and good intentions. This was fortified by experiences with my own marriage and with counseling fellow Christians whose marriages were in trouble. Absent was any systematic theoretical understanding of why marriages did or didn't work and of how to help couples effectively.

Although I met with couples conjointly, I applied techniques of individual counseling, working first with one spouse and then another— thinking I was "modeling" how to communicate well. I assumed one spouse would see my communication with his or her mate and would learn to communicate better. Then, because I knew intuitively that couples must communicate with each other, I would gesture for the couple to talk to each other. I believed that communication must improve if the marriage were to flourish. My vague communication theory sometimes worked.

I now sometimes think that it worked in spite of me rather than because of me. I refused to acknowledge that it only worked about one-third of the time. Many couples either did not return after a few sessions or simply did not change. The more gracious couples assured me of my help, but those times were too infrequent.

Being a Christian, I was convinced that marriage is vitally important. Committed to counseling couples, I decided to learn to do it competently.

I began a study group among psychology graduate students at Virginia Commonwealth University. We scoured the journals for research on marriage counseling and discussed articles each week. We then began to counsel couples and have group discussions of the counseling. Meanwhile, I began supervising counselors in marriage counseling—at first, in conjunction with a trained marriage and family therapist. I taught a course to graduate students on "Theory and Research in Family and Marriage Counseling." The following year, the course became "Theory and Practice of Family and Marriage Counseling," and the third year (and thereafter) it became "Marriage Counseling and Therapy: Theory, Practice and Research." I read the major theories of marriage and family therapy, studied research on marriage counseling each year, and began a vigorous research program in marriage dynamics, enrichment and therapy, which continues to date.

Gradually, I have refined my thinking, drawing techniques and rationales from major theorists and researchers. I explored them with over 200 couples I have either counseled in my private practice or seen through the graduate students and community professionals that I supervise. I have tested many of these ideas with over 600 couples in numerous research projects that I and my students have conducted.

I have been most influenced by numerous behavioral marriage therapists (Jacobson, Margolin, Stuart, Liberman, Patterson, Gottman, Alexander and others) and family systems theorists (Haley, Madanes, Minuchin and Guerin). With these primary influences, my eclecticism is clearly tilted toward a problem-solving, direct and straightforward brand of marriage therapy. My understanding of marriage has been most influenced by McCubbin and Olson, and my cognitive-behavioral view of individuals was influenced most by Meichenbaum. Each of these professionals would recognize some of their ideas in this book, and I acknowledge their inspiration and help. I hope that I have blended theories, techniques and research in a way that has professional integrity and is consistent with Scripture.

My goal is to articulate a *practical* theory for professionals working with couples who are not antagonistic to Christian principles. My approach was developed for counselors and therapists working with both marriage partners conjointly. It could be adapted for cotherapy (two counselors); however, I recommend a single counselor simply because it is less expensive (in terms of professional time and money for clients) and because I, like most therapists, generally practice alone.

Usually I see the couple jointly, though the practicalities of counseling make this an ideal rather than a rule. When I see spouses individually, I usually try to see the couple together for ten minutes, the partners apart for twenty minutes each, and the couple together for ten minutes to wrap up the session.

This book is intended to benefit the professional helper—psychiatrist, psychologist, minister, social worker or counselor—who may counsel couples over a number of sessions. I hope the book will be used: (a) in seminaries for either pastors returning for graduate work in counseling or in seminary courses on counseling; (b) in graduate schools of psychology, social work, or counseling as one of several approaches to marital counseling or therapy; and (c) as a resource for practicing pastors, pastoral counselors and mental health professionals.

The benefits that professionals derive from the book should extend to their clients and ultimately to strengthening Jesus Christ's church. Most of the book will interest married people within the church, who are interested in understanding their own marriage and how some counselors might do marriage counseling, but they might find some parts tedious (such as the summaries of various theories of counseling found in the appendix). Overall, I want to strengthen the church and the marriages of the saints. To Jesus be the glory.

Acknowledgments

I am indebted to many people for their help and support with this book. I am deeply blessed to have so many good friends.

My parents have been good models of commitment to each other. They have been devoted to and supportive of each other and their three children through many trying times.

My wife's parents also showed me that a couple could richly enjoy each other during years of joyful marriage—even with a large family.

Kirby, my wife, taught me to communicate. When we married, I would pout and "guilt-make" if I didn't get my way. Kirby did not allow me to manipulate, regardless of how cunningly I tried. She talked to me and encouraged me to talk. Although I was a stubborn case, some of her good communication skills took hold. (Unfortunately I still have my moments.) Like the little prince in Antoine de Saint Exupery's fable, she refused to let go of a topic that concerned us until we had it resolved. She's my "little princess."

Since we have been married, our pastors have often talked about marriage and I have learned much from them about what Scripture says about marriage. My thanks to Tom Allport, Jerry Rouse, Buzz Kell and Doug McMurry for opening up the Scriptures to me and for sharing God's wisdom.

Special thanks are due my colleagues at Virginia Commonwealth University (VCU). Stan Strong challenged me and provided the impetus I needed to make a full commitment to the study of marriage and family counseling. John Hill, then chairman of the department of psychology, supported my change. Sandy Olson and Terrie Buczek influenced my thinking through their research in adult development and family counseling. Steve Robbins broadened my horizons by introducing me to ego psychology. Ed Thomas has provided a professional role model of an ethical and compassionate gentleman. Tom McGovern has provided emotional support and encouragement throughout my ten years at VCU. Finally, Bob Tipton has been a research colleague, a supportive boss and a steady friend. Besides providing intellectual stimulation, these colleagues have created a supportive atmosphere for research and productivity.

Students in our psychology program at VCU have also pushed my thinking along by their help and encouragement during our research together on marriage and marriage counseling. Those who have worked in that area with me include Mike Hammonds, Beverley Buston, Don Danser, Cindy Clark, Lynn Marlow, Bob Whitney, Kathy Kozma, Barbara Hawes, Walter Heizenroth, Philip Dupont, Brenda Hawks, Sarah Beck, Sandra Nutall, Matt McTaggart, Glenn Gould, Carol Richman, Dave Morrow, Melinda Queen, Helen DeVries, James T. (Dale) Berry and Cheryl Colecchi.

Lastly, my effort has been continued because I have been surrounded by numerous encouragers. They take an interest in me and give me a reason to write. Chief encourager is Kirby, who is always faithful. Kirby's mother, Rena, and her siblings, Sandi and Wayne, give up part of their house each year to allow me to punish the typewriter. Members of Christ Presbyterian Church are my close brothers and sisters, and I love them. Fred DiBlasio has been a friend and collaborator. Andy Le Peau of Inter-Varsity Press has continually encouraged me to write. He even found something nice to say about a piece of fiction that I once wrote.

"He who finds a wife finds a good thing, and obtains favor from the LORD. . . . There are friends who pretend to be friends, but there is a friend who sticks closer than a brother" (Prov 18:22, 24). I am blessed by God with a good wife and a multitude of friends.

Part **1**

Introduction

1/The Need for Marriage Counseling
by and for Christians

SUMMARY The stage is set for counseling with married Christians. In chapter one, the need for marriage counseling is documented, especially among Christians who value the stability of the marriage relationship. Six needs for a Christian theory of marriage counseling are described briefly, and reflections are offered about what Christian theories are and how the present theory is Christian.

The Need
for Marriage Counseling
by and for Christians

MARRIAGES ARE IN TROUBLE TODAY. CHERLIN FOUND THAT DI-
vorce rates have risen alarmingly over the last 100 years.[1] By
1980, the divorce rate was over fifty per cent: Over one of
every two couples married in 1980 will ultimately divorce! Of
course, such growth rates cannot continue indefinitely. Nonetheless, marriage as a long-term relationship is in trouble.

Most people remarry after divorce—over eighty per cent remarry within
five years of divorce, according to recent statistics.[2] Surprisingly, the divorce
rate in second and subsequent marriages is even greater than in first marriages—over sixty-five per cent.[3] Apparently, the institution of marriage is
not as endangered as some people claim; however, the permanence of
individual marriages is in peril.

People have become wary about marrying. Unmarried heterosexual cohabitation prior to first marriages has risen dramatically over the past fif-

teen years.[4] Cohabitation after divorce or widowhood has also substantially increased.[5] Many who cohabit say they are investigating the stability of a relationship before making a commitment to marriage. Yet even when the "incompatible" couples who cohabit and decide not to marry are removed from consideration, couples who cohabit prior to marriage have equal or higher divorce rates than couples who do not.[6]

Although professing Christians have markedly lower rates of divorce than those not professing Christianity, Christians are not immune to this *crisis in commitment* to marriage sweeping through contemporary society. Even committed Christians end up in divorce courts.

Scripture is clear about divorce. God hates it (Mal 2:16), even though it is permissible under certain circumstances (e.g., Ezra 10:44; Mt 19:9).[7] This creates pressure on couples who treat Scripture authoritatively to seek all avenues to preserve their marriages.

Many such Christian couples seek counseling[8] from both Christian and non-Christian professionals. Over half of the cases seen by clinical psychologists in private practice involve marital difficulties.[9] Arnold and Schick found ten of eleven studies to show that the most frequent counseling done by pastors involves marriage counseling.[10]

Are these Christian helping professionals trained in marriage counseling? Not very many and not very well. Most expertise at marriage counseling has been acquired "under fire." Many assumptions and techniques used by Christians in their counseling office are often incompatible with their clients' and sometimes even their own values. Despite this, marriage counseling is surprisingly effective—more so than many individual psychotherapies.[11] But one must ask, Could counselors be even better with training and with an explicitly Christian-based theory guiding their practice? I believe they could.

Having a theory makes counseling or therapy more efficient by directing the therapist rapidly to areas that are potentially important. It also helps the counselor understand how marriages go wrong, which leads to suggestions for setting them right again. A theory also defines the role of the counselor in helping those seeking help. This book provides a practical model for understanding and counseling Christian couples whose marriages are troubled.

REASONS A THEORY IS NEEDED IN COUNSELING MARRIED CHRISTIAN COUPLES

I have reviewed existing theories of marriage therapy (as distinct from family therapy) in appendix A of this book, including *psychoanalytic marital therapies* (Nadelson, Dare, Willi, Paul), *systems theories of marital therapy* (such as Bowen, Mental Research Institute, Minuchin, and Haley and Madanes), *behavioral marriage therapies* (such as Jacobson and Margolin, Stuart, Liberman) *cognitive theories of marital therapy* (Sager, Epstein, Baucom and Lester) and a *Christian-cognitive-behavioral* theory of Norman Wright. Six conclusions may be drawn concerning theorizing about Christian marriages and marriage counseling with Christian couples.

1. *There is a need for an integrated theory of the marriage* that considers three levels of analysis: (a) individual constructs; (b) the operation of the marriage as a unit (or system); and (c) the position of the married couple in the family cycle. The theory should be conceptually integrated, not just constructed by borrowing concepts from theories that consider each level of analysis.

2. *There is a need for an integrated theory of marital therapy that is based on that theory of the marriage.* The theory should use concepts based on changing (a) individual constructs and (b) operating principles of the marriage, and considering (c) the position of the couple within the family life cycle.

3. *The theories of marriage and of therapy should incorporate distinctly Christian concepts.* The spiritual nature of the individual and of the marriage should be woven into the theory rather than merely applying concepts from secular marriage theory to people who happen to be Christians.

4. *The theory of marriage therapy should be simple enough to be used clinically.* Haley has pointed out that clinicians need simple, powerful theories to guide their interventions and produce powerful changes; whereas, researchers need complicated, complex theories that account for much of the variance in human behavior.[12] Thus, as a secondary goal:

5. *The theoretical underpinnings of the theory of the marriage should be rich and complex enough to stimulate research* (so that the theory of marriage therapy can ultimately be improved).

6. *The techniques should* have at least four characteristics:

a. They should *be related to the theory*.

b. They should *be prescribed and standardized* to such an extent that they are easily usable.

c. They should *be varied and individualized* to be able to help a variety of couples.

d. They should *be clearly applicable* at specified points in the therapy.

The theory of marriage and marriage counseling that I present in this book attempts to fill these needs. Undoubtedly it will fail at points, for there is no perfect theory. Any theory that attempts to integrate theoretical concepts, therapy techniques and research from a variety of theoretical perspectives must be broadly eclectic. I think the strength of this book is the clear explication of many techniques for use by the practicing marriage therapist and the organization of those techniques as they apply to (a) intimacy; (b) communication; (c) conflict; (d) hurt, blame and sin; and (e) commitment. I hope that after reading this book, you will emerge with new interventions to try with troubled marriages. On the other hand, I hope that I am not encouraging indiscriminate eclecticism. We should have reasons for our choice of techniques.

Since I have performed, supervised and taught psychotherapy and marriage therapy, I have noticed that therapists of widely different theoretical persuasions often use the same techniques of therapy. Yet, they do so for different reasons, hoping to accomplish different objectives and hoping clients will learn different things from their interventions. Thus, in a way, techniques are somewhat artificially identified with particular approaches to the therapy. Often it is what the therapist does after the technique has been used, and not what occurs while the technique is being used, that has the most impact on the clients.

The explanation of the technique and the way techniques coalesce into a coherent treatment package is more important than applying a technique "letter perfectly." For this reason, I believe that even if I do not fully explain why I might use every technique, the informed counselor might still learn from and even adapt the technique to his or her purpose. Nonetheless, I hope my theoretical framework and my decision rules about when to use various techniques and what should be derived from their use will permit you to understand my selection of techniques.

WHO CAN USE THIS THEORY OF MARRIAGE COUNSELING?

Having been developed during my private practice of counseling psychology, this theory can be used in most general practices of marriage counseling or marriage therapy. However, therapists who will be most attracted to the theory are those who are generally attracted to other direct problem-solving marital therapies such as cognitive-behavioral or strategic problem-solving therapies (for instance, Haley). Therapists inclined to highly value insight into unconscious motives or understanding the intricacies of inter-generational or childhood effects on the marriage will generally find the theory too limiting.

There are two ways that marriage therapy is usually practiced. In one instance, the couple attends counseling with the sole objective of improving their marriage relationship. That does not mean that counseling will be easy. Some marriage problems are relatively "pure," with no diagnosable individual psychopathology even though both spouses may be depressed, anxious, frustrated or angry because of their marital disturbance. In such "pure" marital therapy, the counselor may use the theory I present in this book.

Besides direct marriage therapy, this theory is useful when at least one spouse has serious psychological disturbance and there is serious marital involvement in the problem. Perhaps the wife is depressed and has been for several months. Her depression was precipitated by the discovery of an ongoing affair between her husband and a neighbor. Although the depression now might have other aspects, the marriage relationship is a continuing contributor to maintaining her depression. In this case, the therapist might decide to treat the wife by marital therapy. Individual therapy might be appropriate too, but marital therapy is certainly a viable treatment option. Whether it is the treatment of choice will depend on the beliefs of the therapists and of the couple, who may want marriage therapy (and not individual therapy) despite the presence of individual pathology. Whether the therapist will be able to convince the husband to attend therapy and will be able to help the couple by using marriage therapy is yet another matter.

Direct marriage counseling is done mostly by pastors and people working in church-based settings or where insurance payments are not involved. Couples are freer to request direct marriage counseling when insurance companies are not involved. Marriage therapy as a treatment for individual distress is used often by psychotherapists, especially when dealing with insurance companies that will not pay for direct marriage counseling but will pay for individual psychotherapy through marital therapy.

I have done marriage therapy successfully (and unfortunately unsuccessfully at times) with couples who have both types of presenting concerns. Once the marriage is implicated and treatment of the marriage becomes one goal of therapy, marriage counseling can proceed as I have outlined in the following pages.

WHAT IS A CHRISTIAN THEORY OF MARRIAGE COUNSELING?

Throughout this book, many readers will find that my theory is "not Christian enough." Others will criticize the theory because it is "too Christian." Each person has assumptions about what a Christian theory of counseling should be. In a review of research on religious counseling,[13] I identified three ideas about what religious therapy involves.

In one approach, the goal of the therapist is to create a "Christian" client (or "Christian" marriage). The therapist believes that Christianity is not a matter of technique but of the heart and of human relationships. Thus, reasons such a therapist, it is unnecessary to use specific Christian techniques in therapy. Some even believe it unnecessary to use secular therapeutic techniques. The therapist believes that Christianity is more "caught" from a loving, caring Christian than it is taught. A Christian therapist who practices this type of Christian therapy might never mention Jesus, God or the Holy Spirit and talk might never turn explicitly to religious matters throughout counseling. Nonetheless, the therapist thinks that he or she is doing Christian therapy. If the client's life changes to embody Christian principles of living, the therapist concludes that he or she has successfully done Christian therapy. If not, the Christian therapy may be seen as unsuccessful.

In a second approach to Christian therapy, the counselor believes that all therapy must have direct scriptural justification or at the least be rooted in practices of spiritual guidance techniques (such as prayer, confession, Bible memory and others) that have been used within the church for ages. Such therapists might criticize the first type of therapist as being thoroughly secular. (Of course, the first type of therapist might criticize the second type also.) Therapists who rely on spiritual guidance techniques usually exclude techniques derived from secular theories of therapy because they did not originate in the Bible or the church.

At a third extreme, some therapists use methods developed by secular theories of counseling but deal directly with the spiritual thoughts, behaviors and lifestyles of their clients. These counselors might use any number of spiritual guidance techniques in their counseling, but their theories of influence are generally based on secular theories of therapy coupled with a belief in divine intervention at the level of the unseen world. If therapy may be divided into the *process* of therapy versus the *content* of therapy, then the third type of therapist uses secular counseling processes but Christian content.

My approach to therapy lies somewhere between the second and third approaches. I draw from many secular theories of marriage counseling and therapy but try to integrate them into a Christian framework. I believe my theorizing is consistent with Scripture even though it is not derived directly from it. As you read my descriptions, you might think them quite secular in places. However, when you read the examples and the transcripts that I have included, you will see how I deal with the Christianity of my clients. I usually use some spiritual guidance techniques in therapy—such as explicit prayer, confession, forgiveness, scriptural exegesis and citation of scriptural references and quotations to explain principles to my clients. Much of this book involves the process of marriage counseling; therefore, much of the book will not deal explicitly with Christianity. Nonetheless, I hope the book is an example of Christian helping. In *When Someone Asks for Help,*[14] I describe four distinctives of Christian counseling:

1. It should be *done by a Christian.*

2. It should be *consistent with Christian assumptions,* such as the fundamental truths of Christianity described by apologists like C. S. Lewis.[15]

3. It should be *consistent with God's revelations*—both his special revelations

(Jesus and the Bible) and his general revelations (the created world and the imageness of God within people).

4. It should *have Christ at the center*. This last requirement means that counseling should be grounded in prayer and in the explicit identification of Jesus as the healer of individuals and the restorer of relationships.

Throughout the book, I strive to make counseling a good example of Christian helping. My hope and prayer is that the book will help you become a better Christian marriage therapist who can work more confidently and competently with the Christian couples who seek your help.

Part **2**

Understanding Marriage

2/Individuals and Their Coupling
3/Principles of Marriage within the Family
4/The Marriage throughout the Family Life Cycle

SUMMARY In part two, a model for the marriage is presented. It is necessary to describe marriage on three levels: the individual spouses, their behaviors as a couple and how couples change throughout their life together.

In chapter two, a cognitive-behavioral-spiritual model of individual behavior is introduced and applied to the decision to marry. The model assumes the need for meaning to be the most fundamental human need, with meaning being found through *intimate relationships* and through *behavior that produces changes in the world* (such as work or control over the environment, called effectance). People also need forgiveness and commitment.

In chapter three, marriage is examined in terms of principles for married life involving intimacy, effectance, communication, forgiveness and commitment.

In chapter four, what happens to a marriage across the family life cycle is presented. Throughout part two, ideas for counseling are advanced. Needs for intimacy and effectance transmute into separateness and conflict for troubled couples. Their behavior patterns become rigid over time. These patterns depend on the stage of the life cycle of the married couple, because couples in each stage tend to have different problems and needs. This description of marriage prepares the counselor to assess couples and intervene to produce changes in intimacy; effectance (notably patterns of communication and conflict); hurt, blame and sin; and commitment—which will be described in parts three, four and five of the book.

2

Individuals and Their Coupling

MARRIAGES ARE COMPOSED OF INDIVIDUALS WITH UNIQUE NEEDS, thoughts and behaviors. When individuals marry, the relationship often becomes different than might be expected from knowing the individuals. Yet treatment of a marriage cannot be complete apart from considering the individuals.

This chapter develops a model for understanding individuals and what happens when they marry. It describes their needs and motivations, especially within marriage. In subsequent chapters, which describe marriage counseling, we will draw repeatedly on these ideas.

THE INDIVIDUAL

We are a needy people. We need God at the center of our lives, though   **Basic Needs** some people do not yet know this. God created us with a fundamental yearning for permanent, intimate and productive fellowship with him, and our natures reflect this need.

We experience a direct yearning for God, knowing that there must be more to life than daily existence. We desire the beautiful, the sublime, the subjective feelings of transcendence of the mundane and of time.[1] Created for love and eternal fellowship with God, we want to do something with our lives, something lasting, something eternal, while on earth. We often act on earth consistently with how God created us to act forever.[2]

We experience an indirect need for God, too. Because God created us with his nature stamped upon us (that is to say, "in his image"), we strive to fulfill yearnings for permanence, intimacy and productivity in our relationships with other people. Through intimacy and work we achieve a sense of meaning that reaches its completeness in our eternal relationship with God through Jesus Christ.[3]

Unfortunately, since the fall of Adam and Eve, people have failed to live up to the image of God within them. It is not through lack of knowledge about what we should do but is through willful perversion of our God-given needs for permanence, intimacy and productivity that we fall short of what God intended for us. We substitute immediate selfishness for permanence, we opt for cheap sexual relationships and illicit romance rather than for fulfilling sexual and emotional intimacy, and we desire power and influence rather than productivity. These substitutions constitute sin in our lives and lead to hurt, blame and estrangement from God and from people. We need God's forgiveness for willingly turning our backs on his design for fruitful living, and we need the forgiveness of others—especially the others with whom we live closely—for exercising our selfishness, lack of intimacy and power at their expense.

As with other needs, God fills our needs for forgiveness and heals hurt and blame when we turn to him rather than away from him. Yet, we also need forgiveness from others, and we need to forgive others who have hurt us and whom we blame. God is gracious. He can help us forgive, by following his example and his initiative.

We were created to be in committed relationships, first with God, then with a spouse and finally with a covenant people. We meet the needs of others and have our own needs met in committed relationships through communication. We also pervert our needs through communication. Consequently, communication is the fundamental tool with which we accomplish the purposes of God in our lives and through which our commitments often falter.

Throughout this book, the basic needs of humans within loving relationships are the focus: the need for intimacy, for seeing we can produce effects (effectance), for commitment and for forgiveness when we fail. Through understanding these needs, their perversions and the ways they are made manifest through communication, we know what to assess and treat in troubled marriages and in the troubled individuals within the marriages.

People are complex creatures who try to meet their needs and who have their needs met through their spirits, cognitions (thoughts and imaginations) and behaviors both alone and in the presence of others.[4] Because people are whole, their "parts" are merely explanatory tools. Behaviors do not exist apart from cognitions or spirits. Behaviors do not exist in a vacuum but occur in social or physical contexts and can only be fully understood within their context.

A Model of the Person

A model of the person, then, is obviously a simplification that helps a person understand behavior in order to accomplish a specific purpose. For example, if we are trying to understand humans for the purpose of evangelizing, we might use a model of the person that considers the person's body, soul and spirit. If we want to treat physical disease, we might create a physical, physiological or anatomical model of the person. If we are trying to explain memory, we might describe a model that talked of a person's sensory store, short-term memory and long-term memory.

As a marriage counselor, we want to use a model of the person that explains how he or she develops distressing marital problems and how we can help solve them. I have found it most useful to focus on the spirit, cognitions, environment and behavior of the individual and the spouses within a marriage relationship.

A spiritual, cognitive, environmental and behavioral model of the individual is shown in Figure 1. Behavior arises from cognitive events, which are momentary thoughts and images that enter consciousness. They may be slowly pondered or thought so quickly that they are unnoticed. Cognitive events are influenced by the spiritual world (that is to say, by God, Jesus, the Holy Spirit or even Satan "talking" to us), by environmental events or structures or by cognitive structures. Intervention by God, Jesus or the Holy Spirit into a person's thoughts has scriptural precedent (Num 7:89; Deut 4:12; 8:20; 1 Kings 19:12; Ps 29:3-9; 81:5b-11; Jn 8:47; 10:3-4, 16). So does intervention by Satan (Mt 4:3; Jn 8:38, 44; 10:5; 1 Cor 7:5) into the thought life. Although such phenomena are ignored by secular theorists, the presence of a supernatural world and the intercourse between the natural and supernatural worlds are the distinctives that have set Judeo-Christianity apart from naturalistic philosophy for centuries.

Environmental events are momentary occurrences that people perceive. The event can be an interpersonal interaction, either observed or participated in, or an impersonal occurrence, such as a fire.

Environmental structures are enduring parts of the physical environment. One type of environmental structure is the physical make-up of our home, work place and places of usual recreation, involving physical surroundings and people. For example, if we work with five co-workers, they are part of the environmental structure in our lives. Importantly, environmental structures also include repeated interpersonal interactions.

Cognitive structures endure and can be (to some extent) called into conscious awareness by thinking about them. For example, if I ask you to describe your personality, you draw upon a self-concept that was not in your conscious awareness until you thought about it. Cognitive structures are not arranged willy-nilly; they are organized. They involve (a) our view of the world *(Weltanshauung)*, which contains our fundamental assumptions about life; (b) values, which describe the relative importance we place on portions of our *Weltanshauung;* (c) expectations; (d) plans for living; (e) cultural and subcultural norms; (f) attention-focusing styles; (g) perceptual styles; (h) cognitive processes; and (i) our memories. Cognitive structures may be moved into consciousness by using any of three triggers: another thought, an environmental event or communication from a spiritual source.

Once behavior occurs, it is followed by consequences or outcomes, which are simultaneously environmental events when they are observable.

Figure 1
A Spiritual, Cognitive and Behavioral Model of the Individual

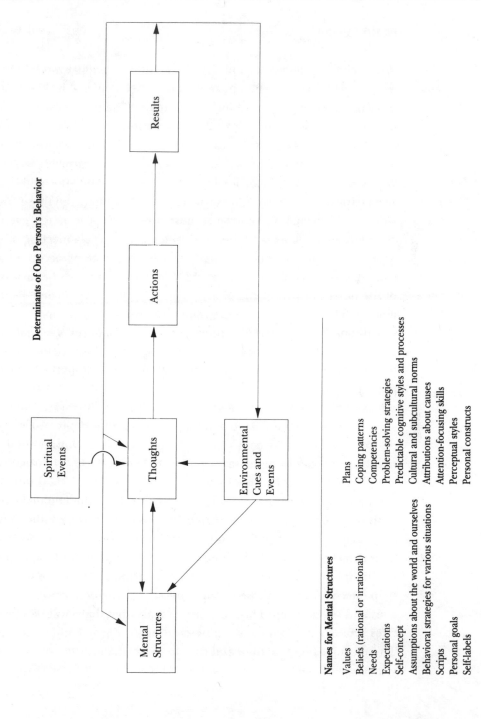

Determinants of One Person's Behavior

Spiritual Events

Thoughts

Actions

Results

Environmental Cues and Events

Mental Structures

Names for Mental Structures

Values
Beliefs (rational or irrational)
Needs
Expectations
Self-concept
Assumptions about the world and ourselves
Behavioral strategies for various situations
Scripts
Personal goals
Self-labels

Plans
Coping patterns
Competencies
Problem-solving strategies
Predictable cognitive styles and processes
Cultural and subcultural norms
Attributions about causes
Attention-focusing skills
Perceptual styles
Personal constructs

COUPLING

Overview   When people marry, they unite. It is as if the individual model described in Figure 1 were fused into a combined model, depicted in Figure 2. Most basically, the two people are united spiritually. Their spirits are inextricably joined before God and with God into a three-fold cord (Eccles 4:9-12), so that their spiritual lives affect each other in ways we cannot understand.

They also bring to marriage numerous cognitive structures: world views, values, expectations, plans for living, and cultural and subcultural norms. Even early in the marriage, spouses share some similarity in these cognitive structures. Throughout marriage, most couples want to reach even more complete agreement about their fundamental beliefs—a meeting of minds.

Finally, as spouses interact, many of their interactions become habitual shared environmental structures and events. Each spouse's behavior is part of the other's environment. Many patterns of behavior become as predictable as the presence of the house upon returning from a trip.

A troubled marriage is disturbed in each area. Spouses' spiritual lives are usually disrupted. Sometimes one spouse becomes closer to the Lord while the other pulls away. Sometimes both may coast away from the Lord. Rather than a meeting of the minds, there is a parting of ways, with bickering, arguing and fighting over whose beliefs and values will govern the relationship. A spouse's natural need to affect the partner becomes an exaggerated desire to dominate or control the partner. Shared environmental events may become openly unpleasant or the couple may cease to interact in fresh ways, leading to a humdrum existence.

One of the marriage counselor's tasks is to help the couple reunite. If positive changes are to be permanent, the *structures* of the couple's life must be changed: both cognitive and environmental structures. (God faithfully maintains the spiritual link, though we can strengthen it.) It is not enough for the therapist to induce momentary behavior changes. He or she must help the couple build those changes into the permanent structures of their lives and relationship. This, of course, means that there will be few "quick fixes" for couples who have longstanding conflictual lifestyles together. These couples require time and care beyond whatever might happen during an emotional and helpful part of therapy.

For a moment, imagine Peter and John approaching the temple for prayer (Acts 3:1-16). It is three o'clock in the afternoon, and a man, over forty, who has been lame from birth, begs for money from them. Instead of giving him money, they give him Jesus, who heals him in one miraculous, spectacular moment. As Peter later said, "And his name, by faith in his name, has made this man strong whom you see and know; and the faith which is through Jesus has given the man this perfect health in the presence of you all" (Acts 3:16). This man was healed and restored to perfect health through Jesus.

But what happened to him when he awoke in perfect health the following morning?

He had been lame since birth and had no skills except begging with which to earn a living. He saw himself as a beggar, dependent on others. He was nonassertive. His friends and family probably did not alter their behavior toward him right away. He *did* have a head start on change: he had a new spirit and his *Weltanshauung* had been drastically, but not totally, revised. He began to associate with Christians more, and they helped change his environmental structures.

In summary, even if God does a miraculous, spectacular and instantaneous work in a relationship, the healing must be solidified into a changed lifestyle. When Jesus heals a troubled couple's marriage, they will need vigilance, perseverance, self-control and the other fruits of the Spirit before they ultimately present their marriage to the Lord as sanctified (Eph 5:25-27). They will also need support in making these systematic changes. In the remainder of this chapter, we examine in more detail the parts of the couple's lives that are affected when they join in marriage: their shared spiritual lives, their meeting of minds, their shared environmental events and their shared environmental structures.

Shared Spiritual Lives

■ *Marriage is a mystery.* God created marriage to help people transcend their egocentrism and to mirror his faithfulness to people. In his wisdom, God makes babies totally unable to care for themselves. They must depend on someone greater and more competent than they are for their lives. Psychologically, babies unite with this greater being (parent). As they grow, their consciousness of self develops as they notice how events have an

Figure 2
The Coupling of Two Individuals in Marriage

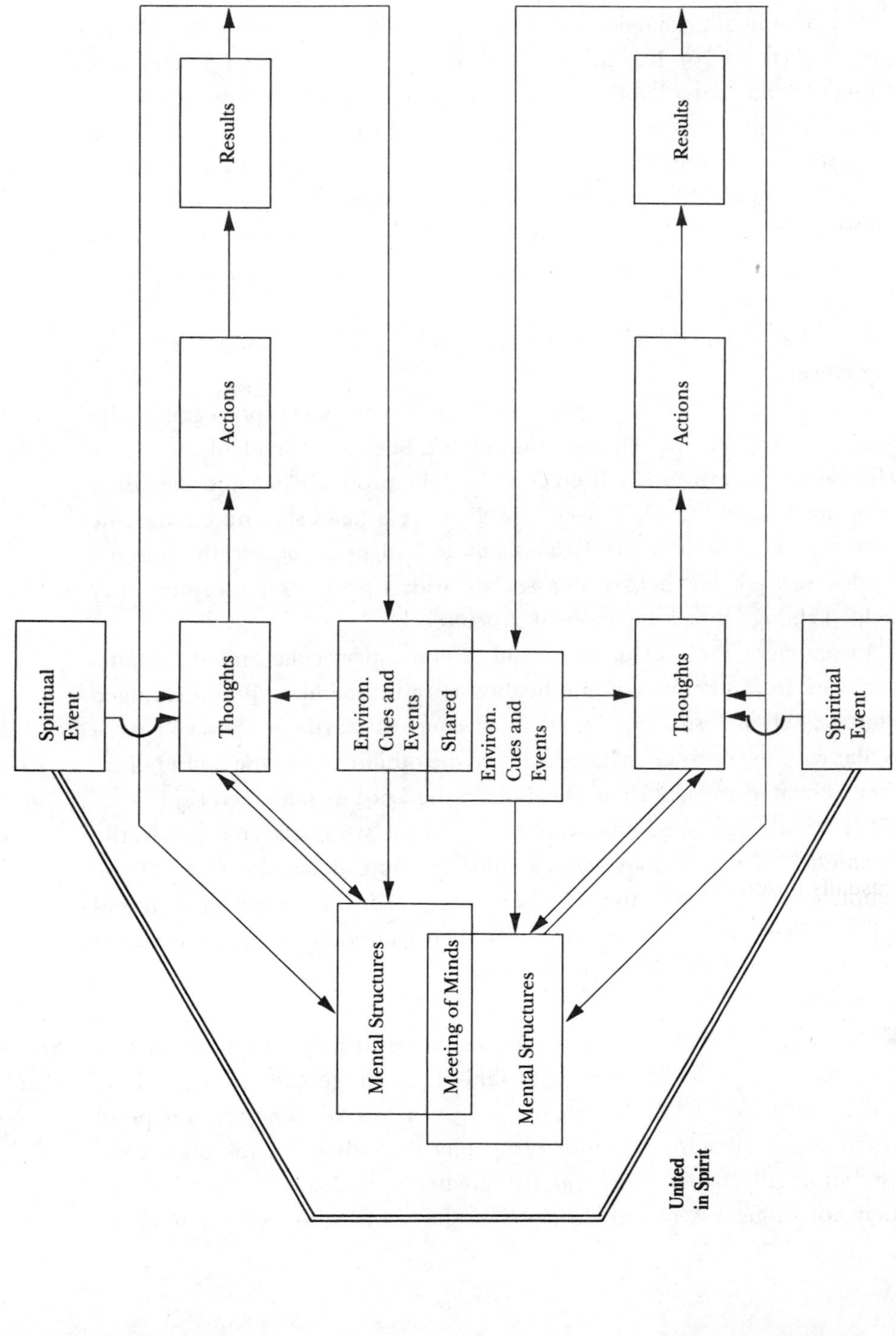

impact on them. From initial dependence on the parent, the child quickly develops a sense that, like his or her consciousness, the whole world is organized to meet his or her individual needs. This is called egocentrism.

For the egocentric person, the perspectives of others are relatively unimportant if they are noticed at all. The adolescent during the early teen years becomes capable of overcoming the egocentrism, but as parents of most adolescents will tell you, the typical adolescent does not always exercise this capability. Life events are evaluated almost exclusively according to their importance to the adolescent. One of the main developmental tasks of adolescence is to establish romantic and other relationships, which help reduce egocentrism as the adolescent learns to care for others. Still, even in early adulthood, the individual is largely egocentric. When people marry, one would suppose that it is a result of having overcome egocentrism and of having been willing to accept another human being as equal and as spouse. Unhappily, this is not often true. People usually marry their own image of their spouse rather than marrying a spouse as an individual who is accurately perceived.[5]

After the first several months of marriage, disillusionment usually sets in, as each partner realizes that the spouse is actually different than the premarriage conceptualization of the spouse. The fundamental task of early marriage is then to learn to transcend one's own egocentric picture of the object of love and transform it into a true object of love.

Developing this capacity to see another human being as he or she really is rather than as we would like for him or her to be is necessary to being able to know God better. Unfortunately, our conceptualization of God is usually based on the idea that he is there as our personal servant. In our minds we know that to be an egocentric and inaccurate picture, but experientially, we live as if that were true. Marriage helps free us from the idea that God is exactly as we would like him to be. Rather, as we see that the reality of our spouse is different than our conceptualization of our spouse, we can come to adjust our conceptualization of God to fit his reality rather than expecting him to change his personality to please us.

By itself, marriage does not work this wonder. In fact, many married people have an egocentric picture of God even after many years of marriage. However, marriage makes it easier for us to accept the occurrences in our lives that fly in the face of our naive understanding of God and emerge from the disillusionments with deep love for God.

God also instituted the mystery of marriage to mirror his faithfulness to people.[6] God will never forsake us. Nor will Jesus (Jn 6:37-39). His commitment is absolute. To weave this truth into the fabric of our lives, he created marriage. Paul speaks of marriage saying, " 'For this reason a man shall leave his father and mother and be joined to his wife, and the two shall become one flesh.' This mystery is a profound one, and I am saying that it refers to Christ and the church; however, let each one of you love his wife as himself, and let the wife see that she respects her husband" (Eph 5:31-32).

Because marriage is the earthly, ritualized way God gave for us to apprehend his eternal commitment to us and our need for commitment to him, marriage should not be expected to last beyond life on earth (see Lk 20:34-35). Believers will have eternal fellowship together, though, as they swap their earthly marriages for the true marriage for which they were created, the marriage with the Lamb (Rev 19).

Because God made marriage important to understanding spiritual truths, he joins people together spiritually when they marry. This joining is permanent, intimate and more powerful than we realize.

■ *Marriage is permanent.* The joining is meant to be permanent and to involve commitment. God's faithfulness is never changing. Jesus (Mt 5:31; 32; Mk 10:2-12; Lk 16:18) and Paul (1 Cor 7:10-11) teach against divorce. Divorce is explicitly forbidden in these passages, with one exception (Mt 19:9; Deut 24:1-4). Of course, people do divorce, though in the eyes of God, it is unclear whether the spiritual bond between spouses is ever broken— even by divorce (Mt 19:9).[7]

Spiritual joining is based on covenant. The relationship between God and Abraham was cemented by a covenant (Gen 15:9-11, 17-18). The relationship between Jesus and his church is based on a covenant (Lk 22:20). The relationship between a husband and wife is also based on a covenant (Mal 2:14).

Before Jesus came, when two people made a covenant, they took a living animal and cut it in half from top to bottom, shedding its blood and symbolizing the death of individual rights of the covenant-makers through the

death of the animal. Then the covenant-makers passed between the two
halves of the animal, symbolizing their union (see Jer 34:18-20). When God
made a covenant with Abraham, he walked between the split animals alone
while Abraham watched, for God and Abraham were not equals.

The traditional marriage ceremony symbolizes the covenant made between man and woman when they unite. Generally, the family of the husband and the family of the wife sit on opposite sides of the church. The
husband and wife walk between the divided body after they have taken
their vows of commitment. The wedding takes place under the auspices of
the church, signifying that Jesus has shed his blood as the sacrificed animal
by which the couple pledge their fidelity. By the marriage ceremony, the
couple agree individually to give up their rights over themselves and to
place the welfare of the spouse as of more importance than their individual
desires. Each declares himself or herself dead to self and alive to the one
flesh that they have pledged to share permanently (see Heb 9:16-17).

Each of these covenants is referred to as a marriage covenant.[8] Throughout Scripture, God is referred to as the husband and Israel as the wife (see
Jer 31:32; Hos 2:16; 3:1). Christ is referred to as the husband and the
church as the wife (Eph 5:25-33). Jesus is referred to as the husband and
the believer as the wife (1 Cor 6:16-17). Covenants are designed to bring
about permanent union—between God and Israel, God and believer, believer and believer and husband and wife.

■ *Marriage is intimate.* The joining is so intimate that it is usually referred
to in Scripture as becoming one flesh (Gen 2:24; Mt 19:5; 1 Cor 6:16; Eph
5:31). This implies that the needs of one partner are linked without differentiation to the needs of the other. What hurts or damages one, affects the
other. What nourishes one, nourishes the other. The two spouses might
perform different functions within the marriage as do heart and head, but
both are part of the same body, the same flesh. Paul argues that this spiritual tie is so strong that a believing spouse can be the vehicle through
which an unbelieving spouse can be consecrated to the Lord (1 Cor 6:16-
17).

The intimacy of marriage, in which spouses are described as being of one
flesh, graphically tells the main purpose of marriage. Marriage is a relationship of separation and union designed to produce growth and fruit.[9] It is

a continual exercise of unity and separateness. Spouses unite sexually and then separate. They experience emotional closeness and then distance. This parallels our relationship with God through Jesus. Although we are to become one with them (Jn 17:22), we are to maintain individual identities. We experience diversity as well as unity. The goal is not total unity as it is within some Eastern religions. This is reflected in marriage, where physical and spiritual unity are meals to be savored when we need food, not orgies of nonstop gluttony.

■ *Marriage is powerful.* The joining is more powerful in its effects than we realize. With two people's spirits joined together, we as counselors cannot afford to underestimate the effects of our marital counseling. We are Jesus' agents, promoting reconciliation between spouses. We strive to promote forgiveness and reconciliation with all our energy, and only with tears do we accept divorce when our clients willingly and knowingly insist. The divorce of Christians can be enormously powerful, sending shock waves throughout Christendom. Christians are all of one body. At the very least, an entire congregation suffers when two of its members dissolve their marriage, and I have seen the faith of people in faraway countries shaken by the divorce of well-known Christians.

Shared Cognitive Structures: The Meeting of Minds

■ *World view and values.* Most married Christians hold in common with their spouses fundamental assumptions about the existence of God and the Lordship of Jesus. Other assumptions about life might differ. The husband might be pessimistic and the wife optimistic. The husband might easily trust people, while the wife finds it harder to trust. In general, though, you will only infrequently find a couple that differs widely in world view. Despite the adage that opposites attract, most marriages are forged among people attracted by similarities.[10]

For the counselor, fundamental differences in world view between spouses are problematic but not insurmountable. It is possible for a couple to declare that certain topics are off-limits and avoid talking about them. There is a myth in modern society that people cannot be totally happy unless they communicate fully about whatever comes to mind. Research does not support this cultural myth. Generally, happy couples maintain several areas that they feel would be harmful to their relationship if they discussed them with their mates. If each spouse believes that the other values and trusts him or her, happiness seems to be affected more by *how* communication takes place than by the exhaustiveness of the communication (see Stuart, for a summary[11]).

What spouses value is vital to their happiness. Basic value concurrence in areas such as commitment, faithfulness, time alone and time together, input from each other and forgiveness makes harmonious marriages more likely.[12] Much of partners' Christian life will address potentially conflictual issues—roles of human authority, Scriptural authority, and value of identification with a Christian denomination.[13] Agreement on these and other salient issues will prevent power struggles over theology. At a minimum, couples should agree to disagree without continual attempts to persuade the other to change his or her opinion.

■ *Expectations.* There are two types of expectations: those due to general culture or subcultural groups and those due to each spouse's personal history. Lederer and Jackson, in their classic book *The Mirages of Marriage,*[14] discussed what often happens when people marry.

According to their reasoning, marriage is like saving money for a long-awaited vacation to Florida. When your plane lands, however, you are confronted by people in lederhosen speaking German and organizing a tour of the Alps. You could say, "This is terrible. I didn't want to go to Switzerland. I hate cold weather. I get acrophobia on a stepladder. This is going to be a miserable vacation. I refuse to have any fun, and I want my money back." Or you could take another tack, "Well, I certainly didn't sign up for a trip to Switzerland, and I'm a little disappointed about arriving at a place that I did not bargain for. However, I might enjoy learning to ski. I have never done winter sports, and I bet there are many things that are enjoyable about them." Lederer and Jackson's thesis is similar to this predicament. We each have expectations about our marriage and our mate, which are often incorrect—sometimes in surprising and troubling ways. (Like the woman who said to her counselor, "I married my ideal, got an ordeal and want a new deal.") If we are aware of the likely departures from our expectations, we can turn disillusionments into something positive.

Lederer and Jackson identified seven cultural "myths" about marriage. Each belief is not true and is potentially damaging for couples who hold it.

1. *People marry because they are romantically attracted to each other.* Not wholly true, assert Lederer and Jackson. They do not deny that people who marry usually feel romantic attraction. They merely point out that people marry for numerous *additional* reasons, such as financial security, loneliness, sexual attraction, parental pressure and others.

2. *Most married people are romantically attracted to each other.* Not true. Most married couples experience substantial decline in romantic attraction within six months after marriage.[15] People stay together for other reasons than the periodic episodes of romance.

3. *Romantic attraction is necessary for a satisfactory marriage.* Not true. It is certainly nice, much nicer than not being romantically attracted to one's spouse. We should try to maintain as much romance as possible, but romance is not *necessary* for a good marriage. Many couples love each other deeply without romance, say Lederer and Jackson.

4. *Marriage troubles are due to the differences between men and women.* Wrong. Men and women certainly differ. They have different physical capabilities, and they have been socialized to value different things at different times in life. However, happily married men and women are just as different as those unhappily married.[16] Differences don't cause problems; how the differences are dealt with causes problems.

5. *Children improve a troubled marriage.* This statement is usually false.[17] If one's sole desire were to have maximal marital happiness, one would be well advised never to have children. However, one of the fruits of marriage is often children, who provide joys and fulfillment in their own right. Therefore, life satisfaction and family satisfaction often remain high even when marriage satisfaction is not.

6. *Loneliness is cured by marriage.* Not so. Two lonely people who marry will most likely be two married lonely people. This is probably because loneliness has more to do with perception than with objective circumstances.[18]

7. *People who have good marriages never fight.* This is definitely false. Gottman's research shows that almost all couples sometimes disagree, and most discuss these disagreements with great feeling. More important is *how* they fight and whether they resolve disagreements without damage to their relationship.[19]

These are the cultural expectations that are often problematic for couples. I would add three others that I have seen in my work with Christian couples.

8. *Christians don't have marriage problems.* Couples who believe this often bury their conflicts and let them fester until they grow to relationship-threatening proportions. These people may put off seeking counseling until help is almost impossible.

9. *God can heal our marriage miraculously without human intervention.* This is true. But even when he heals it, there is much work to be done in relationship negotiation. Often a professional or lay counselor can help during and after the healing of a relationship.

10. *Submission to my partner means squelching my feelings and instantly doing what he or she wants me to.* Perhaps it does. Numerous interpretations of submission have been advanced and countless marriages have been stressed, strained, broken and even healed because of each interpretation. I do not know exactly what Paul and Peter meant when they wrote that wives should be submissive to their husbands, though I have some strong opinions concerning it, based on my study of Scripture. But whatever *submission* means, I do *not* believe it involves lack of communication of feelings from wife to husband. "Submission" is an issue that most Christian counselors confront with many Christian couples.

Couples bring to marriage other expectations, those that have arisen from each person's family and personal history. These expectations are more personal than cultural. Personal expectations are more likely than cultural expectations to govern perceived needs for intimacy and for effectance with the spouse. Thus, personal expectations are frequently behind disagreements over intimacy, power and control within marriage relationships.

For example, early in my married life, I was working at home when it began to rain. Kirby ran upstairs and bounded in the room. "Let's go walking barefoot in the rain," she said.

"It's wet out there," I said. "I think I'd better stay and get some work done."

Her face crumpled and the tears flowed.

"What?" I asked. "What did I say?" I followed her downstairs.

"You used to go walking barefoot in the rain before we got married.

You've always been so *spontaneous*. We used to just take off for the mountains when we were in college. What happened?"

"Well, I have a confession to make. I really didn't just take off to the mountains all that spontaneously. I planned those trips in advance."

"But they always *seemed* so spontaneous." She couldn't have been more shocked if I had admitted to Fruit Loop addiction.

"What difference does it make? We went to the mountains either way. We had fun either way. What does it matter whether I planned the trips or we just spontaneously went?"

But it made a difference to Kirby, for she felt that she had married a "spontaneous" man, only to discover a calculating planner. She was in Switzerland after having bought a ticket to Florida.

Shortly after that incident, I too became disillusioned over some inconsequential event. In both cases, once the mismatch between expectation and reality was uncovered, our insecurities were activated. We each wanted the relationship on our terms, and we tried to influence the other to make that happen. At first we were unwilling to put aside our own expectations, so we experienced conflict. In time, we accepted each other, but we had some anxious moments during that first year of adjustment.

■ *Plans for behavioral strategies.* Growing up in a family, we each develop ideas about what family life should be like. For example, by observing our parents disagree, we learn how to disagree with our spouse or how not to disagree. Or if we never see our parents disagree, we might conclude that married partners should avoid disagreements. The difficulty, of course, is that our parents and our spouse's parents probably differed from each other in important areas. We bring into our marriage two separate plans for marriage.

Kirby grew up in a family where the members were vocal about their love for each other. Consequently, for Kirby, love was to be shown by telling each other, "I love you." She told me that she loved me twenty-five times a day. On the other hand, I grew up with parents who showed love to each other through physical action. Only infrequently did they *say,* "I love you." They were not as bad as the man who said, "Well, I told her I loved her when we got married twenty years ago. I'll let her know if I change my mind," but they were not in the twenty-five-times-per-day category either.

So, each day I showed Kirby that I loved her by bringing her things and by giving her affectionate pats and hugs while she told me of her love for me. Both of us had doubts that we were really loved.

Of course, neither of us understood what was going on. She probably thought something like, "Doesn't he love me? He hardly ever tells me. He just wants to paw me all day." Meanwhile, I was thinking something like, "How come she doesn't show me that she loves me? She just wants to talk about it."

We were practicing the Golden Rule in a self-centered way. We were showing love as we wanted it shown to us, rather than showing love as the other person could understand it.

When we enter marriage with different plans for marriage, conflict is inevitable to the extent that we try to control our spouse without being willing to accept reciprocal influence.

■ *Cultural and subcultural norms.* Norms are standards for behavior that are set by groups. For the Christian couple, a war exists concerning the norms for marriage. Societal norms hold that marriage depends on romance and mutual attraction, that happiness is each person's right, that divorce is a valid way to increase our happiness if we have a troublesome marriage. Norms of the Christian church are different. Marriage depends on agape love (laying down one's life for the other). Jesus promised us eternal joy but not necessarily happiness on earth; happiness is a blessing, not a right. Divorce is to be forsaken in favor of forgiveness and agape love.

Couples who seek divorces are being influenced by the standards of the world. Yet, as counselors, our job is neither judge, nor prosecuting attorney. Neither are we value-neutral. We promote values of Christianity: love, forgiveness, seeking first the kingdom of God rather than selfishly seeking our own happiness. This positive value stance makes it unnecessary to threaten a couple with eternal judgment if they do not conform to Christian principles.

■ *Attributions of causality.* God created people to find meaning in life that is in him; therefore, people (by nature) seek the meaning in whatever happens to them. We continually try to find *why* things are happening: Why did God let me experience this? Why does my wife get angry so easily? Why does my husband still love me after I treat him so despicably?

We generally have no peace until we have answers. People explain causes differently depending on their situation.[20] In a discussion, the active partner will say, "I got angry when she called me a 'turkey,' " or "I yelled when she threw the pan at the wall." A participant explains the cause of an event as due to the things he or she can see or hear. As a result, each spouse tends to ascribe the cause of his or her own behavior to the other person who is easily seen and heard.

When interactions are positive, this is not troublesome. In fact, it might help marriages stay together. A happy spouse says, "She makes me happy. Her love keeps me going. Her support makes me feel good." However, when the interactions are unhappy, the same attributional pattern can create an ever-worsening effect. "She makes me unhappy. She never shows love. She doesn't support me." Such attributions blame the other and, because both spouses are looking at the other's behavior and blaming each other, fights over who is the *real* cause of marital problems are common. Both people feel justified in proclaiming that the partner is to blame for their unhappiness because they can see the spouse's behavior more clearly than their own.

One goal of counseling is to reduce blame and to help each spouse take responsibility for his or her part in negative interactions. For this to occur, spouses must empathize with each other. They must see things through each other's eyes.[21]

Substantial research has shown that couples have unique relationships with each other.[22] Even the poorest-communicating spouse, when told to communicate with a stranger of the opposite sex, can produce enviable communication.[23] In most instances, couples know how to communicate. They do not lack skill in communication. They do not suffer from a personality deficiency. They simply have developed well-rehearsed patterns of communication with each other.

Consequently, in marriage counseling rarely will we "teach" clients something that they do not know nor change the personality dynamics of one or both partners. Rather, we seek to make lasting changes in behavioral patterns: to break up old patterns, to induce couples to initiate new patterns (or resume patterns that they had previously used but had since abandoned), and to solidify new patterns into permanent parts of the couple's lives together.

For most people, the most powerful determinant of their behavior is what they see, hear and feel just before they act. These, environmental events powerfully affect behavior and its consequences and also stimulate thoughts about the meaning of the behavior. A counselor helps couples experience different environmental events. The most direct way to do this is to get them to act differently. During the counseling session, your influence is greatest. *You* are the most important stimulus in their environment during that session. Use your influence. When they leave your office, your impact is dramatically lessened because you are no longer directly visible to them. Of 168 hours in a week, they see you for only one. Successful counseling must extend beyond the counseling hour and must involve indirect influence during the remainder of the week. Develop methods that last throughout the week, including homework.

Shared Environmental Events

Environmental structures involve the permanent objects we respond to. This can include such things as our living accommodations and the layout of the house. The most universal stressor on marriage is disagreements over household tasks. Across the life cycle, this stressor is mentioned repeatedly by spouses and parents as an aggravation.[24] In some cases, this is the battleground on which the wars of power and control are fought. One couple I counseled had a major disagreement over whose responsibility it was to clean the basement. Making changes in that environmental structure involved great passion for each one. Although that was not the only issue over which they disagreed, it was a symbol for how they would work out their disagreements. Their marriage improved substantially after they were able to resolve that issue—with little help from me other than bringing it up weekly.

Shared Environmental Structures

Environmental structures also involve habitual patterns of behavior, such as the ways the couple handle sexual intercourse, treat special anniversaries or events, discuss the mundane events of their workdays, argue, solve problems and resolve differences. Troublesome patterns must be changed if the marriage is to flourish. Pleasant patterns need strengthening. New patterns must be started.

This implies that the counselor should carefully assess enduring environmental structures, both behavior patterns and structures in the physical environment. Helpful environmental events should be initiated. Only in changing the structures of the couple's lives will the marriage operate smoothly after counseling is ended.

SUMMARY

People are created in God's image, needing intimacy, effectance, commitment and forgiveness. We meet these needs through communication with God and with people. Marriage is especially important in meeting human needs.

Individuals have spiritual, cognitive, environmental and behavioral aspects to their lives. Marriage counseling addresses each aspect of the individual while working to improve the marriage.

When people marry, they unite in an earthly commitment and heavenly mystery. They develop shared spiritual lives through a permanent, intimate covenantal relationship. Further, they forge a meeting of minds on several levels. By living together over time, they also share environmental events and structures, the most important of which can be their practiced interactions.

Marriage counseling attends to each of the shared parts of the couple, simultaneously respecting each individual. The whole of the marriage operates according to predictable principles. In the following chapter, I outline the structure and operation of this God-given relationship of marriage.

3

Principles of Marriage within the Family

I N THE PREVIOUS CHAPTER, I IDENTIFIED FOUR HUMAN NEEDS—commitment, intimacy, effectance (the need to produce discernible effects) and forgiveness. Each need was shown to be met in our relationship with God and in a "laboratory" he established for living out our lives and simultaneously learning more about him—the marriage relationship.

Each of the four needs permeates every aspect of marriage. In this chapter, we will examine the structure of marriage, the operation of marriage and the principles of change in marriage, and we will find how the four needs are involved in each part of the marriage.

STRUCTURE OF A MARRIAGE

The most popular metaphor for describing a family within the secular   **Commitment** literature is to liken it to a biological system. A system is an organized group. This group may be a married couple, a family group, a family plus extended family members, or even a larger group, such as a church community or whole society. Actually, systems go beyond mere groups of people. General systems theory explains the operation of any type of system; however, here I will use the term more loosely than in the strict scientific sense.[1]

One of the main characteristics of a system is that its members are mutually dependent on each other. Small units within the system, called subsystems—such as the marriage partners or the children—are intimately tied to each other to produce a functioning whole.

In a sense the parts of a system are normally inseparable. Haley[2] has shown how difficult it is for children to abandon their commitments to their parents and vice versa. Even divorce usually does not separate parents from children or even husband from wife. Interactions between a divorced husband and wife often continue for years after divorce, though they may be characterized by strife and acrimony. Commitment and permanence of relationship is a fact of marriage, even from a totally secular viewpoint.

From the spiritual viewpoint, commitment is a certainty. God speaks of becoming one flesh, and Jesus says that no one should be allowed to put that aside. Marriage, like our relationship with God and God's relationship with Israel, is designed to last.[3] It is viewed by God as lasting.

Intimacy

The structure of a relationship is based on intimate love. C. S. Lewis has written authoritatively about different types of love;[4] Sheldon Vanauken,[5] of the romance in a Christian marriage; Erich Fromm,[6] of the elements of love—knowing, respecting, caring for, meeting the needs of and committing to the beloved. Each of these books merits study.[7]

Intimate love is the building block on which the structure of a marriage relationship is erected. In the familiar love chapter, 1 Corinthians 13, Paul argues that the most fundamental characteristic of the Christian is love. He bases his argument on the knowledge that we will exist eternally in a love relationship with Jesus. Faith and hope, which also characterize the Christian while he or she is on earth, are only temporary qualities because they will ultimately pass away when we see Jesus face to face. We are urged to practice love. The placement of this admonition within its scriptural context is significant for married Christians. The church at Corinth was stirred by controversy and divisiveness. In 1 Corinthians 12 and 14, Paul discussed one of the main points of contention. Squarely in the midst of the discussion comes his admonition to love one another.

Intimate love is "upbuilding" and necessary for proper "growth." Both of these metaphors, used by Paul throughout his letter to the Ephesians, speak to the structure of relationships—with God (Eph 3:14-19), with family members (Eph 5:21—6:4) and with other Christians in the church (Eph 2:19-22). Intimate love is like building stone by stone. It is often hard work. Sometimes the stones must be shaped. Give and take is provided by the cement between stones. But in the end, there is the pride of having constructed a building that rests on a solid foundation, who is Jesus (Eph 2:20). Intimate love is also like growing. It requires continual feeding on the proper foods. One cannot grow healthy on mistrust, irresponsibility, hurt, blame and criticism. Growth requires balance between muscles, bones, joints and tendons. Both the internal and external must be nourished.

Paul says, "Rather, speaking the truth in love, we are to grow up in every way into him who is the head, into Christ, from whom the whole body, joined and knit together by every joint with which it is supplied, when each part is working properly, makes bodily growth and upbuilds itself in love" (Eph 4:15-16). Love builds itself on intimate caring.

Effectance

Loving means that we often serve each other, assuming various roles to bring about the tasks we must accomplish. To create proper effects in marriage, families organize into hierarchies.

Families are ordered so that people function differently.[8] Children are to be obedient to their parents. Wives are admonished to be submissive to their husbands. Husbands are directed to love their wives in the same way that Christ loved the church. There is a clear generation line drawn between parents and children, while husband and wife operate within the same level of authority but have different functions within that level.

Marriage was created to produce growth and fruit in three primary areas: knowledge of the triune God, love (learning to give oneself for the other), and children.[9]

Marriage helps us gain knowledge of God. From the Garden of Eden, God gave man a woman who was different from the man and who could complete the man. This helps both the man and woman understand and love someone who is different than they. A man must not only understand a separate, unique person, but must understand a person who sees things differently than he does because the woman is different from him. The same is true for women. Carol Gilligan has shown that men and women tend to be socialized differently.[10] Men are socialized to value accomplishing tasks; women are socialized to value relationships. As men and women learn to understand each other, they develop the capacity to understand God, who is Other. God is Other than humans because he has a dual nature—human and divine. Understanding the otherness of our spouses helps us understand the Otherness of God.

Marriage helps us love our spouses. Marriage requires self-sacrifice. People are naturally egocentric. Living with another human who depends on us helps us learn to sacrifice our desires for the other.

Marriage provides for the birth, rearing and nurture of children. Throughout the centuries, the Roman Catholic Church has been the most insistent on the purpose of marriage being to raise children (for instance, see Roman Catholic Canon Law, canon 1013: "The primary end of marriage is the procreation and education of offspring").[11] However, even some of the respected Roman scholars have recognized that other purposes for marriage were ordained by God. For example, St. Augustine offered three aims of marriage: offspring, fidelity and sanctification.

Each of these three tasks of marriage are blueprints for the structure of marriage. To build the structure, families organize into different roles.

Forgiveness   The final component of the structure of marriage is forgiveness. People's egocentrism is the force that threatens the structure of marriage with disintegration. It pulls the partners apart. It thrusts the partners against each other. Like the steel bars in reinforced concrete, forgiveness acts against the force of disintegration to hold the structure strong and secure. When individualism weakens commitment, forgiveness rebuilds it. When the desire to do our own thing erodes intimacy, forgiveness calls us back into more intimate interaction. When lust for influence, power and having our own way regardless of the cost thrusts spouses violently against each other, forgiveness helps us lay down our lives for our mates. Forgiveness holds the structure together.

OPERATION OF A MARRIAGE

Commitment is simultaneously an ideal characteristic of a good marriage **Commitment** and a realistic description of interrelationship among family members. Within the day-to-day operation of a marriage, commitment is manifested in many ways.

Commitment involves maintaining a shared spirit. If each spouse strives to maintain a close covenant walk with the Lord, the couple will continue to be bound together into the threefold cord with Jesus.

Commitment involves thinking of ourselves as permanently joined to our spouses. Couples should never let the thought of possible divorce enter their minds. If spouses catch themselves thinking about "what could have been" if they had married another, how things might be if they were divorced or how things don't look as if they will improve, then the spouses should consciously attempt to put these thoughts behind them. Without the possibility of divorce, there is a drive to improve the relationship. When thoughts of divorce are entertained, the daily practice of commitment is eroded. Troubled couples often object to the practicality of stopping thoughts of separation or divorce. I usually counsel them, "You can't stop Satan from coming to your door, but you don't have to invite him in and entertain him." Unwanted thoughts often beset us, but we can control whether we dwell on them.

Commitment involves the environmental events that we share with our spouses. Usually this means the ways we talk to our spouses and the things we do for them. We can build commitment by constantly telling our spouses of our love. We can show we are committed by never flirting with another person, by spending time with our spouses and by being faithful in all our actions.

Commitment involves shared environmental structures. We can arrange our home and office so that we are continually reminded of our commitment and fidelity to our loved ones. We can place pictures of our spouses on our desks. We can arrange our homes to proclaim to all who enter them that we are married. The wedding ring, of course, is an ever-present environmental structure that proclaims to all we meet that we are faithful.

Intimacy

People try to meet their needs for intimacy by the way they use their time. Individuals' preferences for amount and type of intimacy differ. Most women desire more intimacy than most men, but some women prefer more distance and less intimacy than some men. The amount of intimacy or distance needed by each family member is vitally important to the operation of the family.[12] People try to regulate their intimacy through their activities.[13]

All activities have *functions*—that is, they have effects on others.[14] A behavior may (a) produce no effect on intimacy or distance; (b) enhance intimacy; (c) enhance distance; or (d) regulate the distance or intimacy. Regulation means that some intimacy is achieved while at the same time keeping the other person at some distance. As an example, imagine a husband and wife at home alone. They have a quiet dinner, then he reads in the living room while she watches television downstairs. Later, they make love quickly and both fall asleep immediately. Their small-talk over dinner was coactive but not intimate. Most of their evening was spent alone, creating distance between them. Only a brief sexual interlude provided any intimacy.

We would need to observe many interactions to determine the full picture, though. If we find that the husband works two jobs; rarely communicates about his hopes, fears, values or emotions; and wants to make love with his wife only infrequently, we might conclude that he seeks to keep distance between them. Importantly, the wife probably collaborates with the husband in this distancing. For example, she may often complain that she needs more intimacy from her husband. She may gripe and nag about his being a workaholic until she makes it unpleasant for him to seek more intimacy. What she says is not as important as how she acts. Even though she says she wants intimacy, the function of her behavior is distancing. Some common behaviors are listed in Table 1 along with the function that the behavior usually accomplishes.[15]

Table 1
Common Normal and Problematic Behaviors in Marriage and Their Effects on Intimacy or Distance between Spouses

Normal Behavior

Distance	Regulation/Coaction	Intimacy
Reading silently; listening to music thru earphones	Participating in sports, other games; attending movies together; working together	Having sex; talking about values, emotions, hopes and fears
Working two jobs or overtime away from family	Maintaining relationship with kids by attending their sports functions, music recitals, etc.	Asking for help
Sending kids to camp	Raising child in middle years	Caring for baby
(For teen) Spending time with peers, having a steady date, getting driver's license, going to college	Double-dating or only going out with spouse when other friends are present	Communicating feelings

Problematic Behavior

Distance	Regulation/Coaction	Intimacy
Having extramarital affair	Flirting in order to manipulate	Being dependent
Experiencing severe depression	Experiencing agitated depression	Experiencing mild depression; making suicidal gestures; having nightmares
Exhibiting obsessive-compulsive behavior	Exhibiting psychosis	Psychosomaticizing
Working excessively; being overinvolved	(For material provider) being insensitive to dependent's emotional needs	Being dependent; clinging; acting incompetent; worrying; being solicitous
Exhibiting psychopathy	Exhibiting hysteria, alcoholism	Leaving drugs around to get caught

Marriages operate according to repeatable patterns of behavior. Some patterns of behavior occur so frequently that it is *as if* the marriage were governed by rules.[16] Marriages are not really rule-governed, but it is as if they were. There are three types of "as-if" rules. The first involves behavior

Effectance: Rules and Power

patterns explicitly discussed by the husband and wife. For example, in our house I cook breakfast and Kirby cooks dinner.

The second type of rule describes behavior, but spouses are not consciously aware of the rules. For example, a husband may make a decision only after he is prodded by his wife. This is not something that the couple agreed upon explicitly. It is a pattern that developed over time. Although the couple were not aware of this "rule," if it were pointed out, both people would probably agree that it accurately describes their behavior.

The third type of rule describes who usually makes the rules under what circumstances. This rule describes the balance of power. If the husband usually makes most of the decisions, then the husband defines the relationship. Defining a relationship is not the same as controlling one's spouse. For instance, a woman can announce, "Dear, I am totally submissive to you." Afterwards, the woman might be totally controlled by her husband, while *she* has totally defined the relationship. Power in such a relationship is complex. The husband *apparently* has the power. After all, he gives the orders. Yet, he does so because his wife told him to, so she has definitional power.

A misconception has recently arisen concerning power. Power in a relationship is sometimes seen as reflected by control of resources. For example, if the man makes more money than his homemaker/wife, he is seen as being more powerful. This certainly has effects on the relationship.[17] The spouse with less resource control is usually willing to make more concessions to preserve the marriage, whereas the one with more resource control usually demands more changes if the relationship is to continue. But the stuff of relationships also turns on the more ephemeral question of "Who has the power to say what our relationship will be like?"

Disagreements over rule-making cause emotional arguments. However, people are generally unaware that they are disagreeing over who defines the relationship. The topic of their argument is so emotionally charged that if asked, people say they are fighting about finances, sex, in-laws, child discipline or areas as mundane as where to squeeze the toothpaste or which way to place the toilet paper on the dispenser. They do not report disagreeing over who makes the rules. But that is the root of the disagreement.

Generally, when there is disagreement over rule-making, people will mentally rehearse past or future conversations with the person. These disagreements happen in most relationships; however, in relationships that have become troubled, such disagreements are often heated and frequent, and they follow a predictable development and outcome. This is called a *power struggle*. Troubled relationships almost always involve power struggles.

Within the daily operation of marriage, forgiveness requires self-sacrifice. Part of the nature of God is self-sacrifice: Jesus gave himself for us. We were created in God's image and thus share the propensity to sacrifice. Sometimes, though, self-sacrifice is detrimental to a marriage. Self-sacrifice is harmful when (a) it is self-destructive and (b) it keeps the couple from changing. Sometimes each spouse may simultaneously sacrifice himself or herself in ways that maintain the current conflict. For example, in one couple I counseled, the woman sacrificed her intellect. She reacted emotionally and illogically to whatever her husband said. She chided him for being a cold machine. When her husband was not in the room, she was logical and bright. On the other hand, her husband removed all emotion from his demeanor. He was all rationality, chiding his wife for being stupid. When his wife was not present, he was sensitive and emotionally expressive. Both sacrificed parts of themselves to preserve the relationship, despite saying frequently that they wanted to change their relationship. **Forgiveness**

One task of the counselor, then, is to help people use their propensity to sacrifice themselves for others to change their behaviors rather than to preserve their current troublesome behaviors. In later chapters, I will discuss several ways to accomplish this. I usually couch it in terms of "laying down your life for the other." Laying down your life involves stopping demands that the other person do things your way, ceasing to blame the other, seeking the will of God rather than one's own pleasure. It is the essence of confession, repentance and forgiveness.

CHANGE WITHIN MARRIAGE

If spouses were not committed to each other, there would be little pain in marriage. It is the risk that is inherent in commitment that causes pain when **Commitment** our spouses disappoint us.

Pain helps a troubled couple seek help. When a marriage begins to be troubled, blaming begins. As spouses blame each other, hurt and pain are inevitable. "Pain is God's megaphone that rouses the ear of a deaf world," said C. S. Lewis.[18] Pain results in defensiveness, retaliation and bitterness if it is not soon responded to, but it also alerts the couple that help is needed.

Most people seek help from a friend or member of their family of origin. Friends and family members, being told of the relationship from only one spouse's perspective, generally encourage the spouse to persevere in their course of action. Whereas the advice of friends and family is helpful to people with individual problems,[19] it is often destructive to individuals with marital difficulties because support intensifies differences.[20] As the pain increases, the couple might seek help for their marriage difficulties from a counselor. Counselors must be alert to the other helpers involved with the couple.

Intimacy

Couples can actively change their intimacy through changing their interactions with each other and the ways they apportion their time schedules.

One of the universal rules governing the behavior of couples is the principle of reciprocity. In Scripture, this is known as sowing and reaping (Gal 6:7). If a person sows trust with his or her spouse, the person will reap trust. If the person sows compliments and appreciation, he or she will reap them. If the person sows criticism and hostility, that too will be returned. Researchers have found that troubled couples are more likely to retort negatively to criticism from the spouse than are untroubled couples.[21]

This leads to a modification of the principle of reciprocity, which might be called "laying up treasures." Having positive interactions with one's spouse is like making deposits in a bank account.[22] When an account has a large positive balance, then one withdrawal—one negative interaction—does not affect the balance appreciably. However, if a couple has a balance of positive interactions that is close to zero, then any withdrawal produces anxiety, anger and pain. So, if couples lay up treasures with each other, then their few negative encounters will be hardly noticed, but if people lay up debts, then positive encounters make little difference. If the balance is in the red or is close to zero, then even the threat of a withdrawal is enough to produce pain and to provoke an emotional reaction, like a run on the bank.

Treasures are subjective. The husband might prefer to be left alone when he returns home from work. If the wife thinks that her husband wants to be talked to, she might do the very thing that displeases him in her attempt to store up treasures with him. People must ask their spouses what pleases them. Then they can apply the Golden Rule.

Because relationships are generally governed by hierarchies and rules, mar- **Effectance**
riages generally resist change. When a couple is threatened by change due to normal transitions (such as birth of a new child, job changes, moving, graduation or death), they are thrown into an unstable time in which they are reluctant to forsake old behavior patterns and develop new rules. People are generally apprehensive of the unknown and seek to avoid uncertainty that comes with change. Thus, there is a tendency to use old behavior patterns even when they might be inappropriate.[23]

Yet, changes are inevitable in the development of a family, and the healthy marriage must adjust to changes with minimum turbulence and with solutions that work well and protect the integrity of the individuals.[24] The couple who cannot adjust to changes will face unhappy days or will produce family members who develop psychological symptoms. When transitions occur, it soon becomes apparent that change *must* occur. Sometimes couples abandon themselves to change. The problem is that the direction or goal of the change is unknown. Imagine awakening in a small motor boat at sea. It is cloudy and a squall threatens. You realize that if you stay in the impending storm, you are in danger; yet, you have no idea of the direction of shore. Faced with the certainty of destruction if you remain immobile, you fire up the motor, point the bow in some direction that you hope takes you away from the storm and head off frantically. You might be heading toward shore, but chances are higher you are moving either parallel to shore or out to sea.

This example illustrates the dilemma of the troubled couple. Sometimes they awaken to the storm in their marriage and head for change at full throttle. Running from the storm, they may head in precisely the wrong direction. They need direction to their energy.

How is this delicate balance between resisting changes and adapting to necessary changes maintained? Through individual decisions by spouses. One of the great advances in family theory has been the use of systems theory in understanding the operation of the family. Yet, by adopting systems theory, psychologists have downplayed the role of individuals in accomplishing the objectives of the family. Individuals are energized by motivations, thoughts and emotions. Individuals make their decisions not only because of environmental pressures, but also because of their enduring cognitive structures. As a counselor, you must mobilize and direct each individual to change.

Forgiveness   In marriage, confession and repentance usually precede forgiveness. When the bride of Christ (the church) worships him, the celebration of marriage occurs. Many elements of worship are also elements of marriage. Worship involves praise and enjoyment. It involves reading Scripture (listening to God) and prayer (talking to God). It involves announcements or passing mundane information to keep the bride informed. It involves sharing special meals. It involves affirming one's commitment to the other. It involves showing and saying that we love the other. It involves ritual, though some churches are more explicit than other churches about labeling repeated behaviors as ritual. It may involve emotional expression and healing. Worship also involves confession, repentance and forgiveness.

Confession is admitting we are wrong and agreeing with God that we have sinned. Repentance is turning our back on the sinful behavior and not sinning again. Forgiveness is God's part, which he does when we bring our sin under the blood of Jesus through confession and repentance. The stuff of forgiveness is mercy (not giving us what we deserve) and grace (giving us what we don't deserve).

In marriage, we should expect the same elements as in worship—praise, enjoyment, communication, information exchange, shared meals, affirmation of commitment, demonstration and expression of love, ritual, emotional expression and healing of sickness and brokenness. We should also expect confession, repentance and forgiveness.

Confession comes first. This is contrary to the troubled couple's thinking. They each usually believe that the other person is to blame for difficulties. Their focus is on what has been done to wrong them. But, for forgiveness to occur, they each must lay down their natural inclinations and think about how they have wronged the partner. They each confess to the other (see Mt 5:23; Jas 5:16). They must also express and follow through on repentance. Finally, they must avoid provoking each other.

When one spouse confesses and repents, the task of the other is to forgive (see Lk 6:37; 11:4; 17:4). Forgiveness is difficult, and the troubled couple will need to practice this often. When Jesus told his disciples that they were to forgive their brother repeatedly, regardless of how many times the brother sinned against them, their immediate response was, "Lord, increase our faith." As a counselor who deals with couples in conflict, you will continually attempt to increase their faith until they can truly "lay down their lives" for each other.

The conflicted couple will be reluctant to believe that the spouse has repented. They are not to wait until convinced that the spouse is truly penitent. They are to forgive when the spouse merely says that they repent (see Lk 17:3-5). After saying that they forgive the spouse, they will find it easier to truly forgive the spouse. After saying that they repent, spouses will find it easier to repent. Such is the power of commitment.

SUMMARY

Marriage is a structure. It operates according to principles. Its structure and operation can be changed.

Marriage involves commitment, intimacy, effectance and forgiveness. Troubled marriages have problems in one or more of those areas, while each of the areas provides fulfillment in the happy marriage. The marriage counselor must understand the ideal, normal and problematic operation of marriages in each of the four aspects so that the accurate assessment can be made and powerful interventions can be designed to correct difficulties in each area.

Marriages must be understood in terms of their spiritual portions, cognitive aspects and environmental interactions and structures. In addition, each marriage will differ depending on the stage of life of the marriage partners and on the stage of the family life cycle of the marriage.[25]

4

The Marriage
throughout the
Family Life Cycle

INDIVIDUALS ACHIEVE MEANING IN LIFE THROUGH INTIMATE RELA-
tionships (with God and with humans) and through demonstrating
to themselves that they can effect desired outcomes in work and
relationships (called "effectance"[1]). Intimacy and effectance are
exercised most fully in marriage and family life and in life in the church
body. However, intimacy and effectance are exercised in different ways at
different times in the life cycle. The effective counselor must identify each
couple's needs and intervene in a way that accounts for those needs.

All developmental theories may be divided into two types: stage theories
and transition theories. Stage theories tell what happens during a relatively
long period of time in the life of an individual, couple or family. Generally,
these theories identify tasks that must be accomplished during each stage.
The best-known stage theories that describe individual development are
Freud's[2] oral, anal, phallic, latency and genital stages, Erikson's[3] eight psy-

chosexual stages of development, Piaget's[4] stages of intellectual development and Kohlberg's[5] stages of moral development. Evelyn Duvall[6] has
identified stages of family development.

Transition theories have been proposed more recently. Instead of concentrating on what happens during a stage, they describe what happens in
moving from one stage to another. The most well-known transition theory
was popularized by Gail Sheehey in *Passages*.[7] Transition theories are more
interested in change; whereas, stage theories are more interested in stability. Transition theories are generally "process" theories; whereas, stage
theories are generally "content" theories.[8]

SATISFACTION, INTIMACY AND CONFLICT DURING THE STAGES AND TRANSITIONS OF MARRIAGE

Stages of Marriage

A number of theoreticians and researchers have investigated what couples
can expect at various points in their lives. Duvall[9] divided the family life
cycle into eight distinct stages and described the tasks of each stage. Others
have used other numbers of stages to describe the family life cycle. For
example, Olson, McCubbin et al.[10] used six stages; Aldous[11] used seven
stages.

In Table 2, I have summarized some of the tasks that must be performed
at each stage of the family life cycle. Using a number of theories, I divided
the tasks into individual tasks and tasks of the couple. I also describe the
tasks that children face in the family. Furthermore, I summarize findings
of Olson, McCubbin et al.[12] who surveyed over 1000 families in the Luth-
eran Church throughout the United States. In the last column of Table 2,
the most common strains on the family are listed. Generally the pattern of
strains changes as the couple ages, but many of the same strains appear
throughout the life cycle, in such areas as finances, in-laws, sex, child
discipline and household responsibilities.

Strains always exist in marriages, but sometimes the effects are more
disruptive than at other times. For instance, several research studies have
shown a consistent pattern in marriage satisfaction across the family life
cycle (see Figure 3). Generally, marriage satisfaction is highest in couples

Table 2
A Summary of Tasks and Strains for Stages in the Family Life Cycle

Approx. Age[a]	Stage[a]	Transition Points[b]		Developmental Tasks[c]			Family Strains[d,e] within Stage
		Family (Includes Marriage)	Personal: Vocational, Biological, Psychological	Family	Personal		
					Adult	Child	
17-21		Courtship (Cohabitation, 15-25%)	H.S. graduation		Intimacy vs. isolation		
21-25	1. Young couples without children	Marriage; "Honeymoon" 6 mo.-18 mo.	College graduation; first job	Separate from parents, balance couple allegiance with allegiance to family of origin; Establish couple "rules" of relationship; Establish household; Establish mutually satisfying marriage; Adjust to pregnancy	Intimacy vs. isolation (continued); Establish work identity, commitment to productivity, formulate the "dream"; Stabilize sexual identity, bond, establish sense of personal worth; Establish adult status, formulate world view, detach from parents		Work-Family (40): Change jobs, low satisf. with job, difficulty with someone at work, responsibilities at work; Financial (30): Loan, purchase a car, strain on money for necessities; Intra-Family (20): Husband time away from home, tasks not done; Illness (10): Someone close becomes ill
24-30	2. Families with pre-schoolers	Birth of first child; Birth of subsequent children; Discipline of toddler	Wife might stop work (or stop and then return); Change jobs; Promotion; Moving; Buy first home	Make decisions about economic status of family; Resettle into new community: adjust to new physical, economic and social conditions; Make decisions about family size; Child bearing	Intimacy vs. isolation (continued); Generativity vs. absorption; Commitment to career; Develop sense of self-worth; Act out priorities	Trust vs. mistrust; Autonomy vs. shame	Financial (50): Loan, major purchase, strain on money for necessities; Intra-Family (20): Children's "outside activities," tasks not done; Work-Family (10): Satisfaction with job

Table 2
(continued)

Approx. Age	Stage[a]	Transition Points[b]		Developmental Tasks[c]			Family Strains[d,e] within Stage
		Family (Includes Marriage)	Personal: Vocational, Biological, Psychological	Family	Personal		
					Adult	Child	
					Cope with energy depletion	Autonomy vs. shame	Illness (10): Someone close becomes ill Pregnancy (10): Wife gives birth
28-35	3. Families with school-age children	First child enters school; Last child enters school (midlife?)	Buy new home; Wife may (re) enter employment, if not already employed	Balance multiple roles (work, mate, family, community); Childrearing; Social integration of family members; Fit into community in constructive ways	Generativity vs. self-absorption; Readjust career goals, seek "success" in career; Come to view parents as fellow adults; Develop family intimacy, redefine primary relationship; Adjust goals and dreams to reality	Industry vs. inferiority	Intra-Family (50): Husband away from home, outside activities of children, tasks undone, conflict among children, difficulty managing children Work-Family (30): Satisfaction with job or career change Financial (20): Major purchase, strain on money for necessities
35-45	4. Families with adolescents	First child enters adolescence; Subsequent children enter adolescence	Re-evaluate career; Peak work commitment; Menopause (wife)	Time of lowest satisfaction with marriage (reassessment of marriage); Stabilization of family resources; Acknowledgement and acceptance of individual differences with mate;	Generativity vs. self-absorption (continued) Redefine work roles; Shift in view of life to "time remaining"	Identity vs. identity confusion	Financial (60): Strain on money for necessities, strain on money for medical, educational, other major purchases; loan Intra-Family (30): Children's outside activities; difficulty managing adolescents

Table 2
(continued)

Approx. Age[a]	Stage[a]	Transition Points[b]			Developmental Tasks[c]		Family Strains[d,e] within Stage
		Family (Includes Marriage)	Personal: Vocational, Biological, Psychological	Family	Personal		
					Adult	Child	
				Restructure power-influence hierarchy (adolescent power)			Work-Family (10): Promotion or new responsibilities
45-55	5. Launching families	"Important" child leaves home	Children graduate from h.s. or college; Children might marry; Wife might retire if working or might reenter work force or change jobs;	Turning loose of children; Refocus more attention on spouse; Family responsibilities change; Maintaining a supportive home base	Generativity vs. self-absorption; Mentor younger work colleagues; Male-female orientation reversal (male to relationships, female to achievement); Consciousness of physical vulnerability	Intimacy vs. isolation; Married children pull away from family and establish own cycle	Financial (40): Loan, major purchase, strain on money for necessities, education; Intra-Family (20): Kids outside activities, tasks undone; Family Transitions (20): Young adult left home or began college; Work-Family (10): Change job or career; Illness (10): Someone close seriously ill
46-65	6. Empty-nest families	Last child leaves; Grandparent dies/grandparent dependent; First grandchild born	Menopause (wife)	Changing sexual expectations; Relearning to live as a couple; Grandparent role; Relinquishing authority to children as adults; Preparing for retirement	Generativity vs. self-absorption (continued)	Intimacy vs. isolation; Generativity vs. self-absorption (continued)	Financial (30): Major purchase, strain on money for necessities; Illness (20): Someone close seriously ill; menopause

Table 2
(continued)

Approx. Age	Stage[a]	Transition Points[b]		Developmental Tasks[c]			Family Strains[d,e] within Stage
		Family (Includes Marriage)	Personal: Vocational, Biological, Psychological	Family	Personal Adult	Personal Child	
							Losses (20): Death of grandparent; close friend of family dies
							Marital strains (10): Difficulty with sex
							Intra-Family (10): Tasks undone
							Work-Family (10): Satis. w/job or career
65–	7. Families in retirement	Death of spouse	Retirement; Move; Institutionalization	Huge changes in lifestyle; Re-establish social network; connections with adult children; Dealing with loss of spouse (rebound with companion or support group vs. choosing isolation); Adapting home to aging	Integrity vs. despair, disgust; Satisfactorily using leisure time (cultivating avocations); Vigor; Illness and frailty; Accept "subculture" status; Comprehensive life review and reminiscence; Consolidation of world/life view	Generativity vs. self-absorption (continued)	Financial (40): Major purchase; strain on money for medical, other necessities
							Illness (20):
							Parent/spouse become seriously ill, close relative or friend seriously ill
							Losses (20): Death of parents, close friend of family dies
							Intra-Family (10): Tasks undone
							Work-Family (10) Retirement

References   [a]Olson, McCubbin et al. (1983); Duvall (1977); Hill & Rodgers (1964)
[b]Riegel (1975); Haley (1976)
[c]Duvall (1977); Erikson (1976); Wortley & Amatea (1982)
[d]Olson, McCubbin et al. (1983)
[e]Numbers in parentheses are per cents of families within the stage who identified the strain as the most difficult source of strain.

before they bear children. The husband generally is lowest in marriage satisfaction when the children are adolescents. The wife is lowest in marriage satisfaction just after the children leave home but before retirement.

Figure 3
Marriage Satisfaction across the Family Life Cycle for Husbands and Wives

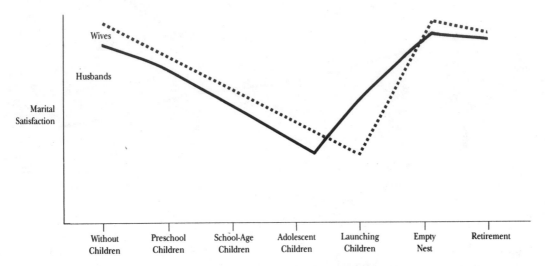

Happy and unhappy couples have different patterns of marital satisfaction[13] (see Figure 4). Unhappy couples have lower marriage satisfaction at all points in the family life cycle than happy couples. The major difference in the two types of couples comes after the children leave home. Unhappy couples have even lower marriage satisfaction after the children leave home than before. Happy couples, to the contrary, generally recover to previous levels of marriage satisfaction after children are launched.

Satisfaction across the Life Cycle

   Although marriage satisfaction generally follows the "U-shaped" curve shown in Figures 3 and 4, there is more to the story. Couples were asked by Olson, McCubbin et al.[14] to rate their family satisfaction (see Figure 5) and their satisfaction with life in general (see Figure 6). Both ratings changed little across the entire life cycle. Of course, each individual experienced ups and downs, but as a whole, no time of life outshone the others. Apparently, couples can experience some strain with each other and still have a fulfilled life.

Figure 4
Marriage Satisfaction across the Family Life Cycle for Happy and Unhappy Couples

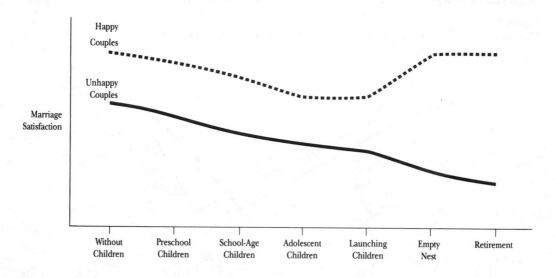

Figure 5
Family Satisfaction across the Family Life Cycle for Husbands and Wives

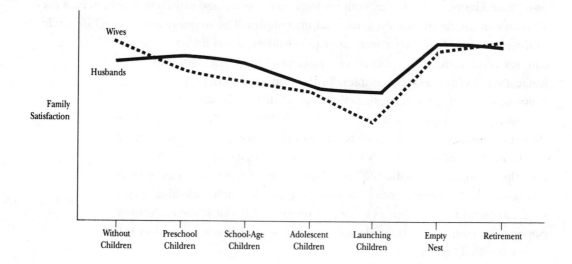

Figure 6
General Life Satisfaction across the Family Life Cycle for Husbands and Wives

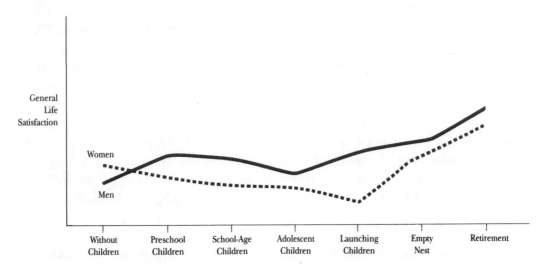

The effects on couples of different stages in the family life cycle can be best understood by recalling that humans must meet their needs for intimacy and for effectance to be fulfilled. They must also continue their mutual commitment and their mutual forgiveness of perceived hurts by the spouse. Generally, normal life transitions most strongly affect the couple's intimacy and effectance.

Factors Involved in a Happy Marriage

Couples meet their needs for intimacy through structuring their time to provide a balance of intimate, coactive and distancing activities. People have different needs for intimacy, coactivity and aloneness, and they meet their needs by adjusting their whole schedules—not just their time with their spouses.

People meet their needs for effectance through demonstrating that they can affect the world, usually through work or ministry at church. Inevitably, though, people look for evidence that they are able to affect their spouse. Ideally, each person wants the spouse to love and to agree with him or her. Within the marriage, efforts are expended to that end. If the person becomes frustrated at achieving this effectance within the marriage, the person may either (a) redirect effort elsewhere or (b) increase efforts. Conflict reflects intensified effort to satisfy needs for effectance.

The patterns by which spouses satisfy their needs for intimacy and effectance become the rules of the marriage. They result in shared cognitive structures (the meeting of minds) and shared environmental structures (for example, enduring patterns of behavior in each other's presence). These influence the marriage satisfaction of each spouse. As the couple ages and the pattern of responsibilities changes both within and outside the family, there is an ebb and flow of intimacy and conflict and thus of happiness with the marriage.

Transitions

Of particular import in a marriage are times when the couple moves from one stage to another. Transitions generally disrupt normal functioning. A couple's response to a transition depends on three factors: disruption in time schedules, the number of decisions in which there is initial disagreement and the initial level of conflict.[15]

Transitions often disrupt well-established time schedules, thus affecting the balance of intimacy, distancing and coactivity. During the transitional period, the couple must rearrange their time schedules to meet their needs for intimacy. Thus, the transition provides both a threat to happy marriages and a simultaneous opportunity to more fully meet each person's basic needs.

Transitions also necessitate making new decisions. Because spouses come from different families, disagreements over new decisions are inevitable. Some transitions require few decisions involving initial disagreement while others require many. Some transitions require decision making in vital, emotion-laden areas while others require only routine decisions. With each decision involving initial disagreement comes a test to the couple's rule system—their structure. Will the same power rules be used to make decisions or will someone be so involved in the decisions or in outside pursuits that he or she takes more or less power than previously? Again, there is a simultaneous threat to stability and opportunity to evolve new, improved rule systems.

Response to a transition depends, too, on the initial level of conflict. If the couple has numerous conflicts over rules, then any transition will likely intensify their conflict. If the couple has fundamental agreement over rules, then they will usually adjust to the changes. However, likelihood is not certainty. Some couples with frequent conflict might find that a new era of life has made the topics of conflict passé. Some couples who never previously argued might find an irreconcilable difference in the demands of the new stage. Transitions are uncertain times.

STAGES AND TRANSITIONS IN MARRIAGE

Generally, the couple that is unmarried will be only infrequently seen *for counseling* by the Christian counselor. A pastor often sees such a couple for several meetings as preparation for marriage, or the church might prescribe that a couple intending to marry attend classes to prepare them for marriage. Such classes, however, are vastly different from marriage counseling with troubled couples. Preparation-for-marriage classes are informational and are rarely involved with negotiating differences and rebuilding intimacy.

Courtship

In fact, one difficulty with the "preparation for marriage" notion is that its purpose is ambiguously defined.

☐ Is the purpose of such "counseling" to help the couple get along better after marriage?

☐ Is the purpose to help the couple get to know each other better so they can decide whether they even want to marry?

☐ Is the purpose to build communication skills in the couple?

☐ Is it to build knowledge about marriage?

☐ Is it merely to inform the couple about the ceremony?

☐ Is it to watch over the Christian couple to insure that they are behaving appropriately?

The lack of clarity in the purposes of preparation for marriage has resulted in only small gains for the couples who attend such sessions.[16] Research has shown that more helpful gains can be realized by couples who, *after* they are married, attend counseling to adjust to marriage and transform their differences into workable relationship rules.[17]

One special instance of courtship involves couples who are living together without being married. Many such couples now exist[18]—dramatically more than existed in the late sixties and seventies. Even among conservative Christians, some couples cohabit before marriage. Although this is in clear violation of God's law and thus is not good for the individuals, both spiritually and in their earthly life, it is nonetheless a fact of modern life.

Most counselors will be confronted with an occasional couple who are cohabiting. This calls for difficult value decisions by the counselor. The counselor must ask himself or herself, "Am I to counsel this couple who is deliberately sinning or am I merely to inform them of God's laws (which they undoubtedly already know) and of the consequences of disobeying God deliberately? Will the counsel I give differ from the way I would counsel a married couple? If so, how?" Obviously, these questions are complex—too complex to consider here. Through asking and answering such questions, though, the counselor defines the criteria he or she uses to determine whether to counsel, admonish or refer.

I generally will counsel a troubled cohabiting couple. I make my values known to them by telling them the risks that they are incurring, both spiritually and physically, by cohabiting. I work with them to better their relationship (though I refuse to do sexual counseling with the couple) and my desire is to guide them to decide to end their cohabitation either through marriage, breaking up, or moving apart and discontinuing sexual relations.

When counseling a cohabiting couple, the greatest challenge to effective counseling is usually their ambivalence about making a commitment to each other. Unlike the couple who knows they are married and need to work the problems out of their relationship, the cohabiting couple is continually thinking, "If it doesn't work, we'll just end our relationship." This wait-and-see attitude makes it almost impossible for either person to risk changing his or her behavior. Rather, each partner decides to change only if the other partner changes. The result is that when cohabiting couples have relationship difficulties, they rarely work them out so that they can continue in their relationship.

Marriage Ceremony: A Transition

When a couple marries, things change. Before they were married, a man and woman say that they are together because they love each other. If asked why they are together after they are married, however, they have two explanations. They might love each other just as much as before marriage (or even more), but they know that they are also together *because* they are married.[19]

The knowledge that there is a legal and moral tie binding spouses to each other creates uncertainty over how much they love each other. The more a spouse thinks about this legal obligation of marriage, the less likely the spouse is to think of his or her love for the other. Some couples, by taking their marriage commitment to each other so strongly, can kill the romance from their marriage and can establish a feeling that they are trapped in their marriage. Other couples who undervalue their commitment to each other can wind up with divorces simply because one or both spouses becomes displeased with the other.

The tension between romantic attraction and permanent commitment remains throughout marriage. At times each couple emphasizes one part of this teeter-totter more than the other. The enduring and fulfilling marriage continues to return to center and to affirm both truths—undying love and undying commitment under God.

Something else happens after the couple marries. Prior to marriage, the couple usually spends time together in mostly intimate and coactive activities. They talk together about their hopes and dreams and about their childhood memories. They explore their sexual feelings toward each other. They date by attending activities together. But when their dates are finished, they each return home and pursue distancing activities away from the date.

Upon marriage, though, when they finish a date, they are still in the presence of the spouse. Whereas before marriage their time together had almost no distancing activities, after marriage there is substantial distancing. The amount of intimate and coactive activities might have even increased, but the balance has shifted. This shift usually prompts each spouse to wonder whether the romance is still there. "You never *used to* read the newspaper at the breakfast table," he wails, forgetting that before their marriage he never saw her at the breakfast table. "You don't love me anymore," she says. "All you do is watch television when you get home from work." She doesn't know that he has watched television each weekday night for five years before they were married but she was not around to see it.

Thus, one danger in the early marriage is that the couple will become dissatisfied with their "love" for each other because they are privy to a spouse's distancing activities that they had never previously observed.

The Honey-moon

After the marriage ceremony, newlyweds want desperately to get along with each other. But they have come from two different backgrounds, two different families. The behavior, roles and communication patterns within their families of origin likely differed. Shortly after marriage, one of the spouses tells or asks the other to do something that is not in line with his or her idea of "proper" behavior within a family. During the honeymoon phase, which might last anywhere from one minute to one year but usually lasts from three to six months, the person who receives the "improper" request might think something like, "Well, it's not really a man's work to empty the kitchen garbage, but I love her and I'll put up with it this time," or "I really don't understand why we need to make a budget, but this time . . ." or "This is really not the proper way to make love, but . . ." During the honeymoon, disagreements over the rules of the new marriage are generally glossed over. Each person feels a little upset that things are not being done "correctly," but the person puts aside his or her feelings to maintain harmony in the relationship.

The Honey-moon Is Over: A Transition

Differences mount throughout the honeymoon phase. One day one of the spouses objects, and the couple has conflict over what the rules of the relationship are, who can say what the rules are and how the rules will be negotiated. This first disagreement over relationship rules is often a disillusionment over expectations that one spouse held for the other. The topic of disagreement is sometimes trivial. The couple is not really arguing about the topic so much as they are beginning to meld the rules of two families of origin into the rules of their marriage.

In some of my research comparing happy and unhappy couples across the family life cycle, I found that unhappy couples had more conflict and less intimacy than happy couples at all points of the family life cycle except one.[20] In the first three years of marriage, happy couples had both more disagreements and more intimacy than did unhappy couples. I interpreted this to mean that couples who did not work out their differences early in marriage through having some disagreements over the fundamental rules of their relationship, would probably have more conflict throughout the remainder of their marriage. Further, in this research I found that unhappy couples, despite having less overt conflict than happy couples, had more private feelings of unhappiness with their partners. I interpreted this as meaning that when couples did not disagree during the early years, they still had unpleasantness in their lives.

When counseling couples early in marriage, the goal is *not* to prevent conflict but to teach the couple how to disagree so that they can resolve their differences without hurting one another. Newlywed couples have established less well-ingrained patterns of behavior and communication than couples who have been married for over three years. They might be helped fastest by inducing them to change their behavior *first* and then verbalize the rules that govern their behavior. Older couples usually have firmly established verbal rules that govern their behavior and often require communication training *prior to* behavior change. This is consonant with research on counseling with newly marrieds versus long-marrieds.[21]

Most divorces occur in the third year of marriage.[22] In the troubled marriage, the first six months are a honeymoon. The next year involves frequent and escalating conflict. Separation occurs in the second year; divorce in the third.

The Couple Alone

However, many couples do not follow that pattern. After increasingly intense conflict, the couple begins to agree on some issues that had been sources of disagreements. They begin to solve problems in ways that work for them, establishing their relationship rules, their patterns of behavior. They gradually achieve a meeting of minds and share more pleasant environmental events. Their behavior patterns with each other become pleasant environmental structures.

As research on marriage has repeatedly shown, the time prior to children is the period of highest marriage satisfaction for many couples.[23] Generally, the spouses have free time. With no children to occupy their nonworking hours, the couple can do activities alone, together or with other couples who also generally have few responsibilities besides work. This promotes high intimacy, for the couple can structure their time together to get to know each other better. With little conflict and high intimacy, the couple is usually quite happy.

**The First
Child Is
Born: A
Transition**

Into this stable two-person system, a child is born.[24] Children require care, and child care requires time. Thus, schedules must be rearranged. This can potentially disrupt the balance of intimacy between husband and wife. The most common complaint of new mothers is exhaustion. They try to do what they were doing before the birth and take care of the child's demands too. The most common complaint of new fathers is that they feel neglected by their wives. Furthermore, both husband and wife complain that their intimacy decreases. No longer can they spontaneously eat out or drive to a nearby resort for an intimate weekend alone. Backpacking for the weekend is out. Trips to Europe just aren't the same. And walking around the block to talk about their day requires the planning and preparation of a move to a new city.[25]

There are many decisions to be made about the newborn. Most couples experience some conflict, but it is not usually pronounced unless they had high conflict before the birth.[26]

Of course, each subsequent child forces the family to adjust in new ways, to rearrange their schedules and to work out new rules; but generally, the first child is the most disruptive.

**The Terrible
Two's: A
Transition**

Newborns grow older. As they age, they fortify the parents' belief in the inherent fallenness of humans.[27] At some point, usually during the child's second year, the couple realizes that the child has a will of his or her own which differs from the will of a parent. Decisions must be made about when and how to discipline the child.

Humans dislike discipline. It is an emotional issue with a family history. Actually, two family histories. As a child, each parent was disciplined differently for different reasons, and each parent has strong feelings about the way that his or her parents disciplined. Dissatisfaction or satisfaction with one's parents' child-rearing methods both produce an enduring influence on parents.

The terrible two's, thus, have more potential to be terrible for parents than for the child. The parents must now face emotional decisions about when and how to discipline each time the child does something displeasing to a parent. Agreeing on which punishments fit which offenses and which rewards fit which behaviors will alleviate much disagreement, but the rules that are worked out in practice, with each decision about discipline, are sometimes different than the couple's verbal agreements. New and highly emotional decisions about child rearing might intensify conflict over who makes the rules of the marriage or might destroy the previous balance of power.

Generally, the couple who comes to counseling concerned with child-discipline problems will focus more on conflict than on intimacy issues. Parenting training by behavioral counselors, Parent Effectiveness Training, Bill Gothard's Basic Youth Conflicts and James Dobson's techniques have been helpful to couples with disagreements about child rearing. These couples can listen to an "expert" and can use his or her advice to settle disagreements, which bypasses some of the power struggles between the couples.

Entering School: A Transition

When the child is five or six, he or she enters school. Suddenly, the family, through the child, is on public display. Authorities at school will judge the deportment of the child and make inferences about the parents' child-rearing ability. If parents are still contesting child rearing, reports from the school can rekindle open conflict between the parents.

In addition, the parents and the school may find themselves in conflict over the child. Parents may disagree with the teacher's evaluation of the child's performance. Parents may object to decisions by school officials about whether a child is to be passed, held back or skipped or about whether a child is to be placed in a special class for gifted or for disturbed children. Conflicts with the school might also trigger disagreements between the parents.

When a child enters school, time schedules change. If the child is the only child or the last child at home, changes can be large, necessitating renegotiation of intimate relationships.

Throughout the School and Adolescent Years

Raising children during their school years is often difficult, primarily because parents are so busy. During child-rearing years, career awareness is high for men and women. Often the woman is either beginning a new career or is devoting herself to child rearing. Because they are concerned with both family and career, the couple has little time for intimacy.

Their needs for intimacy are unchanged, but they are working most closely with either children or other career-conscious adults who are involved in their own careers or families. The middle years are difficult years to meet intimacy needs. People often report being lonely in the middle years, and they yearn for close friends who have time for intimacy. Unfilled intimacy needs often make a person ripe for an affair.

The novelty of an affair provides instant intimacy. The pseudo-courtship maintains the illusion that the relationship with the lover is more fulfilling than the relationship with the spouse. The lover is seen only for intimate and coactive activities. Distancing is accomplished by returning home to the family. Thus, the illicit relationship seems more rewarding than the relationship with the spouse. If the person pursues the illicit relationship by divorcing the spouse and remarrying the lover, the person soon finds the same pressures and cares of the previous marriage. The divorce rate for second marriages is greater than for first marriages.[28]

First Child Enters Adolescence: A Transition

When the first child enters adolescence, numerous changes occur within the family. The increasing independence of the adolescent forces the family to re-evaluate its rules, giving the adolescent more responsibility. Adolescents usually believe themselves to be more ready for independence than parents do. Parents can lessen conflict by giving the adolescent independence gradually *before* the adolescent demands it. The adolescent gains freedom while the parents retain control over dispensing freedom.

Demands for freedom by the adolescent can trigger conflict between the parents. This is especially true if conflict between parents already exists.

Adolescents wrestle with several individual concerns. They are defining their sexual identity and are experiencing changes in their bodies' appearance and functioning. This comes when parents are concerned about their own sexual identity. The wife might have just experienced menopause, and she wonders what its ramifications for the marriage will be. The husband notices that while his adolescent child is increasing in sexual attractiveness, he is getting bald and grey and is perhaps putting on weight.

While the child discusses career concerns with parents, the mother and father often re-evaluate their own careers. The father might be at a crossroads in his career and might have to make a major career decision soon. Although the father is usually in his prime earning years, the expenses of a family with adolescents can be a strain, especially when college expenses begin to be felt.

Often the emergence of one child into adolescence signals the entry of the last child into school. When all the children are in school, the mother's time schedule is often rearranged. Many women re-enter the work force, which generally affects everyone in the family. Mother no longer can do as many household chores, so additional demands are made on other family members to care for the household.

In short, adolescence is a time when family rules are challenged, when family structure is changed, when intimacy patterns are disrupted, and when individual concerns over sexual identity and work identity are paramount for both children and adults. Is there any wonder that adolescence is a time of lower marriage satisfaction for both husband and wives than most other times of life?[29]

When each additional child enters adolescence, many of the same struggles are repeated, keeping personal and family issues highly visible as long as adolescents are in the home.

Children Leaving Home: A Transition

As children leave the immediate care of their parents, there usually is little change in the intimacy patterns in the family. If the adolescent has been given increasing responsibility throughout adolescence, then he or she is ready to take the step into physical independence. That step should be small enough that it does not influence the family's schedule, and thus intimacy, very much. Psychologically, the move away from home is often traumatic, especially for the mother. Because they usually have strong identity feelings as a mother, women often are forced to re-evaluate the meaning of their lives and vocations when each child leaves home. The mother's effectance needs have been met through her role as a mother, and she must re-establish other ways to meet her effectance needs.

When the adolescent leaves home, there are generally few changes in family rules if the adolescent has been gradually allowed to have more responsibility. Thus the largest personal adjustment will usually come from the struggle of the mother to re-establish meaningful work in her life.

The parents, though, have a difficult adjustment to make as a couple. They must redefine their relationship with each other. Whereas, for the past twenty or so years they have related with each other as parents, they must re-establish their relationship as spouses. Many unresolved power struggles can resurface as they negotiate how to spend their last twenty-plus years.

Until now I have described what might happen with harmonious marriages if parents had given the adolescent increasing freedom as the adolescent matured. Unfortunately, many households have great conflict—between husband and wife and between parents and adolescent. In families with tension between the parents, one child will often sacrifice his or her own well-being to prevent the parents from having open conflict that is severe enough to precipitate a divorce. This child "helps" the parents through difficult times by getting into trouble. This child is often labeled the "black sheep" of the family, though his or her role is more accurately as a "sacrificial lamb."[30]

For example, the Milner's have four children. The first two are "angels" and Ron, the youngest, is often described as "very sensitive." The third child, Stuart, is continually in trouble. He wet the bed until he was ten years old. He had periodic asthma attacks and frequent trouble in school, being described by his teachers as hyperactive and requiring medication throughout adolescence.

When Stuart is fourteen, Mr. Milner is offered a transfer and promotion. Mother and father disagree heatedly about whether the promotion will be accepted. One night, while Stuart is supposed to be at the bowling alley with some friends, the parents receive a call from the police. Stuart has been arrested for public drunkenness and auto theft. The family is thrown into crisis, but they pull together to get past this emotional time. Things stabilize, but Stuart is soon expelled from school for using drugs on school property. Because this violates his parole agreement, he is placed in a special reform school, which he reports liking better than he did public school. The family limps along for three years while Stuart is under the custody of the juvenile authorities. Mother and father are worried to distraction over what will become of Stuart. They have forgotten, or at least laid aside, the conflict over the promotion. (How could they move when Stuart was still here?) They are so exasperated with Stuart, in fact, that they have very few arguments and life at home is relatively smooth. After three years, Stuart is placed on work release; he loads trucks for a meat-packing house. He is suddenly killed in a freak accident.

After a period of mourning by the family, conflict again surfaces between mother and father. As the tension mounts, Ron begins to have difficulty at school. His marks decline, and he becomes clinically depressed. Father and mother—worried about the effect of their fighting on Ron and disturbed because Ron does not seem to be making much progress, despite weekly counseling sessions—stop discussing the topics that they had been arguing about.

As should be clear from this example, which is not far removed from some actual clients I have counseled, this couple will probably have difficulty when their adolescent children leave home—if they ever leave home. A counselor for this couple would be interested not only in the relationship between Mr. and Mrs. Milner, but also in their relationship with their children, especially with Ron. Ron seems to have taken the "black sheep" role left vacant by the accidental death of Stuart. In this family, the counselor would expect that the couple might request counseling to resolve some long-standing marital difficulties, but a family crisis would erupt and the couple might end counseling because of the more pressing concerns of the crisis. They would describe themselves as "doing a lot better" and as "not really needing counseling anymore." The counselor's task is to concentrate on their conflictual relationship.

The Empty Nest

Once all the children have left home, most couples spend many years together. Some divorce.

Couples who divorce often say that they merely stayed together "for the kids"; however, generally they divorce because they could not readjust to a two-person system from the larger family system. Conflicts that were displaced onto children while the children were at home suddenly must be faced, and the couple is unwilling to resolve their different roles.

For the counselor facing such a distressed couple, the immediate task is to reduce their conflict. Merely attempting to increase their time or intimacy together usually produces even more conflict. In younger couples, whose conflictual patterns are not so well ingrained, the first treatment might be to increase their opportunities for intimacy. But the reverse is true for the older couple.

On the other hand, some couples have had little conflict throughout their life together. These couples might come to counseling because they are experiencing more conflict than in the past or because they feel that their relationship has "lost the romance." These couples must be dealt with by first increasing their intimacy and later alleviating conflict.

In general, the empty-nest years have high potential to be some of the happiest years of married life, since career demands are usually lower than at other times and children occupy little attention of the spouses. If the relationship rules can be re-established to govern the husband-wife relationship, the couple can have a strong base of mutual support with which to cope with the inevitable transitions that occur in the remaining years of their lives.

Becoming an In-Law: A Transition

The effect on the marriage of having a child marry depends on the proximity of the newlyweds to the parents and on the amount of contact between the two families. It also depends on the response of the parents to the struggles of the new couple.

Parents usually identify most closely with their own child, which is important when the child has a disagreement with his or her spouse. Meaning well and sincerely trying to help the child, parents can become involved in a coalition against the child's spouse that can make it difficult for the child to solve his or her marital difficulties.

Scripture advises newlyweds to leave their parents and to cleave to each other (Gen 2:24). It does not provide an exception clause, such as leave their parents until they become dissatisfied with their spouse. Conflicts between spouses are inevitable. Parents, while loving and supporting their child, must gently refuse to become embroiled in their children's marriages.

Counselors generally do not see parents coming for counseling because they are overinvolved with their children's marriages. Rather, counselors see newlyweds who are in conflict and learn through the couple about the destructive influence of the in-laws. At that point, the counselor must decide whether to invite parents to counseling sessions or whether to work with newlyweds alone to disentangle the parents.

When a couple's children have children, the couple must accept changes in the structure of their own family. For some parents who have already "let their child go," the transition to being a grandparent is easy. However, grandparents who have kept tight control of a child even after the child is married often find themselves immersed in the structure of their child's family. They must accept their status as advisors and peers to their children rather than continue to run the life of the adult child.

Becoming a Grandparent: A Transition

Especially dangerous is when grandparents form a coalition with the grandchild against the parent. One case that I supervised involved a husband and wife, Sam and Fran. Both had been previously married and Sam had custody of his pre-teen daughter, Jenny. They sought counseling because of Jenny's misbehavior. One of my students, Tim Tehan, wanted to learn Jay Haley's strategic family counseling, so we approached the case in orthodox strategic therapy fashion.[31]

It soon became evident that pre-teen Jenny and her father, Sam, had formed a coalition against stepmother Fran. Jenny would misbehave. Fran would correct her. After several corrections, Sam would upbraid Fran, calling her an incompetent mother. Fran would withdraw. Sam would try to correct Jenny's misbehavior, but he could not control her effectively. He would become increasingly exasperated until he lost his temper and asked for Fran's help. Jenny would continue to misbehave, and Fran would correct her. After several times, Sam would again upbraid Fran and the cycle would repeat . . . for years.

Following Haley's recommendations, we tried to break up the coalition between father and daughter by getting mother more involved in helping the girl. Tim (the counselor) defined Fran as the "expert" on misbehavior because as a girl she had had similar problems. Sam was gently moved to a less central place of involvement with Jenny.

During one week, however, Jenny became upset with her father and ran away to her paternal grandparents' house. With the grandparents involved in the child discipline, Tim asked about their role in Sam's and Fran's lives.

A new dimension to the case opened up like a flower in the spring.

When Sam had obtained a divorce from his first wife, he had been only eighteen. He had joined the army and had been stationed in Germany. Because the first wife did not want to rear Jenny, Sam left her with his parents during his time in the army. The grandparents became attached to Jenny, and they transferred their love from Sam to his daughter. The closeness had continued after Sam married Fran. Whenever Jenny did not get her way at home, she complained to her grandparents, who called Sam and threatened to remove him from their wills if he did not "treat Jenny better."

Thus, two simultaneous coalitions were operating in the family. The coalition between the grandparents and Jenny paralyzed Sam from effective discipline, while the coalition between Sam and Jenny paralyzed Fran, making her impotent as a disciplinarian.

Death of a Grandparent: A Transition

When a grandparent dies, especially the first grandparent on one side of the family, the family often is placed under strain.

The grandparents provide each other with most of their support. They satisfy most of each other's needs for intimacy and effectance, yet they depend on outsiders for meeting some of their needs. A representation of the grandparents' system is shown in Figure 7a. The grandparents have friends who interact with them as a couple. Other friends interact with only one member of the pair.

When one grandparent dies (see Figure 7b), the survivor's social support system undergoes drastic revision. Besides losing the spouse, the surviving grandparent loses interaction with people who were the spouse's friends and those who were friends of the couple. The only remaining support system involves the friends of the surviving spouse as an individual, which includes the survivor's children.

The grandparent still needs intimacy but has a vastly reduced network for meeting those needs. The children will likely be called on to meet those intimacy needs. The grandparent might move in with the family or might require financial assistance. The grandparent might require frequent visits or telephone calls. All of these demands place strains on the couple because they require time previously used in other ways. Intimacy can easily be disrupted.

Figure 7a
A Representation of Grandparents' Social System

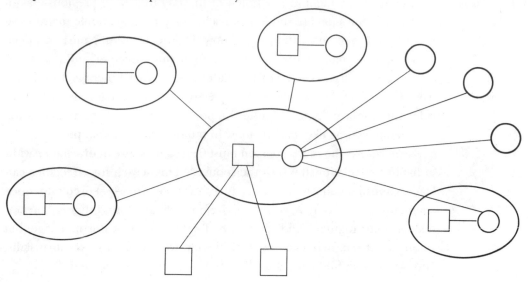

Figure 7b
A Representation of One Grandparent's Social System after the Death of the Other Grandparent

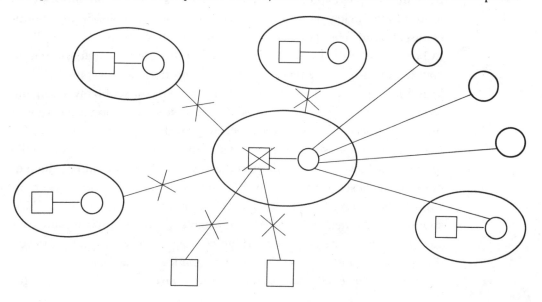

**Retirement:
A Transition**

When one or both members of a couple retires, large changes in time schedules occur. Eight to ten hours of the day that were previously associated with one's job are suddenly unscheduled time. A couple might have more time for intimacy than they know what to do with. Numerous decisions must be made about how to use their time together and apart and about how to survive on the often inadequate financial income they derive from social security, retirement and personal savings. Each decision provides the opportunity to redefine the power structure of the relationship. Retirement can be like starting anew in building a relationship.

Furthermore, the retired person must find some sense of effectance within his or her relationship with the spouse.[32] This search for effectance can lead to unusual behaviors. For instance, a wife of a newly retired man once complained, "As soon as he retired, he immediately found that *my* kitchen needed rearranging. I had scraped by for fifty years of our marriage, but when he retired, he moved into my kitchen with all of his executive skills, and now I can't find a thing and I can't keep him out of my hair."

**The
Retirement
Years**

The biggest struggle during the retired years is to satisfy needs for effectance.[33] The social system is structured so that senior citizens often are treated as helpless and are considered as almost useless appendages onto a productive society. Furthermore, for most retired people, financial difficulties abound. The standard of their living is often changed drastically as inflation erodes their retirement savings. In this environment, the retired couple must find some feeling that they can affect the outcomes of their lives. Sadly, too few find this feeling. One of the major problems during the retired years is depression. Depression can take on additional meaning if one spouse becomes depressed largely to provide a sense of effectance for the other. One spouse achieves effectance through being "caretaker," while the other achieves a sense of effectance by protecting the other. The tendency for spouses to "protect" each other can establish a stable system in which *both* spouses lament the depression and loneliness of the troubled spouse, but the depression seems intractable. A counselor is usually contacted because of the depression. If the marriage is to be changed, however, the counselor must provide a sense of effectance for both spouses.

On the positive side, the retirement years have enormous potential for intimacy. Work demands are nonexistent, and family demands are greatly reduced. The couple can structure their time to meet each's needs for intimacy. Friends outside the marriage often take on importance that they did not have during earlier years of life, and old friendships are often rediscovered. Yet, with intimacy comes pain as friends and other family members are often lost through death.

WHY TRANSITIONS AFFECT SOME COUPLES MORE THAN OTHERS

Stages and transitions between stages throughout the entire life cycle are summarized in Table 3. The table lists for each stage and transition the expected level of intimacy and open conflict for most couples. It also summarizes transitional disruptions to time schedules, and therefore to intimacy, as well as likely disruptions to relationship rules occasioned by new decisions about which the couple initially disagrees. Additional disruptions characteristic of each stage or transition are also noted in the last column.

Effects of a Particular Transition

Each couple experiences a transition differently, so the marriage counselor must treat each couple individually. However, it is helpful to understand the effects of transitions on most couples in order to begin assessment of particular couples.

Three assessments are fundamental to understanding couples' responses to transitions: the degree of disruption in their time schedules, the number of new decisions about which there is initial disagreement and the level of ongoing conflict prior to the transition.[34]

Generally, if the degree of disruption of time schedules is great, the couple will experience great upheaval in their lives. During that time, spouses will be disoriented and will struggle to get their lives back in order. They will feel overstressed and little able to cope with the changes in their lives.

If the number of decisions about which there is initial disagreement is high, the couple will have many disagreements. Some will be relatively minor, but others will loom larger. With each disagreement, the rules about how decisions are to be made and who has the most say in the decisions will be in question. The couple will test their old patterns of problem

Table 3
A Summary of Disturbances throughout the Life Cycle

Stage	Transition	Level of Intimacy	Level of Open Conflict	During Transitions		Other Effects
				Likely Disruption in Time Schedule	Likely Disruption in Rules (conflict)	
Courtship		High	Low			
	Marriage	High-Mod	Low	Suddenly sees distancing	Rules must govern all of life, not dating	Becomes *legally* married
Honeymoon (0-6 mo.)	(0-6 mo.)	Mod	Low			Conflicts are internal
	Honeymoon is over	Mod	Mod-Hi	Little disruption	Conflict becomes overt; rules being worked out	Expectations violated
The Couple Alone		High-Mod	Low			High satisfaction with marriage
	1st child born	High-Mod	Mod	Very high; couple activities curtailed, exhaustion in mother, time schedules overhauled	Some; new rules for 3-person system must be formed	
Child (0-2)		Mod	Mod			
	Child discipline begins	Mod	High	Little additional disruption in schedule	Discipline policy formation is emotional	
Child (2-5)			Mod (Depends on congruence between "policy" and actual decisions)			
	Child enters school	Mod	Mod-Low	High (if only child or if last child)	Some, if decisions are required about placement of child	Possible conflict w/ authorities might pull couple together or push them apart
Child in School Years		Low-Mod (High "career" involvement; friends also over-involved)	Low-Mod			Low intimacy makes affairs a threat

Table 3
(Continued)

Stage	Transition	Level of Intimacy	Level of Open Conflict	During Transitions		Other Effects
				Likely Disruption in Time Schedule	Likely Disruption in Rules (conflict)	
	Child enters adolescence	Low	High (conflict may be with both spouse & adolescent)	High (teen begins to want more freedom, schedules become more uncertain)	High (demands for autonomy force changes in family structure)	Threats to parents' sexual identity; Threats to parent & child body image
Throughout Adolescence		Low (High "career" involvement; friends also over-involved)	Mod-High			
	Launching	Low (Mother loses involvement with child)	Mod	Little (Esp. if adolescent has been given increasing freedom)	High (Moving back to a 2-person system)	Change in self-concept from parent to spouse
Empty nest		Mod-High	Mod-Low			Happy couples become happier; unhappy couples become unhappier
	Becoming an In-Law			Low-High, depending on proximity	Low-High, depending on amount of interaction with newlyweds	Must change self-concept from parent to peer
	Becoming a grandparent			Low-High	Low-High	Must change self-concept from parent to advisor
	Death of grand-parent			Mod-High, depending on support system of surviving grandparent	Low-High, depending on proximity of surviving grandparent	
	Retirement			Very High	High	Need to reestablish effectance
Retired		High	Low			For happy couples who work out rules, can be happiest time; for unhappy couples, can be most unhappy time

solving and forge new ones.

Relationships with many new decisions to make will often be characterized by spouses with short tempers and little patience with each other. They
might feel as if their basic rights are being violated or that they are not
understood or appreciated. They usually complain that their opinions are
not valued the way they have been in the past. Anger, frustration and
depression are often the spouses' dominant moods.

If the pre-transition level of conflict has been high, this usually signi-
fies that whatever conflicts occur during the new transition will be more
emotional and harder to resolve than they would be if the pre-transition
level of conflict has been low. High pre-transition conflict usually means
that the fundamental power rules in the relationship are being contested;
thus, any disagreement is usually interpreted by both spouses as a bid
for additional power by the other spouse. Such relationships are usually
characterized by mistrust and suspicion. In addition, the problem-solving
behaviors of the couples are characterized by coercion and threat. There
is little effort to reason together. One spouse may use rational arguments as a persuasive strategy, while the other spouse usually uses emotional tactics. Despite the reasonableness of the arguments of the "rational" spouse, the couple is generally not interested in solving problems equitably. Rather, they are interested in solving problems so they get their own
ways. Conflict and stress both stimulate people to greater levels of egocen-
tricity.

For any particular couple, disturbances may or may not occur in any of
the three areas. For example, one couple might have a first baby and
experience little change in their time schedules, few decisions about which
they disagree and low levels of initial conflict. The couple is likely to find
the transition to parenthood to involve little difficulty. A second couple who
were also having little conflict prior to the birth of their first child might
have their time schedules greatly disrupted and might have to resolve many
new issues. That couple will usually find the transition to parenthood to be
stressful. On the other hand, the first couple, who sailed through the transition to parenthood, might be utterly devastated when their first child
enters school because they had different ideas about how to make decisions
over homework, teachers and child discipline.

SUMMARY

The second part of the book has argued that three considerations are important to understanding marriage. Each of the three considerations will be used in the remainder of the book as the basis of assessing and treating troubled marriages. The three considerations involve different levels of analysis, so the marriage counselor must conduct the assessment and treatment of couples using the three levels at the same time rather than sequentially.

At the most basic level, fundamental human needs dictate attention to commitment, intimacy, effectance and forgiveness within the relationship. These needs must be met for the relationship to flourish and for the individual to feel fulfilled.

1. *When commitment goes awry,* marriage is characterized by mistrust and feelings of betrayal and unfairness.

2. *When intimacy is not fulfilled,* the marriage is characterized by aloofness, lack of interest and coldness (or coolness) of the partners toward each other. Problems in intimacy might also be characterized by feelings of being overwhelmed and overstressed.

3. *Problems in effectance* result in an overconcern with power, with who is right or with who has wronged whom. Arguments are frequent and are often catalyzed by minor incidents. Conflict tends to escalate over time, and disintegration of the relationship can occur if the couple cannot resolve their differences in power within the relationship.

4. *Problems in forgiveness* result from hurt and egocentrism of the party who was hurt. A relationship characterized by unforgiveness is built on mistrust of the spouse and either an air of martyred affliction or a desire to hurt the other person in return. Often, Christian couples can confess forgiveness, but still tend to act in ways that provoke their spouses. Over time, lack of forgiveness can lead to bitterness.

Overlaid onto assessments of commitment, intimacy, effectance and forgiveness are determinations of the effects of each partner's spiritual life and cognitions, and of the couple's shared environmental events and structures. I have selected these areas as important because I (and others who hold to cognitive-behavioral theories) have found them useful for all kinds of couples—from the mildly disturbed to the severely disturbed. The marriage counselor must attend to the current status of the couple's spiritual involvement with other Christians, with each other and privately. It is my belief (and it is supported by the Bible) that the seen world and the unseen world interact, affecting each other in ways that people do not always understand unless God gives them particular revelations. Focus on thoughts, behaviors and environment are consistent with a cognitive-behavioral perspective. Special attention must be paid to the communication and other interactions between spouses. Communication forms the largest part of the environmental events that each spouse must cope with in the marriage.

Finally, the marriage counselor must attend to the stage of life of the couple with whom counseling is taking place. Special considerations are necessary at each stage and at each transition between stages. These considerations must be accounted for, especially in the ways that they affect the commitment, intimacy, effectance and forgiveness of the couple.

Yet, it is not helpful for a counselor to aim solely at helping couples understand the major parts of a marriage relationship and how problems can occur. Most couples who are disturbed enough to seek marriage counseling can benefit little from mere information. Usually, they have received information and advice from many "counselors" prior to seeking help from a pastor or other mental health professional. The professional counselor must stimulate change systematically with concentration on the crucial areas of marriage and with the use of powerful techniques of change. The third and fourth parts of the book provide a theory and method of counseling that will use the background presented here to help you help couples change their relationships.

Early Phase of Counseling Troubled Marriages

SUMMARY Counseling is divided into assessment, intervention and termination phases—even though the phases are intimately intertwined and are each dependent on the counselor's understanding of the marriage. The primary goals of the early phase of counseling are to join with the couple in a working alliance, assess the marriage so that changes can be attempted and set goals for change based on the assessment. The primary goal of the second phase of counseling is to help the couple change. The primary goal of the last phase of counseling is to promote commitment within the couple.

Part three begins with an overview of counseling (chapter 5) and a discussion of its three phases. Chapter 6 offers instructions about how to create a working alliance between counselor and couple. In chapter 7, assessment, both how and what to assess, is given special attention because the couple's willingness to participate in the counselor's suggestions for change is dependent on the credibility of the suggestions. Guidelines are given for assessing intimacy; communication; conflict; hurt, blame and sin; and commitment. Thorough assessment builds credibility. Finally, the counselor will formulate goals for change and present them to the couple (chapter 8). A set of working goals must be negotiated prior to the intervention phase of counseling. Finally, concrete guidelines are given concerning how to conduct the two assessment sessions and the feedback session that compose the early part of marriage counseling (chapter 9).

Overview of Counseling: Assessment, Intervention and Termination

THE COUNSELING I DESCRIBE IN THE FOLLOWING PAGES IS NOT for every couple that walks through your door. It is best applied under three restrictions:

1. The couple *specifically request marriage counseling* and are *seen conjointly*.

2. Counseling is *relatively short term* (approximately three assessment sessions and from eight to sixteen counseling sessions).

3. The counselor works *without a cotherapist*.

Given these restrictions, marriage counseling generally follows a regular progression.

THE STRUCTURE OF COUNSELING

See Couples
for Marriage
Counseling

One of the first tasks with any person who seeks your help is to *determine who the client is,* which is not always easy to do. For instance, Mrs. Johnson contacts you because her twelve-year-old son, Rob, is misbehaving at school. At your first appointment, all the Johnsons—mother, father and son—arrive at your office. Each of them wants Rob to behave better at school. By the end of the first interview, it is apparent to you that substantial conflict exists between Mr. and Mrs. Johnson, and Rob is terrified that they will divorce. Assume that you take as your main goal to help Rob behave better at school. Who is your client?

☐ Is it Rob? His behavior is the focus of the outcome of your counseling. Creating observable change in his behavior will determine the parents' and possibly the school's evaluation of your effectiveness as a counselor.

☐ Is it the mother? She contacted you. She is the primary caretaker for the boy and is likely to have substantial influence over him.

☐ Is it the father? He attended counseling unbidden. He pays the bills for the counseling, and he lets you know this early in the session.

☐ Is it the marriage? True, Mr. and Mrs. Johnson did not request that you change their marriage, but your clinical sense tells you that as long as they experience conflict, Rob will misbehave.

☐ Is it the family? It's your aim to restore stability to the family while helping members change their self-destructive behavior.

☐ Is it the family/school interaction? Perhaps you suspect that Rob is caught in the crossfire between parents and school authorities who are making different demands on the boy.

Obviously, you would like to help everyone be happier. Unfortunately, this rarely (if ever) happens. Frankly, counseling just isn't that powerful. You can hope to make some limited changes that relieve immediate discomfort and set the people involved on a road that will be less painful than the road they were traveling prior to counseling. But you will probably not solve everyone's problems. If you enter counseling without deciding exactly who your client is, though, your chances of helping anyone will be reduced.

Counseling generally starts with gusto and progresses well until the first major intervention. In the Johnson's case, after some parent training, Mrs.

Johnson returned depressed. The counselor, not wishing to see her unhappy, focused on her depression. The initial intervention was forgotten. Over the next few weeks Mrs. Johnson's depression improved, but school officials wrote notes home about Rob's behavior. The counselor returned to the original direction of counseling. Having lost momentum, a new intervention had to be built.

That's how counseling often proceeds. The counselor tries to "help the family get better," but counseling is unfocused and helter-skelter and little progress is made.

Because of this, almost all of my counseling is with one clear objective: to improve the marriage relationship. Clients might seek help because they have lost enthusiasm for their marriage—that is to say, they are bored, have no common interests, don't love the spouse any longer. They might seek help because they argue and fight. They might seek help because one spouse had an affair. They might seek help because one is symptomatic (depressed, anxious, beset by career indecision) and the other is disturbed at the chronicity of the problem.

Regardless of why they seek help, I try to be clear early in counseling.

My belief is that your marriage is in trouble. I will gladly work with both of you to improve your relationship. If your relationship improves, I would expect your other difficulties to bother you less. If you agree with me that you want to work primarily on your marriage, then I would be glad to help. If you have a different idea about what you would like counseling for, then I would be glad to refer you to any of several Christian counselors in town. What do you think?

My goal is not to coerce people into accepting my goals, but to select clients whose goals are in line with my interests and talents.

Naturally, I want to do more than help people have better marriages. I want to help the anxious or depressed spouse become less anxious or depressed, but if I frequently change the focus of my counseling, I likely will accomplish *neither* the bettering of their marriage nor the improvement of their psychological functioning.

If I have been counseling a couple for marriage difficulties and one spouse arrives at a session depressed, I will certainly take time to help the spouse. However, I try to do that only if the person is so distressed that our usual counseling will be unhelpful *and* only if I can reserve the second half of the session to continue with marriage counseling. This acknowledges the importance of the spouse's emotional state while affirming the central importance of the marriage counseling.

See Couples Together

Marriage counseling is most effectively done when both spouses attend sessions together. Couples who attend individual counseling to work on marriage concerns have less than a fifty per cent success rate. Those who attend counseling conjointly have about a two-thirds success rate.[1]

Some counselors insist on conjoint attendance, preferring to cancel a session rather than see only one spouse. I generally tell couples the statistics I just cited and then I say:

> It is to your advantage to attend counseling together. I know that emergencies happen and only one of you might be able to attend a session. As long as this does not happen regularly, I don't believe it will interfere with successful counseling.
>
> I must say, though, that if I do see one of you alone, I would like for you to treat it as if the other person were present. Anything that you tell me, assume that I might share during a future session with your spouse. I think this is important because in the past I have faced some very delicate situations. For instance, one time a woman told me, after getting my assurance that I would not tell her husband, that she had had a one-time sexual encounter. The next session, her husband casually mentioned that if he found out she had an affair, he would kill her. That secret hung over all of our counseling together like a dark cloud. I felt caught in the middle and unable to do anything to promote forgiveness between them. Needless to say, I would prefer not to have something like that happen again, so I think that we are best off treating all of our counseling knowledge as being known by all three of us.

In practice, it is sometimes impossible to continue counseling without seeing partners individually. One couple I saw was very emotional. The husband demanded that I see him alone, refusing to participate in counseling unless he was able to talk to me without his wife being present. After about twenty minutes I relented. However, I stipulated that I would see each of them individually for fifteen minutes for them to tell me whatever they wanted. Because they could not agree on who would see me first, I flipped a coin.

In his private session, the husband told me that he had already decided to pursue divorce, but he had been afraid to tell his wife for fear she would commit suicide if he told her. She had a history of suicide attempts, and her present state suggested that his fear was reasonable. He adamantly refused to participate in marriage counseling because his mind was already made up. My task became one of getting the wife into individual counseling to support her through the announcement of the imminent divorce and the aftermath of that announcement.

I generally begin counseling with a statement that I want the couple to agree to three sessions during which we will assess their marriage—its difficulties and the resources for solving those problems. I stress that the couple is not committed to continue counseling after that time and that I, too, am free to decide whether I think I could help them or whether someone else might be of more help. **Set Time Limits**

If the couple elects to continue counseling after those three sessions, we usually agree to from eight to sixteen counseling sessions (depending on how severely disturbed I estimate their relationship to be) followed by a re-evaluation of their relationship. I provide written evaluations of their marriage and my recommendations. Most of the time, counseling is completed in the agreed-upon time, but sometimes we will recontract for additional time.

Although some counselors insist that counseling occur weekly, I generally am flexible about the frequency of sessions. One couple recently met with me for fifteen sessions over twelve months. The same week that couple ended their counseling, another couple also finished, having met with me for ten counseling sessions over eleven weeks.

There are six reasons why limits should be set for counseling.

First, short-term counseling is as effective as or more effective than long-term counseling (for a review see Stuart, 1980).[2] In fact, Stuart suggests that most of the benefit of counseling is derived from the first five to ten counseling sessions.

Second, short-term counseling also keeps the clients motivated. Most couples seek counseling because they experience a crisis. During the emotional period of the early crisis, the couple is acutely motivated to ease the pain and to prevent crises from recurring. Later, motivation may wane.

Third, time and money are important to clients. Most clients want their discomfort to cease with as little time and energy expended as possible. Even when insurance covers all or part of the fees, the couple expects rapid treatment.

Fourth, most clients expect rapid treatment from an active counselor.[3] I once saw a couple in which the husband originally presented himself as the client. On the form he completed before the first interview, he simply and clearly answered the question, "What do you think the problem is?" He said, in capital letters, "GROSS CHARACTER DEFECT." In the initial interview, he explained that he had lost control of his temper and struck his wife. His wife had demanded that he seek counseling and had consented to attend counseling also if the counselor thought that necessary. I explained a way to help him control his anger, saying that it should take about seven weeks of counseling. To this, the man with the GROSS CHARACTER DEFECT replied, "I didn't think it would take that long." He had expected to eliminate his GROSS CHARACTER DEFECT in only two or three weeks.

Fifth, a limit on the number of sessions gives the clients a target for change and allows them to concentrate their efforts.

Sixth, a time limit on counseling motivates the counselor to help quickly, which helps the counselor plan interventions.

Short-term counseling does not mean frantic intervention. Freud called too-rapid intervention "wild analysis" and claimed it was ineffective.[4] Of course, Freud's standards and objectives were quite different from marriage counseling. A couple sought counseling from me after two months of marriage. I made some bad assumptions about the couple. I assumed that their patterns of conflict were not well entrenched, that they were similar to other couples with end-of-the-honeymoon rule negotiation, and that if I intervened quickly, the couple would respond quickly. I omitted my usual three-session assessment phase and began to treat them during the first session. Progress was herky-jerky. After seven sessions, the couple was little better off than before beginning counseling. They pointed out (with some eloquence and feeling) the error of my assumptions and my lack of helpfulness. This couple was more difficult and resistive than I initially realized;

however, I would have known that had I not tried to cut corners by omitting my usual assessment. In the long run, good assessment saves rather than wastes time.

Generally, a good marriage counselor has a genuineness, a caring attitude and good skills of empathy. Trustworthiness, expertness and attractiveness are also important.[5]

The Effective Marriage Counselor

In marriage counseling, some specific behaviors have been found to be unhelpful.[6] Counselors who do not structure the early sessions risk losing the confidence of their clients. Counselors who intervene too quickly by bringing up highly emotion-laden materials in the first two sessions or by confronting the couple too early can drive the couple away from counseling. Clients may terminate or simply tune out. By labeling unconscious motivations too early, counselors can lose the confidence of the clients, probably because clients assume that you cannot know them well enough to know their deep motivations if you have met with them only once or twice.

Finally, marriage counselors must walk a fine line in stimulating interaction between the spouses. The counselor can err through not stimulating enough interaction between the spouses or by not actively preventing destructive interactions between the spouses. Couples apparently want to know that you will allow them to work out some of their difficulties, but they want to feel secure that you have counseling under control.

My experience suggests that couples respond to a good sense of humor when it is used appropriately. When couples make jokes and sarcastic remarks at each other's expense, however, do not participate. My experience also suggests that the marriage counselor must be more active and directive than in individual counseling. In individual counseling, sometimes it is appropriate to listen to long explanations and "soliloquies" by the client as he or she relates an experience or a feeling. In marriage counseling, the interchanges between counselor and clients must be shorter and more energetic. In individual counseling, when the client stops talking, the counselor can begin. In marriage counseling, when the husband stops talking, the wife begins. When she stops, he starts. A timid marriage counselor will not be able to control the couple.

The clients want to believe that you can help. They want to believe that you can handle the spouse that they cannot handle, that you can help them control the anger, frustration and bitterness that they cannot control. They want you to be confident and competent. Justify their trust in you.

STAGES OF COUNSELING

Five Stages of Any Helping Relationship

In a previous book, *When Someone Asks for Help,*[7] I described five stages that any helping relationship passes through. In stage 1, the counselor must understand the problem from the point of view of the clients and then communicate to them that he or she understands. Having the warmth and empathy of a Carl Rogers is not necessary. Albert Ellis, who is definitely not known for his warm, empathic demeanor, is clearly able to establish the belief that he understands his clients. Effective helping is built on the cornerstone of clients' beliefs that you understand them.

Help them rethink their problems (stage 2). As a counselor, you are objective. This does not mean that you have no values, beliefs or even biases. It means that you are not intimately involved in clients' problems—you have no vested interest in guiding them a particular way. "Proof" of your objectivity is your ability to help clients rethink their problems in different ways. Clients usually think they understand why they are having difficulties. Their understanding usually centers on blaming the spouse. The way they are thinking about their problems is not helping solve their problems. Help them think about the problem differently.

Based on this new way of understanding, help them create and try out different action plans (stage 3). The labor of counseling is the continual creation and re-creation of action plans based on the new conceptualization of the problem. The clients will try out each plan—either within the session or as homework. They will be successful or unsuccessful with the plan, and you will provide support (stage 4) and will follow up their change attempts (stage 5). Based on their performance with the plans, help them create new action plans and try them out. In general, marriage counseling follows the same five stages, but I will discuss them more specifically as they apply to marriage counseling.

The first stage of counseling is physically and psychologically set apart from the remainder of counseling. It involves a thorough assessment and culminates in a written report to the couple. If the couple elects to pursue counseling, the second stage is entered. I call this, "Increasing their faith," because of the similarity to Luke 17. Jesus was discussing what to do whenever someone wronged his apostles. When Jesus demanded that the apostles forgive the person who had sinned against them, even seventy times seven times (an unlimited number), the apostles immediately saw the difficulty of the command and responded, "Increase our faith" (v. 5).

The married couple in conflict is in this very position. They each perceive frequent hurts from the other, even when none are intended. One goal of counseling is to increase the faith of the partners so they can repent of their hurtful attitudes and forgive each other—even if the spouse sins against them repeatedly. Forgiveness is a spiritual need as well as relationship need.

The couple can be helped to increase their faith through two types of interventions: building intimacy and bettering their communication (including reducing their conflict). In each instance, the counselor must help them (a) break old patterns of behavior and (b) build new ones. The order of intervention is determined by the needs of the couple, considering their position in the family life cycle and their individual patterns of behavior.

Generally, you will work simultaneously on each area, but you will emphasize one more than the other. For example, with a young couple, you will usually begin by attempting to build intimacy. As the couple acts more intimately, you will try to reduce their conflict and work out rapprochement, or reconciliation, in areas of difference. With a couple that has been married longer and has established rigid patterns of conflict, you attempt to reduce their conflict before you help build intimacy. Prescribing intimate activities too early will likely increase their conflict and undercut their confidence in you.

A general rule is to make the beginning of counseling as pleasant and conflict free as possible to increase the couple's hope and confidence that you can help.

In Figure 8, I have shown stage 2 as building intimacy and communication in parallel, with the understanding that the actual emphasis on

Stages of Marriage Counseling

Figure 8
Stages of Marriage Counseling

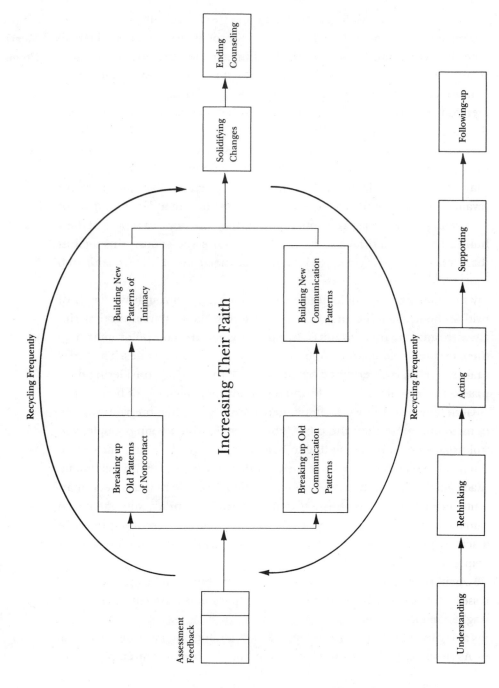

each stage is determined by your assessment of each couple.

The third stage of marriage counseling is to help couples maintain their changes. Of course, this occurs continually throughout the second stage, but it will occur with more regularity if you give explicit help with making changes more permanent. Without careful attention to maintenance and generalization of change, the couple might not make lasting changes.

The final stage of counseling is termination. During termination, I generally do at least four things. I space out the meeting times so that there is more time between sessions, provide a written evaluation of what gains have occurred and where the couple needs continued work, have a verbal evaluation with the couple in the final session and say good-by.

The middle two stages of marriage counseling, increasing the couple's faith through building intimacy and communication and maintaining their changes, require frequent recycling. Interventions are assigned, tried (or not tried) by the couple, discussed in the following session and followed by additional interventions. During the middle of marriage counseling, like with individual counseling, the labor of counseling is having the patience and creativity to stick with the couple as they try to make changes and as they "do not do what [they] want, but [they] do the very thing that [they] hate" (Rom 7:15). Only by your prayers, perseverance with interventions, patience and powers of persuasion coupled with God's grace will the couple realize gains through counseling. Even then, progress is not like climbing a mountain. It is more like riding a wild roller coaster with its slow climbs followed by sometimes dizzying plunges and then other laborious climbs.

Couples' Responses to the Stages of Marriage Counseling

Each couple is different, presenting new challenges and responding differently to interventions. Each couple requires an individually tailored plan, though there will be fundamental similarities in clients' goals. Yet, despite each couple's uniqueness, some generalizations are possible about what to expect from couples throughout treatment.

■ *Assessment.* Most of my clients have been enthusiastic about the two assessment sessions and the feedback session. Couples often say, "It's amazing! It's almost like you had been living with us." Or, they might say, "That's us all right." Or, "You seem to understand us better than we do."

Assessment is the cornerstone of treatment. It gives the clients confidence in your ability to handle them. It provides the initial structure to counseling that clients expect and that predicts success with marriage counseling. It provides self-discipline that inhibits you from intervening before you understand what is happening with the marriage.

■ *Intervention: the S-E-R cycle.* Clients generally increase their hope after the assessment, which gets counseling off to a good start. Hopeful clients usually try what you suggest. Early interventions are usually marked by a surge forward in the couple's relationship.

After the initial surge, some couples feel euphoric and stop coming to counseling because they think that their relationship is completely restored. An unwary counselor will terminate the couple as successful. This is a danger. Many couples will experience a relapse after the first surge of progress. If the couple has terminated counseling, they might be even worse off than before counseling because they might reason either (a) they cannot maintain changes if they are not in continual counseling or (b) counseling produces at best only temporary gains.

Couples usually go through at least one Surge-Euphoria-Relapse cycle, sometimes two. Actually they may go through even more, but if they have stuck through counseling, they have learned to expect and cope with them. So additional cycles are not as damaging as experiencing cycles without warning. When they begin to progress, I generally warn the couple about their need to continue in counseling. I might say, "You are doing very well. You seem to be enjoying each other more than you did a few weeks ago, and you are recapturing some of the romance you had early in your marriage. Without dampening your enthusiasm, let me encourage you to keep working. Even though things are going well right now, I have found that we need to keep working in counseling through at least two or three weeks more to make sure these changes are lasting. After all, we want to have these changes last and just not fade away once your enthusiasm decreases."

I do not imply that their changes will not last. I encourage them to make sure the changes do last. This positive expectation helps the couples then act confidently in expressing their new behaviors as indications of real love for each other.

If the couple does relapse, however, I talk with them about the usual progress of counseling. To enhance their belief that this is a regular happening, I show them a chart (see Figure 9) that I have constructed showing a typical progression of counseling. I point out that not every couple relapses because each couple is unique. Relapses are to be viewed as another challenge to be conquered rather than an indication that the couple can't progress. I stress that for each couple the degree of relapse is variable. Some plunge even below where they were before they sought counseling. Some can arrest the relapse quickly. Positive lessons from the relapse are stressed. The ups and downs of life together are paralleled with ups and downs in our spiritual life with Jesus. I remind them how God is faithful even when we coast away from him. Sometimes we discuss each person's spiritual history, showing them that the course of their spiritual history and their relationship history is similar. The necessity to "press on toward the goal for the prize of the upward call of God in Christ Jesus" (Phil 3:14) in our relationship with the Lord is likened to a need to press on to an upward movement in the relationship with the mate God provided.

■ *Termination.* Couples differ in the ways they say good-by. Since we usually agree to a given number of intervention sessions, I experience few "premature terminations." If couples agree to eight counseling sessions, they usually point toward that number and make tangible accomplishments during that time.

Generally, couples terminate after the allotted sessions. Few couples continue even if they have not reached their goals. Thus, the initial contract and goals should be set with care. If they are, termination will generally be pleasant. Couples feel a joint sense of pride in what has been accomplished with their, your and the Lord's efforts.

If goals have been too optimistic or if you poorly estimated the number of sessions, there will be ambivalence in the termination. Termination is often a time of uncertainty and ambivalence anyway, and mistakes in goal setting can make termination a time of intense feelings.

SUMMARY

In this chapter, I have provided a bird's-eye view of the structure and stages of counseling. Counseling is structured as an intensive, time-limited agree-

Figure 9
The Surge-Euphoria-Relapse Cycle: A Typical Progress in Marriage Counseling

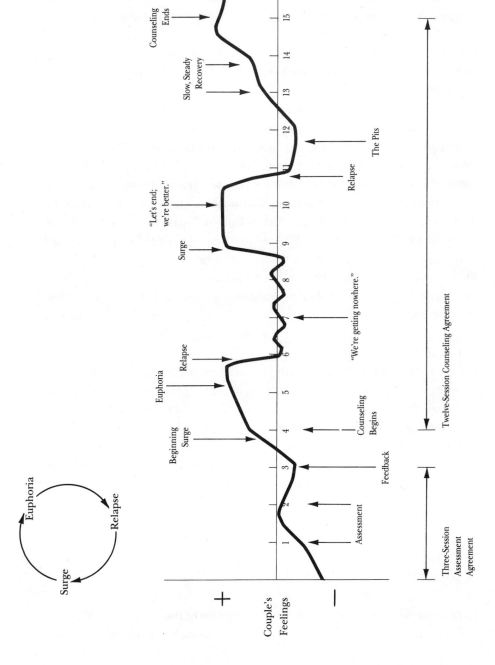

ment to work directly with a couple on their marriage relationship. Counseling begins with a formal, three-session assessment agreement. At the end of the sessions, the counselor formulates clear goals with the couple for the focus of intervention. During intervention the counselor helps the couple break up unhelpful patterns of poor intimacy, conflict, communication, lack of commitment and unforgiveness. Then, the counselor helps build helpful patterns. Relapse is an unfortunate part of marital counseling, and the counselor must be prepared to teach the couple to view relapse as a challenge instead of a defeat. In the final stage of counseling, the work with the couple is terminated in a final evaluation of the gains of counseling and suggestions for the couple to continue work on their relationship.

Crucial to helping the couple benefit by counseling is the counselor's ability to join the couple. In the next chapter, I suggest effective ways to join the couple and to handle common problems in joining.

Joining the Marriage

J OINING MEANS MAKING YOURSELF IMPORTANT ENOUGH TO THE COUPLE
that they will heed your suggestions both during counseling sessions
and when they are at home. Joining involves establishing a good
working relationship with the spouses individually and with the couple as a unit. When you establish yourself in their eyes as a competent
helper who can keep their conflict under control, you can work with them
to help reach their goals.

In one sense, joining continues throughout counseling, for the counselor
can never neglect the therapeutic relationship with the couple; but the
major work of joining occurs from the initial contact through the first
counseling session. Successful counseling depends on successful joining.

In this chapter, I discuss four tasks during joining: creating positive expectancies, creating a cooperative attitude, creating confidence in you as a
counselor and creating momentum for success. Then I will discuss how to

accomplish your tasks and finally some common difficulties with joining.

YOUR TASKS IN JOINING

Create Positive Expectancies

Four positive expectancies must be established.
1. Change in the marriage *can* occur.
2. *Counseling* can help the couple change.
3. *You,* their counselor, can help promote this change.
4. Your specific *suggestions* will be helpful.

Each of these expectancies must be promoted. Generally, the couple will develop more or less positive expectancies without your explicitly addressing them, but by exerting deliberate effort toward creating these positive expectancies, you can make their adoption more efficient and stronger.

Positive expectancies fuel counseling by creating a willingness to do what you suggest and by propelling couples past the times when their relationship is not doing well. Positive expectancies create a self-fulfilling prophesy, through focusing the attention of the spouses on positive change rather than on their difficulties.

Create a Cooperative Attitude

Strange as it may seem, most couples do not start counseling willing to cooperate eagerly with the counselor's suggestions. They enter counseling blaming their partners for relationship difficulties. They are involved in power struggles that they fear will be decided in the favor of their spouse by the counselor's interference. Generally, they are wary of unknown landmines that might be exploded by counseling. These fears prompt them to resist the counselor. On the other hand, couples dislike the pain and distress of marital troubles, and they are willing to invest their time, energy and money in marriage counseling. These factors impel the couple to cooperate with the counselor. Pulled in two conflicting directions, the couple is ambivalent about counseling.

One of your tasks is to promote the couple's cooperation—rather than their resistance—to counseling. To accomplish this, avoid hints that either partner is more to blame for the difficulties than the other. Rather, be clear that spouses are mutually responsible for their marriage. Assure them of your impartiality. Let them know that you will not take either partner's side consistently, though you might support one or the other on any particular issue. Try to reduce the fear of the unknown by telling them reasons for your suggestions and by explaining what will happen throughout marriage counseling. Finally, let them know that you believe they have made a wise decision in seeking counseling.

Your use of good relationship skills helps your clients have confidence in you. So does performing a thorough and accurate assessment.

Create Confidence in You as Counselor

The assessment report conveys, in writing, many of the things that the couple told you during their two assessment interviews. These facts must be accurate. During interviews, carefully write details such as the spouse's ages, the names and ages of any children, the number of years married and other information about the couple's history.

Having a couple look up from your assessment report to them and say, "Actually, we have *four* children, not three," is embarrassing for you and them, and it undermines their confidence in you. Having Mrs. Nastyweather smile sweetly and say, "I'm only thirty-seven, not forty-five. I mean, do I *look* forty-five?" produces feelings only rivaled by being informed by your dentist that he needs to do four root canals or by being told by the IRS that you are being audited for the three years relating to the receipts you threw away last week. Be *thorough* and *accurate* on the assessment report.

You can also create confidence by being *insightful* in your assessment report. You must do more than tell the clients what they told you. You must demonstrate some insight into the dynamics of their marriage that you infer from their behavior and inventories. How to make such inferences will be discussed in the following chapter on assessment.

Assessment is not merely assessment. It is part of treatment too. By getting the couple to cooperate in completing assessment inventories, you make it more likely that they will follow other directives. You are defining your relationship as one in which you can give directives which they follow— for their benefit. By directing the couple to argue in front of a tape recorder (as you will do in one assessment interview), you prepare the way for using other tape recordings to help them change their communication. By steer-

Create Momentum for Success

ing the couple through an informative and positive assessment, you create the momentum to repeat the positive experience during intervention.

Momentum, in physics, is the tendency of bodies to remain in motion once they are put in motion. By inserting movement and energy into your relationship with the couple, you create a trust in counseling that will often carry the couple past doldrums and will push them through the valleys in their feelings.

HOW TO PROMOTE POSITIVE JOINING

Your Behavior

How do you accomplish these objectives? You have five primary tools with which to forge the link between the couple and yourself: your behavior, verbal information, written information, assessment tasks and counseling technology.

From the first contact, usually over the phone, you must be friendly, competent, appropriately humorous, confident, helpful, sincere, genuine, understanding and empathic. In short, wear your Super-Counselor suit.

Some concrete behaviors illustrate your positive attitude.

1. *Be courteous, friendly, but businesslike* on the phone. If your secretary or answering service takes calls for you, check to see that he or she is presenting a competent, professional face to the public.

2. *Answer questions* about your counseling style, theory, policies or fees without defensiveness and without "over-justifying" your decisions.

3. *Start and end appointments on time.* This shows respect for your clients' schedules. Extending past the usual ending time of a counseling session is not always considered a favor by the clients, who might have other commitments.

4. *Give clients clear information* about how to find your office and about where they can park.

5. *Shake hands* at both the beginning and the end of the first interview.

6. *Greet clients* by coming to your door or into your waiting area.

7. *Clearly designate where they are to sit* as a couple rather than individually.

8. Before the couple arrives, *arrange the chairs* so that the couple's chairs

are closer together than either one is to your chair. (Throughout, I assume that you counsel from three easily movable chairs. The mobility of the chairs allows you to use spatial distance as a metaphor for emotional distance in certain interventions.)

9. When you sit, *slide your chair forward slightly.*

10. *Don't look at your wristwatch while the client is talking.* If you cannot see a clock unobtrusively, look at your watch only when you are talking.

11. *Introduce yourself* the way you would like the couple to address you. Establish immediately whether they prefer to be called *Mr.* and *Mrs.*, or to be called by first names. Some counselors prefer to be called by their titles *(Dr., Pastor, Mr., Mrs.* or *Ms.)* throughout counseling because it enhances the perception of their expertness. Others prefer to be called by first names because it enhances the perception of their individuality and friendliness. Others begin by having clients call them by their titles and move to first names after a personal relationship has been established.

12. At the end of sessions, *walk the couple to the door and repeat the time of your next appointment.*

13. *Apologize if you are late* for an appointment or if you must cancel an appointment.

Verbal Information

You can reduce fear of the unknown and build a cooperative attitude by the information you give to the couple verbally. Strike a balance between optimism and realism. Demonstrate hope and belief that the couple will improve. However, avoid blind, groundless reassurance, such as "Things will get better," or "You will get past these difficult times." They are harmful rather than helpful. Far from reassuring the couple, blind optimism undermines your credibility. The couple believes that their relationship is seriously troubled enough to require the expense of counseling. A sanguine attitude by the counselor devalues the clients' problems.

Giving couples clear, thorough rationales for directives not only promotes compliance with the directives, it also communicates that you consider them intelligent, free-choosing adults who can rationally decide what is best for them if they have pertinent information. It also establishes them as responsible participants in counseling rather than "patients" on which *you* will operate. Besides this, research shows that people frequently resist directives that are not accompanied by thorough rationales.[1]

Another important way to gain cooperation is to talk about counseling in ways that people can understand. Generally, that means using numerous examples, analogies and metaphors to illustrate your points. For example, to help a couple get through a relapse, I describe counseling as if it were a roller coaster ride, with slow, laboring ups and rapid—sometimes terrifying—downs which are followed by other ups. If a couple has not yet made such progress, I have them visualize a bowl turned upside-down on a table. On the rim are two ants. As they begin to climb, the way is very steep and the going is slow. But later they find that they are making progress and that the climb is easier. By making concepts understandable to the couple, you again show that you respect them enough to put concepts in their language.

Written Information

Acclimate couples to counseling by telling them what it will involve. Generally, this is done naturally as counseling progresses, but initial ambivalence of deciding to attend counseling can be reduced by giving information early.

When the couple contacts me for assessment, I do not give written information, but when assessment is complete and the couple has agreed to six to twelve sessions of counseling, I give them some pre-counseling information (see Figure 10, "Introduction to Marriage Counseling").[2]

In the "Introduction to Marriage Counseling," I use the techniques that are involved in good counseling: a clear description of goals for counseling, seven suggestions for getting the most out of counseling (illustrating them with analogies when appropriate), indication that responsibility for change is the couple's and specification of the limits of my responsibility.

Some counselors like to use treatment contracts to define expectations for counseling and limits of responsibility. Personally, I find the idea of a contract somewhat implicitly devaluing, but this does not mean that clients or other counselors will respond similarly. I prefer to transmit the same information in a way that conveys my positive expectation that the couple will behave responsibly. There is value in having the couple make a public commitment to counseling,[3] but I prefer the less formal verbal agreement (letting our *yes* be yes) to the more formal written contract.

Figure 10

Pre-counseling Information Given in Written Form to Couples after Assessment But before Counseling Begins

Introduction to Marriage Counseling

By electing to have marriage counseling, you have agreed to a period that will undoubtedly be difficult, require your time and effort and, at times, be emotional. But with the risks come the opportunity to make changes that could positively affect the rest of your life.

The goal of marriage counseling is *not* to change your partner or to change you (though both might occur). The goal is *not* to help you endure an unsatisfactory marriage. The goal is to help you *build a more satisfying, more intimate and less conflictual marriage.*

This probably will not happen all at once. Suppose you were in Los Angeles looking toward Richmond, Virginia. Then you changed your direction by only a single degree of the 360 degrees in a full circle. With only this small-but-fundamental change in course, instead of arriving in Richmond, you would pass north of New York City. There is a world of difference between Richmond and New York City! In the same way, I hope that counseling will help you and your spouse make small-but-fundamental changes that make a world of difference in your marriage.

Here are some suggestions to help you make the most of the time you spend in counseling.

1. Counseling takes time and hard work. I will ask you to do things, to make changes in the way you are currently acting. It will not be easy to change. Be assured, however, that the couples who benefit the most from counseling are those who willingly do what I suggest with a genuine desire to help their marriage.

2. It takes time and patience to change your current behavior to make your marriage happier. If you break your leg, a physician places your leg in a cast to allow it to heal. It is not natural to have your leg in a cast. It feels awkward, and you sometimes resent it. But you do not take off the cast. When your leg is healed, the cast is no longer necessary. In the same way, your marriage needs healing. Many of the things I ask you to do might seem unnatural, awkward or perhaps silly. You might resent following my suggestions. Some things I suggest are not meant to be permanent. But for maximum effectiveness, they should be followed at least while you are in counseling so that your marriage will have the opportunity to heal.

3. During counseling, there will be ups and downs in your relationship. Only rarely does progress quickly gained last long. Be prepared for swings in your feelings about your spouse and about the benefits of counseling.

4. Don't quit too early. You are likely to feel that you want to end counseling if you experience two or three good weeks. If you end there, you might run into problems later if conflict again erupts. Or you might want to end counseling if you can't see progress. Sometimes counseling gets "stuck," and it takes several weeks to free it. If you feel "stuck," tell me.

5. Don't expect perfection from your spouse. Assume that your spouse is trying to do what is best, but is human, just as you and I are. At times, we will all fail. Practice forgiveness instead of judgment.

6. Change first. When a marriage becomes troubled, there is a tendency to think, "I'll change when I see that he (or she) is serious about changing." This attitude is much less helpful than thinking, "I am responsible for my own behavior. I must change my negative behaviors without being concerned about what my spouse does."

7. It's worth the risk. Perhaps things have not been well with your marriage for a long time. You might think, "It's not worth the risk. Why should I try to love her (or him) one more time when it looks as if I'll just be rejected again?" You might be correct in your thinking, but if you don't take the risk—using counseling to really show your love to your spouse—then your marriage will almost surely fail.

As your counselor, I can't guarantee success. I wish I could. I am like a hunting guide who contracts to lead hunters to where they are likely to find the game they desire. All the guide can do is use his or her expertise and knowledge of the terrain so that the chances for success are as high as possible.

I want you to be successful at improving your marriage. I know you both want the same success and happiness. I am looking forward to working with you in this venture.

/signed/
Everett L. Worthington, Jr., Ph.D.
Psychologist (Counseling)

Assessment Tasks

Assessment tasks establish the norm that the couple will share personal information with the counselor, who will use the information to help the clients. The inventories are particularly valuable for they are completed at home, which in a sense brings the counselor away from the counseling session and into the couples' weekly lives.

Assessment also provides a miniature version of the counseling agreement that is to follow. The couple and counselor agree to a task, carry it out with mutual trust and openness, and a product is produced. The written assessment is usually easy for the couple to evaluate, and they can project into the counseling sessions a sense of the competence of the counselor. This "projection" from assessment to intervention phases is encouraged by structuring counseling similarly to assessment in that an agreed-upon number of contacts is established to be concluded by a formal assessment of the relationship. The couple has seen it work once, and so they can expect a positive outcome again.

TWO COMMON PROBLEMS IN JOINING

The Reluctant Spouse

Sometimes, one spouse—usually the husband—is hesitant to come to counseling. Usually this is because he or she (a) has not been asked; (b) thinks counseling will be unhelpful; (c) thinks it is the spouse's individual problem; (d) is involved in an affair; (e) has already decided on divorce; or

(f) is involved in a power struggle with the spouse and counseling has become an issue over which they are struggling. Obviously, you cannot do conjoint marriage counseling if only one spouse will attend. So you must either persuade the reluctant spouse to attend counseling or use a different type of counseling.

Sometimes the issue arises on the initial phone contact. The wife usually calls, announcing that she is depressed over her marriage and saying that she understands you do marriage counseling. She says, however, that her husband won't come to counseling. My response is usually:

> *Mrs. Robbins, I usually see couples together because research has shown, and my own experience validates, that couples benefit more when they are seen together than when only one is seen. However, sometimes that just isn't possible. This might be one of those times. I think you should come to counseling alone this week to talk about your situation. I think we should consider this a one-session consultation visit during which we will decide what your options are about further counseling. What do you think of that?*

I try to avoid saying or implying that we will *persuade* her husband to come to counseling, for statements like that often get back to the husband. I also try to be clear that I am not accepting her for counseling until after we have talked. If she balks at a consultation, I offer to make a referral. Getting the wife to counseling is a first step, because it allows you to gauge the reasons for the husband's reluctance.

Ask the person why his or her spouse will not attend. Often, that spouse will either not know or will be incorrect or incomplete in his or her knowledge. You might have to call the reluctant spouse. You can usually get permission to call from the attending spouse by referring to some successes you have had in the past with other reluctant spouses.

When you talk to the reluctant spouse, propose assessment, not counseling.

When you call, say:

> *Mr. Robbins, your wife has come to a consultation session about her unhappiness in marriage. I, of course, don't have your side of the story. I am not really interested in affixing any blame on you or her for what goes on in your marriage. I usually find it best when marriage concerns are brought up, though, to assess the marriage before having someone decide to attend marriage counseling. I was*

wondering whether you might consider participating with your wife in a three-session assessment of the concerns the two of you might have about marriage.

The main attractions for the reluctant spouse are the promise of a limited assessment period and the assurance that you are not allied with the attending spouse. Usually, after attending the assessment, the reluctant spouse will no longer be reluctant but will be able to make an informed decision with his or her spouse about whether to enter counseling.

You must decide whether a reluctant spouse should be invited to counseling. If the spouse has already determined to divorce, in most cases there is little to be done to improve the relationship. Since I do not feel comfortable doing "divorce counseling," though I have done it when circumstances dictated, I usually do not take the case when divorce is a foregone conclusion.

Another time I am hesitant to persuade a reluctant spouse to enter assessment or counseling is when the reluctant spouse is in an ongoing affair. When I discover that an affair is in progress, I usually say:

If you are to attend counseling, I would like you to consider putting a moratorium on seeing the person you are having an affair with. No marriage in the world can compete with an affair for excitement and romance, so it isn't fair to see someone else for romance and intimacy exclusively while spending your alone time, your busy-work time and your conflict time with your spouse. By setting up such a comparison, you are predetermining the outcome, and it is a waste of money to pay for counseling. Counseling under those circumstances would only give the illusion that you have worked to save the marriage when, in fact, you are working to justify ending your marriage. So if you want to continue with the affair, I am afraid I cannot, in good conscience, provide marriage counseling.

If the reluctant spouse thinks that the problem is his mate's problem, I usually suspect three things: (a) that he is worried about being blamed for his wife's problems; (b) that he is defined as the "strong" one and she as the "weak" one—thus, if he is threatened with stress and is in danger of collapse, she will protect him through exhibiting her symptoms; or (c) that she could be under stress (and not he) and she became symptomatic to elicit support, understanding and help from him. Having conflicting hypotheses, I look for evidence before deciding which hypothesis to believe. In any event, I like to have both partners attend counseling for marriage problems.

I try to judge which explanation he will be most open to. I might say that I need his help to solve her problem, or that part of her problem is unhappiness over the marriage and he can help her get over her problem faster by attending than by having her seen in individual counseling. I might say that even if she gets over the problem in individual counseling, he can help maintain her gains and avoid future problems by participating in marriage counseling. In most cases, all of these reasons are valid, so my first attempt at persuasion will be determined by which one I think the man is most likely to accept.

Some counselors have suggested being more devious. Haley,[4] for example, suggests that sometimes it is appropriate for the counselor to say things to the attending spouse that the counselor knows will be objected to by the reluctant spouse. The attending spouse is invited to share with her husband what went on in counseling. The counselor then might offer to have the reluctant spouse attend counseling so that the record can be set straight.

Some counselors invite the spouse to counseling as a "helper" for the attending spouse. Spouses can help conduct individual counseling, and I have asked them to attend. However, when such an arrangement is made, I consider it improper for me to conduct marriage counseling. My primary goal, in such instances has been symptom removal for the individual. An improved marriage might be a by-product but is not the explicit focus of counseling.

When a spouse refuses to attend counseling *because* his or her spouse wants marriage counseling, you have an excellent opportunity to help the marriage by resolving this impasse and getting the spouse into counseling. The difficulty, of course, is that to get one spouse into counseling you must side with the other spouse, which undermines the couple's confidence in your impartiality. The solution is to get the person into counseling without siding with either spouse. The following is one way I've attempted this.

Mr. Robbins, your wife tells me that she wants marriage counseling but you adamantly refuse.

"That's right. It won't do any good at all."

I was going to say, Mr. Robbins, that I disagree with your wife.

"You were?"

I sure was. I don't think marriage counseling is for everyone, even though I think it can be a lot of help to the people who need it.

"Are you saying that we don't need it? Boy, will that surprise . . ."

No. You're getting a little ahead of me. You see, I don't know whether you might benefit from it. To be fair, you might not know either . . . unless you have attended counseling for your marriage before and are convinced that you are in the same boat now as then.

"Well, no. Ellie and I haven't ever been to marriage counseling, but we've had some friends who went to counseling and got a divorce anyway."

Those things happen. In fact, many couples who attend marriage counseling don't get better. But your experience might be quite different from your friends'.

"It might," he said, sounding skeptical.

I detect a note of skepticism in your voice. Let me make you a proposal and see if you consider it reasonable.

"Okay."

Instead of starting counseling, how about agreeing to a three-session assessment of your marriage. You both would see me for three sessions; at the end of that time, I'll give you my opinions from an informed point of view about whether counseling might help and what I think you could do on your own even without counseling. You wouldn't be committed to any counseling because of these assessment sessions. After they were over and you had my opinion, you and your wife could then decide whether you thought counseling would help you accomplish your goals for your marriage. What do you think of my proposal?

"Well, that's interesting. I'll give it some serious thought."

Good. Your wife has already told me that even though it was not exactly what she wanted, it was okay with her if it was okay with you. You think it over and decide what you want to do. How about if I call you tomorrow evening around this time? Is that too quick?

"No, that's fine."

The struggle between Mr. and Mrs. Robbins is probably a replica of most of their power struggles. The couple is arguing over who can say whether they attend counseling. As an impartial third party, *you* can say, without tipping the balance of power. If you are diplomatic, you likely can get the couple to cooperate with you, especially if they both want to do what you suggest but are constrained by their relationship dynamics not to agree to the suggestion if made by the spouse.

In this case, the separation of assessment and intervention allows for a creative compromise between spouses and enhances the couple's expectations that the counselor can promote agreement where there previously was none. This also sets up the counselor as a peacemaker, which is beneficial in the *early* stages of dealing with conflict, though it is not a stable role that the counselor wishes to perpetuate.

Power Imbalance

Besides the reluctant spouse, the second common problem in joining the marriage system occurs when an apparent power imbalance exists. Peter Steinglass[5] recounts "the oft repeated story of the wife who attributes the stability of her marriage to the fact that her husband makes all the important decisions (such as who should be elected president and what our stance should be in the SALT negotiations), while she handles the minor things (where they should live, where they should go on vacation, and what they should spend their money on). . . ." (p. 328). On one level, in Steinglass's example, the husband has power (verbal description of him as powerful), while on another level (behavior), quite the opposite is occurring. Both husband and wife are satisfied and the marriage is stable. Another couple said they had an equal distribution of financial power. The husband said with pride, "I make all the money; all she does is spend it."

This is not to say that power imbalances do not exist. Power is ephemeral, abstract and always in flux. Sometimes one spouse grossly abuses his or her power. Such relationships are usually unstable and short-lived. Stable relationships, even though they may seem to the observer to be unfair, generally have hidden payoffs.

Sometimes, both spouses will feel that one spouse has more to lose than the other. The "stronger"—whether husband or wife—spouse will likely demand concessions—*or else* (divorce, drop out of counseling, etc.). The "weaker" spouse will more likely accede to the demands, though the negotiation will often be heated and long. In such instances of coercion, joining poses particular problems. Siding with the powerful spouse keeps the couple in counseling but perpetuates and empowers the coercive lifestyle. Since one aim of counseling is usually to realign harmful power imbalances, siding with the more powerful spouse can be countertherapeutic.

Haley[6] strikes a good balance. He recommends paying special attention and extra respect to the spouse who has the power to bring the couple back to counseling, but giving first priority of talking to the other and gently trying to shift the power structure through directives that make small but fundamental changes.

Joining a mixed religious marriage is especially difficult when you are clearly identified as a Christian. From the outset of counseling the non-Christian spouse expects you to support the Christian spouse. This is especially difficult when the couple heatedly disagree over religious issues and the Christian spouse whirls toward you and says, "What is your opinion about this issue?" If you have not had the perspicacity to initiate a pre-emptory swoon (or some equally clever maneuver), you are suddenly caught in the middle of a power struggle with the necessity to remain true to your beliefs. Joining this couple means assuring the non-Christian that, though you have clear opinions about religious issues, you will respect the clients' rights to have different opinions. And, while agreeing at times with the Christian spouse, you will not systematically impose your power on the side of the Christian spouse. Again, Haley's advice is valuable: Give more respect to the person whose side you are less likely to support.

SUMMARY

Effectively joining the couple to become a unified problem-solving team is crucial to all aspects of counseling. You can join effectively by using good relationship-enhancing skills to create positive expectancies, a cooperative attitude, confidence in yourself as counselor and momentum for success. Joining is accomplished through assessment and paves the road on which progress is made. We will examine the crucial assessment process in the next chapter.

Assessing the Marriage

BOTH PRACTICALLY AND CONCEPTUALLY, TREATMENT OF A MAR-
riage depends on its assessment. What and how you treat
depend on what you look for during assessment, even though
some modifications occur during counseling.

In this chapter, I will describe how to prepare for assessment and the
sources of data to use. Then, I will discuss what to assess: intimacy; effectance (communication and conflict); hurt, blame and sin; commitment; and
other crucial areas. In chapter 8, I discuss goal setting and in chapter 9, I
describe how to conduct each assessment session.

PREPARING FOR ASSESSMENT

Your clients are unique individuals who have unique marriages. A couple's
relationship is unlike anyone else's—even your own. One temptation of

**Know Your
Clients'
Positions in
God**

marriage counseling is to share our wisdom about what works with our marriages. Our marriages are good sources of *suggestions* for other couples, but what works for us might not work for someone else. Our clients are the reigning authorities on their desires, values, wants, expectations and thoughts. This is helpful for me to remember when I become impressed with my clinical acumen and diagnostic ability—which, alas, I sometimes do.

Our clients are also complex people with complex motives and needs. The complexity and diversity in our clients is sometimes forgotten as we apply our clinical theories to their lives. We tend to act as if we understand the essence of the clients, when we are merely applying a useful conceptual scheme to make limited but important changes in their lives.

Finally, our clients are people inhabiting God's world. They are bearers of his image, reflecting his nature. They are valuable, whether they make decisions to divorce, to abuse their spouses or to harm their children. At the same time, they are fallen and we, as members of the body of Christ, are called to strengthen, exhort, confront, support and impel them in their walk with the Lord in his world.

Know Your Clients' Likely Presenting Problem

Generally, when couples begin counseling they usually already have certain ideas about the cause of their relationship difficulties. There are four common assumptions.

■ *"It's his (or her) fault."* Problems are attributed to the other person's behavior, personality or parentage. This is probably the most common assumption, but it makes people look bad to voice it. So, spouses usually present one of three other assumptions to the counselor.

■ *"It's because we had to move (or had a baby, etc.)."* Couples who have generally led a happy life together until some major life transition will blame the transition for their difficulties. They assume that if the event could somehow be undone, the marriage would repair itself. This is unlikely. The transition disturbed the couple's balance of power and intimacy. Further change would merely disturb them again. Often the couple that attributes their problems to a specific external event are more likely candidates for successful counseling than those who complain of general relationship malaise.

■ *"We're incompatible."* Couples who make this claim are often difficult candidates for counseling because they have decided that their marriage will not work out. Usually, they have diffused blame by accepting the "inevitability" of their divorce. This is not always the case. Young couples who are psychologically sophisticated and have been exposed to popular writing that preaches no blame for relationship problems might proclaim that they are incompatible, while holding personal opinions blaming their spouse for their marriage difficulties.

■ *"I'm the cause of our problems."* Spouses who blame themselves are often either depressed or guilty over an overt transgression (such as an affair). Counseling will often involve work on their individual problems within marriage counseling.

Your assessment must go far beyond the causes couples present at the outset of counseling. There should be a number of characteristics of the assessment. Stuart[1] identifies five.

Know the Characteristics of a Good Assessment

1. *Assessment must be parsimonious.* It should be quick and efficient, yet complete enough to provide a good base for intervention.

2. *Assessment must be multidimensional.* Stuart recommends diverse methods by varied observers (counselor, spouse, family members, friends, co-workers).

3. *Assessment should be linked to a theory of intervention.* Assessment instruments should be used because they are relevant to treatment, not just because they provide interesting information about the couple.

4. *Assessment must be situation specific.* Stuart cites evidence to show that family members behave differently in the presence of different family members. The practical implication of this is that if the couple want to improve their marriage interaction, invite them both to counseling. Then, realize that you presumably have joined their subsystem and the way the couple behaves in your presence is not the way they will behave when you are not there. Thus, use homework judiciously to help the couple change their behavior when you are not there.

5. *Participation in assessment must be of value to the couple as an end in itself.* The couple must be interested and engaged by assessment and must be given useful information by the end of assessment.

**Know the
Areas to
Assess**

As we discussed in part two of this book, problems are likely to occur in four areas: (1) intimacy; (2) effectance (including both communication and conflict); (3) hurt, blame and sin; and (4) commitment. Obviously, each area is composed of numerous aspects. Problems can show up in each area— in the spirit of each marriage partner or in their cognitions and behaviors. Problems also arise in the environmental events they share and in the environmental structures with which they contend.

SOURCES OF DATA FOR ASSESSMENT

**Information
during the
Clinical
Interview**

During the interviews, you ask questions of the couple and encourage them to discuss their perceptions of their marriage. Much of your assessment report involves recall of the information they have provided. Record notes to yourself as they give information.

**Observation
during the
Clinical
Interview**

Much of your data will derive from the two assessment sessions with the couple. You will see the couple interact with each other; and you will see how they present themselves to an outsider. If you direct them to discuss a topic, you may see how they attempt to persuade each other about an issue. Observe how close they sit to each other and how they refer to intimate and conflictual issues. You will also see how they talk about each other to a third person.

While listening to them and recording notes, listen for data about the key issues that will be useful in their counseling. Find out (a) their commitment to each other and to the Lord; (b) their methods of controlling their intimacy and distance needs; (c) the ways they meet their effectance needs; (d) the ways they have conflict with each other; and (e) the stage of family life they are currently in.

**Prescribed
(Videotaped
or Audio-
taped)
Discussion**

During the second assessment session you will direct clients to discuss for seven minutes a topic about which they disagree. Analyze the videotape or audiotape of the discussion. The discussions are revealing even when couples question their authenticity. Although the intensity of the struggle might not be reflected clearly in the tapes, the techniques of arguing that appear on seven minutes of tape are usually confirmed as soon as the couple begins to be counseled for conflict.

I usually listen to the tape at least two times. The first time I listen to understand the content of each person's arguments. I want to know how logically each person presents arguments and how clearly he or she thinks through what is advocated. I need to be able to summarize each person's arguments. The second time through I concentrate on the syntax (style), semantics (meaning) and pragmatics (effects) of the communication.[2] (For more explanation of these terms, see pages 337-38.)

☐ How much does each talk?

☐ How does one gain the floor?

☐ How clearly does one communicate?

☐ How emotional are the arguments?

☐ How provoking are the arguments?

☐ What kind of power relationships do the arguing styles reveal?

On this second time through the tape, I frequently stop the tape and make notes about the communication. Sometimes I must rewind the tape and listen to portions again. Altogether, it generally takes thirty to forty-five minutes to analyze the seven-minute discussion.

When I am having particular difficulty understanding what is happening, I divide my paper into three columns, headed *His, Hers* and *Comments*. As I listen to the tape a third time, I make short synopses (three or four words) of each person's utterances. Also, as they occur to me, notes are written under the "Comments" column.

Inventories

I use the Couple's Precounseling Inventory (CPI)[3] and the Personal Assessment of Intimacy in Relationships (PAIR),[4] which are tied to the areas in which I intend to intervene: commitment, conflict and general communication for the CPI and five types of intimacy for the PAIR. I use the CPI mostly for my information and hypotheses and because some couples find it easier to write their complaints than to talk about them (which suggests that for those couples homework directives that have them write thoughts to each other might be effective). I use the PAIR to demonstrate to the couple that they need to build intimacy. The profile sheet of the PAIR provides graphic and dramatic evidence of the difference in actual intimacy from each spouse's ideal level of intimacy.

It also shows that some types of intimacy need more work than others. The use of the PAIR, and going over the results with couples, improves compliance with homework to build intimacy. It is possible to convince the couple that they need to become more intimate, but one picture is worth a mound of explaining in persuading the couple to carry out homework.

Daily Log

A daily log, sometimes called a behavioral diary, is a record of when certain events occur and what conditions surround their occurrence. If the couple complains about fighting but cannot tell what brings on a fight, you might assign them each to keep a daily log for two weeks. This might bring to light the events that trigger fights. Although I have used behavioral diaries with individual clients, I have never used them with couples; so I refer you to Jacobson and Margolin[5] or Liberman et al.[6] for a discussion about their usefulness.

Behavioral Monitoring

Occasionally, I might want a couple to provide an accurate count of a particular behavior, such as disagreements, compliments or "mental rehearsals" of arguments with the spouse. If the behavior occurs frequently and if I do not care about the events surrounding the behavior, I might ask a couple to keep a numerical count of the behavior. Usually it is rewarding for the couple to see the graph change as counseling progresses, though it is difficult to get the couple to continue to keep records longer than two or three weeks unless you are willing to make this a major test of your power in counseling. Since I am unsure how much good it does to have such accurate counts of specific behaviors, I am usually not willing to pay the price for long-term compliance with self-monitoring.

Diagnostic Games

Liberman et al.[7] recommend several diagnostic "games" to assess aspects of the marriage. These games are often structured sentence stems that each partner must complete. For example, each spouse must say, "I like it when you . . . because it makes me feel. . . ." Spouses alternate until the counselor calls it quits. Another diagnostic game is to have the partners identify positive resources and assets in the other person, or to have, for instance, the wife identify one of her husband's needs and tell what she could do to meet it. Another is to name three things the partner likes and does not like about the spouse.

These exercises seem particularly suited to group counseling, and they might be useful for some couples in individual counseling. Like all assessment devices, the particular techniques chosen should contribute to your general plan for counseling.

ASSESSING INTIMACY

Satisfaction

Knowing where to look for assessment data, we turn now to what to assess. Satisfaction with the marriage is one of the first variables to assess. The couple's satisfaction with the marriage can be assessed with proven reliability and validity by using either of two inventories: The Locke-Wallace Marital Adjustment Scale[8] or Spanier's Dyadic Adjustment Scale (DAS).[9] Although I have used the DAS for research with numerous couples, I do not believe that it yields enough information that is directly usable in counseling to justify the time required by clients. I look at the first item on the CPI,[10] which is taken from the DAS. This single item gives a good index of marriage satisfaction.[11] Spouses indicate their and their spouse's satisfaction with their marriage. Couples who are not severely dissatisfied and can closely predict their spouse's feelings are likely to benefit by counseling. Other spouses experience more difficulty in making changes in counseling.

Satisfaction can also be assessed simply by asking couples how they feel about their marriages. Contrary to some questions that have socially desirable (or perhaps theologically desirable) answers, asking about a couple's marriage satisfaction usually draws a thoughtful response.

Intimacy

For most couples, one goal of counseling will be to increase their intimacy. Almost always, couples who seek counseling would like more intimacy. I treat intimacy as a multifaceted concept, trying to assess each facet through interviews and inventories and then designing interventions for the facets that the couple are most dissatisfied with.

In the first interview, I begin to get a feel for the capacity of the couple for intimacy by their description of their pre-marriage activities and by the description of their early married life, prior to the development of problems. Individuals differ in their needs for intimacy and can adjust their needs for intimacy within limits. Because it is essential to determine the *total* intimate contact that each spouse is getting—from friends, family and work as well as from the spouse—it is essential that the entire time schedule of the couple be reviewed during the second assessment session, not just the time they spend together.

The PAIR[12] identifies five types of intimacy. For each type of intimacy, each spouse rates his or her actual and ideal amount of intimacy that he or she is currently experiencing. The results are graphed on a profile sheet that makes it easily used in a counseling session.

In Figure 11, I have shown a profile for a couple I will call John and Mo. The *x*'s represent John's scores on each of the five types of intimacy. They are connected by dashed lines. The dots represent Mo's scores on each type of intimacy. They are connected by solid lines.

First notice that John's and Mo's lines are similarly shaped. They see the relationship with similar eyes, even if they are not entirely happy with it.

Second, each one's scores are on approximately the same level. Large differences in level indicate that one person is likely to describe the relationship in extremes—either bad or good. The exact level (high or low) is usually not important except that it gives valuable information about how the spouse might talk about the relationship. More important is the pattern of differences between each person's ratings of ideal and actual intimacy. If the differences are similar for the partners, even though the absolute values of the scores differ, then the partners are in fundamental agreement about how they perceive the relationship. For John and Mo, except for emotional intimacy and (to a lesser extent) recreational intimacy, they agree about the pattern of intimacy.

For emotional intimacy, the couple disagrees about how closely their ideal is being met. John feels a little dissatisfaction with the emotional support he is getting, but Mo experiences a lot of dissatisfaction. The first interview revealed that John perceives Mo as being too emotional and as requiring too much support. He complains about her moodiness, and he withdraws when she demands that he support her. John's career demands are high due to a governmental contract that his firm recently received, and

Figure 11
A Typical PAIR Profile for John and Mo, Revealing Their Ideal Amounts of Intimacy and
Perceived Current Amounts of Intimacy

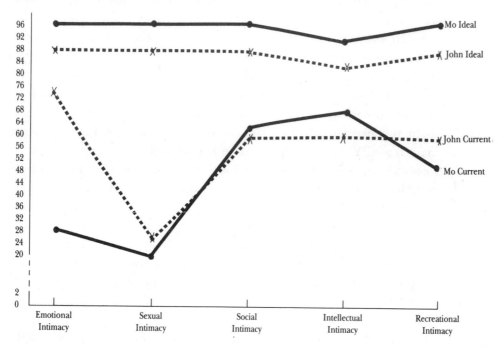

he resents the time Mo demands from his career. On the other hand, Mo
said that she never got the support she wanted, even before the firm got
the government contract.

Their sexual intimacy is far different from the way each would like it to
be. There may be a number of reasons for this: not making love often
enough, not enjoying it when they do or other difficulties. The exact source
of the problem must be identified through interviews so that appropriate
remedial action can be taken. The impression that the couple is dissatisfied
with their sexual life is fortified by the answers they provide on the Couple's
Precounseling Inventory. They are unable to identify how frequently each
approached the other to initiate sex in the last month, and they state that
they only had intercourse once during the last month. During the end of
the second assessment session, both John and Mo related that intercourse

is generally unsatisfying to Mo, who complains of being irritated when John sexually stimulates her. Because of her complaints, John snaps at her and they argue. Based on the interviews and assessment instruments, a consistent picture emerges of their sexual life.

Social intimacy, the degree to which the partners socialize together, is perceived similarly by both John and Mo. In the same way, intellectual intimacy, the degree to which the partners share important ideas with each other, has good agreement. There are some differences in the way John and Mo perceive their recreational intimacy. Because the differences are slight, you might or might not call attention to this area during your assessment report. Your decision would be based on the presence of other information that supported the idea that this was an important issue for John and Mo and on the number of other areas of potential treatment of John and Mo.

The feedback sheet of the PAIR allows you dramatically to convey your understanding of their intimacy to the couple. It also gives concrete, visible justification for working to resolve the couple's differences in intimacy. Coupled with interview information, the PAIR profile is a powerful therapeutic tool.

Boundaries

The boundaries of a marriage are determined by the ease with which the spouses do activities with other individuals or alone versus the ease with which activities are couple-oriented. The ideal structure for each couple varies, but some generalizations can be drawn. Generally, prior to the birth of their first child, a couple has a more rigid structure than after they have children. By virtue of living in the household of the couple, children force their inclusion as triads or larger groups. Prior to children, couples solidify their structure by doing couple-oriented activities, whether that means getting together with other couples or going hiking or shopping together. After launching the children, couples again pull together as they age and their work and recreational activities become more restricted.

A detailed survey of the spouses' time schedules should give you a rough idea of the couple's structure. Furthermore, their behavior during the interview can tell you whether they easily incorporate a third person into their subsystem. Do they sometimes speak as a team, in unison? Does one spouse let the other speak for him or her? Do they give you the impression that they are a couple or two individuals? After two interviews, you will probably have a good hypothesis about the firmness, looseness or even rigidity of the boundaries around the couple.

ASSESSING EFFECTANCE: COMMUNICATION

Rules of Communica- tion

Besides assessing intimacy-related issues, we must attend to effectance-re- lated issues: communication and conflict. We first consider general aspects of communications. Couples' communications are not *really* rule governed; it just seems that way.[13] "Communication rules" are a counselor's way to explain the repetitive patterns of a couple's communication. Therefore, do not hastily infer rules from a couple's behavior. One instance of an inter- action is not a rule. Nor are two instances. But after you have observed several instances of a particular pattern, or if the couple describes their behavior as *usually* following a certain pattern, then you can make tentative hypotheses about the "rules" of their relationship.

The rules of most interest during assessment—and indeed throughout treatment—are (1) those that describe methods of conflict; (2) those that are at issue; and (3) those that prescribe the couple's behavior and lead to relationship difficulties. Be especially alert to determine the power rules that describe who can make the rules, and how and under what circum- stances the rules are made. Generally, the couple is unaware of their power rules, yet those rules are the source of most disagreement.

It is essential to determine these communication rules to design effective treatments. But do not include these rules in the assessment summary! There are three good reasons to withhold your understanding of their communication rules from the couple. First, when you point out power rules to the couple, they will almost always argue that you are wrong. They will argue that they are fighting over *issues,* not over who is to make the rules. Acknowledging power rules threatens the couple.

Gurman and Kniskern have shown that if a marriage counselor con- fronts threatening material early in counseling, the counseling is likely to be unsuccessful.[14] Second, Haley recommends not only that you do not discuss power rules with the couple during assessment, but that you *never* discuss them with the couple.[15] He claims that discussing power issues will make them more rigid and harder to change. Third, after two sessions, you cannot possibly have accurate evidence that the behaviors you have observed are rules and not isolated instances. You might be right; they might be rules. If you are an astute clinician, you might be correct seventy-five or eighty per cent of the time. But if you are wrong twenty per cent of the time, you are likely to do irreparable damage by guessing incorrectly in an area so threatening and important to the couple.

I suggest you keep your hypotheses about the power rules of a relationship to yourself during assessment.

Roles in Communication

Roles are formal summary statements of rules of a relationship. Roles are generally taken by the couple with their awareness, as opposed to the power rules, which are usually outside the couple's immediate awareness. Roles may be rigidly or loosely followed. Determine the rigidity of the roles during assessment.

Couples will often say they act out certain roles, but their behavior does not support their claim. For example, Judy and Stan might say Judy is submissive and Stan is the head of the household, but the opposite may be apparent from your observations. When you encounter such inconsistency, do not immediately comment on it. Remember that you are observing their behavior only one of the 168 hours per week. Decisions may have been made at home and may be merely acted out in your presence.

Even if you are correct in your observation and the couple is behaving differently than they say they are behaving, this inconsistency probably serves some function in the marriage. It would be unwise to call the inconsistency to the couple's attention without having any idea of the ramifications in their life.

In the case of Judy and Stan, suppose that Judy is struggling with her faith. She is particularly wrestling with the question of how literally to take Scripture. Having studied the portions of Scripture dealing with submission and headship in marriage, Judy has concluded that the man should be head of the house and she should be submissive to him. At the same time, however, Stan is unwilling and perhaps incapable of functioning as his wife's head in the way that they each understand that passage of Scripture to suggest. Previous attempts to implement their understanding of the Scripture have led to serious relationship turmoil and to near divorce. Over the years, the couple have adopted a "family myth" that they were behaving differently than they in fact were.

With this couple, it would be unwise to expose the "family myth" during assessment. The couple might be catapulted into relationship difficulties beyond those for which they sought help. Also, Judy might experience spiritual unrest by casting additional doubt on her perception of Scripture. In this analysis, I am not saying to avoid such thorny issues throughout counseling. I am arguing simply that it would be unwise to expose a "family myth" without having a good idea of what will happen when you do.

Another time that roles loom important in a couple's life is near transition points. The roles for different stages of life are often culturally prescribed. It takes time for individuals to learn the new behaviors that are required of them.

It will repay marriage counselors to study the work of Pauline Boss, from the University of Minnesota, who has written clearly and extensively about the role and boundary changes that occur with each stage of family life. In her work, she has also provided a bibliography of books and articles describing others' work on each stage.[16]

Patterns of Communication

Your task throughout counseling is to identify and change unhelpful patterns of communication. During assessment you formulate hypotheses about the regularities in communication that you observe. Many of these hypotheses you will convey to the couple during the assessment report. To avoid labeling a pattern of behavior incorrectly, I will often speak only generally of the behavior during the assessment summary, such as "Andy and Margaret often use humor as a double-edged weapon—to sting the other but also to add liveliness to their relationship."

It is tempting during assessment (and even more so during intervention) to be provoked by a blatant, harmful communication into correcting the couple when that is not in your plan for the session. During assessment, note the interactions but resist the urge to intervene too early.

Amount of Communication

For each communication that seems important, ask yourself several questions.

☐ How often does this behavior occur? Does it occur too much or too rarely? (frequency)

☐ How long does it last? (duration)

☐ How long does it take before the partner responds? (latency)

You might ask these questions, for example, when the husband teases the wife and does not know when to stop, continuing until he provokes her to anger, or when the wife reminds the husband of his responsibility so often her reminders become nagging. Perhaps the husband fails to answer his wife when she asks a question. Perhaps she fails to respond to a criticism or he responds too quickly, flying off the handle at any suggestion of criticism.

Besides involving issues of frequency, duration and latency, the "proper" amount of communication also depends on its context. Obviously, you cannot work on all aspects of a couple's communication. There isn't time. So, consider the seriousness of the communication problem so that you know which difficulties to call attention to during assessment and intervention.

Valence of Communication

The valence of the communication is your estimation of whether it produces a positive or negative effect on the relationship. Assess the overall tone of communication. Is it largely negative? Then any suggestion of a negative comment by either spouse will likely provoke the other to respond. Is the overall tenor of the relationship positive? Then the couple will likely have resilience for negative interactions.

Also assess the valence of particular communications. Some that seem negative to you are not perceived negatively by some couples. Likewise, others that appear to be compliments are perceived negatively by some couples. Do not assume that you can judge the impact of a communication better than the couple. Look for their reactions.

Openness of Communication

In our culture, we laud honesty and truth in communication—sometimes without considering the need for sensitivity. Completeness of communication is extolled. Unfortunately, at times, honest, truthful, complete communication can destroy a relationship.

One couple that I counseled, David and Margaret, progressed very well through six counseling sessions. They responded positively to intimacy and communication-building interventions used both inside counseling sessions and as their homework. They responded better to videotaping their communication than any couple I had previously counseled. Whatever was suggested, they immediately tried with boldness and courage. By the sixth counseling session, they had made enough progress that I considered terminating before our agreed-upon eighth counseling session.

At the seventh session, however, they reported an absolutely disastrous week, filled with long, emotional arguments and much pain and regret. The counseling session was interrupted on three occasions by angry and hurtful accusations and reprisals. At the eighth session, David and Margaret reported another week of the same. I had timed the contract with David and Margaret so that we would end counseling before I was to leave town for two months. The eruption of turmoil in their relationship two weeks before I was to leave created a delicate situation.

They were adamant that they did not want referral to another counselor for the two-month hiatus in their treatment. They asked for advice, so in a direct way, I told them my observations over the last two weeks.

I think your problem is that you are too *open with each other. You found out how to communicate well on some touchy issues through the work we did together, and since then, you have tried to tackle every little difference that ever existed between you. The result is, your marriage is falling apart. No relationship can take that much strain in so little time. You took several years to develop differences but are trying to solve them all in two weeks.*

"Yeah, but isn't it good to get our gripes out?" asked David. "I mean, until now I have been dishonest with Margaret."

I certainly think it is important to tell each other if something bothers you. But not everything at once. And maybe not ever *everything. A good relationship is based on a realistic appreciation for each other. That foundation supports some of the harder things you have to say to each other. But, flooding each other with criticism in the name of "honesty" or "openness" is guaranteed to put an enormous strain on any relationship.*

"Well, what should we do, then?" asked Margaret.

I would recommend not bringing up any differences or any criticisms of the other during the two months I am gone. That will be hard. Maybe impossible. You are now so sensitized to criticism from each other that anything either of you says is grounds for an immediate fight. I think you need to let some of the wounds you have inflicted on each other grow scabs so they can heal underneath. Stop picking at the sore spots. That is not helping your relationship even if it is "honest."

They agreed to try. I emphasized that eventually we needed to deal with some of the differences, and I suggested that it might be appropriate to renegotiate our contract upon my return to Richmond.

Upon my return, I called them. They related that they had lived pleasantly during the two months I was absent. They had had three or four arguments but described them as "normal disagreements." They said that they had decided that they had lived for years being different people, and that they did not need to try to change all of the differences.

Research supports the idea that it is not beneficial to share all of one's negative feelings. Stuart reviews research that shows the independence of positive statements and negative statements in marriages.[17] He found that too many negative statements are more associated with distressed marriages than too few positive statements. From this he concludes that one goal of counseling should be to reduce the negative statements spouses make to each other.

Degree of Understanding in Communication

Assess whether communicational messages are being understood by both spouses. Especially during disagreements, when both spouses have their minds on what they are going to say rather than what the other spouse is saying, the counselor usually finds that the couple is not understanding each other. During assessment, you can assess mutual misunderstandings especially from the tape-recorded disagreement and from the way each spouse responds to the information conveyed to you by the other spouse.

Communication of Feelings

Because couples are well advised not to express *every* negative feeling does not mean they are to stifle expression of all feelings. There are times when expression of negative feelings is appropriate and necessary. Assess not only how negative feelings are expressed (verbally and nonverbally), but also assess the abilities of each spouse to determine the timing and method of expression of negative feelings. Usually when a couple seeks marriage counseling, getting them to express negative feelings is not difficult. In fact, during assessment the challenge is often getting them *not* to express the negative.

Another challenge during assessment can be getting a couple who are at loggerheads to express positive or tender feelings for and to each other. In fact, even some happily married couples have difficulty expressing positive feelings toward each other.

You are most likely to see how the couple handles their positive feelings when they discuss their courtship. Often this is a time of fond remembrance, and they might not have engaged in such pleasant nostalgia about their relationship in years. Sometimes, if the couple seems to have a good sense of humor, I will ask them if something funny happened on their honeymoon. Almost invariably the couple recounts some humorous event.

During the assessment period, by calling the couple's attention to the positive and the humorous within their relationship, I can motivate the couple to work harder on their relationship to recapture the pleasant days. Behavioral marriage counselors try to keep the assessment completely pleasant. Although I agree with this ideal, I have found it difficult to do. I try to make the assessment *as pleasant as possible* but try not to let the task obsess me.

Communication of Requests

Requests by one spouse of the other involve the power rules of the relationship. During the two sessions of assessment, try to note at least three requests that each spouse makes of the other. Look for commonalties in these requests. Commonalities may reveal the power rules of the relationship.

Sometimes couples will make few requests of each other, or one spouse may make requests but not the other. Often these reveal the distribution of responsibility in the relationship. If *you* must direct the couple to make requests of each other, their behavior will likely differ from their behavior in their home.

Some spouses are aggressive, too demanding or too passive with their requests. Others fail to acknowledge requests from the other spouse, fail to ask clearly for what one wants (expecting the other to read one's mind), couch requests within criticisms or accuse the spouse. Calling the problem "poor assertiveness" does not consider the complexity of the problem. By localizing the problem within one person—such as saying the wife is not assertive enough—you obscure the interactive nature of the rules of the marriage. This may lead to being puzzled, later in treatment, if the couple fails to respond to your interventions for building assertiveness.

Negative Patterns of Communication

Communication theorists have identified a gaggle of patterns of communication that are generally disruptive and produce distress in most couples who use them. Transactional Analysis, which analyzes transactions between spouses, has summarized many of these patterns and given memorable names to them. By perusing a number of sources of communication training, I have compiled a glossary of poor communication techniques (see Table 4). These definitions merely touch the surface of the many ways people can communicate poorly.

Sometimes poor communication patterns are not necessarily as harmful as theorists say they are. For example, mind reading, or operating on one's expectation of the spouse rather than asking the spouse directly, is not always bad. Gottman's research[18] has shown that happy couples "mind read" regularly. All couples try to guess what their spouse wants and try to meet the spouse's needs without always going through formal inquiry. This is necessary for economy of effort. However, distressed couples may persevere longer without checking out an assumption that doesn't seem to be working than do non-distressed couples.

Another example of good communication according to most communication theorists is *meta-communication*. Meta-communication is communicating about how you are communicating. For example, when James and Hedda are arguing about whether to have dinner at Hardee's or at The Ritz, Hedda might interrupt James by saying, "Don't raise your voice to me!" That is a meta-communicative statement: it communicates about their communication. In itself, it is not bad. Distressed and non-distressed couples meta-communicate in this way. Distressed couples might then argue about whether or not James *really* raised his voice or whether he was justified in raising his voice. Their conversation might take on a did-not/did-too/did-

Table 4
Glossary of Poor Communication Techniques

I. Introduction: Not only can dirty fighting be a casual interest, a pleasant pastime and a creative outlet, it can also become a way of life. Besides adding hours of excitement and entertainment to an otherwise-drab existence, dirty fighting can give you what people want most but are often least able to get: *your own way.*

While fighting dirty is practiced as a matter of course in homes and offices, at school and play, it is often thought that people's abilities to engage in underhanded warfare is natural and no real endeavor. However, all people do not come to the arena of human interaction equally equipped to do battle. To the contrary, many people find themselves unnecessarily crippled by moral, ethical and temperamental biases that inhibit self-expression and leave them to face the world at a profound disadvantage. To make matters worse, our educational system has largely ignored this important area. It is for these reasons, in an effort to make up for these unfortunate deficits, that this modest work has been created.

II. Some General Considerations:
A. The Importance of Good Timing: Many potentially lethal dirty fighters miss golden opportunities because they are unaware of the value of proper timing. Begin an argument just before your spouse leaves for work. Strike out at your spouse at bedtime after a tiring day—especially if your spouse has to get up early the next morning. Pester your children with household chores or homework just as they sit down to watch their favorite TV program or before they go out to play.

In general, keep in mind that it is best to attack others when their guard is down, when they least expect it or when they are least able to defend themselves.
B. Developing the Proper Attitude: There are a number of circumstances that automatically qualify you as being right and/or justified. The following are a few lead-ins that can be used to get you started on the right track.
(1) Parent: "I'm your father (mother), and I know what's best for you."
(2) Family wage-earner: "I'm working to pay for it, so the discussion is over."
(3) Person in authority: "That's the way things are. If you don't like it, that's just too bad. As long as you're here, you'll do what I tell you to do."
(4) Friend: "I wouldn't think of bothering you unless I really needed your help. I'll be really hurt if you refuse."
(5) Loved one: "I shouldn't have to ask you to do things for me. You should know how I feel without my having to tell you."
C. Developing a Winning Style: Many people win arguments, not because they are right, but because they have a style of arguing that is unbeatable. Choose the style that best suits your personality:
(1) Monopolize the conversation. Don't let anyone get a word in edgewise. If the other people try to speak, either ignore them completely or accuse them of cutting you off before you are finished.
(2) Meander. Make short stories long, make mountains out of molehills, talk about things irrelevant to the issue. Do not, under any circumstances, come to the point.
(3) Don't listen. While the other person is talking, use the time productively to think of how you are going to answer back. When it is your turn, ignore any and all concerns that may have been mentioned and go right on to the point you would like to make.
(4) Be a problem solver. This style is useful when the main concern is the other person's feelings. The approach here is to ignore the feelings and simply hand down decisions, solutions or suggestions. Once you have offered a solution, that is all that need be said; the issue is closed.
D. Power Plays: Power plays are often used to win arguments. Sometimes the players establish a pattern where one person seemingly has all the power. (This is an illusion, but it serves the function of letting the more powerful person feel superior and the less powerful person feel martyred or wronged.) In reality, the

power is distributed well. Merely the tactics used to fight are different. Here are some tactics used by one-up players and one-down players.

(1) One-up: Play to win. Start small and increase the power. Threaten, coerce and finally beat your opponent into submission. Starting power plays includes (a) "I've arranged everything the way I want it," followed by, if your opponent objects to your arrangement, (b) "If you can't prove it, you can't do it."

Middle games power plays include (c) sulking and making 'em guilty.

End game maneuvers involve physical might, either passively, (d) "I ain't budging," or offensively, (e) "Shut up or I'll shut you up."

(2) One-down: Don't try to win. Just make life so miserable for your opponent that he or she will give up. (Hint: You must keep this up for years because a one-up player almost never gives up.) Your one-down measures include: (a) techniques to arouse guilt, such as not saying anything but just crying (or drinking); (b) techniques that hurt (such as, saying "I didn't have an orgasm, you know"); and (c) techniques that waste the other person's time, money or energy (such as saying, "We don't have enough money to pay for this new wardrobe? Honest, honey? You'll have to get a second job? Oh, I am sorry." Smile to self.)

(3) Pitched battle: Both opponents use the full range of tactics—usually one-up tactics, but occasionally one-down. For such battle, a wider range of strategies is necessary. (The following section offers further suggestions.)

III. Some Specific Techniques:

A. Collect Injustices: Collect slights, hurts, injustices, inequities. Let your anger build up to the point where you explode over relatively minor issues. Then, when you've had enough, shout, scream, terrorize, even hit. You will be surprised to learn how good it feels to get things off your chest. An added benefit of collecting injustices is that you can then rationalize anything you may later wish to do, like getting a divorce, quitting your job or having an affair.

B. Help with a Vengeance: There are countless opportunities to tell people what they should do, how they should feel, what they should think—all in the interest of being helpful. It doesn't matter whether or not they have asked your opinion; go right ahead and give others the benefit of your experience. If they should object to your unsolicited suggestions, point out to them that you are only saying things for their own good and that they should be able to accept constructive criticism.

C. Don't Get Mad, Get Even: Anger expressed openly can be uncomfortable for all concerned, so learn to find other ways to channel your feelings. Get revenge by sulking, having an affair, going on shopping sprees, rejecting the other sexually, etc. In general, it is always a good idea to find ways to undermine the other's confidence or independence; this tends to increase the effectiveness of your anger.

D. When the Going Gets Tough, the Tough Get Going: If the other person is saying something you don't like, it is time to get going. Walk out of the room, clam up, refuse to talk about it. With children, send them to their rooms. No need to hang around an unpleasant situation. No matter how much others feel their complaints are justified, no issue is so important that it can't be walked away from. Better yet, refuse to acknowledge that the situation even exists.

E. Play Psychiatrist: This is closely related to the previous technique but extends the concept somewhat. Analyze others, point out their shortcomings and hang-ups and, where possible, explain in psychological terms the weaknesses you see in their characters. Example: "You have a mother complex" or "The reason you say that is because you're basically insecure." The real secret in playing psychiatrist, however, involves the skillful use of labels. (For example, *egomaniac* or *dominating witch*.) With a little forethought, you can find a label for any behavior you don't like: if people are drinking to relax, they are "potential alcoholics"; if they don't want sex they are "frigid" or "impotent." By the way, if they object to your clinical evaluation, it is undoubtedly because they have "inferiority complexes" or they "can't face the truth."

F. Never Back Down: Backing down can only be seen by the opposition as a sign of weakness. Right or wrong, you have to stand up for yourself. If you don't, who else will? By the way, when was the last time you were *wrong* about something anyway?

G. Never Accept an Apology: Just because others have said they are sorry, right away they expect you to forget about it. Never let others think that they are forgiven. How else will they remember the next time? Learn to hold grudges—for years, if necessary. People's misconduct can be thrown up to them over and over again, giving you a decided edge in future disagreements.

H. Put the Other Person in a Double Bind: Criticize your spouse for gaining a little weight, not keeping up his or her appearance and the like. Then when your spouse dresses up and looks especially good for a party, accuse the person of trying to impress people or flirting. Hound your children about hanging around the house too much. Then, when they are getting ready to go out to play, remind them of some chore they were supposed to do or tell them it's too close to supper. The idea is "damned if you do; damned if you don't." Double binds artfully used can, and do, literally drive people crazy.

I. Devastate with Humor: Keep in mind that the most devastating remarks are often said in jest. Therefore tease and humor your opponent. Be sarcastic but always smile to show it's all in good fun. If the other person begins to get defensive, you can accuse him or her of being overly sensitive. This is an excellent tactic to use in public because it shows you are a fun-loving person with a sense of humor and the other person is a spoilsport.

J. Play One against the Other: When out with your spouse, always take a long, wistful look at passing strangers of the opposite sex. Compare the success of others to those of the person you are with. A parent should never miss a chance to hold up the accomplishments of one child to another. A child should likewise never miss an opportunity to play one parent against the other.

K. Play the Martyr: Go out of your way to sacrifice your pleasure for others, even to the point of letting others take advantage of you. Later, when you want to get your way, preface your remarks with statements like: "How could you do this to me? After all the things I've done for you" or "See how I've suffered because of you?" You will be amazed at the power a little guilt gives you. The possibilities are limitless.

L. The Kitchen Sink Technique: Throw everything into the argument but the kitchen sink. No need to stick to the issue at hand; now is the time to bring up all the other incidents that have been bothering you. Talk about his or her past failings, defects in his or her character, past injustices, unsettled issues from the last argument, etc. Before long, so many irrelevant issues will have been brought up that the other person will begin to feel that winning an argument with you is next to impossible.

M. Ambush—The Art of Getting the Other Person in a Corner: Be on the lookout for situations you can capitalize on later. Go through your spouse's wallet; listen in on the telephone extension; quiz your children's friends to find out what your kids have been up to. You will be amazed to find how much ammunition you can gather for your next fight. Once you have become proficient in this tactic, others will think twice about bringing up even the most legitimate grievance.

N. Chinese Water Torture Techniques: This heading is a grab bag for a number of techniques that are meant to exasperate the opposition. Here are a few possibilities; make up your own variations.

(1) Be a chronic forgetter. Never keep a promise; forget to do an errand. Act surprised when the other person gets upset, as if to imply it didn't matter anyway. Forgetting birthdays and anniversaries also adds a nice touch, as does forgetting to call when you are delayed.

(2) Be a procrastinator. Delay carrying out promises or obligations. The more others are depending on you, of course, the better. If there is a complaint, take the tack (a) "What are you getting excited about? I said I would do it, didn't I?" or (b) "You're always nagging me about something; no wonder I never have a chance to get anything done." Being a procrastinator makes you look good because it gives the impression that you have so many important things to do that you don't have a chance to get all the trivial things done as well. (Note: *Important* means important to you; *trivial* means important to the other person.)

(3) Promote misunderstanding. Never be clear about your likes and dislikes, plans, times, dates and directions. When people fail to do what is expected of them, use the opportunity to get angry, make them feel guilty or call them stupid.

O. Use Children and Money as Weapons: Here are some potentially devastating tactics often overlooked by inexperienced dirty fighters. The beauty of this method is that you can use either a direct frontal assault or an indirect sniping attack with equal effectiveness. The following remarks, listed by category, have been used successfully by dirty fighters for generations.

(1) Money: "If you would go out and work for a change, you wouldn't be complaining about needing _____ (fill in the blank)."

"How do you expect us to get along on the piddling salary you make?"

(2) Children: "What kind of father (mother) are you anyway? What kind of example do you think you're setting?"

"If it weren't for your spending so much time with your friends (or doing other unacceptable behavior) Johnny wouldn't be having nightmares (getting poor grades, etc.)."

P. Mind Rape: Never allow the person to be right—even about his or her own thoughts or feelings. For example, if the other person says, "I'm furious," you should object—very benevolently, of course—saying, "Now, now. You're not *really* furious, you're just a little *frustrated.*"

Q. Guilt Making: Do something self-destructive and blame it on the other person. Above all, never examine the harmful effects to yourself. For instance, after an argument, say, "I'm going out and get drunk, and it's your fault." Better is the implied threat. If you have a history of suicide attempts (drug abuse, depression or psychotic behavior will do just as well), say, "This argument makes me very depressed. I don't think it's ever been this bad."

R. Non-Engagement: When you sense a disagreement coming on, state your position and then announce, "I refuse to discuss it." Then leave the house. It makes others furious, but what can they do? A nice variation is to allow the others to talk, yell, threaten and get red in the face, while you merely smile at them (or continue to read the newspaper).

S. Closure Block: When an argument gets well underway, you should unilaterally say, "You're losing control. I don't want to talk about it anymore." This is especially effective immediately following a "Kitchen Sink" maneuver. The effect is nice if you have used the "Kitchen Sink," but it has a flavor of justification if the other person has just "Kitchen Sinked" you.

T. Always and Never: Make absolute statements such as, "You never take me out," or "You are always so nasty" or "Nobody makes love like that." This is not a good way to win an argument since undoubtedly the other person immediately will come up with one time that refutes your absolute statement, such as "Oh yeah? Well, in 1946 we went out to eat." This tactic is a good way to keep from losing an argument after your opponent has scored heavily because it diverts your opponent from the point-producing argument and directs attention to finding the exception to your absolute statement.

U. Threat of Abandonment: This maneuver can be used in many forms, but usually it is the big gun in the arsenal because most times the abandonment threatened is relatively permanent. (For example, you can threaten separation, divorce, suicide or going crazy.) This is effective because you don't really expect others to take you up on the threat. You think they will give in. Most times this works. Unfortunately, the first time it doesn't work the game could end (through actual divorce, suicide, etc.). And ending the game would be a shame.

V. Concluding Remarks: Study this outline and memorize the points thoroughly. Use the tactics whenever possible. Then practice catching your spouse fighting dirty. Don't give up fighting dirty yourself, but expect your spouse to stop. That way, it will be even easier for you to get your way. . . . And that's the important thing!

Adapted from "Dirty Fighter's Instruction Manual" (supplement to the film *The Failing Marriage,* Alan Summers, producer), by Transactional Dynamics Institute; *Scripts People Live,* by Claude Steiner; *Intimate Enemy,* by George Bach and Peter Wyden; and other sources.

not tone, completely obscuring the original issue. Non-distressed couples, however, can acknowledge the meta-communication and get back to the original issue, not getting caught in what Gottman calls meta-communicative loops. For instance, James might reply, "You're right. I am raising my voice. I'm sorry. I do think we should eat at Hardee's, though, because we have so little money that even the cockroaches in our house are starving to death." He acknowledges Hedda's complaint, but gets back to business.

One negative pattern of communication involves the frequent use of sarcasm and put-down humor. When challenged, the couple might even defend the use of the humor. At least, the user of sarcasm defends it while the other sits passively.

The problem with such humor is that it contains both negative and positive elements. It is thus difficult to criticize. The injured party can complain, but the one who used the humor merely claims that no harm was intended.

Often, the ambiguity of put-down humor typifies a relationship. One couple I counseled involved an alcoholic husband. Alcoholism is a lifestyle that allows the person to be ambiguous about his or her true feelings. Under the influence of alcohol, the person can be amorous or vicious, and the spouse remains uncertain whether the alcoholic really means it.

In this particular couple, the man would frequently use cutting humor at the expense of his wife. When she would protest, he would laugh and act as if she were deranged and paranoid in seeing any hostility in him. He then proclaimed his undying affection for her "despite her condition." Much of this man's life was characterized by ambiguity and mixed messages. His use of cutting humor was consonant with his style of life.

Another client would deliver a particularly devastating sarcastic dig at his wife, then look at me and wink as if he were involving me in a huge joke. His playful manner was meant to convey ambiguity to me and to co-opt me into his destructive interactions.

A problem with giving mixed positive and negative messages is that the negative message usually has the most impact on the person hearing the message. Although the person using sarcasm might emphasize his or her playfulness, it is the sting, not the smile, that lasts longer. Sarcastic humor is like mixing vinegar and ice cream. The vinegar spoils the ice cream, regardless of how good the ice cream is.

ASSESSING EFFECTANCE: CONFLICT

The Cause of Conflict

When patterns of poor communication develop, spouses do not feel validated. Each feels as if the spouse does not care about him or her, that the spouse will not meet his or her needs. Their sense of effectance—being able to produce a desired effect on the spouse—is at low ebb. To restore their feelings of effectance, people make stronger requests. If the requests are not heeded, they escalate to rigid positions, which are often held without compromise and can appear to the spouse (and the counselor) as demands. When one or both spouses attempts to gain or regain a sense of acceptance at the expense of the other, the result is conflict.

Topic of Conflict

Generally, the easiest part of assessing a couple's conflict is to determine the areas of conflict. These may be gleaned through the interviews and through the Couple's Precounseling Inventory.[19] For most couples the areas of conflict are similar, though particular arguments within the topics may vary. The most common areas of disagreement are (a) household chores; (b) decisions concerning money; (c) child rearing and discipline; (d) sex and affection; (e) use of leisure time; (f) involvement with in-laws; and (g) style of communication.[20]

Besides determining the areas of conflict, you should be able to summarize the positions taken by each spouse on the topics at issue between them. Usually each spouse has not listened to the other's arguments very well. Your ability to summarize will demonstrate that *you* understand. On the assessment summary, list the topics of disagreement but don't summarize each spouses' arguments. The summary of the arguments will be useful during intervention.

Levels of Conflict

On a battlefield, with wounded soldiers everywhere, a medic arrives. His first task is to "triage" the survivors of the battle. A triage is a three-category classification system. Survivors are denoted as: (1) those not needing immediate treatment; (2) those that immediate treatment may save; and (3) those likely to die regardless of whether or not they are treated.

Similarly, couples in conflict might be triaged to help you set reachable goals for them. Guerin[21] recommends that couples be classified into one of four categories, depending on the level of conflict the couple exhibits. According to Guerin:

1. *Level I conflict* involves couples who have problems that are of recent origin or that are issue-focused rather than rule or meta-rule focused. These couples generally will benefit most from counseling and will usually respond positively to communication training.

2. *Level II conflict* has become serious. It involves well-entrenched disagreements over the power rules of the relationship. The atmosphere of the household is turbulent and angry. Fights can be vicious, loud and long.

3. *Level III conflict* is characterized by weary despair. The couple fights but never expects to convince the other of anything. The entire household is usually depressed. Turmoil is always beneath the surface. Hope is deeply submerged. The prognosis for couples typically exhibiting Level III conflict, Guerin estimates, is lower than 50-50 of ever resolving their differences in ways that can produce much happiness.

4. *Level IV conflict* has an even worse prognosis. At least one spouse has already engaged a lawyer. Since the legal system is adversarial, dealings with an attorney will most often push the couple farther apart. Level IV conflict is dead-end conflict. The couple might or might not still argue, but most arguments give the impression of being well rehearsed with a foregone conclusion. Guerin estimates that these couples will resolve their marriage difficulties less than twenty-five per cent of the time, and in over half the cases, they will soon divorce, despite any efforts on the part of the counselor. Often the couple's goal in Level IV conflict is to justify the divorce to themselves and their friends—to be able to say, "We tried everything, but nothing would work. We even went to a Christian counselor." Or the goal might be divorce counseling, to ease the pain of the dissolution of the relationship.

Some research supports the accuracy of these stages of conflict. Level II couples have been found to have less satisfaction with marriage, less intimacy in all five areas of the PAIR, less self-reported intimacy, more conflict and more evidence of disagreement over meta-rules than couples in Level I.[22]

Rausch, Barry, Hertel and Swain (1974) proposed that specific arguments could be categorized into three groups:[23]

■ *"First degree" arguments.* These arguments stress a specific issue. Both spouses employ tactics that enhance mutual gain, rather than tactics that promote winning at the expense of the other. There is specificity of problem definition, and when problems are clearly defined, they are solved most of the time (sixty-seven per cent). When problems are only vaguely specified, they are solved only eighteen per cent of the time. Attention of the couple usually remains on the problem during first-degree arguments.

■ *"Second degree" arguments.* During a second degree argument, the focus changes from the (usually) ill-defined specific problem to the inadequacies of the spouse. Almost any discrepancy in viewpoint quickly becomes linked to some core issue. Accusations such as "You never . . ." or "You always . . ." frequently scorch the air. Each spouse tries to force the other into agreement through using coercion, bullying, tears, physical complaints, psychological symptoms and other manipulative tactics. Spouses devalue the relationship—"Why try to preserve a relationship with a person as troubled (wrong or evil) as my husband (wife)?"

■ *"Third degree" arguments.* These occur when the relationship begins to be criticized regularly. At this stage, the couple begins to make divorce threats to coerce the other into submission. Because both partners are unwilling to give in on the power rules, they may be impelled toward a divorce that neither really wants. Once they begin to make divorce threats in earnest, they no longer try to resolve differences because they are thinking in terms of splitting up rather than making up. Conflict tactics tend to become more and more personally destructive until the couple divorces.

Whatever way you classify the level of conflict,[24] it is helpful to think about exactly how serious the arguments of the couple are. Only after making this assessment can you determine the proper duration of counseling and the likelihood of achieving certain goals during the allotted time.

Styles of Conflict

As pointed out in the appendix to this book, various theories of counseling focus "communication training" on different aspects of communication. Behavioral counselors, Rogerians (such as Guerney and proponents of the

Minnesota Couples Communication Program), Gestalt counselors (such as Virginia Satir) and cognitive counselors generally focus on the semantics and syntax of communication. Such counselors will have couples talk to each other quite often. The counselor will usually interrupt the couples frequently to give feedback about how to communicate better. They will have couples check out whether they understand each other and will strive to insure that each is hearing the other's meaning as well as the words. They will be aware of how much each is speaking and how clearly. They will also be interested in whether particular verbal and nonverbal messages are congruent and whether both are congruent with the context.

Counselors who spring from the roots of the Mental Research Institute, such as Haley, Minuchin and their followers, emphasize the pragmatics of communication. They want to know the effects of communication in a relationship. They are interested in the couple's power rules and in the power structure revealed by communication and in other practical effects of communication. These counselors will have couples speak to each other less frequently than counselors concerned with syntax and semantics of communication. When couples do converse, they will generally be allowed to talk longer without interruption. The counselor is more interested in the meaning of the communication for the couple's structure and power than in changing specific utterances.

I tend to look at the pragmatics of communication more than the semantics or syntax of communication. Like all counselors, I am not "pure" in my focus, for communication is too complex always to fit into neat conceptual boxes. Still, I generally do not rush to have couples talk with each other early in assessment or treatment. I also tend to wait for a minute or two of their conversation before I make suggestions about how they can talk differently.

Like all who are concerned with pragmatics of communication, I know that it is almost impossible to alter the broad patterns of power and rule structure through mere insight. Communication patterns are too well ingrained for that. Rather, couples change their rules and their power structures because they modify important specific utterances or specific patterns of utterances. Thus, to effect change, the words of the couples must be changed.

Assessment, then, is geared to understanding the specific sequences that couples go through that reveal their rules and their power strategies. I try to identify the couple's problems over their relationship and power rules. Some potential problems are:

1. A couple may disagree because there are no rules about a particular area, such as when a couple enters a new stage of the family life cycle involving tasks that have never before been required of them.

2. A couple may have different views on what the rules are.

3. A couple may agree on what the rules are, but one person is dissatisfied with the rules.

4. A couple may agree on what the rules are, but both are dissatisfied in different directions.

5. A couple may agree on what the rules are but disagree about how they got to be that way, such as disagreeing over who got to say what the rules were.

6. A couple may disagree about the rules and disagree about how they got that way.

7. A couple may agree about the rules (at least outwardly) but is upset because someone frequently violates agreed-upon rules.

Disruption in "Normal" Rules

Because I tend to emphasize relationship rules over other conflict concepts, I also assess how much the current status of the relationship differs from the status prior to the onset of the problem. To make this determination I use the couple's description of the relationship history. If the couple has recently undergone a life transition, you might elicit information about previous rules by asking each person, "What do you see as different in the way you have discussions (resolve differences, act with each other) now compared to before (the transition)?"

ASSESSING HURT, BLAME AND SIN

Blame

Problems in intimacy, satisfaction, general communication and conflict can result in hurt, pain and anger. People often respond by blame, lack of forgiveness, bitterness and self-indulgence. When a couple enters counseling, you need to assess their previous and current responses to the hurt, pain and anger they have experienced at each other's hands.

It is natural to attribute the cause of one's relationship difficulties to the spouse, who is the most prominent figure in a person's perceptual field. Blame is nearly always present in couples in distress. Generally, you will detect blaming patterns throughout assessment. The most difficult part of assessment for me is to *resist confronting* the problems I observe *during* the three assessment sessions.

When I see a couple blame each other, I want to shout, "Stop it! That's destructive." I want to confront the behavior on the spot. "I'll just point out that they are blaming each other," I think. "That won't cause any problem." But it does. Besides using valuable assessment time, intervening too early creates resentment and defensiveness rather than cooperation. Confrontation of highly emotional topics too early in therapy predicts lack of success in counseling.[25] Therefore, to be effective, I stifle urges to intervene until I have joined the couple and provided a credible assessment.

Spot the blame in each partner. Note what each blames the other for. Determine the times when each is likely to lay blame. Catalog those findings in your mind or in your case notes. But do not point out instances of blame and do not try to change the patterns . . . yet.

Lack of Forgiveness

Spouses who blame each other have not forgiven the other for perceived transgressions. But, lack of forgiveness is more than mere blame; it can be secretly harbored without the knowledge of either spouse. Or it can be a bitterness spoiling otherwise sweet waters of marriage. Some friends who had been happily married for twenty years had their marriage poisoned by bitterness. The man had an affair. He terminated it and asked his wife for forgiveness. She held onto her hurt and unforgiveness. Finally, after years, she worked through her unforgiveness, but her husband could not, then, forgive her for her tardiness in forgiving him. Both spouses' pride and unforgiveness poisoned twenty years of good marriage.

You must recognize signs of the festering sore of lack of forgiveness beneath the skin of the couple's behavior. Deal gently with the person rather than condemn. Insure that the hurt and lack of forgiveness are dealt with during counseling.

Bitterness

Bitterness is due to long-lasting lack of forgiveness. It shows up as cynicism by either party and by an unwillingness to take risks to make the marriage better. Bitterness is a disease of the soul that has consequences for the body. Although I have no experimental evidence to support such conjecture, I would propose, on the basis of my experience, that bitterness is often revealed in diseases of the body. Certain expressions in common parlance reflect this. For example, a "stiff-necked people" are rebellious. When I see a client complaining about a stiff neck, I wonder (to myself) whether she or he is rebellious. A "pain in the tail" is a person who continually aggravates one. When I see a client with lower back pain, I hypothesize that the client has been continually aggravated. "He's always on my back" might indicate someone who is frequently "riding" a person. I might suspect that a person who experiences back pain might be nagged frequently. I treat these as merely hypotheses for investigation. If the client denies any connection, I assume that he or she knows better than I what is happening in his or her life and I drop the topic. For me, the physical symptoms are often an indication that bitterness *might* be operating in a person's life.

Self-indulgence

Pain in a marriage often impels the couple to seek help. It also focuses their attention on self-protection. In each spouse's headlong flight from additional distress, he or she thinks mostly about himself or herself, not the needs of the spouse. No longer will a spouse give in to the other.

This self-indulgence violates the cardinal rule of a happy marriage. This rule was told me by my father-in-law on my wedding day. I was in the Navy in California. I got weekend leave to get married in Florida, where Kirby was living with her family. Flying in on Saturday, I was jet lagged, excited and exhausted. I wouldn't say I was nervous—just incredibly alert. So alert that I couldn't stop my right leg from shaking. In this state of heightened attention, Kirby's father gave me some good advice. "Sit down, boy," he boomed from his six-foot four-inch athletic body. He stood in front of the couch and talked while I stared unblinking, stunned.

"Marriage is *not* a fifty-fifty proposition," he began. I swallowed my chewing gum. "It's a hundred-hundred proposition. There will be times when Kirby is going through difficulties and you must give one hundred per cent to her. Don't think of your needs at all. Those times may last for years. Don't think of yourself. Think of her. There will be other times when you will be having difficulties, and she'll be giving one hundred per cent. Don't ever worry who has given the most. It'll all work out in the long run. Got it?"

I nodded—alertly—and have not forgotten.

Marriage difficulties make people forget about their spouse and become consumed with their own lives. During assessment, notice how this happens so that later, during intervention, you can help each spouse focus on meeting the needs of the other instead of indulging the self.

ASSESSING COMMITMENT

Spiritual separation from God can also affect your clients and their treatment. For the Christian counselor, there is the same (or more) concern over the clients' future when the client is apart from the True Vine (Jn 15:1-11) as when the client has psychological difficulty. The moral imperative for the counselor is to try to assist the client in being grafted into (or back into) the True Vine.

Spiritual Commitment

However, the situation is different than with psychological problems. With psychological problems, an assessment and recommendation by the counselor of the client's psychological state is generally appreciated and received. A non-Christian or Christian who has backslidden might resent the counselor's attention to spiritual matters if the implicit or explicit contract of counseling does not make room for the counselor to share spiritual matters.

If you are an explicitly Christian counselor and your clients know that, your assessment can easily include spiritual questions. In fact, for explicitly Christian counselors, more discomfort might be aroused if you did not address spiritual concerns than if you did. If you are not explicitly identified *by your clients* as a Christian counselor, you will probably want either to bring it up yourself or to avoid spiritual questions until the topic either arises at the initiation of the couple or comes up during counseling.

Assess first whether each person identifies himself or herself as a Christian. Often committed, theologically conservative Christians will broach the topic before you do. Generally, the more theologically liberal Christians will not but will respond with enthusiasm to your inquiries. Next, assess each spouse's commitment to the Lord. Commitment may be shown by their (a) church attendance; (b) frequency of considering God's will in making decisions; (c) involvement in ministry; (d) personal expressions of love and commitment to the Lord; (e) familiarity with the Bible and conformity to God's Word (Jn 14:15, 23); (f) example of love and care for others (Jn 13:34-35); and (g) unity with other Christians (Jn 17:21, 23).

Your task is not to administer a theology test, but to assess the couple's commitment to the Lord to determine how much you can rely on explicitly biblical principles during counseling. You will also want this information in order to help you estimate how to help the people better their relationship with Jesus Christ.

Commitment to This Marriage

Christians often proclaim their commitment to the permanence of marriage. Yet they divorce. They separate their commitment to marriage in general from their commitment to *this* marriage. They say, "Of course, I took him 'for better or for worse.' But he was worse than I took him for."

You must determine how likely they are to work to preserve their present marriage despite the cost of time, effort and distress. Simply asking each spouse whether he or she is committed to making the marriage work will not suffice, for there is strong social pressure to give an "acceptable" or "correct" answer. Yet ask anyway. Researchers in social psychology have shown that making a verbal commitment—even if the person does not fully agree with the statement—helps the person carry out the commitment.[26]

To assess their actual commitment to the marriage, however, look beyond their words.

☐ Are they considering alternatives to the marriage? How detailed are their considerations?

☐ Is there romantic involvement with someone outside of marriage?

☐ Are there children involved? Do the children pull the couple together or apart?

☐ Has the person lived by himself or herself prior to or since marriage?

☐ Have they talked of separation or divorce? To what extent?

Some counselors like to assess commitment to the marriage by using the *Marital Status Inventory.*[27] This fourteen-item inventory lists progressive steps to the dissolution of the marriage. The items are specific, ranging from considering divorce or separation to contacting a lawyer. I don't often use the *Marital Status Inventory*. Since I counsel Christian couples almost exclusively, I do not want to set the expectation that a marriage may not be improved through hard work. I do not want a couple to think of divorce from the outset of counseling. Once it becomes clear that a couple (or one spouse) is considering divorce seriously, I might administer the *Marital Status Inventory* to determine how seriously each spouse is thinking of divorce.

Besides spiritual and marital commitments, which were discussed earlier, assess the couple's commitment to counseling.

Commitment to Counseling

One indication of their commitment is their willingness to complete the assessment tasks. One couple I counseled recently had difficulty completing the two instruments—the CPI and the PAIR. As always, I did not schedule the feedback session, telling them that whenever I received their inventories, we could meet for feedback. After about a month, the wife called me. She asked whether I would talk to her husband about the uses to which the inventories would be put, for he was reluctant to complete the inventories. I called him and reassured him that the forms were to provide an accurate assessment. He asked whether the forms could ever find their way into a court of law, explaining that he was afraid that they might be used against him someday by his wife. This man was, at best, unsure of his wife's commitment to the marriage, but more likely, he was uncommitted to the marriage. Counseling with this couple was unlikely to produce positive results in their relationship.

One additional consideration in using the forms as a measure of the couple's commitment to counseling involves individual differences. Some people just don't like to fill out forms and make lists. For others, completing inventories is effortless. It is thus helpful to know the person's attitude toward questionnaires before drawing conclusions about their motivation to work in counseling. However, inventories are vital to good assessment. Whether a person *likes* to complete inventories or not, I expect them to be completed. In fact, I will probably ask each spouse to do a number of tasks that he or she does not like to do before counseling is completed. If the couple is to benefit, they must do the tasks.

There is much a counselor can do to help a couple comply with suggestions to change. But, much as we hate to admit it, there are limits to our effectiveness. Some couples are rigid. They resist suggestions despite what we do. They resist almost any change that attempts to foist itself on the marriage.

Sometimes this rigidity is adaptive. Transitions that send some couples reeling barely affect these rigid couples. They can absorb the birth of a child or the death of a relative or a job change without anyone outside the family realizing it has happened. But when a transition *does* affect such a couple, they are often hardest hit. Accustomed to stability at any price, they flop around like a fish on land seeking to cope with loss of breathing space. Coping with change is made even more difficult because the couple tries to re-establish the conditions they were used to, which are inappropriate for their new situation.

Thus, assess the couple's rigidity or resilience to change.

☐ Does the couple typically adapt, or do they crack under strain?

☐ How often have they faced crises before?

☐ Have they had difficulty coping with previous transitions or have they been able to change to meet the new demands of the new stage of life?

These are easily assessed during the couple's relationship history. A simple question like, "How did you find that change, easy or hard?" is often enough to see how the couple coped.

The couple's rigidity can often be assessed through observing their reactions to some of the small directives that you give throughout assessment. When you direct them to talk to one another in a way that is different than they are accustomed to, can they follow your directives? Are they capable of different styles of interactions, or do they present the same face to everyone? Do they vary from day to day in the type of conversations they show you or are they consistent? Do not place a value on their consistency or rigidity. Consistency has both advantages and disadvantages. Your task is to discern how consistent, or rigid, the couple is so that you can know how to set goals appropriately for intervention.

The opposite end of the continuum from rigidity is an almost total lack of structure. The couple that is so adaptable that they are chaotic is as hard to help as the couple that is excessively rigid. Trying to change an amorphous, structureless couple is like trying to hog-wrestle a Jell-O pig. If the couple gives in too easily to your suggestions, expect slow and tortuous progress.

Although "resistance" is something that you as counselor have some influence over, it is not solely an interpersonal matter. Some individuals develop a lifestyle that is oppositional. Such people are difficult to work with, whether they resist actively through disagreement and arguing, or whether they resist passively through appearing to cooperate but sabotaging or failing at whatever you ask of them.

It is difficult to discern whether a couple is made of two resistant people or whether you are provoking resistance. Usually couples in distress are in such an extreme power struggle that any suggestion you make for change triggers resistance. I can tell only after several weeks whether resistance is due mostly to my provocation, their power struggle or to an oppositional personality. If I determine that the couple is resisting each other, but not necessarily me, I try to get the couple to cooperate with me. If I determine that the couple is habitually resistant, even with others besides me, I might use a paradoxical intervention to see whether their resistance can be made to work for them rather than against them.

Some people have difficulty relating to authorities. This might have been created by their interactions with parents, school teachers, employers, military officers, pastors or other authority figures. Regardless of the reason, the person acts either too rebelliously or too compliantly toward authority figures. Some clients assign authority status to a counselor. Most couples will treat you on your own merits, but for some people, your authority is an emotional, personal issue.

Be alert early in counseling to whether each partner responds consistently to authority. Does one spouse rebel against God, the pastor, the employer, the government, the Bible and the partner? Then expect that person to rebel against you too. If the person values authority—especially legitimate authority such as the authority of Scripture or of his or her pastor—then perhaps you can use this later in counseling. One danger is that you might interpret Scripture differently from the person. If so, prepare for conflict.

ASSESSING OTHER CRUCIAL AREAS

Assessing Individual Problems

Individual psychological problems can precipitate marriage problems and can be a source of continual aggravation for the couple. Some theories of marriage counseling see individual psychiatric symptoms as due to marriage or family strains. I find that for some clients the "systems" view fits; for others it doesn't. Whether or not marriage difficulties are caused by or cause individual problems (or both), the presence of individual psychological symptoms in a troubled marriage is one of the most difficult instances of treatment.[28]

Depression is the most common psychological symptom in tandem with marriage problems.[29] To treat the marriage and the depression, it is essential to diagnose depression and determine how severe it is. Assessing depression and other psychiatric difficulties is beyond the scope of this book. See Beck, Rush, Shaw and Emery[30] for a book about the assessment and treatment of depression from the framework of individual cognitive therapy.

You are responsible for assessing the degree of depression or other symptoms so that you can decide whether to do marriage counseling. Individual counseling for psychological problems usually damages *the troubled marriage* because the counselor becomes the advocate for the individual client and disturbs whatever tenuous balance of power existed prior to counseling. However, if the client is seriously depressed, marriage counseling may not be what is needed at that time to protect the client. I thus recommend that the client pursue individual counseling (usually with a different therapist so that the depressed client and I will not form a special bond that impedes future marital counseling) until the depression is under control. Then the couple should return for marriage counseling with me.[31]

If the depression is not severe, I usually treat the couple for marital difficulties and include individual counseling within the marriage counseling. The difficulty is keeping clear who the client is—the marriage or the individual. Confusion can make counseling unfocused and ineffective.

In some rare cases I have given a couple marriage counseling at the same time that one spouse was receiving individual counseling from another professional. This is usually not a good idea. Inevitably two counselors make recommendations that are slightly (or sometimes more fundamentally) incongruent, which confuses the couple, divides their loyalty, allows the couple to use the different suggestions to avoid any unpleasant change and creates power dynamics that are unnecessarily difficult to work with. Haley suggests that only one counselor give professional help at any time.[32] My experience validates his advice.

Another individual problem that commonly occurs in conjunction with marriage difficulties is alcoholism. I have found such cases to be most difficult. If alcoholism has been denied and has not received treatment, family members are often hostile to each other and threatened by labeling the alcoholism. If the problem has been recognized and dealt with, the person is usually involved in Alcoholics Anonymous. The family might also have been involved in Alanon.

AA and Alanon have been the best treatment developed for the treatment of alcoholism. I am not disparaging their work. However, the effects of the AA model on the family often make them particularly resistant to treatment. They are inculcated into a way of thinking about and dealing with alcoholism which they often transfer to any behavioral problem. If you take a different approach to treatment, usually substantial portions of treatment will be spent "undoing" some of the teaching of AA that the couple are applying to their detriment.

As with depression, alcoholism in a marriage can confront you with value decisions about which problems are the most urgent to treat. Failing to recognize individual problems can hamper your effectiveness with the couple and can endanger your clients' well-being.

Assessing the Severity of Difficulties

Couples with severe problems usually require more sessions and usually improve less than couples with less severe difficulties. But what is a severe difficulty?

Based on my experience, there are at least eight important predictors of poor counseling outcome. It is my guess that the more of these critical indicators experienced by a couple, the less success the counselor will have.

1. Ongoing affair that one spouse refuses to terminate.

2. Either or both spouses uses overt threats of divorce, and a lawyer has been contacted.

3. Presence of severe personal problems such as chronic depression or alcoholism.

4. Both spouses are non-Christians or involved only on the fringes of the organized church. If one spouse is bitterly opposed to Christianity and the other is actively involved in it, the effect is similarly pessimistic, though the couples will tend to have different problems.

5. Lack of intimacy and pleasantness in the couple's interaction. This is distinct from the presence of hostility and negative affect.

6. Stage III or IV conflict according to Guerin's[33] stages of conflict. This indicates that conflict patterns are harmful, overlearned, well rehearsed, deeply disturbing and demoralizing. Conflict involves power struggles that are well entrenched. During conflict, the couple attacks each other personally and disparages the worth of the relationship.

7. Continual focus on the problems with the relationship and with the spouse. If the couple returns to the deficiencies in the relationship and the spouse, even when the counselor persistently induces them to discuss other topics, the relationship will require more effort than if the couple cooperates with the counselor.

8. Involvement of "helpers" who encourage individual spouses to protect themselves in the relationship. In-laws tend to become involved easily in supporting one spouse against the other. One can understand their proclivity to protect their offspring through advice and sometimes interference, but their intervention forces the marriage apart. Other parties that can become overinvolved in marriage struggles and make success less likely are: (a) individual counselors; (b) pastors; (c) influential friends; and (d) siblings.

Assessing Your Competence

As Christians, one of the biggest mistakes we can make is to assume that we are to counsel any client that asks us for help. Although God sometimes arranges circumstances to guide us toward his perfect will, this is not a foolproof norm. Generally, we know God's will by concurrence of (a) circumstances; (b) scriptural directives; (c) the "still, small voice" within; (d) the direct guidance of the Holy Spirit; (e) the guidance of spiritual authorities; and (f) our own reasoning (based on the data from *a-e* above).

With each couple, carefully assess their needs and your ability to meet those needs. At times, your assessment of your competence should necessitate a referral. At other times, you might arrange for intensive supervision from one competent to supervise you with that couple. At other times, periodic consultation might be sufficient to meet your deficiencies. In still other instances, you can handle the couple by yourself.

When we feel inadequate to a task, we are faced with the dilemma of faith. Jesus is sufficient to meet all needs. We know that. But is it his perfect will that we step out in faith, trusting him whenever we feel inadequate as a counselor?

My inclination, when in doubt about my ability to counsel a couple, is to pray and consult another professional. If I cannot arrange coverage sufficient to help me feel that the clients are protected, I refer.

An honest evaluation of our counseling competence is in order with each case we see. Responsible action is necessary on the basis of our assessment.

Assessing Your Own Attitude

Evaluating people and their marriages is a responsibility and a danger to the counselor. I sometimes judge my clients harshly for their sins and failures. Although each counselor must evaluate individuals and couples, we must not judge them. When I catch myself thinking I am superior to my clients, it drives me to repentance. That is one thing I love about counseling. It so often reminds me of *my* imperfections, *my* sins, *my* failings. Who am I to judge anyone? I am totally dependent on the grace of God for what I have and what I am. This knowledge continually impels me to seek God. When I am reminded of the ugly motivation to power that lurks within me, I am driven to Jesus for healing.

Oh, gracious Lord. Help us to be insightful with the couples you lead to us. Let us see with your eyes and help with your wisdom and your hands. And while we do your bidding, protect us from pride and from judgment. Drive us to you and to total dependence on you for life. Amen.

SUMMARY

Prepare for good assessment by realizing that your clients' spiritual beliefs are important. Further, couples will undoubtedly enter counseling with beliefs about their compatibility and the likely causes of their problems. Your assessment must be complete, multifaceted, tied to your plans for intervention and useful to the couple as an end in itself. Generally, you will assess the couple's intimacy; effectance (communication and conflict); hurt, blame and sin patterns; and commitment using a variety of methods over two assessment sessions.

The couple's intimacy involves not only an assessment of different types of intimacy—emotional, social, sexual, recreational, intellectual—but also determinations of their degree of relationship satisfaction and the permeability of their boundaries as a couple. A couple's sense of effectance comes from their communication and (when things go wrong) from their conflict. Assessing communication is difficult. It involves assessing communication rules and roles; patterns of communication; amount, valence and openness of communication; degree of understanding; styles of communicating feelings and requests; and ways of communicating negatively. Patterns of conflict must also be understood. The causes, topics, severity and style of confict must be determined. Anger and pain within a marriage lead to hurt, blame and sin. When these persist, they can change to the more serious problems of lack of forgiveness, bitterness and self-indulgence in criticizing one's spouse. Finally, commitment must be assessed. The couple's commitment to the Lord, the marriage and counseling are each crucial to the healing of the fractured relationship.

Marriage assessment requires attention to areas besides the marriage relationship. Individual psychological problems can impair marital counseling; thus the counselor must assess the extent of such problems before determining whether marriage counseling is appropriate. Finally, we must each assess our own competence and attitude in dealing with the problems presented by our clients. Only after thorough assessment are we ready to consider what can be accomplished in counseling.

8

Setting Goals

W HERE THERE IS NO VISION, THE PEOPLE PERISH. . . ."
(Prov 29:18 KJV)

As counselor, you help clarify the vision of the couple. When they come to counseling, the couple has distant and infrequent sightings of their direction as a marriage. Their vision is obscured by the fog of problems, the haze of blame and unforgiveness, even the cloud of hatred. Worse, their vision is inwardly directed to self-protection and self-gratification. They know the shoals of marital destruction lie before them, but they rush toward them as if drawn by the siren song of self-justification. The couple are joint captains, ordering different courses to the same destruction. You have been engaged as their navigator to guide them safely past the reefs toward their destination. Thus, at times your working goals are different from the captains', while you hold the same (or even grander) ultimate goals as they.

Goal setting is the activity that as much as any bespeaks the success or failure of counseling. There are three parts of goal setting.

1. *Assess problems.*

2. Using the problems, *identify worthy goals.*

3. *Present these goals* to the couple so that they adopt them.

In the previous chapter, assessment has been explained. The present chapter deals with identifying worthy goals for yourself and the couple and persuading the couple to seek them.

CHARACTERISTICS OF GOALS

Goals Should Be Shared by the Couple
Couples who seek counseling usually have ambivalent feelings about their relationship. They value their marriage yet are dissatisfied and seek changes in it. They want to invest effort to create new strengths but also want to return to the "good old days." They want to understand each other but want vindication of their understanding of the problem too. Change both threatens and confirms their goals. The counselor must throw his or her influence on the side of the couple's positive desires to eliminate problems and improve the relationship.

Inevitably, because the couple has ambivalent desires for the marriage, you will conflict with their wishes. You will probably want more for them than they are willing to express at the moment. At those times, your task is *not* to force the couple into submission to your desires. It is *not* to convince the couple that you are correct or that your goals for them are better than theirs. It is *not* to convince the couple how grand and insightful you are as a counselor. Rather, you should pull back your implicit demands. This isn't the time to push the couple. As they get past their "resistance," you can again give them a vision of counseling that is perhaps beyond their own.

In successful counseling, you and the couple will share goals. This will happen early in counseling, often at the end of assessment and during the first few weeks of intervention. As counseling progresses, you can begin to lead the couple into higher goals.

Most couples want to believe that they can make positive changes in their relationships, so your realistic, yet optimistic, adherence to goals can give them a vision without which their relationships might perish.

Goals Should Be Positive

Your continual goal of counseling, which you want the couple to share wholeheartedly, is to help them accomplish changes that will increase their freedom. Counseling should increase their freedom *from* conflict, problems and distress, and it should increase their freedom *to* love and to grow.

Haley[1] classifies therapies into two groups: "growth therapies" and "problem-solving therapies." *Growth therapies* strive to create positive attributes and shape clients who are somehow "better" than most other people: more "self-actualized," more "insightful," less "repressed," better "communicators" or more "sanctified." Each growth therapy has its own goals for growth. On the other hand, *problem-solving therapies* assume that the people who seek counseling are normal people who are impaired from their normal functioning due to problems. The goal of problem-solving therapies is to help people solve their problems so they can return to their normal lives. I have tried to fashion a therapy that is both problem-solving and growth-oriented. The main goals are two-pronged: help solve problems and help the couple grow; decrease conflict and increase communication; decrease power struggles and increase intimacy; decrease blame and unforgiveness and increase faith.

While setting positive goals, be realistic. Unbridled optimism can cause the couple to lose confidence in your competence. If you do not take their problems seriously, you will create resistance. Implying that problems will be easily dealt with stimulates the couple to resist your interventions; they think, "If this is such a simple problem, we must be pretty incompetent and worthless as a couple not to be able to solve it in all the time we have had. I can't believe that this problem is that simple. We'll see." It is strange how often directives will fail when you have unwittingly insulted the couple by too much optimism. Treat the couple with respect.

Goals Should Be Realistic

On the other hand, some couples want to set goals that are too optimistic. A couple who has waged virtual war for six months since the birth of their first child will argue that therapy should completely eliminate disagreement and return the marriage to the blissful and "perfect" pre-birth state. Such blindly optimistic statements often test the counselor. Some couples unconsciously want to see whether the counselor can be led into areas that they know to be unrealistic. These statements manifest their essential ambivalence about the relationship. They simultaneously want to affirm their positive goals aloud, yet they prevent change by exposing the incompetence of the counselor to help them change.

When a couple wants to set goals that are too optimistic, I generally talk with the couple about the difficulty of changing well-established patterns of behavior. I urge the couple to modify their goals *for counseling,* to be less ambitious. I let them argue that they can achieve the optimistic goals. I express doubt that they can achieve "*that* much change in so short a time," but I say that if they want to set that goal for themselves, I can't stop them. I usually say, in a challenging way, that "I want you to be successful with counseling, so let's just take stock of where you are starting from. I'll go along with your goals, though it's against my better judgment. At the end of counseling, let's be sure to recall where you are now, so we can see how far you've come."

Besides being honest about my assessment of their potential for change during the relatively few weeks of counseling, I use the interaction around goal setting with the too optimistic couple to accomplish other therapeutic objectives. I tell them directly that counseling means hard work and that change will not come easily. I also challenge the couple to make more progress than I think is reasonable by using their desire to prove me wrong (by improving) rather than stimulating them to resist improvement. I induce them to verbalize their optimism about the relationship, rather than pessimism.

At the same time, though, I am not pessimistic. We are disagreeing over degrees of optimism rather than optimism versus pessimism. Finally, I (reluctantly) accept their goals—if I think they are within reach at all. (If I do not think that the couple's goals are remotely achievable, I am much stronger in my insistence that they not set unreachable goals. In the last resort, I might have to argue for two sets of goals—their set and mine.)

Goals Should Be Derived from Assessment

Goal setting should follow from assessment. Rarely do the couples I see ever disagree with the goals I propose for them in the assessment summary during the feedback session. Problems are described based on specific observations and questionnaire results. Goals are aimed at eliminating problems and providing growth. The conduct of the assessment and the assessment summary pave the way for acceptable goals.

Goals that are specific are more likely to be reached than those that are vague. However, most people seem to believe that the more specific a goal is, the less meaning it has for the relationship as a whole. I set general goals during assessment but throughout intervention try to make goals more specific. **Goals Should Be Specific**

For example, during the assessment summary, I might state as a goal to improve the couple's intimacy. However, once we have begun counseling, I assign the couple to spend time together doing something pleasant. Beginning with twenty minutes a day, I might ultimately hope for them to spend at least five hours together each week doing things that are intimate or coactive. I continually justify specific goals by referring to the general goal of increasing intimacy.

Conflict often erupts in several prominent areas: sex, in-laws, money, child rearing and household responsibilities. For some couples, conflict is widespread; for others, it is more circumscribed. Goals involving reduction of conflict will often be set for several areas, but counseling will not deal with each area. In much of counseling, the couple defines one area as the (implicitly) agreed-upon battleground. Conflict is waged in that area. **Goals Are Usually in Predictable Areas**

One couple had several conflict areas, but the issue we focused on in counseling was disagreement over household responsibilities. Discussing this problem, the power struggles in the relationship surfaced and the resolution of the problem—coming to an equitable arrangement about the household chores—removed much of the competition from the relationship.

Although the couple still had some rather heated disagreements, they had accepted a parity of sorts through the one issue worked on. Having gotten past a difficult time in their relationship, that couple then helped countless other couples in their church, applying some of the lessons they learned in therapy to a ministry with other couples.

However, sometimes the area about which a couple disagrees is a *metaphor* for a more serious and enduring problem that they have implicitly agreed not to fight about because it would severely threaten the marriage. Madanes[2] describes one case of a couple who had fundamental disagreement over acceptance of the husband's son by a previous marriage. Being too threatened to disagree about that topic, the couple began to have conflict over their sexual relationship. Whereas they had previously had sexual intercourse frequently, they now had sexual intercourse only rarely, and the wife complained that it was not even pleasurable. Madanes relates how a strategic therapist helped solve the sexual problem and the problem with the son. The couple never talked in detail about their past resentments and hurts around the original problem, but simply followed the directives of the counselor.

Most other counselors seldom work the "magic" of the strategic therapist. My approach in this case would probably have been to work on the sexual problem, even though progress might be sporadic, in order to gain the couple's confidence. After the couple trusted me with the more threatening problem, we would work to resolve it, and then return to the unfinished business of the sexual problem.

GOALS THROUGHOUT COUNSELING

Not all goals are of the same specificity or on the same level of importance. Parloff[3] has distinguished between mediating goals and ultimate goals. Mediating goals reflect the counselor's assumptions about the necessary steps and stages through which counseling must pass to be successful. Ultimate goals go beyond mediating goals by describing the outcomes desired from counseling. Gurman has compared psychoanalytic, Bowenite, communications and behavioral marriage counseling theories on twenty-one mediating goals and twelve ultimate goals for counseling using two succinct tables.[4]

We need to distinguish among types of goals. I have identified three categories of goals, which I call ultimate, mediating and working. (See Table 5 for a summary of each type of goal.)

Ultimate goals reflect the primary aims of counseling: to resolve presenting problems and to increase the couple's faith (or more precisely, to resolve the couple's problems and thus be a vehicle through which the Lord increases their faith).

Mediating goals use theoretical constructs such as intimacy, conflict, commitment, boundaries, sin, forgiveness and others to describe how the two ultimate goals will be reached.

Working goals describe the specific tasks that must be accomplished throughout counseling for success to occur. In the following sections, each type of goal will be discussed.

Table 5
Three Types of Goals in Marriage Counseling

U l t i m a t e   G o a l s

☐ Resolve presenting problems	☐ Increase the couple's faith

M e d i a t i n g   G o a l s

☐ Increase intimacy	☐ Solidify marriage boundaries
☐ Improve communication	☐ Increase adaptability to future stresses and strains
☐ Reduce conflict	☐ Increase awareness of biblical norms, guidelines and principles
☐ Restructure power imbalances	
☐ Improve positive and negative expressions	☐ Help spouses meet their individual needs

W o r k i n g   G o a l s

☐ Structure assessment sessions	☐ Induce confession and repentance for one's own hurtful behavior patterns
☐ Assess problems efficiently	
☐ Establish a working alliance	☐ Induce each spouse to forgive the other
☐ Specify problems clearly	☐ Provide clear rationales for directives
☐ Set reachable goals	☐ Build new behavior patterns through suggestions and directives
☐ Prepare the couple for counseling via precounseling information	
☐ Structure counseling sessions	☐ Stimulate the couple to a "vision" of a happy marriage for them
☐ Build recognition of individual responsibility for problems and for change	☐ Provide understanding of why change occurs
☐ Orchestrate a meeting of minds (common understandings and goals)	☐ Provide opportunities for practicing new behaviors
☐ Break up old patterns through directives in session and out	☐ Inspire the couple to "press on to the high calling" of a better marriage and a more vibrant faith

Ultimate Goals

Couples seek counseling for relief from marital distress. The success or failure of counseling depends on the resolution of presenting problems. Because I as a counselor am explicitly identified as a Christian, though, an implicit goal of counseling is to help the couple with their spiritual lives. This goal is achieved through using explicitly Christian techniques and those techniques compatible with Christian values and goals. The primary goal of resolving presenting problems must remain as the focus of counseling.

Most distressed couples do not seek counseling for their spiritual growth. They want help with their marriages and assurance that their fundamental Christian beliefs will be valued. For such a couple, spiritual growth is only a side benefit, not a primary goal of counseling. For the counselor, spiritual growth for the couple is a likely secondary goal, achieved by aiding the marriage. Merely aiding the marriage will not produce spiritual growth. However, being open about your assumptions, beliefs and values and using techniques that direct the couple's attention to their Lord will make spiritual growth more likely.

Mediating Goals

Where the ultimate goals often form the *implicit* treatment agreement between you and the couple, mediating goals will usually be described *explicitly*. They will be written into the assessment summary. These goals describe the problem areas that you assess. Not every couple will have problems in each area.

I describe mediating goals simply and clearly. As far as the clients are concerned, these are *the* goals of counseling. I never make distinctions to clients between ultimate, mediating and working goals. I merely call the mediating goals, "our goals."

Working Goals

Whereas mediating goals are used to understand what is expected from counseling and why the counselor is asking the couple to perform certain directives, working goals are exclusively for the counselor. They describe the *tasks of the counselor* in bringing about the mediating goals. These tasks of the counselor differ in each stage of marriage counseling: assessment; between assessment and intervention; during intervention, consolidation and termination.

During assessment the counselor has five working goals: structure assessment sessions, assess problems efficiently, establish a working alliance (join the couple to promote cooperation), specify problems clearly and set reachable goals. Accomplishing all of these goals will not ensure success at counseling, but it will create confidence in the counselor and a collaborative feeling between clients and counselor. These will make cooperation better later in counseling.

Between assessment and counseling, the counselor can help prepare the couple to benefit from counseling through using the "Introduction to Marriage Counseling" (Figure 10 in chapter 6). This information helps the counselor and clients have similar expectations about counseling and provides a positive rationale for what is likely to happen during intervention.

During the intervention sessions, the counselor pursues ten working goals. Counseling sessions must be *prepared for* and *structured*. A plan is devised for each session, and a clear goal is established for each session.

Some of the counselor's working goals will be aimed at getting the couple to change their cognitive structures. The counselor will try to build a recognition in each spouse that he or she is responsible for part of the problem with the relationship and that a workable solution depends on each spouse taking responsible risks. The counselor also seeks to orchestrate a common understanding of the problems, goals and means for reaching mutually beneficial outcomes. The counselor also helps break up patterns of behavior that maintain relationship difficulties. Old patterns of communication and intimacy must be changed. Habits that are destructive must be recognized, confessed and repented of, and each spouse must forgive the other for past wrongs and hurts. New patterns of behavior must replace the old. This requires that the counselor give clear suggestions, directives and persuasive rationales for making the changes.

Throughout intervention the counselor helps the couple get a "vision" of where they are going with their marriage. The counselor's directives and lucid explanations help clients identify and understand pathways to their destination.

During consolidation, the counselor's working goals include explaining why change occurred and providing opportunities for the couple to practice the behaviors that have been built into their daily routines. Because both explanation and action are necessary to consolidate change, both should occur throughout counseling.

During termination, the main task of the counselor is to inspire the couple to continue their work toward a better marriage and a more vibrant faith. If you have used the techniques of counseling to good advantage, you will not only have helped the couple eliminate their presenting problems (your main goal), but you will also have stimulated more awareness of God. The couple will use their Christianity even more than they did before counseling to guide their daily lives. They will rely more on the power of the Holy Spirit to lead them into truth about their lives together. If you can aid the couple in that increased faith, as well as help them with their marriage, you can consider counseling truly successful.

THE ASSESSMENT SUMMARY

Structure of the Report

The assessment summary is a written report to the couple that conveys the results of your assessment and suggests goals and a timetable for counseling. I generally follow a rough structure for writing the reports, deviating from the usual if the couple's situation requires it.

Each couple is different. The purpose of each assessment summary fits the couple. In some cases, I assure the couple that there is hope for their marriage. In other cases, I try to jolt the couple from their complacency to see that they need to work on their relationship. In some cases, I suggest broad changes meant to challenge the couple. In other cases, I describe a grim picture of a stagnant, diseased marriage that will require great effort to achieve modest changes.

The assessment summary is begun by describing the facts of the couple's lives—their ages, years married, number of children, and other information. Presenting problems are also stated. It is essential that this information be accurate. As far as the couple is concerned, the "faithful in little, faithful in much" principle is at work.[5] If you cannot be relied on to keep the easily verifiable facts of their relationship straight, then why should they trust you with the more difficult intricacies of their emotional lives?

The second section of the assessment summary describes the couple's relationship history. In your summary of their history, be accurate but selective. Describe the positive times of the relationship, the onset of the problems in the context of their time in the family life cycle, and how the problems decrease intimacy and produce conflict.

The third and following sections of the assessment summary describe the strengths and problems of the couple—one section for each major category of problem. It is necessary (in most cases) to enumerate at least as many relationship strengths as you do problems or weaknesses. In discussing problems, one section might discuss the couple's current lack of intimacy and mention the evidence you used to deduce this. Another section might discuss their communication patterns, especially their conflict. A third might discuss the incessant power struggles or the lack of forgiveness by each spouse or the tentativeness of commitment to the relationship. For each couple, the report will differ depending on the issues that trouble them.

The next section of the assessment summary will contain your recommendations, including whether you recommend counseling. If you recommend counseling, suggest goals. Your statement of goals will parallel the discussion of the problems in the earlier sections of the summary. Statements of goals will generally be similar in specificity to the mediating goals, that is to say, increase their intimacy, reduce their frequency and intensity of conflict, etc. Finally, suggest a reasonable treatment plan for accomplishing the goals. Finally, recommend the number of counseling sessions you think it will take to accomplish the goals you identified.

I sometimes suggest that the couple not begin counseling immediately (depending on the severity and urgency of the disturbance). I tell them:

You now have my ideas of the problems of your relationship and the goals I think are reasonable for you to work toward. You might want to try to work toward these goals on your own. This is often a good idea. It can make your marriage strong if you work on your goals together. However, if you try to make the changes and find that you are unable, then phone me and we'll work on the goals together. What do you think?

Some people will try to achieve the goals on their own, but usually if their relationship has troubled them enough to seek counseling assessment, they are convinced that they are unable to change without the counselor's assistance. Most couples begin counseling immediately. When a couple tries to make changes without my aid, they will sometimes succeed. Most of the time, though, they phone shortly after the assessment to initiate counseling. I generally consider that a good sign for counseling. They have admitted to themselves that they are unable to reach their goals on their own, making them more receptive to my suggestions than couples who hold an unspoken belief that they could do it on their own but choose to go on with counseling anyway.

The final section of the assessment summary is a statement of hope and motivation. I almost always state that I believe that the couple can achieve the goals I suggested "if [they] work hard." Following the suggestion of Jacobson and Margolin, I stress that success in counseling is usually experienced by the couples willing to do the homework, take risks and work hard on their marriages.[6] I affirm that we will not work on the marriage alone, but can expect that the Lord, who is vitally interested in marriages and fidelity, will be the main power impelling success.

Examples

I have selected three examples of assessment summaries to illustrate the style of the report as well as the variety of aims that are addressed. I have, of course, changed numerous details to protect the identities of my clients. Each report has a different objective.

The first report (Figure 12) describes a young couple. The wife was unhappy with the marriage, but the husband could not recognize any problem. After assessment, one goal of feedback was to convince the husband that there were substantial problems with the relationship so that he would be shocked into action. Rather than emphasize the positive aspects of the relationship, I emphasized the problems.

The second report (Figure 13) describes a couple in their early thirties with two young children. They had some conflict, but the main problem with their relationship was that it had lost its sparkle and its intimacy. My objectives were for them to recall the positive aspects of their relationship and to stimulate them to recapture those times while reducing the conflict that had developed.

The third report (Figure 14) describes a couple in their early forties with three adolescent children and one adult child, though only the two young-

Figure 12
Sample Assessment Summary for a Couple with an Unhappy Wife and Husband Who Is Unaware of Difficulties

C O N F I D E N T I A L
Tim and Sue Gray

Tim (twenty-four) and Sue (twenty-four) have sought counseling in order to improve a marriage relationship that has shown signs of strain. The difficulty seems to be almost entirely a relationship problem, with both Tim and Sue functioning well despite the employment pressures to which each is exposed. Both have good self-esteem and are not subject to debilitating psychological problems or mood disturbance.

Nature of Presenting Complaints

Tim and Sue share the view that their relationship could be improved; however, they have different views of the nature and the severity of the problems within the relationship. In itself, this difference in perception indicates that attention needs to be paid to improving the relationship. Tim views the disturbance as relatively mild. He feels that communication could be improved, that he could control his temper better during disagreements, that he could be a better listener and could be more understanding when Sue has a rough day at the office and that they could argue less and show more outward signs of their love for each other. Sue views the marriage as in more trouble. She complains of frequent arguments that are sometimes loud and long, of being afraid to argue with Tim at times because of his strong reactions, of an emotional pulling back where physical presence or closeness is no longer experienced as emotional closeness, of Tim not listening to her and not taking seriously what she says, of not having enough affection (not just sexual contact) and of not doing enough things together.

Sue reacts to this by expressing her dissatisfaction with Tim. Though she tries to present suggestions in a positive way, they sometimes come across as accusatory, placing Tim on the defensive. My perception of Tim's behavior is that when he gets defensive, he jokes and makes light of the situation to try to diffuse the threat. If that fails, a heated argument often ensues. Tim's defensiveness and Sue's (sometimes) accusatory style perpetuate the cycle of arguing, for Tim's joking merely strengthens Sue's belief that he doesn't take her complaints seriously.

Concerning the seriousness of the relationship disturbance, I am inclined to side more with Sue's perception that the relationship has some disturbance that needs considerable attention—if for no other reason than *she* believes the relationship to be in some trouble. However, though I see some room for improvement in the marriage, I do not believe that Tim is the primary cause of the trouble. Rather, I attribute the cause of the trouble to some habits that *both* have in their relationship with each other—habits that can be changed *if* both are willing to work on changing.

Relationship History

Tim and Sue have known each other for a little over four years. They met and dated for six months before getting engaged. They were engaged for sixteen months—a period that they described as being one of their best periods, though they fought sometimes during this period. During their period of dating, they described their sexual relationship as very pleasing for them both.

They have been married for eighteen months. Their honeymoon was enjoyable though they had a large fight on the first day back from their honeymoon. Their life together after marriage has been characterized by a good deal of work by both of them. Both have jobs and are trying to move ahead. Both jobs are intense and draining, leaving them tired when they get home from work on most nights. They have different days off. This means they have less time together than if both were off on the same day; yet this also allows them to have alone-time to do work around the house.

This past May they noticed that their relationship was changing in ways that were not pleasing for them. Two things happened at that time that affected their intimacy. First, they bought a house and that entailed extra duties beyond those of apartment dwelling. Second, a friend of Sue's came to live with them. Some of her habits increased the tension in the household, forcing them to adjust to the presence of a third person and interfering with the intimacy patterns that had been established. She has recently moved out; however, a future brother-in-law has moved in—though his presence is less disruptive to them than the friend's was.

Relationship Strengths

This relationship has numerous strengths and has the potential to be a permanent, satisfying relationship for both Tim and Sue. One strength is that Tim and Sue respect each other. They are visibly proud of being with the other and are very supportive of each other. Another strength is their commitment to sticking with the relationship and working the problems out rather than being willing to abandon the marriage at the sign of needing some hard work. Furthermore, both Tim and Sue seem to enjoy being with each other, and they have more common interests than the average couple. One of the biggest strengths is that they now actively seek to please each other. In general, they have a good knowledge of the things that make the other person happy, and they often seek to provide those things for the other person. An important strength is that they enjoy a mutually pleasing sexual relationship. Another strength is that they have members of their families of origin in town to provide support. (Paradoxically this can also be problematic if they depend on family members during marital disagreements rather than sticking around and working out the difficulties.) One additional strength is demonstrated on the Couple's Pre-Counseling Inventory. Except for a few areas, both Tim and Sue gave evidence that they shared the same values and perceptions of their life together.

In short, this relationship is built on a relatively solid foundation.

Relationship Weaknesses

There are three weaknesses in the marriage that seem to be the root of the problem: intimacy, communication and conflict-resolution style. Improvement in these areas would, I believe, solidify a relationship that largely has a lot going for it. Failure to attend to these differences, I believe, could be *disastrous* for the relationship and for each individual's self-esteem.

Intimacy. Most of the information about intimacy is derived from the PAIR Inventory. Five areas of intimacy were assessed. One general observation from the inventory is the marked differences in Tim's and Sue's perceptions of the current relationship. In general, Tim seems to report that the relationship is going pretty much as he would like. Few changes are seen as necessary. On the other hand, Sue sees the relationship as being in some serious difficulty and does not seem to feel that she is getting her needs met. This is especially true of emotional intimacy. These inventory results fit with their general style of behavior during counseling sessions and with their presenting complaints. In my opinion, this large difference in perception is cause for quite a lot of concern. It shows that there is a problem with communication and that there are forces at work within the relationship that could make differences that now exist become increasingly problematic if something is not done fairly soon.

Communication. Besides the responses on the PAIR Inventory that indicate some problems in communication, observations of the couple during assessment sessions indicates that communication styles are going on that are detrimental to the relationship. Both people are contributing to this problem, so both people need to change their communication patterns if the marriage is going to continue and improve.

A repeatable pattern of communication involves Sue, while sincerely desiring to help Tim, offering criticism about his behavior or complaining about something. Generally, Tim responds by laughing to try to keep the atmosphere light. This is interpreted by Sue as Tim refusing to take seriously her complaints. She escalates the complaints or criticisms. This ultimately provokes Tim to respond by defending himself. As the criticism-defense cycle continues, Tim escalates his responses, becoming louder, as does Sue. The emotional intensity of the arguments threatens and frightens Sue, who becomes reluctant to engage in future discussions with Tim for fear that she will provoke a fight. Therefore she tries to get Tim to change by making helpful suggestions (criticisms), which continues the cycle.

After the problem-solving discussion that was videotaped, the mood of the session shifted. Before, the mood was fairly cooperative and congenial. Afterward, negative feelings were vented and periodic "barbs" were exchanged. This is of some concern to me, for it indicates that disagreements do not get resolved and that the disagreements might be "poisoning" the interactions that occur after any agreement.

Another area of communication that needs attention includes sexual communication. The Grays need to communicate their sexual desires clearly and unambiguously because there seems to be an inability to read the other's signals. This is most obvious from the Couple's Pre-counseling Inventory. When asked about how many times during the past month they had initiated sexual contact, Tim said five times but Sue only recognized one advance. Sue said that she had initiated sexual interaction four times but Tim only recognized one advance.

Problem Solving. Based on the videotaped discussion of an area in which disagreement occurred, with instructions to come to some resolution about the issue, a number of difficulties in problem solving were discovered. First, the problem was never clearly defined and they jumped from topic to topic. Second, most of the time was spent in cross-complaining; there was no attempt to specify exactly what the problem was or to arrive at any kind of solution. The problem was discussed mostly in the past (about who caused the problem) or was localized within the personality of one person. (Sue defined the problem as something wrong with Tim.) Positive comments about one another that occurred within the conversation were generally vague and unspecific; negative comments were quite clear. The result is that generally the couple is better able to know what is wrong with them than what is right with them.

Recommended Treatment Goals
Intimacy.

1. Increase the emotional intimacy. Tim needs to listen carefully to Sue and to identify her feelings and acknowledge them. Sue needs not to criticize Tim and to create a positive support for him.

2. Increase the frequency of sexual contact, given that the quality of the contact is good (when it occurs).

3. Set aside a regular time that the couple can be together and talk about intimate things.

Communication.

1. Increase positive interactions.

2. Use the videotape to improve communication styles.

3. Spend more time in each other's presence.

Problem Solving.

1. Use videotaped practice to learn to communicate problem solving in ways that will get to some resolution of disagreements and will not carry over into other interactions.

2. Read a good book on problem solving, *Getting to Yes,* and learn to employ the method of problem solving that is outlined in the book.

Overall

Even though this marriage is in trouble at present, it has a lot of potential to be a fulfilling marriage for both Tim and Sue. Both love each other and both have common values. The problems in this relationship reside in the communication patterns and the behavior patterns that have evolved in the relationship. These are certainly changeable if Tim and Sue are willing *to work hard on their relationship* and are willing to set aside their self-interests in order to work out a satisfying and long-term relationship which will in turn be fulfilling. Their chances of success depend almost entirely on *how hard they are willing to work* and on whether they are willing *to take risks and be vulnerable.*

/signed/

Everett L. Worthington, Jr., Ph.D.

Figure 13
Sample Assessment Summary for a Couple Whose Main Complaint Is Little Intimacy

CONFIDENTIAL
Ray and Cheryl Peck

Ray (thirty-seven) and Cheryl (thirty-five), parents of two children (four, two), have sought counseling to improve a marriage that has lost the freshness and sparkle of a vibrant relationship. The problem appears to be almost entirely a marriage problem, with the children apparently uninvolved in the unhappiness. Emotionally both Ray and Cheryl have reacted to the awareness of the relationship discord by feeling frustration, anger, exasperation, powerlessness to effect substantial changes in the relationship and depression (Cheryl seems considerably more depressed than Ray).

The situation is exacerbated by the illness of Cheryl's mother, who has cancer and who has come to live with them. This additional stress, besides taking an emotional toll on all those involved, increases the emotionality of all in the household. This makes arguments more likely and heated (or possibly inhibits arguments while not preventing conflict, thus increasing hostility and making it easy to avoid working on marriage problems when the illness is of such immediate and apparent concern to all).

On the other hand, the crisis serves a useful function in that it provides a clear way for providing emotional support within the family, since it is obviously an emotionally taxing time. Having a relative come to live in the house forces a certain amount of disruption and reallocation of the time schedules of family members. This can be a force that is positive (if the schedule changes promote intimacy) or negative (if the schedule changes further isolate Ray and Cheryl from each other).

Relationship History

Ray and Cheryl began their early relationship in the context of the church. Much of their early pleasant interaction centered on a solid sexual relationship, though no premarital intercourse was involved. The passion that attracted them and held them close to one another throughout the early years of marriage is a definite relationship strength which, if rekindled, can provide pleasant interactions throughout their future life together.

The early years of marriage were relatively conflict free, which is in marked contrast to the usual marriage in the United States. This too suggests that there is a strong bond between the two that works for unity in their marriage. My guess is that their early relationship continued to be fueled by a spontaneous and gratifying sexual relationship and by a fundamental agreement over important values. Furthermore, there was an atmosphere of mutual support and upbuilding.

The major transition point in the relationship history came with the beginning of their life as a family. A number of traumatic events and disruptions happened at that time, and it appears that the relationship never fully recovered from those strains. The sexual relationship, which had been a great source of mutual satisfaction, became less spontaneous and more volitional, tied closely to a rigid schedule. This reduced the pleasure of the sexual encounters somewhat and directed the attention of both partners to some of the dissatisfactions in the encounters that had previously been of little importance. Of particular importance was the lack of orgasm experienced by Cheryl. Although this apparently did not bother Cheryl, Ray seems to have begun to interpret this as a continual indictment on him—especially since his first wife, too, was inorgasmic. Thus, while not intentionally trying to, Cheryl can put Ray down through her own failure to ever reach orgasm.

On the other hand, Ray has experienced a lowered sexual desire for Cheryl. This is accompanied by his letting her know in several ways that she is not measuring up. For example, Ray sometimes refers to other women, usually in the context of benevolence or compliments about the other women. The loss of sexual desire, which cannot really be controlled by Ray, achieves the same outcome as Cheryl's lack of orgasm—it puts Cheryl down through Ray's failure.

One result of these unintentional symptoms—orgasmic failure and failure in desire—is that the sexual area, in which lies one of the greatest relationship strengths, has become a battleground. True, both Ray and Cheryl are exasperated by the sexual problem; both are distressed and both would like to be able to enjoy their lovemaking as they used to. However, both are unwillingly locked into repeating their painful behavior (painful to themselves as well as to each other) by their unwillingness to risk new sexual behaviors that might resolve the tension. One of the encouraging aspects of their sexual relationship is that when they do engage in intercourse, they still seem to be able to have satisfactory experiences (which only become contaminated with negative feelings when talk or thoughts turn to orgasm).

Relationship Strengths

This relationship has a lot going for it. It is stronger in many ways than many happy relationships.

1. The sexual area is a real strength.

2. There is similarity in important values.

3. Both Ray and Cheryl have a strong commitment to Jesus, who is Lord of their lives and Lord of their family. This unity in the Holy Spirit looses a powerful force that promotes unity within the family.

4. They are unified in child-rearing practices—an area that often divides couples.

5. They communicate well and they understand accurately how the other person views the relationship.

6. They can discuss their problems in very open terms, including their feelings about the problems.

7. They both take care of the smooth functioning of the marriage and family tasks, keeping the day-to-day operation of the family proceeding smoothly.

8. They both love each other and are interested in working on the relationship rather than letting it sit in an unproductive state until the children feel the effects of it at full force.

Relationship Weaknesses

1. There is conflict over sex, which both enjoy, in that unintentional personal failures indict the adequacy of the spouse.

2. There are expressed needs for improvement in the emotional, sexual, recreational and intellectual intimacy of the couple.

3. There is little communication about how to solve the problems that are discussed so freely.

4. There has been a decrease in affectionate behaviors.

Treatment Goals

1. To revitalize the marriage.

2. To increase the self-esteem of Ray and Cheryl.

3. To eliminate the depression of Cheryl (especially).

4. To rekindle the fire in their sexual relationship.

5. To increase the positive feelings each feels for the other and for the relationship.

6. To promote effective problem solving rather than problem discussion.

7. To increase intimacy—sexual, emotional, recreational and intellectual.

Overall

I am encouraged by the prospects of improvement in Ray and Cheryl's relationship and in their personal lives. The key to how much their relationship improves, though, will rest largely with how hard Ray and Cheryl are willing to work and on how courageous they will be in trying risky behaviors. They have a mighty God on their side, and it is his will, I am convinced, that they work on their marriage and on aspects of their personal lives that are interfering with their relationship with him. Their relationship can be healed, by God's grace, through persistent prayer and hard work.

/signed/

Everett L. Worthington, Jr., Ph.D.

Figure 14
Sample Assessment Summary for a Couple in Severe Conflict

CONFIDENTIAL
Win and Betty McNabb

This report summarizes two assessment sessions with the McNabbs.

Win (forty-four) and Betty (forty) have been married for twenty-four years. They were recently separated and agreed to live together again after four months of separation, under the condition that they would pursue marriage counseling. They have four boys: Cal (twenty-two), Don (eighteen), Bret (sixteen) and Frank (twelve). The problem appears to be largely a marriage problem. The boys add some additional strain with their problems at school and with a neighbor and with conflict over discipline; however, most of Win and Betty's relationship strain centers around two main issues: little intimacy beyond their sexual relationship and frequent conflict (exacerbated by a communication style that seems adversarial and an unwillingness to resolve the differences between them).

Relationship History

Betty and Win met when Betty was fourteen and Win was seventeen. They dated, sometimes against the advice of her parents. Their physical attraction for one another was one of the strongest attractions in their relationship. They related that taking long drives while they were dating was one of the pleasurable activities of their early relationships. Three years after they met, they were married.

During their first year of marriage, they had few problems. Cal was born after they were married for eighteen months. There were some difficulties at this point due to conflict with Betty's parents. During the early years of the relationship, the McNabbs moved frequently. Although this involved some instability, it probably also strengthened the relationship by causing them to pull together to adjust to the instability.

Win's drinking became a problem as the relationship continued. The drinking provided the battleground for different expectations Win and Betty had for the amount of intimacy in the relationship. Win has since sought treatment for the drinking and much of the social contact they now have is with Alanon and AA groups.

About three years ago, Betty began to attend church, after which there were several changes in their relationship. For example, she stopped drinking and began going to Alanon meetings, and she stopped sexual relationships for about two months to persuade Win to stop drinking. Over the last three years, the relationship has been quite stormy, punctuated by the recent separation.

Relationship Strengths

1. One of the McNabbs's main strengths is their sexual relationship. Although this has not always functioned smoothly, it appears that this is one area where they can usually agree and share intimacy. Furthermore, their sexual relationship was a primary force in their early relationship; it has withstood the test of time.

2. Another strength is their faithfulness to each other. They have not only been faithful to each other sexually but have also stuck by each other even though there have been some serious mar-

riage strains (with Win's drinking and some troubles with their boys). This faithfulness is a strength to draw on.

3. The willingness of each to attend counseling is another good indicator that they are willing to try to hold the relationship together.

4. Finally, the cooperation they have maintained while raising four teen-age boys is noteworthy.

Difficulties

Having three teen-age children and one young adult child places the McNabbs in a stressful time of life. Traditionally for wives, the period when children leave home is the time when life is most stressful and marriage satisfaction is lowest. For husbands, traditionally the most stressful time of life—and the time with the lowest marriage satisfaction—is when the children are going through adolescence. With two children at home who are adolescents and two who have left home, the McNabbs are *each* in the most difficult time of life for most couples.

Also, there are substantial problems between the McNabbs that must be resolved if they are to be happily married once they get past this time of life. Major disagreements center around communication difficulties and lack of intimacy. The communication difficulties involve several aspects:

1. Win ignores Betty's feelings and uses aggressive rational arguments. Betty ignores his arguments and uses her feelings to manipulate.

2. Each person justifies himself or herself by blaming the other person for something done wrong instead of taking individual responsibility for changing his or her own behavior.

3. Each person mistrusts the other. Win does not trust Betty to maintain confidentiality about what happens in their relationship. He expects she will tell her church friends, a counselor or others. Betty does not trust Win to continue not to drink. She feels that she has to structure his time to make sure that he will not drink.

4. They correct each other about most things they discuss, "winning points" if they can catch the other at any wrong detail. It is as if they believe that if they can find a detail that is incorrect in whatever the other says, then they do not have to listen to *anything* that the other person says.

5. Win sometimes "needles," "teases" and "aggravates" Betty. Betty sometimes tries to control Win and treats him as if he were "sick."

6. Each has, at times, used withdrawal of sex to punish the other or coerce the other. This is dangerous, since sex is the most positive aspect of their relationship together.

Recommendations

1. I believe that they can improve their marriage if they are willing to work very hard and are willing to put aside their present ways of communicating and practice new ones. This will not be easy, since they have used the present ways of communicating for years. They can expect numerous failures on the part of each person. In order for them to succeed, they must be willing to substitute a forgiving attitude for the blaming attitude that seems so prevalent in their present relationship.

2. I believe that they should concentrate their efforts on building intimacy by setting aside time to do things together *that both enjoy*. At present, they seem to do things individually more than together. There has to be new balance established between activities done alone and those done together. And the activities done together should be mutually satisfying (such as going out to eat; go-

ing for drives; visiting cultural attractions, parks, historic buildings; etc.).

3. I believe that they should also concentrate on changing their communication patterns and developing a pattern of forgiveness and trust.

4. My belief is that counseling would be most effective using about twenty counseling sessions at weekly (or at most every-two-week) intervals. The counseling would be effective *only if both Win and Betty were willing to cooperate with the counselor and work hard at doing things that might feel uncomfortable.* Just going to counseling in itself will not help if both are not committed to working on the relationship and taking risks. At the end of the twenty sessions, an assessment of the future of the relationship would be in order.

/signed/

Everett L. Worthington, Jr., Ph.D.

est remained at home. Both younger children were involved with school authorities. Conflict permeated the marriage. The husband was alcoholic. The couple had different religious commitments. The prognosis for the couple was not good. My primary objective was to convey the difficulties that lay ahead of the couple and thus temper the hope of counseling with realism about the gains that were achievable in time-limited counseling.

As you read each assessment report, look both for similarities and differences. Evaluate how well you think I achieved my objectives and how you might have written the report differently. In addition, look for how the assessment summary—by focusing the couple's attention on intimacy, communication, conflict, individual responsibility and commitment—prepares the couple for interventions in those areas.

After you have read the summaries, you might think, "Good grief! I don't have time to write a report that long for every client."

Indeed, I have sometimes found it wearisome. However, I believe that I don't have the energy *not* to write such an assessment summary. For one reason, putting my assessment on paper clarifies my conceptualization of the facts of the case, the nature of the problem, the strengths and complaints in the marriage and the likely time frame of counseling, all of which help me plan my counseling so it is more efficient and focused. For another reason, the tangible assessment report—that clients can look at and carry away with them—gives them confidence in me and my willingness to work to help them. They can check my understanding of their relationship with theirs and can correct me where I am incorrect. They know my beliefs about the scope and duration of therapy, and they can negotiate a different understanding if they choose.

For all of these benefits, it takes perhaps an hour to write and edit each report. To me, that is one of the best-spent hours in therapy.

SUMMARY

During two sessions of formal assessment and one feedback session, which uses a written report, I assess the couple, identify reachable goals and present the goals clearly to the couple. For best results, goals should be agreed upon by both partners; goals should be positive, realistic, specific and derived directly from assessment. Generally, goals will be to: increase intimacy, improve communication, reduce conflict and increase commitment to God and to each other. Ultimately, goals should both solve problems and promote growth. To accomplish these general goals, the counselor uses working goals throughout counseling.

Goals are presented to the couple during a feedback session structured around a written report. The report summarizes the facts and history of the partners. It usually gives equal attention to strengths and weaknesses in the marriage. Goals are set to reduce weaknesses and emphasize strengths. Usually, the counselor gives hope that the marriage can improve through prayer and hard work by the couple.

Conducting Assessment and Feedback Sessions

THE COUNSELOR SHOULD HAVE A GENERAL PLAN ABOUT HOW TO conduct each session. Each part of counseling—assessment, intervention and termination—is conducted differently. Good counseling is both planned and flexible, so that the couple and the counselor can attain their goals. In this chapter, I describe a method of conducting each of the two assessment sessions and the feedback session. In the next part of the book (Part four, chapters 10 through 14), I discuss methods of intervention.

ASSESSMENT SESSION ONE

I greet the couple and introduce myself to both husband and wife. We might exchange acknowledgements about the person who referred the couple to me for counseling, or we might get right down to business.

I'm glad to meet each of you. Most people want to know something about me before we begin to work together, so let me tell you some things about myself. I'm a Christian, first of all, and the counseling that I do is based on Christian principles. So that you can understand a little about where I am coming from, let me tell you that I consider myself a Bible-believing Christian who loves Jesus. I'm also happily married, since 1970, and have four children. As far as counseling is concerned, I am a licensed clinical and counseling psychologist here in Virginia, and I teach at Virginia Commonwealth University. I hope that gives you some of the basics about me so you can feel more comfortable with me as we work together. Is there anything else you'd like to know before we start?

Because my clients are referred to me for my private practice, at least one spouse is usually a Christian. Generally, Christians have been more interested in my beliefs than in my professional qualifications, though I believe it is important to assure them that I have been properly trained and licensed to counsel. Some research that Suzanne Gascoyne and I conducted shows that many Christians, especially those with conservative theologies, evaluate counselors more on the similarity of the counselor's beliefs to their own than on the counselor's style or approach to counseling.[1] When I introduce myself, I mention first the information most clients want to hear. Then, I talk about how I conduct counseling.

I've found it useful to take counseling a step at a time. I would like to meet with you for three assessment sessions so I can find out about your marriage. I'll interview you for two sessions and ask you to fill out some questionnaires. In a third session, I'll give you a written evaluation of your marriage, its strengths and what might be improved. I'll also make recommendations about whether I think counseling would be helpful and what might be accomplished. This three-session agreement gives you a chance to evaluate whether you want to work with me and it gives me a chance to see whether I think you can benefit from my help. Only after the third session will you decide about counseling. How does that way of working sound to you both?

One goal of the first assessment session is to help the couple think of some of the positive aspects of their relationship. However, if I start the session by asking about the good parts of their life together, the couple usually becomes puzzled and resistant. Generally, they have come to counseling

with problems on their minds. So, I first ask what brought them to counseling.

> *I'd like to hear what each of you sees as the main problem with your marriage.*
> *I'll give each of you a chance to say your opinions from your point of view. Let*
> *me begin with you, Fred.*

I usually begin with the person who *did not* call to set up the interview,
under the assumption that this person is less invested in counseling. I want
to involve him or her immediately. This person might wonder what the
other person told me when setting up the appointment, so I want to give
this person a chance to have a say before the other person talks.

After hearing a brief summary from the first spouse, I paraphrase the
main difficulties. I ask the other person, "Now Marge, would you describe
the problem from your point of view?" From the beginning, I try to establish
that problems are from *someone's* point of view. I do not correct a person
who says, "The problem *really* is that . . ." I simply paraphrase the statement
as, "So you think the problem is . . ."

After both have given their perceptions of the problems, I summarize
their statements and give a rationale for describing the history of the relationship. I might say:

> *Now Fred, you see the problem as being Marge's controlling, overprotective*
> *attitude; while you, Marge, see the problem as stemming from Fred's drinking.*
> *Well, I can see that this problem did not develop overnight. I think it would be*
> *helpful for me if I had a clear idea of exactly how your entire relationship*
> *developed from the time you met, so that I could put this problem into its proper*
> *place. You understand your history, but having just met you, I need some history*
> *of your relationship to put these current difficulties into context. Does that make*
> *sense to you? Good. Tell me, how did you meet each other?*

I wait until one of them begins talking. As they tell about their history, I
try to steer the couple away from criticism and blaming and help them
recall times of happiness and intimacy. This is, of course, easier to say than
to do. A determined couple can find almost anything to criticize, but I
interrupt and refocus continually until they finish their history.

With a couple late in the life cycle, history-taking can use the remainder
of the session and sometimes a portion of the next. Substantial time is spent
talking about dating and times when the couple was happiest. I generally

remark in an offhand way that it would be wonderful if they could recapture some of the initial fire and romance.

By the end of the relationship history, the session is usually nearing its end. I give the couple two inventories to complete before the next session. The inventories I use are (a) the Personal Assessment of Intimacy in Relationships (PAIR)[2] and (b) the Couple's Precounseling Inventory (CPI).[3] In assigning the inventories, I say,

> *These inventories are important to my having an accurate picture of your relationship so we can plan how to help you. Fill them out completely and carefully. They take quite a while, possibly one and one-half hours, so leave time to complete them before the next session. You can give them to me at the beginning of the next session.*

We then set the time for the next session.

ASSESSMENT SESSION TWO

Prior to beginning the second assessment session, I prepare a list of questions, leaving sufficient space to write notes. The interview is conducted from the list, and the notes become my case notes for the second session. A typical list is shown in Figure 15. (The space between questions is reduced in this example to present the sheet in a smaller space.)

After greeting the couple and asking how their week was (but not pursuing the details of their week), I collect the completed inventories. About seventy-five per cent of the couples have completed the two inventories correctly. Glancing at the inventories to make sure that they have been completed fully, I commend the couple on their prompt completion of the task and say that I will study their inventories later. If the couple (or one spouse) has not completed the questionnaire, I say, "I must have the questionnaire before I can make a good assessment of your relationship. I need to have the completed inventories about a week before we meet for the feedback session so I can have time to score them and write the assessment summary for you." Thus, I suggest that whenever the couple gets the completed inventory to me, we can schedule the third assessment session.

The first question I ask the couple is usually one that (a) they can both

Figure 15
A Typical List of Questions Prepared Prior to the Second Assessment Session

Fred and Marge Smith
December 6, 1987
Session #2

☐ Collect PAIR and CPI.
☐ Describe the last time the two of you did something together as a couple. What happened? Was it enjoyable?

☐ Notes for conflict task: Discuss in front of the tape recorder a topic about which you often disagree. Try to come to some agreement.
☐ What happens in a typical week? Describe in detail each hour of the day of each day of the week.
☐ What other recreational activities do you usually do alone, with others or with your spouse?
☐ What kind of close or intimate activities do you enjoy doing together?
☐ How does a typical sexual episode proceed? Who initiates? How do you know that the other person wants to make love? What happens after the person initiates? How long is your foreplay and what does it consist of? Do you each reach orgasm? How often? What happens when you finish making love?

☐ Set time for next session.

discuss; (b) is pleasant; (c) builds a willingness to talk; and (d) requires less than five minutes to discuss. For example, I might ask, "What did you do this week together that you enjoyed?" After this discussion is completed I get a sample of how the couple argues. I introduce the task by saying:

To better understand what happens when you disagree, I would like to set up a task. I'm afraid it won't be very pleasant, but I have found that even though it seems a bit artificial and contrived, it gives me valuable information. Pick a topic about which you frequently disagree—I don't care what topic it is; it doesn't matter—and discuss it and try to come to some agreement. I know that if you have not been able to agree before now, the chances are that you won't agree during the next seven or so minutes. But I want to hear how you talk with each other about the topic. Now, to make the task more realistic, I am going to leave the room while you have your discussion. So I would like to videotape (or audiotape, if video is not available) your discussion. The recording is solely for my use and no one but me will see it (or hear it). I know it seems unnatural to have a discussion like this, but it is helpful for me. Can I have your permission to videotape you?

Often couples want additional reassurance, and they say that they do not think the discussion will be informative, but I assure them that *I* have found it useful whether they see the use or not. Most couples agree.

Before leaving the room, I repeat the instructions and close the door, taking with me their completed PAIR and CPI inventories. During the seven or eight minutes I spend waiting, I look over the CPI, which gives an overview to how they each perceive the satisfaction, commitment, strengths, problem areas, intimacy, conflict and goals of their relationship.

When I return to the interview room, I ask how their discussion went and whether it was similar to talks they have at home. Usually, they are surprised at the similarity but comment that it was more controlled and less emotional than at home.

Then I initiate probably the most useful task of the second assessment session. I ask each spouse to describe in detail, hour by hour, how he or she spends the entire week. My intent is to assess the amount of time each spends in activities that produce distance, coactivity or intimacy. (I usually find that couples spend little time together in either coactive or intimate activities.) This task usually consumes twenty to thirty minutes. I continue to ask for details after the task becomes repetitive and boring.

Detailed explanation of use of time is well worth the energy. It provides a solid base for understanding how, how often and under what circumstances the couple interacts, and it allows me to design directives that are more likely to be carried out because I know the times that are available to the couple and can tailor directives to each couple.

The remainder of the interview proceeds relatively quickly. I ask about additional recreational activities of each person, done alone, with others and with the spouse, and about close or intimate activities they enjoy with each other. This generally leads to a discussion of their sex life. If it does not spontaneously come up, I ask about it. Most people do not talk freely about how they have sex, so it is helpful to prompt them with specific questions.

Your task is to understand whether their sexual life has potential for improved intimacy and how satisfied the couple is. Often, when queried verbally, the couple will say that they have a satisfactory sex life, but on the CPI they will have identified in writing some dissatisfactions with it. By pursuing the details of their sex life to the extent necessary to formulate any therapeutic goals in the area, you understand what intimacy actually occurs.

Inquiring into the couple's sex life after only two hours of contact is sensitive—especially in Christian circles—for both counselor and clients. However, since the sexual relationship is a frequent source of conflict and of positive interaction, the clinician can ill afford to make assumptions about that area.

After the discussion about their sexual life, many couples feel uncomfortable and vulnerable. I thus conclude the session by saying,

> *You have been a very courageous and trusting couple today. I have asked you to do some threatening things and you have carried them out excellently. When a couple is so willing to take risks to help improve their relationship, I am very encouraged and hopeful. The factor that best predicts whether a couple will make their marriage better through counseling is their willingness to work hard, to take risks and to expose the parts of their relationship that are often very secret. You have done that today. This week I will ponder the things I have learned from you over the last two weeks and will have a written report for you at our next meeting. At that time, I'll make recommendations about your relationship. We need to set a time for the meeting. . . .*

FEEDBACK SESSION

After the initial greeting and settling in, I generally summarize the procedure that we have gone through and restate that I have prepared a written summary of my assessment. I give *both spouses* a photocopy of the assessment, which they read. I explain the inferences I made and show the couple their profile of the PAIR, which describes five types of intimacy, graphically illustrating the similarities and the differences in their perceptions about intimacy in their marriage.

I summarize briefly the improvements that can be made in their intimacy, communication, conflict and perhaps commitment, and I call attention to the goals I have recommended for counseling. We discuss each goal and my estimation of the time necessary to achieve the goals. One rule of thumb is a minimum of six to eight intervention sessions. With couples married more than six years, I add an additional session for each year or two of marriage over six (up to a maximum of about sixteen counseling sessions).

I close saying,

Let me remind you that we have been talking about what might happen if you attend counseling with me. When we first met, we agreed to meet these three times for an assessment. I said then that you were under no obligation to attend counseling after the assessment. Now that you see what counseling will involve, you must decide whether you wish to enter counseling or whether you will work on these goals on your own. You don't have to decide today, unless you want to. I want you to decide without feeling pressure from me. If you wish, you can call me and tell me what you decide and we'll go from there. What would you like to do?

About half of the time, the couple immediately states that they want to attend counseling and the duration of counseling is negotiated if the couple does not agree with my estimation. I have never had a couple who stated outright that they did not want counseling. About twenty per cent of the time, the couple elects to call me later, and either they never call or they call and say they decided to try it on their own. Occasionally, one of these couples will seek a different referral from their pastor or someone else. About thirty per cent of the time, the couple calls back within a week to a month and says that they want counseling. These couples are generally motivated to follow suggestions because they found that they could not achieve their goals alone.

SUMMARY

In this chapter, I describe the procedure I follow in conducting each assessment session. I assess the couple in the areas that I anticipate problems: intimacy; communication; conflict; commitment; and hurt, blame and sin. The sessions are carried out so that the couple is readied for treatment in the areas they have most of their problems.

After assessment, the couple is poised to begin trying to change their relationship. Goals of clients and counselor should be clear and should be in harmony. But it is never as easy to promote change as it sounds.

Part **4**

Changing Troubled Marriages

SUMMARY One difficulty with many books on counseling is that the authors share theory and philosophy freely but describe and illustrate few techniques that put the theory into practice. In part four, I hope to avoid that pitfall. In chapter 10, a brief overview of my understanding of change is offered, stressing the need for counselors to promote changes in the couple's cognitive and environmental structures. In chapters 10 through 14, I describe numerous techniques to change the couple's patterns of poor intimacy (chapter 11); poor communication (chapter 12); conflict (chapter 13); and hurt, blame and sin (chapter 14).

These chapters are heavily oriented toward delineating techniques. However, Christian counselors do not depend on techniques to induce change. Rather we depend on the Holy Spirit to work change in our clients. Prayer is our chief weapon in this warfare—prayer for our clients and prayer for our discernment, wisdom and obedience to the leading that God supplies. Yet, God works through techniques as well as through our personalities and through his miraculous intervention. Thus, as careful stewards of grace, we must learn to apply the techniques of counseling competently. We strive to master and build our repertoire of techniques. Then, as Minuchin and Fishman suggest, we try to "forget" the techniques,[1] so that our counseling is not counseling-by-rote or by formula but is counseling that is spontaneous, tailored to our clients and Holy Spirit-led.

Procrustes was a mythical Greek innkeeper, determined to fit captives perfectly to their beds. To accomplish this, he stretched or shortened his victims until they fit their beds. Let us not force our clients into a Procrustean bed by applying rigid techniques. Rather, let us strive to make the bed of techniques moldable to the service of our clients.

10

Promoting Change through Counseling

U NTIL NOW, MOST OF MY ATTENTION HAS BEEN ON ASSESSMENT of the marriage as a probable prelude of counseling. I have not explained a theory of change in counseling beyond the fundamentals given in chapter 2 ("Individuals and Their Coupling") and chapter 5 ("Overview of Counseling").

The present chapter describes how the counselor uses assessment, intervention, consolidation of gains and termination to induce couples to change their marriages. There are many ways that couples can change unhappy marriages, including direct intervention of God, following their own self-directed efforts, seeking the help and advice of friends and family and numerous other ways. This chapter deals only with how a counselor can help the couple change.

Simply put, the counselor must get the spouses to change their cognitive structures so there is more agreement ("a meeting of minds"). The coun-

selor must also get the spouses to change their shared environmental structures—primarily their behavior, but also their physical and social environments—to produce more harmony, cooperation and love.

The structures, cognitive and environmental, must be changed if improvement is to be maintained after counseling is ended. The changed
structures, in turn, will result in new behaviors and new shared environmental events.

Areas of Change

As I have stressed repeatedly, most change will be needed in five areas,
which derive from the fundamental human needs for meaning achieved
through intimacy, effectance, forgiveness and commitment. The five areas
of change are intimacy; communication; conflict; hurt, blame and sin; and
commitment. Assessment and techniques of intervention are aimed at
affecting cognitive and environmental structures in each of these five
areas.

Tools of Change

What tools does the counselor have to accomplish this task? Only what can
be done in the counseling session. The counselor can engineer environmental events, which must be powerful enough to change the couple's
cognitive and environmental structures. The environmental events provided by the counselor are what he or she says, does and directs the clients
to do both during and after the session.

Techniques of Change

The counselor's directives to the couple are called techniques. Techniques
have been developed by counselors with a variety of theoretical persuasions
and often come to be identified with certain schools. For example, family
sculpting was developed by Virginia Satir and tends to be identified with
her family therapy; whereas, paradoxical directives have been popularized
by Jay Haley and Mara Selvini-Palazzoli and tend to be identified with their
family therapies. Yet, these techniques are not necessarily wedded to the
theory of the originator or popularizer of the technique.

Rather, in my experience a technique produces fruit on the basis of how
it is introduced prior to its use and how it is explained after its use, not by
virtue of the content of the technique per se. For instance, suppose a couple
is directed to discuss their vacation plans. Before, during and after the

discussion, the counselor could have numerous objectives. The counselor may focus on:

☐ The ways the couple will enhance their intimate interactions

☐ The manner in which the couple communicates about their hopes, dreams, fears and plans

☐ The way the conflict develops and is (or is not) resolved

☐ The hurt experienced by each partner as he or she tries to "win" the conflict and the need for forgiveness by each partner

☐ The potential for enhancing commitment between the partners

Clearly, a counselor with each goal in mind will try to orchestrate the couple's discussion differently but all will use the same "technique"—the couple's discussion.

Techniques, then, are not only *not* inextricably wedded to a particular school of therapy, they are also not wedded to achieving any particular therapeutic *objective*. Nonetheless, I have found that some techniques lend themselves more easily to producing intimacy than to helping resolve conflict or to ameliorating hurt or blame. In the following chapters, I have grouped techniques according to the area to which each technique easily contributes.

Process of Change

Rarely does something change directly from one stable position to another stable position; usually an unstable position must be an intermediary step.[1] Troublesome patterns of thinking and acting do not suddenly disappear to be instantly replaced with new patterns. There must be some intermediate instability.

In each chapter, techniques for changing marriages will be organized into three steps: increasing a couple's awareness of the problem, breaking up their old behavior patterns and building new behavior patterns.

Given my cognitive-behavioral problem-solving approach to counseling, I believe change is enhanced when people are aware of their need to change and of the goals for which they must aim. Techniques from a variety of theoretical schools of therapy promote a couple's awareness. Even more than the technique per se, the *therapist* promotes awareness of the problem by the way he or she discusses the couple's behavior before, after and during the use of the technique.

There is a time of breaking old patterns. As they break, the couple experiences distress and discomfort. They want to end the discomfort and return to the comfort of the misery they know. As old patterns break, prepare for the couple to be discouraged and resistant.

As old patterns break, you must help build new patterns. To do this, use techniques that are consistent with your goals in therapy. More than this, though, motivate the couple to build new patterns. Infuse them with hope. Give them a clear vision of their goals. Provide an escape hatch from their unease. Suggest new behavior patterns, then ingrain and strengthen them.

PRODUCTION OF CHANGE

How does the counselor use the session to accomplish these tasks? There are four ways: stage dramatic events, present a positive conceptualization, direct and enforce changed behavior and get the couple to act differently outside of counseling. Each general method has a myriad of techniques associated with it.

Stage Dramatic Events

Events of counseling must be memorable and must provoke cognitive and behavioral involvement throughout the week. Though events of counseling must be similar to other events in the couple's life to facilitate generalization, they must be unlike other events to increase their impact.

One way to make counseling dramatic is to use videotape recording whenever possible during counseling. When it is not possible to use videotapes, I use audiotape recording. Couples can then behave normally, but under strikingly non-normal conditions. Videotape (and sometimes audiotape) recording is threatening to most people. Good. If it were not, it would be far less useful. Being different from the normal, the mild threat makes counseling have greater impact.

Another reason that counseling is dramatic, yet somewhat similar to normal life, is because clients do things in the presence of a virtual stranger—the counselor—that they have probably never done before except in private. They talk about their plans together and their intimate lives. They discuss in detail their failings and their successes at living together.

They argue about personal topics. They discuss their sex lives. Since these are done in front of a third party, they often have enormous impact on the couple in terms of convicting them of a need to change poor or sinful behavior and in terms of enhancing their commitment to behave better toward each other.

A third example of increasing the drama of counseling is to use role plays, role reversals and structured feedback about the couple's behavior. When you direct a couple to role play a conflict (for example), they have certainly had conflicts previously. However, under your direction and in the presence of you and your tape recorder—which misses nothing—the context is changed. An observer increases self-consciousness and helps each spouse concentrate on his or her behavior and thoughts in ways that he or she might never have done before.[2]

These are only three examples of increasing the drama of counseling to enhance change in the couple's cognitive and environmental (especially interactional) structures.

Present a Positive Conceptualization

Provide consistent, systematic conceptualization and goal focus; promote positive thoughts and interactions instead of the old destructive thoughts and interactions. During counseling, attention is focused toward constructive goals. The counselor continually reconceptualizes and reframes the meanings of events and behaviors. The counselor pursues a clear conceptualization of the problems with logical, persuasive interventions that are expected to solve the problems. Through this, the counselor keeps the couple task-focused. During the session and even between sessions, the couple's attention is pulled back repeatedly to how they can make their marriage better. Powerful counseling should command attention and response from the couple.

Direct and Enforce Changed Behavior

While presentation of a positive conceptualization and adherence to clear goals are aimed at changing cognitive structures, we must also change environmental structures. During a session, the couple must behave differently toward each other. Most people know what they *should* do to make their marriage happier, but they do not do it because of practiced, overlearned behaviors and because of sin in their lives (see Rom 7).

Therefore, to ensure that they are able to behave as you wish (which will foster practicing better behavior and make the couple more willing to comply with homework), direct the couple and enforce their behavior in accord with the directives. This might require repeated trials, frequent feedback and several explanations of the benefits of the behavior we want the couple to do and of the ways that the behavior contributes to the goals of counseling. It might require your insistence that the couple follow directives. Importantly, couples must practice new behaviors during the counseling session, not just be told to behave differently.

Some people learn best through being told why they are to behave in certain ways. Others learn best through action. Use *both* explanations and actions with a couple, which should produce better results than using either singly.

Get the Couple to Act Differently Outside of Counseling

During the counseling hour you generally have the undivided attention of the couple. What about the other 167 hours of the week? If for no other reason than the weight of time, homework is important. It keeps the couple involved with counseling between sessions.

Actually, though, this is the least important reason for using homework. The most important reason is that eventually the couple must leave counseling. If they return to their natural environments which are largely unchanged, they will likely fall back into old behavior patterns. Such is the power of the environment over behavior. For example, consider your behavior when you enter a church. Do you dress in a sweat suit, run around the isles, jump over the pews and spit on the carpets? (If you do, I know a different book you should read.) How about on the racquetball court? Do you dress in a suit or dress, walk and talk quietly, read your Bible, pray, sing the doxology and confess your sins? I admit to doing some of these on the court, depending on the state of my game at the time, but *usually* those behaviors are more indicative of a church than a sports environment.

The external environment powerfully influences behavior. Try to induce the couple to change their *home* environment and their behavior at home so that when counseling ends, the changed environment will help maintain the gains of counseling.

Much of counseling is aimed at having the couple talk and act differently during counseling sessions. We try to convince ourselves—because we want to believe we are helping—that what the couple is doing during counseling sessions (with us present) is what they are doing at home (without us present). If we are not building in generalization through assigning regular homework to our clients, though, we delude ourselves that we accomplish much. Thus, counselors must assign valuable homework. Couples must do it. A couple's compliance with your therapeutic directives is a vital part of change.

Therapies may be divided roughly into those in which the counselor tries to provoke the client(s) to resist and those in which the counselor tries to promote compliance. Freud believed that progress in counseling could only occur when a client *resisted*. The resistance was seen as a recapitulation of an early conflict, which could then be interpreted to the client *if* the timing were right. Progress in psychoanalytically informed counseling cannot occur unless clients resist.

In the present theory of counseling, I strive to promote cooperation at every turn. I believe that people improve because they behave differently or subject themselves to different environments. They will not behave differently just because a counselor says to. You must create the proper environment for cooperation, and your suggestions must make sense to the client and appear to contribute to his or her goals. In addition, the counselor exerts social pressure through his or her presence and through the explicit and implicit demands made. Cooperation of couples with your suggestions is far from automatic. You must persuade it, nurture it, nurse it, encourage it and very occasionally force it.

Cooperation is built at every stage of counseling.

Joining with the couple is vital. Good joining provides a base from which you can ask for changes. You show that you understand and accept the clients as unique, important individuals and thus bond with them, making it possible to ask things of them in later stages of counseling.

Assessment is designed so that every question you ask, every assignment you make, every inventory you assign is tied to understanding the couple, preparing them to accept your conceptualizations of their problem, joining them more closely, introducing counseling that the couple can trust and showing them a counselor they can trust. Through the efficiency and effectiveness of the assessment, you set the stage for the couple's future cooperation.

By the time to begin intervention, the couple should be acting cooperatively. During intervention, however, you continue to build cooperation, strengthening their faith and thus cementing the bonds between you and them. You can do this in a variety of ways.

1. Give sensible directives and homework assignments.

2. Choose techniques of intervention that produce positive effects in changing environmental and cognitive structures.

3. Explain the rationales for your directives and tell how the directives contribute to achieving the couple's goals.

4. Handle any instance of noncompliance or partial compliance with your directives in such a way that compliance will be *more likely* with future directives, not less likely.

5. Consolidate gains by building on what the couple has accomplished.

6. Remind them of their gains.

7. Terminate by solidifying cognitive changes and understandings of what has been accomplished through using a final summary report.

8. Focus the couple's attention on goals that they can work on alone.

9. Reinforce (reward) the couple for making changes in their behavior and their environmental structures.

Cooperation is not automatic. Build it throughout counseling and the couple will respond to your directives and will change. Cooperation is desirable because it is pleasant, direct and effective. But if the couple insists on not cooperating, all is not lost. Your task is to help the client change structures of the mind and the environment. If the couple resists, try positively reframing their symptomatic behaviors and prescribing the symptoms. If the couple insists on resistance, use the resistance to move the couple away from their destructive behaviors through paradox.

RESPONSIBILITY FOR CHANGE

The Couple   If the couple does not improve their relationship, they will suffer. Husband and wife are responsible for their individual behavior and together for their behavior as a couple. They must each show their willingness to try new behavior within the marriage, and they must each avoid sin and seek sanctification in their personal lives. In addition, the two are "one flesh" and are responsible on some level for the behavior of the other.

When you attempt to join the couple to create a therapeutic triad, you incur an obligation to the couple. They have sought you as a change agent, presumably because the Holy Spirit has led them to you. If you then take them as clients, you agree to try all in your power to aid their marriage and to further their faith. **The Counselor**

If you try to induce change and fail, try again. If you fail once more, try another way. As their counselor, you can ill afford to throw up your hands and say, "Well, I've done *my* job. They are merely a stubborn and rebellious people." It may eventually come to that, but I find that I am far too willing to be self-righteous, thinking, "I've tried. Heavens knows I've tried. But it's *their* responsibility. I am blameless for their plight."

In most cases there are ways that people can be helped if we look for them. Our tendency is to exhort, reprove (we are sometimes especially good at that), encourage and demand that the couple go the way we want them to. If they refuse, we feel self-justified. Instead, keep trying.

God will accomplish his purposes. Who can stand against the will of God? We cannot thwart God's will, but we can refuse to participate in it, thereby losing the blessings he has for us. I believe that the couple's healing is ultimately in the hands of the healer, Jesus. Knowing that he has directed the couple to me in order to accomplish his purposes, I must trust that he will. **The Lord**

I am called to help the couples Jesus leads to me. Of course, not every couple that comes to me is led by Jesus. Rather than seek a definite sign or word from the Lord that I am to help each couple, I assume that I am to help by virtue of his calling me to my profession. Only a definite indication from the Lord can direct me *not* to help. I answer the call enthusiastically. And the Lord will work his will out. That is his job.

SUMMARY

In this chapter, I suggest that God will change people, not us. However, God has chosen to use counselors to stimulate some of the changes he desires. Counselors use techniques to give form to the changes.

Techniques are not tied to any theory of counseling. Rather, the counselor's description of the technique and his or her explanation of what the couple should get from the technique are crucial to the impact of the technique.

I present a straightforward cognitive-behavioral theory of change. The counselor helps stimulate change through providing important and memorable events during counseling and by getting the couple to change their behavior at home and to rearrange other important aspects of their lives together. Specific interventions will be aimed at promoting change in intimacy; communication; conflict; and hurt, blame and sin. In each case, the counselor helps the couple to become aware of the problems, break old patterns and build new patterns of behavior.

11

Changing Intimacy

GOD INTENDED MARRIED COUPLES TO EXPERIENCE INTIMACY.
Through their intimacy, they can feel a shadow of the real
intimacy that they will someday feel with him in glory. Intimacy is described by Scripture as oneness—oneness of spirit,
soul and body.[1] Each person will establish a unique expression of intimacy.
As counselors we should not attempt to prescribe the details of their intimacy beyond what Scripture says.

Most troubled couples desire more intimacy than they are experiencing
at the onset of therapy. To achieve their goal, they need to develop a clear
picture of their destination. The best description of Christian married intimacy that I know is given by Larry Crabb in his book *The Marriage Builder*
(Zondervan, 1982). Crabb describes *spirit oneness* as achieved by trusting God
for our salvation and needs. God is totally sufficient to meet the needs of
his children, freeing them from dependence on others—including

spouses—for need fulfillment. Marriage is seen as unnecessary for need fulfillment, but is seen as God's provision for people to understand and experience how our needs can be met by a loving companion. *Soul oneness* is derived directly from spirit oneness. It consists of ministry to and communication with the spouse. *Body oneness* concerns the sexual joining of spouses in marriage, consummating spirit and soul oneness on a physical level.

Throughout counseling, I often assign or recommend that couples read *The Marriage Builder* as a blueprint for building intimacy. Most of the book stresses having a biblical understanding of marriage. This directs couples as they work in counseling to build more intimacy through changing the patterns of non-intimacy they have developed. For couples who do not like to read, I give a more elaborate verbal summary of Crabb's thinking than I do when I introduce the book. I do not consider it optional for couples to understand Crabb's thinking. It is essential in that it places the techniques I use within a biblical framework.

COMMON PROBLEMS IN INTIMACY

Although couples are unique in the patterns they develop, several patterns occur with such regularity that numerous techniques have been developed to handle them. Recall that people have unique needs for intimacy, distance and coaction. They generally arrange their time schedules, choose their spouses and friends and select their work environments so that they have a tolerable, if not comfortable, balance of intimacy, distance and coaction. Despite their desire to achieve an optimal balance in intimacy-distance-coaction, people cannot always accomplish that desire. There might be a variety of reasons why they cannot.

There might be faulty beliefs involved in their dissatisfaction with intimacy. For example, one common misconception is that the spouse must meet all of the intimacy needs of his or her mate. Inevitably, a person who holds that belief will be disappointed in the performance of the spouse as the couple lives together for years.

Another misconception is that intimacy is characterized by total fusion of two personalities. When people glorify intimate sharing, they set themselves up for disappointment because they cannot hope to achieve total intimacy all of the time.

Further, they often *believe* they desire intimacy but are unconsciously rebelling against intimacy, which results in internal and interpersonal conflict and inconsistent behavior. Another common misconception is that sexual intimacy is the sole source of real intimacy or conversely that sexual intimacy does not really matter.

There might be environmental structures that prevent people from achieving an optimal balance of intimacy, distance and coaction. One family felt enormous financial strains in rearing their three teen-age children. The husband worked at two jobs, and the wife also worked at a secretarial job that paid well but isolated her from contact with others. The couple was unwilling to lower their standard of living. Their environmental structures thus prevented them from being satisfied with the amount of intimacy that they were experiencing.

There might be behavior patterns that have developed over time that prevent intimacy. A man reared in a family in which the father was alcoholic and the mother easily became depressed developed a lifelong pattern of vacillating between intimacy and distancing behaviors. Eventually, he married a woman who complemented his behavior. She tended to become depressed with regularity and also to experience psychosomatic difficulties. Both her depression and physical difficulties allowed her to withdraw at times and to seek assistance at times, effectively regulating her level of intimacy. The man similarly vacillated between helping her when she became depressed and withdrawing into his business pursuits. Over years, the couple developed a push-pull, stimulus-response pattern of intimacy and withdrawal that tired them and left them feeling dissatisfied with their level of intimacy with each other.

Couples present counselors with a number of common problems that have unfulfilled intimacy needs at their root:

☐ Too little intimacy (the disengaged couple)
☐ Too much intimacy (the overinvolved couple)
☐ Too much regulation of intimacy and distance (the distancer-pursuer couple)
☐ Too much negative intimacy (the conflicted couple)

☐ Too little sexual contact, too much negative intimacy surrounding sex, or both (the sexually conflicted couple)

The nature of each problem will be discussed separately in this chapter to help the counselor recognize some common problems affected by intimacy. In a subsequent section of this chapter, a catalog of treatment techniques will be presented from which the counselor can select appropriate interventions based on his or her assessment.

The Disengaged Couple

The disengaged couple has lost the romance of their relationship. They might or might not be engaged in active conflict, but they have certainly lost all positive mutual interaction. They do little together either coactively or intimately. Usually, at least one spouse is overinvolved in outside activities, which might include work, leisure, children, volunteer or even church duties.

With couples who are overinvolved outside of the marriage, there is often a sense of time urgency. Many disengaged couples are not inclined to say they want more intimacy, though at times each partner longs for increased intimacy. Both spouses may complain that they do not get enough love from their partner, but both are relatively unmotivated to pursue more intimacy. Napier and Whitaker hypothesize that the disengaged couple has sublimated their affiliative needs to the outside activities.[2]

The Overinvolved Couple

The overinvolved couple, often called "enmeshed,"[3] has difficulty separating themselves from each other. They talk about themselves exclusively as a couple and tend not to engage in individual activities. Often each spouse confuses personal needs with the needs of the partner, which can create resentment and feelings of being dominated by the partner. Because partners identify so closely with each other, it is not uncommon for both spouses to feel dominated by each other.

In the overinvolved couple, spouses might frequently answer questions directed at their partner and assume that they know exactly how the partner thinks and feels. Boundaries between the spouses have become blurred over time, through mistaken beliefs about the desirability of total intimacy and through using assumptions of similarity to govern behaviors.

In my experience, the overinvolved couple is rarer than the disengaged couple, but of the overinvolved couples I have seen, more have been Christians than non-Christians. The norm in Christian environments is love and intimacy, which promotes overinvolvement.

Philip Guerin (1982) has described the emotional pursuer-emotional distancer problem.[4] In times of stress, the emotional pursuer, who is usually the wife, will move toward the emotional distancer. In response both to stress and to the demands of the spouse for support, the distancer will seek *noninvolvement* with the partner and will often become involved with work, sports or hobbies.

The Distancer-Pursuer Couple

The emotional pursuer usually easily shares feelings and feels responsibility for maintaining relationships. He or she is usually people oriented. Mistakes are usually those of commission, and apology comes relatively easy. Endings and good-bys are typically difficult.

The emotional distancer is usually reserved, steady and predictable and is oriented toward things and productivity. He or she does not regularly communicate feelings—only when pinned down. Mistakes are usually those of omission, and apology comes hard. Endings and good-bys are usually accepted in stride.

Over time, a pattern develops when pursuers and distancers do not explicitly work against their natural proclivities. The pursuer repeatedly demands closeness, support and intimacy, while the distancer continually disengages and becomes over-involved in work or other activities. The pursuer holds the "dark fantasy"[5] that if he or she stopped demanding intimacy, the spouse would leave altogether—emotionally or physically. The distancer usually holds the dark fantasy that if he or she stops disengaging from the spouse, the spouse will flood him or her with emotional demands that he or she cannot handle. Some counselors[6] speculate that *neither* spouse can tolerate intimacy, and the partners have unconsciously colluded to select spouses who maintain a suitable distance between them.

After some time period, which might be as short as weeks or as long as twenty or more years, the pursuer usually tires of pursuing intimacy without receiving an adequate amount or type of intimacy in return. The pursuer stops asking for closeness; he or she gives up, erecting an emotional wall between them. The distancer is suddenly awakened by the withdrawal of the pursuer and makes tentative advances to find out what has happened.

The former pursuer, bitter over what he or she perceives as continual rejection, self-righteously hurls insults and criticisms over the emotional wall, which punishes the spouse for the years of inattention. "Where were you when I needed you?" the pursuer might wail plaintively.

Hurt, the distancer withdraws and erects a similar emotional wall between them. In one instance, a distancer who fit this pattern accurately described himself as lying in bed with his arms around his wife but feeling as if they were separated by a large, cold sheet of steel.

It is important for counselors to note that both spouses collude to keep a safe, semi-intimate distance between them. Counselors tend to blame the distancer for not being intimate with the spouse. Most counselors are people-oriented, active, responsible sharers of feelings. They thus have a natural tendency to identify with the emotional pursuer. To avoid overidentification with either spouse, we need to accurately assess our own relationship tendencies and guard against their intrusion into counseling.

Katherine Guerin discussed the ways that four therapists engage the emotional distancer.[7] Minuchin treats the distancer as the boundary guard of the family. The distancer is approached first and is implicitly asked permission to interact with the spouse. Fogarty gives the distancer lots of distance in the session. The counselor pays polite attention to the distancer without making direct effort to change him or her. The distancer is listened to when he or she chooses to speak. Distancers are thought to evolve rather than change precipitously. Bowen, as do all four of the counselors, spends most of the session with the emotional pursuer. He begins the session by talking to the distancer, but soon moves to the pursuer. Katherine Guerin respects the emotional boundaries of all members of the family, especially those of the distancer. She also talks little to him or her. When she addresses emotionally laden topics with the distancer, she uses an indirect "just suppose" type of question that allows the distancer to answer without feeling personally threatened.

Therapists also deal differently with emotional pursuers. The guideline is never to ignore pursuers.[8] Pay lots of attention to them. Try to get them to change their styles from overmonitoring their emotional needs and their spouse's unwillingness to meet those needs to monitoring the whole relationship.

Jacobson and Margolin recommend a different step-by-step method of dealing with distancers and pursuers, though they call the couple affiliative-independent.[9] Their four steps are as follows:

1. The affiliative spouse must *temporarily accept the partner's independent behavior* without protest. This is thought to stop the reinforcement of the withdrawal by the independent spouse, for previously withdrawal had stopped the spouse's noxious demands for intimacy.

2. The affiliative spouse should *greatly reduce,* again temporarily, *attempts to seduce the independent spouse away from withdrawal.*

3. The affiliative spouse must *cultivate a more independent life,* thus reducing her or his need for affiliation from the partner.

4. The affiliative spouse must *state his or her need for relationship change* directly to the independent spouse. Because of the lessened need for intimacy, expressed by the affiliative partner, the independent spouse now feels less threatened by requests for increased intimacy and will more likely agree than when the affiliative spouse was totally dependent on the spouse for intimacy.

The conflicted couple is characterized not only by low intimacy but also by frequent negative interaction. Generally, this couple cannot be simply directed to do activities together in the hope that the time spent will be perceived as intimate. Conflicted couples will usually turn time together into a negative interaction. Tasks that are used with conflicted couples need to be carefully prescribed and delimited to avoid negative interaction. Also, usually the couple should be involved in conflict management or communication training prior to using most of the techniques that are used with disengaged couples. There are three techniques that I do use with conflicted couples early in their treatment: reading aloud, reframing their conflict and betting them that they cannot have a totally positive week. Each of these three techniques will be described later in this chapter.

The Conflicted Couple

DECISIONS ABOUT CHANGING INTIMACY

As can be seen, changing the intimacy-distance-coaction balance within the couple's relationship is not simple. How intimacy is changed depends on a careful assessment of (a) the individuals' needs and desires and (b) the patterns of interaction most frequently employed by the couple. It is naive to think that any single technique will change the patterns built over years of married life. Rather, the therapist must use all of his or her ingenuity to help the couple become aware of their need to readjust their patterns of intimacy. Then, the therapist must set out to break old patterns of behavior, realizing that people will likely resist changing their established behavior or will relapse easily if they do change. Finally, the therapist must help the couple institute new patterns of intimacy and distance that meet their individual needs and are compatible with the goals of the couple.

A number of decisions must be made before the treatment of the couple's intimacy pattern can be successful.

1. *How much does each spouse's background contribute to the couple's difficulty in establishing patterns of intimacy that are healthy and satisfactory for the couple?* Some spouses may have unresolved psychological conflicts over their own independence from their parents. The spouse may be seen as a parental substitute who activates dependency needs or stimulates desires to rebel and thus differentiates from the parental substitute by force. If the counselor comes to believe that individual issues are preventing the couple from resolving their intimacy needs, the therapist must decide whether to suggest individual therapy, refer the spouse for individual therapy or attempt to resolve the psychological conflicts within the context of marital therapy.

2. *How important is the intimacy problem relative to problems in communication; conflict; hurt, blame and sin; or commitment?* The therapist cannot focus on all problems simultaneously and must make hard choices about which problem areas to assign priority for treatment.

3. *How would the therapist like to see the couple act regarding their intimacy-distance-coaction after successful therapy?* I believe that the counselor will stimulate the most progress in counseling if he or she knows clearly what the final goals are. Thus, it will repay the effort to imagine the desired end state of counseling before embarking on a plan for change. Beware, though: The danger of determining what is "good" for the client is that the counselor will not remain sufficiently open to new information that he or she receives from the couple as therapy unfolds.

4. *How extensive are the needed changes in intimacy, and can they be achieved within the time allotted for counseling?* It is necessary to assess carefully and realistically how much change to expect and to inform the clients about the extent of change you anticipate.

5. *How does intimacy need to be changed?* Are the changes mostly quantitative—requiring more positive activities or less negative activities? Or are the changes more qualitative—involving changes in how to be intimate with each other?

After the counselor has (1) considered the type of intimacy problem experienced by a couple—disengaged, overinvolved, distancer-pursuer, conflicted or sexually troubled—and (2) answered the five questions concerning the spouses' backgrounds, relative importance of the problem in intimacy, the projected goals, the extent of required changes, and the amount or type of change desired, then the counselor can select from a variety of specific techniques for promoting change. Recall that it is usually what the counselor does and says before, during and after the technique is employed that determines the couple's response to the technique.

SPECIFIC TECHNIQUES FOR CHANGING INTIMACY

As with all techniques in the upcoming chapters, those dealing with changing intimacy will be grouped into three categories: those that help increase the couple's awareness of the problem, those that break old patterns and those that build new patterns. Deciding which techniques you will use depends on your assessment of the couple.

The most common way to increase the couple's awareness and motivation is frequently to invite them to talk with each other about their feelings concerning their intimate activities together. The counselor should ask at every opportunity how satisfied each spouse is with the present state of the marriage. When one spouse talks of dissatisfaction, the counselor asks the spouse to explore that further. Generally, the counselor can aim an entire session at the couple's patterns of intimacy in order to *dramatize the deficiencies.*

Increasing the Couple's Awareness of the Problem

Another technique to dramatize the deficiency in intimacy is sculpting. Sculpting is generally used more with families than with couples, but it is still useful with disengaged couples. One spouse is directed to mold his or her own and partner's bodies into postures that depict the couple's emotional status.

While watching the person arrange the scene, the counselor verbally describes the position of the bodies. It is important *not* to comment on the relationship, but to stick to describing the *physical position* of the bodies. After the spouse has completed the sculpting, the counselor briefly discusses the person's view of the couple's intimacy. The person is then invited to arrange the couple's bodies as he or she would *ideally* like them to be. Often the contrast is startling and increases the couple's desire to achieve greater intimacy. The procedure can be repeated with the other spouse doing the sculpting if the counselor thinks that might be beneficial.

Regardless of whether focused discussion or some other technique is used, the counselor usually concludes by summarizing what the couple has "told" him—that the couples' current patterns of intimacy need changing. Before new patterns can be built though, old patterns must be broken up.

BREAKING UP OLD PATTERNS OF INTIMACY

Reading Aloud

One of the first assignments that I give almost every couple is to set aside about thirty minutes to one hour during the week and read a chapter aloud to each other from the book *Getting to Yes: Negotiating Agreement without Giving In.*[10]

The premise of the book is that people stake out positions on issues of conflict and then become wedded to the positions. This prevents people from seeing other solutions to their problems. The book's authors, Fisher and Ury, recommend that people identify the interests of both parties that underlie their positions. The assumption is that there are many ways to meet one's interests, not just the one way that is represented by a person's position. Fisher and Ury suggest that both parties find a solution that meets both parties' interests. In so doing, compromise is unnecessary because both people get what they want and are not forced to give up part of their desires, as they must in a compromise.

For example, suppose Maria and Carlos argue about how often they eat at restaurants. The conflict is characterized by acrimony and each repetitively states his or her position: Maria wants to eat out more often and Carlos says no. To help them identify their interests behind their respective positions, the counselor might ask each, "*Why* do you hold the position you do?"

After discussion, Maria determines that she (a) feels Carlos is ashamed to be seen in public with her; (b) does not want to do the dishes; and (c) enjoys the undivided attention she receives from Carlos when they eat out. Carlos determines that he wants to eat out less because he (a) is concerned over their inability to save money, which makes him feel like an inadequate breadwinner, and (b) believes that Maria prepares better food than most restaurant food.

Instead of allowing an argument to develop between Maria and Carlos about the validity or relative importance of each of their reasons, the counselor can direct them to think of creative ways to meet both of their interests. For instance, Maria suggests that she could be sure Carlos was not ashamed of her if he took her to less expensive restaurants or other enjoyable low-cost activities. Carlos suggests that they prepare special meals at home at least weekly in which they take the phone from the hook and give undivided attention to each other for the night. They agree to wash up after dinner while continuing their conversation. The solutions meet the interests of both partners.

I actually have several purposes in using this read-aloud assignment. I listed it in this chapter on intimacy because the couple is induced to spend time together while accomplishing a pleasant task. This promotes coaction and reserves a time in their schedules that can later be used for more intimate activities. There are other benefits achieved by this task too. As a first assignment during intervention, the read-aloud task starts small and prepares the couple to follow other directives.[11] It also introduces them to some of the principles that will be used to resolve conflict. The book is engaging, easy to read and useful in situations besides resolving marital conflict. Furthermore, because the book was on the best-seller list for several weeks, it is usually available in any popular bookstore.

Because the read-aloud assignment has many uses, it may be introduced as a method of conflict resolution as easily as a method for increasing intimacy. Its use depends on how it is justified and discussed by the therapist.

Reframing Conflict

Reframing is placing a behavior of the couple within a different context from its current frame of reference. One couple, Dick and Jeannie, fought loudly and emotionally. After one session during which they shouted at each other, they rose to leave very discouraged.

"We must really hate each other. We say such hateful things," said Jeannie.

"Well," I said. "This was certainly an emotional time for you, but I disagree that you do not love each other. The opposite of love is total indifference toward the other. What you showed today was far from total indifference! In fact, I would have to say that you are *very involved* with each other emotionally. You just need to channel the emotion a little differently."

The couple laughed at my interpretation, but they fought less after that and worried less about the fighting that they did. Sometimes I think that with that couple, that was the best intervention I made.

Sealed Orders

Roy and Sally had been married for seventeen years and had three children. They initiated counseling because they felt they had lost the sparkle in their relationship. Privately Roy told me that he had frequently had sexual fantasies and felt guilty because of his Christian beliefs. Sally became clinically depressed because she could not find intimate friends. After a year of Roy's withdrawal, Sally became openly critical of Roy's work and of his infrequent attempts at emotional support. She also ignored his requests for support.

I assessed Roy and Sally as being almost textbook examples of the distancer-pursuer pattern. Sally pursued intimacy by demanding help and support while Roy distanced himself by his high involvement at work. I planned the third and fourth intervention sessions to deal with this pattern. In the third session, I broached the topic by picking up on a complaint from Sally early in the session. I mentioned having become aware that Sally had complained several times about Roy's overinvolvement in work.

For about ten minutes, Sally described Roy's overinvolvement in work. Roy was asked about his side of the story. He described the demands of work and vaguely mentioned the demands of the family. When I inquired about the specific demands he felt from family members, he first mentioned the children, then in almost a throwaway statement said, "Of course, it's tough when Sally is depressed too."

"How so?" I asked.

"She needs a lot of time from me. It's hard on me. Sometimes I don't even want to come home. I know it's going to be emotionally draining. And just the same old things, again and again."

"What do you mean?" I asked.

"She asks the same old questions. And I can't answer them. I just listen, frustrated. I feel so *incompetent*. At least at work I feel competent."

When these feelings came out, I had Sally and Roy discuss them. After about five minutes, they had provided a personalized description of the emotional pursuer-emotional distancer pattern. I stopped their discussion and summarized the pattern, referring to a printed chart that graphically portrayed the pattern. They enthusiastically agreed that they fit the pursuer-distancer mode. Having anticipated the general flow of the session, I assigned them homework that I had previously prepared. I withdrew from my desk two sealed envelopes, addressed to each separately. Inside were the following instructions:

> *Roy, this week you are to pick three activities that you consider to be intimate activities. You are to initiate these activities and carry through with them. Whichever activities you select can be performed whenever you wish so long as they are enjoyable to both you and Sally. You are not to tell Sally what is written on this piece of paper, nor are you to ask her what is on hers.*
>
> *Sally, this week you are not to initiate any demands for intimacy or support from Roy. Do not ask him for any help. Furthermore, you are not to criticize him for his behavior—either aloud or silently to yourself. If you find that you are thinking critically about him, pray for strength to avoid criticizing him. You are not to tell Roy what is written on this piece of paper, nor are you to ask him what is written on his.*

After Roy and Sally had read the instructions silently, I asked whether they understood what they were to do during the week. Then I said, "There is a second part of this assignment besides what you are each to do. I want to see if you can figure out what the other person is doing. The catch is that you cannot ask the other person what the assignment was. So, this is a test of your observational powers. I will give you each a hint. Whatever the other person is doing, it should be something that you will like."

At the following session, Roy and Sally reported adhering to their instructions throughout the week. Sally was able to determine that Roy was initiating intimacy. He had taken her out to dinner (arranging babysitting himself), had an after-dinner talk on the porch and came home during lunch to make love during the midweek. Roy was also able to detect what Sally's task was.

The homework for Roy and Sally accomplished several things. First, it helped break up their usual patterns of intimacy. Instead of Sally initiating intimacy, Roy was the initiator. Instead of Sally concentrating on Roy's failure to support her, she focused continually on the positive as she tried to discern the nature of the instructions to Roy.

Second, because the directives were followed, evidence was presented to the couple that their "dark fantasy" was unrealistic.[12] Roy found that he could stop avoiding intimacy without being overwhelmed and Sally found that she could stop demanding intimacy without having Roy totally withdraw. The evidence was meager because Roy and Sally were following my directives, but still there was concrete evidence.

Third, I did not repeat the pattern within the counseling relationship. The cardinal rule in dealing with the distancing spouse is "never pursue a distancer."[13] The counselor's demands for more and more intimacy, more intimate sharing of feelings within the counseling relationship can recapitulate the distancer-pursuer pattern between the counselor and distancer. However, while I did make some demands that Roy be intimate with his wife, I did it in a non-threatening way, using written instructions, treating it as a light game rather than as an emotional task and giving instructions that maximized choice regarding which intimate activities to initiate at which times.

Rearrange Time Schedules

Another technique for breaking up old intimacy patterns that are deemed problematic is best employed with underinvolved couples but is occasionally useful for overinvolved couples as well. Couples negotiate changes in their time schedules.

Couples balance their needs for intimacy, coaction and distance through the ways they use their time. Liberman et al.[14] suggest that rearranging the couple's time schedules might be *the* solution to their problems. Liberman et al. recommend making simple changes in the relationship before undertaking sweeping changes such as communication training.

As a beginning, have the couple make a time budget that shows how they distribute their leisure time. Use four categories: as individuals, as a couple, as part of a social group and as a family. Do not assume that spouses want to change their leisure time in the same way. The husband might want to take the children to a ball game while the wife might want to have the whole family go camping. Consider whether changes in each of the four categories are appropriate.

One couple, Laura and Rob, each needed more time alone. Rob worked for a social service agency and dealt with people all day. Laura stayed home with their three preschool children. By five o'clock, Laura was frazzled. She talked to herself, picked up anything she saw and corrected the mail carrier for incorrect grammar. Meanwhile, at work, Rob helped the destitute, talked to the lonely, listened to the irate and moved five pounds of paperwork across his desk daily. Each day as he drove home, he thought about the prospects of helping children, talking to them, dealing with an irate wife and cranky kids and sifting through five pounds of junk mail. When Rob walked in the house each day, he and Laura would begin a verbal jousting match that extended until after the children were in bed and they could get by themselves.

Rob said that he did not mind dealing with the children, but that he needed some time to unwind before tackling them. Laura said she could hold herself together until Rob got home, but when he walked in the door, it was like showing a bull red: she trampled small objects to get away from the children. Rob and Laura were frustrating themselves and each other through their time schedule. They set up a signal system. If Laura needed immediate relief from the children, she posted a large red flag in the window of the family room. If Rob drove up and saw the flag, he was to come immediately into the house and handle the children. If no red flag was posted, he was entitled to sit in the car for up to thirty minutes and do whatever he wanted to—read, think or even sleep. By this simple signal system, Rob and Laura resolved most of their tension.

Routine jobs also provide an opportunity for increased intimacy. John was responsible for the outdoor work around the house, while Marie handled most of the indoor work. They agreed to divide up one of the jobs from each person's domain and spend one hour on each Saturday helping with the other's job. Marie helped John trim the hedges while John helped Marie with the vacuuming and dusting. During their time together, they discussed the events of their work weeks. John discussed his week while helping Marie and she discussed hers while they worked in the yard.

Hobbies sometimes make good ways to increase spouses' intimacy. Often couples can start new hobbies, such as camping, hiking or boating, that provide increased opportunities for intimacy. Sometimes couples have engaged in leisure activities in their early married years; counseling provided an excuse to resume enjoyable activities.

In using each of these renegotiations of time schedules in counseling, the counselor does not merely ask the couple to decide what they are going to do together to increase their intimacy. Rather, have both spouses make suggestions that are nonbinding on the couple. Then, have the couple decide which things they would like to do. Finally, the couple plans an actual time when the activity will be carried out. This is a crucial step, for all activities take time from busy schedules, so the couple has to agree not only to do the activity but also what they will give up from their schedule to make room for the activity.

Once couples try to place a new time schedule into operation, their usual patterns will be disrupted and the tendency will be strong to go back to the old patterns. As counselor, help them remain motivated to maintain the changes. This will ready them to build new patterns of intimacy.

BUILDING NEW PATTERNS OF INTIMACY

Wish List

Once a couple has decided to increase their intimacy, they naturally want to know how. I generally say:

That's a good question. I'm sure that you have some ideas about how to be more intimate with each other. I would encourage you to try out your ideas at home during the next couple of weeks just to see whether they will work. I have some ideas too, which should supplement the ones you try, and I would like you to try some of my ideas too.

I know that you want to practice the Golden Rule—"do unto others as you would have them do unto you." I also know that you don't want to rush out and do things for your spouse that he or she doesn't interpret the same as you. I remember when Kirby and I were first married, I thought I was showing her love by giving her lots of physical contact. That's what I wanted. Unfortunately, she wanted me to tell her that I loved her. After a few misunderstandings, I realized that what I really wanted was for her to ask me what I wanted her to do. After that, I asked, and she was able to tell me that she wanted more "I love you's."

What I would like you to do, then, is to make up a wish list—things that you would like the other person to do that would show you intimacy. The important point is to get a long list, so let your minds run freely. We'll do that right now. Here's some paper for each of you.

Now I know that you have been married a while and probably know lots of the things that your spouse will put on his or her wish list. That doesn't matter. Go ahead. List everything you can think of anyway. But, I also want you to try to come up with some things that will surprise your spouse—even though you have been married [x] years.

Several purposes are accomplished with these instructions. Spouses make long lists, which can later short-circuit objections that intimate activities are not being freely chosen. You can argue that because of the number of choices available, the spouse is obviously free to choose anything he or she wishes. In addition, the couple is instructed to surprise each other so that the fiction (with some couples) that they perfectly know their spouse will not be *directly* confronted. Confronting shared fictions, especially early in counseling, produces resistance. Later in counseling, if it contributes to the goals of counseling, you might want to confront the fiction. Finally, you are setting the stage for helping the couple achieve "soul oneness"—ministering to each other's needs.

The wish list will be used to inform each spouse of how to show love in a way that can be perceived positively. This can serve as a foundation on which to build positive experiences.

Increase
Positive
Activities

Therapists have created numerous techniques for helping couples increase their positive activities together. I will briefly list and describe ten.

■ *Caring days.*[15] From a list of specific, small, positive behaviors, each spouse selects five to perform daily. Caring behaviors are done, regardless of whether the spouse does his or hers, which is consistent with Christian philosophy that we give despite what the other person does.

■ *Love days.*[16] Couples attempt to double their usual number of positive behaviors for their spouses. Each partner is assigned a separate love day each week.

■ *Pampering your spouse.* Each spouse is assigned to select one day and do things that make the spouse feel "special."

■ *Cookie jar.* Create three jars: his, hers, theirs. Periodically select pleasing behaviors from each of the jars. The frequency of doing the pleasing behaviors is up to the spouses.

■ *The "up deck."*[17] This gives eighty-five activities that might help the spouse feel more cheerful. Each activity is printed on a card, which can be drawn at intervals acceptable to the spouses.

■ *The "fun deck."*[18] Like the up deck, these cards suggest 126 activities that might be fun for couples.

■ *Fifty-two presents.* Carl Miller, a friend of ours, gave his wife as a Christmas present a decorator jar with fifty-two slips of paper, each listing an activity that he could do for her or which they could do together. Each Sunday, Carl carried the jar to Debbie before she got out of bed. Debbie selected a piece of paper from the jar which described the activity to be done during the upcoming week.

■ *The Royal Family Exercise.*[19] Fred DiBlasio, a friend and excellent Christian counselor, has developed a game for families that can be adapted for couples. Each partner is instructed to do three nice things for the spouse during the week. They are to do the nice things surreptitiously. The spouse will be required to guess what was done for him or her at the next session. Fred coaches the couples that they can do as many nice things as they wish and at the next meeting they will give Fred a list of only three activities. The spouse must guess the three that are on Fred's list.

Points are awarded arbitrarily by the counselor, who acts as the "king." The counselor awards points for correct guesses or creative "nice things" so that the couple together receives twenty-five points. At the end of the session the couple is instructed to open an envelope that Fred has prepared prior to the session. The envelope contains a gift certificate to a local ice cream store for two ice cream sundaes—which gives the couple another opportunity to do something together (without additional cost to them).

■ *Catching your spouse doing something nice and letting him or her know about it.*[20] One nice thing is done for the spouse each day. That night the spouse tells what he or she appreciated and the actor reveals what was done.

■ *Planning and having a date.* The couple plans a date that would be mutually enjoyable. They set a night and work out the details *during the session.* They are instructed not to discuss anything negative or conflictual despite what happens on the date. They carry out the date at the appointed time.

Share Intimate Experiences

Some experiences promote intimacy in most couples. Couples can be assigned to share those experiences occasionally. Some of the intimacy-producing experiences include:[21]

■ *Reminiscing about the good ol' days.* Most every couple has a happier time in their past which can encourage them that better days can be before them as well.

■ *Sharing a fantasy or making up a story together.* For example, one spouse starts a story and talks for one minute. The other spouse takes over and talks for one minute. The story must last for ten minutes at a minimum.

■ *Sharing silliness.* One couple used to talk like Ma and Pa Kettle. When they would go to the theater or to dinner, they pretended that they were directly from the mountains and were unaccustomed to such finery.

■ *Sharing a deviant experience.* One couple pretended that they were spies. They drove to a local small-plane airport late at night and skulked around the runway avoiding the spotlight.

■ *Sharing dreams of the future.* Some couples can use their dreams to produce intimacy, but for some couples this provides an instance of conflict. Before assigning this activity, you should have a good estimate of the couple's reaction.

■ *Creating core symbols.*[22] Core symbols are places, rituals or objects that have special significance for the couple. One couple, for example, had a disastrous honeymoon in which they were snowed in with no heat and with a broken car. Although the honeymoon was not fun while they were experiencing it, it was a source of humor and intimacy as they later retold it.

Combating Resistance to Building New Patterns

Disengaged and conflicted couples usually become that way over a long time. They find it difficult to understand how changing momentary behaviors will help them be more intimate. Many disengaged or conflicted couples will subtly or overtly challenge you when you direct them to increase the positive things they do for each other and together and to share intimate experiences. Their challenges are to be expected and even encouraged. I much prefer the couple that actively challenges my directives to the couple who halfheartedly goes through the motions without putting any real effort into them.

Some spouses will object that they can't think of any nice things to do. Their wish list will be short, and they will resist being pleased by almost anything. Usually, I call their attention to some of the already prepared lists, such as those in the book by Gottman et al.[23] I then ask them to select from the over 200 suggestions some that might please them. I suggest that there may be many activities listed that they have not tried, and I encourage them to try the activities before judging whether they are pleasing. I might also share some of the things that Kirby and I do for and with each other as a personal testimony to some of the activities.

Some spouses will object to having a list of pleasing activities. They argue that pleasing things should be "spontaneous" or they are not "real." I might answer, "Each person has a list of activities in his or her head and selects from the list whenever he or she wants to do something pleasing for someone else. These written lists are merely ways to lengthen someone's mental list and are ways to be sure that you have some input into your spouse's list."

Some spouses also argue, "He should *know* what pleases me." This assumption not only paralyzes the couple from carrying out this exercise, but it also promotes mind reading and poor communication.

I generally counter by asking, "How should he know?"

"Well, he should just *see* what I need or he should know just by talking to me," the wife might reply.

"But seeing and hearing you are just nonverbal communication. They are just telling your spouse what to do without using words, which is inefficient and easily misunderstood communication. Why not tell him in a way that has less chance of being misunderstood?"

Some spouses say that trying to create pleasant interactions is merely *pretending* intimacy that they do not feel. The assumption underlying this objection is that feelings drive behaviors and that feelings are more real than behaviors. This is a difficult assumption to combat because, since Freud, it has become enculturated. I usually try to avoid a power struggle over the issue because no one can ever prove whether feelings or behaviors come first.

I sometimes say, "You are right. Under many circumstances feelings must come before behavior, and I should try to behave in accordance with my feelings. But at times, the reverse is true. For example, sometimes I don't feel justified in the sight of God, but I know that if Jesus is my Savior, I am justified. So I have to behave accordingly, even though I don't feel like it."

At times I will state that psychological experiments have shown that sometimes feelings precede behavior and sometimes changing behavior can help change feelings. I urge the couple to "experiment" to determine whether this is one of the times that behaving in a caring way might help them feel more caring.

Sometimes one spouse might object passively by simply not doing anything positive for the partner. This usually creates resistance in the spouse who is following your suggestions. I deal with the passive resister by asking why he or she objects to following my directives. Then, I deal with the reasons as they surface. In instances when the person simply refuses to cooperate, I might ask the person for his or her plan to help build more intimacy.

If the person has a plan, we might experiment with it for a couple of weeks. If not, I might say, "If you don't have a concrete plan that you think will work, then why are you adverse to trying something that I have seen work with some other couples? How am I to interpret your behavior? Perhaps you don't believe it is important to build a more intimate marriage.

Perhaps you don't want to work on intimacy right now—there's something that you think is more pressing."

It is important that the spouse not feel that you are coercing him or her into your program. Rather, be genuinely interested in identifying the roadblocks to building a better marriage. Treat the impasse as a problem to solve rather than a test of wills, and you will model a way to help the couple resolve some of their impasses.

THE SEXUALLY TROUBLED COUPLE

At the beginning of this chapter, I identified five common difficulties in intimacy. The last difficulty, problems with sexual intimacy, I did not describe with the others because sexual problems often require special training of the therapist. *The therapist without adequate training or supervision in sexual counseling is urged to seek such assistance and to refrain from practicing sex therapy until assistance is available.* Because sex therapy is such a large and intricate topic, I cannot hope to cover it adequately in the present section. I will merely touch on some basics of dealing with couples who have non-physiologically caused sexual troubles. These will include only two types: the sexually conflicted couple and the sexually bored couple.

Counseling the Sexually Troubled Couple

There are three fundamental types of problems with sexuality:

☐ Those that result from or can be resolved through sexual technique

☐ Those that must be dealt with through the individual

☐ Those resulting when spouses use sex as a battleground for power struggles in their relationship

Each of these sexual problems requires different counseling techniques. A thorough explication of the techniques of dealing with sexual problems in couples is beyond the scope of this book.[24] In this chapter, I will address only a few techniques for helping couples with the third type of sexual problem—the sexually conflicted couple.

A recent survey has shown that eighty per cent of couples seeking marital therapy were sexually dissatisfied.[25] Even in very happy marriages, about half of the couples report some sexual problems or sexual dysfunction.[26]

Regardless of the origin of sexual problems in couples—whether a result of individual dysfunction, unpleasing sexual techniques or power struggles—most sexual difficulties will soon result in frustration, anger, blame and conflict around the sex act. Many of the techniques I describe will be applicable to the couple regardless of the origin of the problem.

Couples who have a power struggle around sex might fight over the frequency of intercourse, the time of intercourse, the positions or acts one or both demands or assumes, the ability or willingness of one to please the other, the way sex is initiated or the lack of fulfillment in their sex lives. Conflict might be active (involving heated arguments) or passive (involving sabotage of the spouse's or one's own enjoyment of sex in order to frustrate the other). The common threads of the conflicted couple are that (1) both people are distressed over the sexual condition of their marriage and (2) both achieve some payoffs from the current situation, primarily in terms of control over relationship definition or resistance to control over relationship domination.

Annon (1976) has presented a four-tier system for counseling couples with sexual problems: the Plissit model.[27]

Levels of Intervention

■ *Level one of **Plissit** intervention gives the couple **permission** to engage in sexual acts that they have doubts about.*

For example, some people believe that sex should not be enjoyable for the woman but rather is a duty. A permission-level intervention might tell the woman (or man) that God designed sex not only as a procreative function but as fun for a married couple.

Not all permission-level interventions are as straightforward. Many require value judgments. For example, a marriage therapist does not have to practice long before becoming aware of the enormous variety of ways that married couples express themselves sexually. Some sexual expressions are quite idiosyncratic. The marriage counselor must be slow to judge others. Sometimes, though, permission involves affirming the feelings of one spouse not engaging in some sexual act. For example, one couple had conflict over the husband's insistence that mate swapping with a couple that were close friends would improve a drab sex life. By the counselor's affirming biblical standards, the wife was encouraged not to yield to the pressure of her husband in participating in sin.

■ *Level two of Plissit intervention offers* **limited information.** At this level, specific factual information is provided the couple. For example, newlyweds often are uncertain whether the frequency with which they engage in intercourse is "normal." Many married people still masturbate, and you can help them study Scripture concerning the topic.

■ *Level three of Plissit intervention gives* **specific suggestions.** The counselor may suggest what the couple can do to improve their sex life. For instance, the counselor might recommend manual stimulation of the woman's clitoris until orgasm instead of vaginal stimulation by intercourse if the man has difficulty with early ejaculation, if the woman cannot reach orgasm through vaginal stimulation or if the woman simply prefers manual stimulation to reach orgasm (which is actually quite frequently the case).

■ *Level four of Plissit intervention is* **intensive therapy.** At this level, programs of sexual therapy are used with the couple and that is the focus of their marriage counseling. Often, marriage therapy and sexual therapy can be carried out concurrently by two counselors without interference, if one counselor does not feel competent or confident in treating sexual dysfunction. At times, each counselor will operate at each level of the Plissit model. The marriage counselor should be familiar with sexual counseling techniques.

THE SEXUALLY CONFLICTED COUPLE

Separate the Problems

The couple conflicted over their sexual relationship is usually ambivalent. They experience distress, frustration, pleasure and power over their conflict, although the positive feelings about the conflict are usually suppressed because of social norms. You can clarify your thinking about the problem by separating the situation into (a) the sexual act and (b) the sexual conflict. Generally, the sexual act is enjoyed. As counselor, your first task is to (1) increase the couple's pleasure from sexual contact and (2) decrease negative feelings associated with the sexual contact. The second task is to help the couple (1) increase the distress of sexual conflict and (2) decrease the control they gain through using sexual conflict.

Several techniques have been developed to help the couple enjoy their sexual lives more. Generally, activities are assigned so that the couple gradually approximates lovemaking. The couple might start simply by giving each other a nonsexual massage. For example, the couple might be directed to give each other a hand, foot, head or back massage. The recipient of the massage is responsible for giving the spouse feedback about what feels good and what does not. The couple is allowed to communicate about giving pleasure to the other by this activity, which lays the groundwork for increasing the communication during lovemaking. This activity can be done within the counseling session and the counselor can give suggestions about the communication between the spouses. Next, the couple might be assigned to repeat the massages at home during the week, with each spouse giving and receiving three massages.

A second task might be to have the couple recall how they had sexual contact during their premarital interaction. Did they hug or kiss for long periods? Did they park? Was there a romantic hangout that they frequented? After the couple identifies fond memories, they are instructed to pretend that they are again dating. The limits of sexual contact are set by agreement within the session, and intercourse is defined as off limits for the evening. The couple carries out the date, including kissing and hugging.

Some couples might enjoy sensate focus exercises. Designed for couples to become reacquainted with the sensations of sexual contact while not engaging in intercourse, sensate focus exercises provide a systematic program of increasing sexual intimacy for the couple. The couple moves at a pace with which they are comfortable from nonsexual massage to massage of erogenous zones.[28]

Increase Pleasure with Sex

Some women's distress with the sexual act might be due to a physical problem. With most sexual conflict, however, the distress is psychological rather than physical. Spouses fear rejection or failure and are thus threatened by sex. Sometimes spouses complain about being too busy or feeling no sexual attraction for the spouse. There are several ways that these psychological distresses can be dealt with.

1. *Help spouses create a climate of reassurance, acceptance and support within their sexual lives.* Attribute positive motives to both spouses—that they both

Decrease Distress with Sex

want a pleasant sex life and are willing to help the other so they can both be happier. Reinterpret demandingness as a desire for closeness and interpret withdrawal as fear of being overcome by intimacy which impels the person to keep a safe distance between the spouses.

2. *Go slowly.* Do not push the spouses into sexual contact. Rather, restrain them from contact longer than you think necessary. For some time the couple has tried to achieve intimacy through their intercourse and failed. Take the pressure off by forbidding sexual contact for a time. Create frustration and anticipation of sexual contact rather than a dread of it.

3. *Accept the couple's threatened feelings.* Failure to achieve their goals in their sexual lives together has created threat and fear. Encourage them to be courageous rather than admonishing them for their fear.

4. *Help them handle their embarrassment about dealing with their sexual lives with a stranger.* Couples worry that a "Christian counselor" will judge their behavior as wrong as well as judge their prognosis as hopeless. Reassure the couple that you are not embarrassed about discussing their sexual lives. I find that mentioning that about eighty per cent of the couples with marital problems also have sexual problems helps the couple understand that I have dealt with sexual problems with numerous other couples and that they can have confidence in my experience. I assure them that I have seen couples with satisfying sexual lives even though they did a lot of unconventional things in bed, so I do not anticipate that I can be shocked.

5. *Help the couple identify their dark fantasies*—their expectations that terrible consequences will ensue if they solve their sexual problems.[29] Common dark fantasies include fears of being controlled, found to be an inadequate lover, abandoned if the spouse becomes sexually well functioning, being promiscuous or at the mercy of one's overpowering sexual drive, being absorbed into the other person's personality, being taken advantage of and others.

Increase Distress with Sexual Conflict

Mostly counselors think about ways to decrease the distress of their clients. However, one way to help couples get over problems is to increase the distress they experience when they engage in the problematic behaviors. A way to do this is to intensify the couple's dissatisfaction with the problem by having them relive and re-experience the event. Haley calls this a benevolent ordeal.[30]

For example, a couple reports that they attempted to have intercourse during the most recent week, but the attempt resulted in an emotional argument. The counselor might have the couple describe exactly how the argument developed. The couple might even role play the argument and be encouraged to re-experience it in its emotional intensity. After the argument is recounted, the couple is directed to discuss it and speculate about the meaning of the argument for their relationship. By having the couple re-experience the negative emotions, the counselor is making it more costly for the couple to have arguments. If the couple must relive each argument before the counselor, the cost of arguing increases.

Decrease Interpersonal Control Gained through Sexual Conflict

Sexual conflict, which spoils the enjoyment of sex by both spouses, serves as an indirect way of controlling the spouse or resisting the perceived domination of the spouse. Some couples use denial of sex as punishment or as revenge for some slight. Sexual dysfunction can serve the same function.

To decrease the use of sex as an interpersonal control strategy, the counselor assumes control of the frequency or type of sexual interaction during sex therapy. The control exerted by the counselor is not heavy-handed coercion but is direction of the couple's interaction for their good.

Usually couples are initially prohibited from sexual intercourse while the couple re-establishes communication through sensate focus or other communication exercises. The counselor might even determine who is to initiate what kinds of sexual activities. Finally, the counselor usually determines the rate at which couples re-establish sexual intimacy.

If the couple complies with the counselor, they give up some of the power to use sex punitively. If the couple defies the counselor and fails to achieve satisfactory sexual lives, then the counselor gains power by being correct. If the couple defies the counselor and has satisfactory sexual activity against the counselor's advice, then the couple has still achieved their goals and the counselor can easily attribute their success to their efforts.

THE SEXUALLY BORED COUPLE

Some couples are not conflicted over sex but are merely bored because of lack of variety in their sex lives. They report their sex lives as relatively unfulfilling. Generally, sex is a peripheral issue with this couple. To initiate a discussion of sex, I usually tell a story.

> *I think it was Larry Christenson who told (I can't recall exactly where) of the woman who had attended some talks at church about renewing the intimacy in marriage. After a particularly inspiring talk, she returned home late one night, slipped into her flimsiest nighty and cuddled up next to her sleeping husband. He stirred and mumbled, "Whassit?"*
>
> *"Honey, we have to renew our love. We have to recapture the old romance. Rekindle the old flame."*
>
> *"Must we do all this tonight?" he mumbled. "It's almost midnight."*
>
> *"We must." She breathed hotly on his neck, whispering, "Honey, bite me on the ear like you used to when we first got married."*
>
> *"Now? Can't we . . ."*
>
> *"Now. Bite me on the ear like you did when we first got married."*
>
> *"But . . . but . . ."*
>
> *"Please, dear. Bite me on the ear." Then she added in a split second of inspiration, "and bite me on the neck too."*
>
> *"Okay," he sighed, at last warming to the task. "Just hand me my teeth off the table."*
>
> *It is never too late to build a more intimate marriage.*

Through this joke and during our discussion of increasing sexual intimacy, I usually can create some openness to making a small change in their patterns of sexual contact. The humor allows me to confront their usual behavior pleasantly, without putting them on the defensive by telling them what they should be doing. I find that after that joke, most couples are receptive to directives to spend more and more varied sexual time together.

SUMMARY

God intended marriage partners to have intimate relationships. With most couples, changing intimacy will be one goal of counseling. Generally, before intimacy can be changed, the couple must become aware of their deficiencies in intimacy. This is usually accomplished through assessment and goal-setting periods but more motivation can usually be built during the early parts of intervention by directing couples' attention to the discrepancies between their goals and their present behaviors. The counselor then helps the couple identify patterns of interaction that promote unhealthy or unsatisfactory intimacy patterns and intimate interactions that are negatively charged. The couple must be given a picture of the desirability of God's intimacy in their lives together and must begin to break old patterns. Finally, the couple is helped to build new patterns of intimacy through their own efforts and through the techniques presented in this chapter. Most important, the counselor must remain flexible and alert to the couple's needs and not become wedded to techniques, which apart from the intervention of the Holy Spirit cannot please God.

Changing
Communication

COUPLES IN DISTRESS HAVE DISTURBED COMMUNICATION. FEW professionals will argue with that. But communication training programs abound that supposedly help couples change their communication in ways that eliminate or mitigate their other problems. At present, twenty-one books rest on my bed. Each describes a *different* communication training program. Programs include behavioral approaches,[1] empirical approaches,[2] systems approaches,[3] cognitive approaches,[4] psychodynamic approaches,[5] transactional analysis approaches,[6] strategic approaches[7] and eclectic approaches.[8] The approaches are so diverse that the term *communication training* is meaningless. It encompasses too much variety to communicate meaningfully what the counselor is actually doing in counseling.

In this chapter, I do not propose yet another program for communication training. Rather, I identify some of the major theoretical questions that must be addressed by the counselor who tries to change a couple's communication. I state my preferences for answers to the questions but do not prescribe a single way of working with the couple. I eclectically draw from the varieties of theories to address the needs of the couples with whom I work. In the latter portions of the chapter, I describe some techniques that I have found helpful with the Christian couples who have been my clients.

DEFINITION

Communication is any behavior that transmits information between people. Within marriage, most communication makes one's needs known to the spouse and meets the needs of the spouse. Failures in communication usually involve each spouse becoming centered on communicating his or her needs and ignoring the needs of the spouse. Thus, as Crabb identifies, communication problems ultimately stem from self-gratification and self-centeredness.[9] They can be remedied as the couple becomes more other-centered.

Good communication differs from couple to couple. Essentially, good communication is that which effectively accomplishes the goals of communication while being (a) consistent with Scripture and (b) within God's will. Scripture does not describe precisely *how* people should communicate. Neither should counselors. Many theories have described good communication. Research has later shown that both distressed and non-distressed couples engaged in the "good" communication as well as the "bad" communication.[10]

I generally assume that if a couple is in distress, they have developed communication patterns that are not working for them. Those communication patterns must be changed if the couple is to become more satisfied. In addition, the couple must be helped to be more other-centered and more God-centered in their communication. To help people change their established communication patterns, three steps are necessary.

1. The couple must become aware of the problems in their communication.

2. They must break the old patterns of communication.

3. They must build new and better communication patterns—those that help them meet the needs of their spouse and focus on God's will in their relationship.

DECISIONS ABOUT COMMUNICATION TRAINING

The varieties of programs in communication training provide the counselor with many ways to help couples improve their communication. It is possible for a counselor who practices within one "school" of marital therapy to learn only the approach developed by that school. However, the varieties of programs offer the counselor who is not aligned with a single school of therapy a rich smorgasbord of techniques.

Because techniques are based on different assumptions, thorough counselors must carefully identify what they want to accomplish by communication training. This necessitates numerous decisions about how to conduct communication training. I will briefly identify the issues below. In each case, I will italicize the option I favor. Each issue necessarily requires a decision; each practitioner might arrive at different conclusions than I.

■ 1. What is the ultimate aim—teaching or *changing patterns?*

Many theorists assume that the purpose of communication training is to teach the couple new ways of communicating. The danger in this assumption is that the counselor will talk down to the couple, insulting them and provoking them to resist the teaching of the counselor.

I usually challenge this assumption by asking counselors to suppose that they offered the couple one million dollars if they would communicate as a model couple would for fifteen minutes. In this time of psychological sophistication, where television shows, as well as *Reader's Digest,* cover good communication, do we really think that the troubled couples who sit before us *do not know* how they ought to communicate? In actuality, we rarely teach couples what they do not know. Communication training merely helps them do what they already know by providing the constant attention of the counselor and the social pressure of a sanctioned helper who asks the couple to communicate differently.

■ 2. What kind of self-disclosure is desirable—recounting feelings about problems or expressing *positive statements, compliments and problem solutions?*

Research has shown that troubled couples express negative feelings and judgments more freely than non-troubled couples. However, non-distressed couples outdo distressed couples at making positive statements and giving compliments.[11] Self-disclosure by itself is neither good nor bad, but couples should be encouraged to communicate positively rather than negatively. This does not mean that couples should bottle up all negative feelings. Rather, they should build up a "bank account" of positive communication that will give negative comments a positive framework; this way they will be able to express negative feelings in a way that the spouses can hear and respond to them.

■ 3. What should the counselor foster—emotional release or *restraint?*

Again, research has shown that unbridled emotional expression—when the emotion is negative—does not lead to better communication but to worse.[12] If the couple is emotionally upset, they are usually better advised to cool down for a while before they fight. Obeying the biblical injunction not to let the sun go down on their wrath (Eph 4:26), the couple who discusses hot issues should strive to restrain their tongues (Jas 3:6-12) so that they can be angry and yet not sin (Eph 4:26).

Theorists disagree strongly over the role of emotion in communication.[13] For example, Haley makes counselors *apologize* when the couple becomes angry with each other during a session. Bowen tries to detoxify—remove the poison from—the session. On the other hand, Whitaker, Satir and, more recently, Greenberg and Johnson strive for release of emotion and even try to increase the emotion in the session.

■ 4. Should the counselor focus on the semantics, syntax or *pragmatics* of communication?

All communication can be analyzed according to semantics (meaning), syntax (punctuation or style) or pragmatics (effects, especially power relationships) of communication. All counselors will at times address each aspect of communication. Yet, counselors cannot effectively cover all three in depth, so practical choices are made.

In my perspective, much of communication and especially conflict is important to meeting effectance needs of each partner. Power struggles among clients are the best indication of the self-gratification and self-centeredness of the clients (who are struggling to meet their own needs for effectance); thus power struggles are often at the root of relationship difficulties. Therefore, like Haley and the Mental Research Institute therapies, I focus more heavily on the rules of the relationship that are revealed by patterns of communication than on exactly what is being said and whether it is being understood (semantics of communication) or on the style of communication and whether someone is interrupting or filibustering (syntax of communication).

■ 5. Under the counselor's direction, how much should the couple communicate during a session—almost continually or *only infrequently?*

Reasons for each preference are related to other issues in conducting communication training. If one intends to change the words that the couple is using, which would be preferred by those who focus on the semantics and syntax of communication, it is necessary to have clients speak a lot of words throughout the session. If one intends to change the power relationships of the couple, which might be preferred by those who focus on the pragmatics of communication, the counselor is concerned more with overall patterns and will focus on fewer sequences of communication that seem to be often repeated.

■ 6. Should the counselor allow the couple to offer short messages or *long messages* before intervening?

Counselors who prefer to interrupt the couples frequently during a conversation are generally trying to influence the content or style of communication. I prefer to let the couple communicate for around two or three minutes before I intervene by identifying the pattern of communication and helping them change the fundamental power structure that is revealed by the pattern.

■ 7. How much intervention should occur during a session—multiple, frequent interventions covering a variety of points or *limited interventions reinforcing a few key points?*

Some counselors who intervene frequently will bombard the couple with changes that should be made. This is one mistake of inexperienced counselors. Experienced counselors usually have only three or four main points that they try to get across to the couple during a session. The counselor might interrupt the clients frequently but each interruption reinforces one of the main points rather than spreading the changes so thinly that the couple cannot benefit by them.

I intervene only infrequently, and have a limited number of main points to make each session. When I interrupt the couple and identify a pattern that needs changing, we work on that pattern for several minutes. We might observe the interaction on videotape (or listen to it on audiotape). Then we might discuss the interaction and what each was trying to accomplish and how his or her behavior made the other person feel. We might role play other ways of getting across points without hurting the person. I might also suggest a different way of behaving altogether that creates a different structure within the relationship.

■ 8. Should the counselor use *audiotape or videotape* or neither?

Some counselors believe that audiotaping or videotaping destroys the naturalness and spontaneity of the session and inhibits the clients. I find that clients do not stay inhibited very long. They appear to forget about the taping when they become involved in the session. A far greater threat to the spontaneity of the couple is the presence of the *counselor*. Couples simply do not argue or communicate in the same way in the presence of another person as they do when alone. For this reason, there are times when I leave the room during taping. I also use the taping to provide accurate feedback during communication training and to create a dramatic experience that the couple will remember, since few people are used to seeing themselves on videotape.

■ 9. What type of structure should the counselor provide in communication training—a reactive approach, a proactive approach or a *modular approach?*

Some counselors prefer to react spontaneously to couples as communication difficulties are revealed during a session. Other counselors are proactive, creating programs of communication that the couple moves through systematically. The proactive counselors tend to pursue the program of communication training despite the other events of the couple's life, whereas reactive counselors tend to instigate communication about the events of the couple's lives and then respond to the couple's communication rather than the content of the event. Still other counselors use a modular approach to communication training. Self-contained mini-programs are used but are not introduced until the couple exhibits a need for the intervention through their behavior during the session. I prefer the latter approach because of the flexibility it affords while allowing me the security of having preplanned interventions.

■ 10. How often is homework given—never, infrequently or *weekly*?

Some counselors limit their interventions to the counseling hour. They assume that if they make a change during the counseling session, the couple has learned the behavior and will practice it in their lives outside the counseling hour. This assumption is related to the belief that couples have communication difficulties because they do not have enough knowledge about good communication. I believe that the couple's patterns of behavior during their lives outside of counseling must be changed. Thus, homework is always given, and it is always discussed during the following session.

DANGERS IN COMMUNICATION TRAINING

Having made my share of mistakes in about fifteen years of counseling and supervising counselors, I am aware of many common errors made by counselors during communication training. I have included some of them below.

The couple enters counseling wanting immediate relief from their distress. Generally, they are well entrenched in their points of view, so when given the opportunity to discuss a controversial issue, they produce quite a spectacular disagreement. As the counselor observes the interaction, there is a strong pull to intervene and help the couple stop communicating destructively.

Intervening Too Early

Don't be provoked into helping the couple communicate less destructively or more constructively before the assessment is complete or before the couple is committed to counseling. They may not understand that their communication is destructive. Each thinks that he or she is fair but that the spouse is being unfair. If the counselor jumps in too early, trying to change *how* they communicate, they will misunderstand what is going on because they are involved in *what* is being communicated and who is correct.

The counselor must lay the groundwork carefully before attempting systematically to change the couple's communication. This does not mean that the counselor cannot intervene when necessary to stop destructive communication patterns. For example, in the first assessment interview the couple is asked to describe their opinions of their relationship problems. Some couples begin to argue instantly. To stop the argument, the counselor might *interrupt* destructive communication without *correcting* the communication prematurely. In such a case I might say:

> Hold it just a minute, George. I want to hear your side of it, but let's do this in an orderly way. Susan can give her view of the problem and then I'll not allow her to interrupt while you offer your view. It is important that I understand both of your perceptions without having you defend yourselves while you tell me. Does that sound fair?

When Pursuing Other Goals

Another frequent mistake is to be provoked into trying to change the couple's communication in the midst of a session aimed at accomplishing a different goal. Suppose you are trying to help a couple build intimacy through rearranging their time schedules to include more intimate activities. Suddenly, the husband strikes out in anger and the wife retorts harshly. It is easy to be provoked into offering a "lesson" in communication, which incidentally diverts the purpose of the session from attempts to build intimacy.

All counselors occasionally are diverted from their plan for the session. This is necessary to use the "teachable moment." However, if the therapist finds himself or herself frequently provoked by a couple, the therapist must reflect on whether the interruptions are preventing progress in counseling or preventing work on some particular aspect of the marriage.

Too Content-Oriented

When couples begin to discuss an issue about which they have disagreed for years, they lay out their arguments powerfully—sometimes logically, sometimes emotionally. Their presentation is usually compelling. Yet because they are at loggerheads, the therapist is struck by the futility of their pursuing their proposed solutions to their problems. This futility provokes the therapist to think of compromise solutions that would resolve the issue. Because many therapists are logical and skilled problem solvers, they arrive at some very original solutions.

Occasionally the therapist's ability to solve problems will break a dead-lock between spouses. However, more frequently, the therapist's overin-volvement in the content of the problem will not advance the couple's ability to solve other issues. Often, the result is simply a three-way power struggle among husband, wife and therapist over whose solution will be used.

I usually advise therapists to avoid offering a compromise solution. Rath-er, they might deal with a deadlocked issue as follows:

George, you claim that you must have a room for yourself to do all the work required of your job without staying at work late at night and on weekends. Susan, you claim that the spare room is needed for guests, especially your mother who visits regularly. You both feel that the only solution to this dilemma is your way. I know there are several solutions that would be acceptable to both of you, and I am sure that you will be able to come up with one or two—if not today, then soon. But I am more concerned in how *you are arguing with each other than in finding an agreeable solution. It seems almost like a life-or-death strug-gle, that if you don't get your way, it's divorce. What do you think would happen if you had to give in on this issue?*

Notice that the couple's concern over the importance of the issue is not minimized by directly considering their communication style. If anything, the importance of the problem is magnified. But the counselor is not pro-voked into offering compromises that might resolve the issue. It is more important to help the couple practice solving problems than to solve the problem. (Notice that I did not use the old adage that it is more important to *teach* them to fish than to *give* them a fish. George is a skilled labor negotiator and Susan is a social worker. Both know *how* to solve problems. They just aren't doing it with each other.)

Some counselors, especially inexperienced counselors, enter a counseling session clinging to a technique as though it were a lifeline to a space ship about which they were weightlessly floating. For instance, two clients, John and Marie, were particularly resistant. For five weeks they failed to complete their homework assignments. The cotherapists working with them tried reassigning the homework, discussing the reasons that prevented the homework from being done, repeating the assignment, planning with the

Inattention to the Client

couple when the assignment would be done, telling the couple that they had missed a crucial opportunity to solve their problems by not doing the homework. During my weekly supervision with the cotherapists, I planned a paradoxical directive that the cotherapists could use with their resistant clients during the upcoming session.

Confidently, the cotherapists entered the counseling session, only to find that the couple had done the week's homework completely and found it most helpful. Did that daunt the cotherapists from using the paradoxical directive? Not a chance. Enthusiastically, they reframed the couple's (now dubious) resistant behavior and delivered the paradox with a technical mastery that was admirable—especially considering that this was their first case of marriage counseling. We had rehearsed their behavior well during supervision. Unfortunately, though, the couple was completely baffled by the assignment. The confusion took two sessions to undo.

Shotguns Versus Rifles Couples talk about and act out thousands of destructive behaviors during each session. The counselor usually will not find a dearth of intervention points but will rather have to deal with a surfeit of intervention points. Effective counselors, whether they are largely reactive or proactive, will approach problems systematically like a rifle bullet piercing a target, rather than scattering their interventions like shot from a shotgun.

The difficulty usually shows up by having a counselor begin an intervention that should require several weeks to complete and then failing to carry through on the plans. A new plan is initiated at the next session. This generally indicates a lack of confidence in the program or intervention that the counselor is trying. Because of the incomplete application of the technique, the technique rarely works, which justifies the counselor in not following the plan to its completion.

TECHNIQUES FOR INCREASING THE COUPLE'S AWARENESS OF COMMUNICATION PROBLEMS

Only a few techniques can be described in one chapter on changing communication. Numerous sources describe programs of communication training more fully. Counselors should refer to complete descriptions of communication programs before applying their techniques with couples. In this chapter, techniques are organized according to those that increase awareness of problematic communication, break up old communication patterns and build new patterns.

One way to dramatize spouses' styles of communication and thus increase their awareness of their communication is to have them argue as if they were the partner. Sometimes I introduce the role reversal by saying:

Role Reversal

> You each say that you understand each other's position, but I don't see much evidence that you do. Let's see if you can convince me that you really understand your spouse. For a moment, pretend that you are your spouse. We'll have a discussion in which you argue as persuasively as possible for the position of your spouse on this issue. You should also argue in the same way as your spouse, using the same strategies of persuasion as he or she does. What do you think? Can you mimic your spouse?

Couples who become involved in this exercise paint caricatures of the spouse's communication style. When the role reversal is discussed, spouses object that "I'm not really that bad." Yet, usually, they can see enough of the truth in the caricatures that they become aware of what their behavior looks like to their spouse. Besides showing the counselor that the spouses do understand each other's position but are unwilling to agree to their demands, the role reversal makes the couple more tolerant of the other's position.

Stuart[14] has identified a way to help couples become aware of the differences and similarities in their decision-making authority. Couples list areas that require them to make decisions. Stuart usually begins with items on the Couple's Precounseling Inventory, which include sex, money, in-laws, child rearing and duties around the house. The couple adds areas of special interest to them. The list is refined by having couples classify each item as of primary, secondary or tertiary importance to their relationship. Usually Stuart limits the couple to five areas of primary importance. The areas of primary importance are lettered *A* through *E* on Figure 16a and 16b.

Stuart's Powergram

Each area is rated by both husband and wife according to who makes

Figure 16a
Stuart's Powergram: Present Decision-Making Pattern

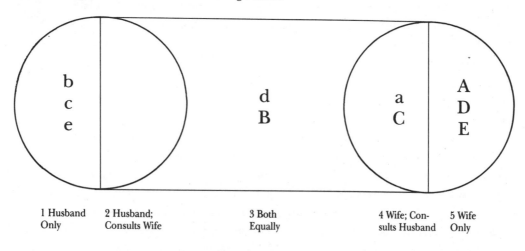

| 1 Husband Only | 2 Husband; Consults Wife | 3 Both Equally | 4 Wife; Consults Husband | 5 Wife Only |

Figure 16b
Stuart's Powergram: Desired Decision-Making Pattern

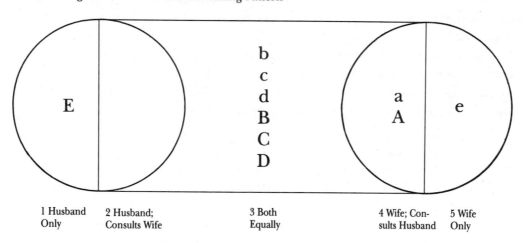

| 1 Husband Only | 2 Husband; Consults Wife | 3 Both Equally | 4 Wife; Consults Husband | 5 Wife Only |

Key to Fig. 16a-b
aA—Child Discipline
bB—How We Make Love
cC—When We Make Love
dD—How We Spend/Save Our Money
eE—Whether Toilet Paper Goes Flap Out or Under

Capital Letters—George
Small Letters—Susan

the decisions: (1) almost always the husband; (2) the husband, after consulting the wife; (3) both share equally; (4) the wife, after consulting the husband; (5) almost always the wife. Both spouses record their answers on the powergram divided into those five sections (see Figure 16a). The husband uses capital letters corresponding to the areas of primary importance and the wife uses small letters (or vice versa). An example is given in Figure 16.

George, represented by the capital letters, believes that Susan makes unilateral decisions about child rearing, finances and whether the toilet paper roll is placed flap out or flap under on the spindle. Susan agrees that she has most of the decision-making ability in child rearing but believes that financial decision making is shared. She also believes that George has unilateral decision-making power about the toilet paper. On the other hand, Susan believes that George is in charge of how and when they make love, while George believes they share decisions about how they make love and believes that Susan actually controls when they make love. George and Susan share different views of the power in their relationship and their arguments are long and loud.

The spouses then rate how they would like the decision making to be distributed by completing the bottom powergram (see Figure 16b). Spouses do not always want more power than they currently perceive themselves to have, nor do they necessarily want equal distribution of power. For example, ideally both George and Susan want to share decision making about how and when they make love and about their finances. Both want Susan to be primarily responsible for child discipline but to consult George. On the toilet paper issue, George wants control and so does Susan. Such is life.

The first part of the powergram reflects the frustration with the current situation, while the second part reflects the issues that are likely to be persistent problems because the couple is striving for different goals. The powergram provides a concrete and graphic way for couples to become aware of some of their differences and similarities.

Broderick[15] suggests that couples who have problems with sexual communication often have different ideas about their desired sexual experience.

Scripts

He has them write a detailed description of the "greatest sexual experience I could imagine." The "script" that each spouse creates can reveal different goals and can set the stage for changing those goals.

Metaphors

Often a couple can be made aware of their communication difficulties through the judicious use of metaphors. When some couples conflict, I have described their communication as conducting a bargaining session in two different languages: neither seems able to understand the other but is nonetheless undeterred in stating his or her own position. Another similar metaphor is to describe their bargaining as if they were conducting business using two foreign currencies.[16]

A third metaphor, though of a different type, is to use the physical space between the partners as a metaphor for their communication. For example, in one recent session Danny and Elizabeth disagreed over household duties. I directed them to discuss their positions with the other. After several interchanges, the discussion became heated. I stopped them and said:

It seems as if you are both firmly entrenched and immovable in your positions. My picture is that you are sitting back to back, each with your arms folded tightly across your chests and talking over your shoulder at your partner. In fact, why don't you assume that position right now? That's right, just turn the chairs around so that you aren't facing your spouse. Good. Now, resume your discussions.

After a couple of additional exchanges, I interrupted again:

I think I got something wrong in putting you in these positions.

Danny commented, "I'll say. It's hard to talk this way."

That's true. It is hard to talk that way, but what I got wrong is that you are still quite far apart on this issue. Move your chairs farther apart. No. Don't turn them back around. I haven't seen any evidence yet that you are less entrenched in your position and are ready to listen to each other.

Elizabeth said, "I think you have made your point."

You mean you are ready to listen more openly? Okay, Elizabeth, if you are ready to listen, you can adopt a position that shows what your attitude is.

Both Elizabeth and Danny turned their chairs facing each other.

So, you are willing to listen to each other. Good. Let's see whether you can get any closer together on this issue.

Awareness of poor communication patterns will not, by itself, change the couple's behavior. In fact, awareness of the differences in positions on various issues might discourage some couples who had maintained the fiction that they were really not far from each other's positions.

Once the couple is aware of their communication patterns, they might continue in them because of the principle of sin operating in their lives (see Rom 7). The pride, bitterness and anger might simply overpower any benevolent motives that they have. Some couples even use their awareness to coerce and weaken their spouses by "calling them" on their poor communication. The counselor who places the tool of awareness in the hands of a bitter couple *must explicitly point out the potential for abuse and define that as reprehensible.*

Awareness does produce some positive effects though. It prepares the couple for your intervention and makes them more willing to follow your suggestions because they see the extent of the problem. It also shows the couple what to pray for, unleashing prayer power on the problem. Awareness also makes the poor communication harder to continue because the communication pattern is explicit. Finally, depending on the counselor's emphasis, each spouse's attention can be focused on the poor behavior of the spouse or on his or her own poor communication. Obviously, the counselor wants to have each spouse become vigilant of personal behavior while being tolerant of the spouse's.

TECHNIQUES FOR BREAKING UP OLD PATTERNS OF COMMUNICATION

Because most people are raised in families and watch their parents behave, they develop expectations about how married couples should relate. Usually, people are not aware of their expectations. When expectations differ in ways that cause crossed communications, you can help the spouses identify their expectations. However, merely identifying each spouse's expectations does not mean that the spouse will change. In many cases, each person believes, "Now that he (or she) knows what I expect, he (or she) will change." If both spouses hold that belief, they could become more entrenched in their positions rather than less. To help break up the power of the conflicting expectations, the counselor can redefine them as demands. Instead of "She expects that taking care of the trash is a man's job," you can say:

> *It seems that she is demanding that taking out the trash is your job. Sharon, say to Will, 'I demand that you take out the trash. It is a man's job, and no one in his right mind could think otherwise.'*

By overstating the expectation and repeating the overstatement of the spouse's conflicting expectation, you help break up the implicit demand that there is only one way to do a task.

Another way to deal with expectations is to use a formula that was developed by William James[17] around the turn of the century.

$$\text{Happiness} = \frac{\text{Performance}}{\text{Expectation}}$$

I write the equation on a piece of paper and ask the couple whether they want to have a happy relationship. I then ask how they could make their happiness increase. The two ways apparent from James' equation are to increase performance and to decrease expectations. I then say:

> *When your expectation is that someone else does things the way you want, it is difficult to increase performance because you are dealing with someone else's performance and you don't have direct control over their performance. However, you do have direct control over your own expectations and your own performance. Work on the things you can control.*

Redefining the Situation
The Christian counselor holds a high view of people and at times tells that view to the couple. Often people are self-sacrificing, protective of each other, desiring to show love as they understand it, morally desiring to do what is right and fair; they are worthwhile (but fallen) people for whom God incarnate died.

Attributing to people positive motives that we know to be true helps break up sinful patterns of behavior. It prevents verbal resistance from the spouses, for few people will take issue when you describe their positive motives. Attributing positive motives to the spouses helps them become aware of the inconsistencies between their motives and their execution, which also breaks up hurtful communication. People usually do have positive motives. Of course, they simultaneously have some less altruistic motives.

By saying aloud their positive motives, you focus their attention on their goals of becoming more Christlike. Their difficulties are then defined as largely in their faulty execution of positive intentions, which can be changed and observed, rather than in their intentions, which are unobservable.

Even in the most vicious communications, the ultimate intent of both spouses is usually to restore harmony to the relationship. Their methods are usually faulty and will not accomplish their desired ends. Thus, when a spouse uses aversive control strategies such as intimidation, isolation, assault or punishment, the counselor should interrupt the sequence of behavior and say:

> *Maria, you seem hurt by Smitty's neglect and it makes you want to lash out. I can see that you care deeply about your relationship and are trying to avoid such neglect happening again, but your method of accomplishing your goal might cause even further resentment and neglect. Rather than use sarcastic humor in hope that you can change Smitty's mind, how about trying to describe the kind of relationship you'd like to have?*

The Pinch

The pinch model[18] is a simple model that can help couples interrupt destructive communication patterns. A pinch is defined as something that hurts . . . only a little. Usually, the pinch comes in the form of a mixed message or sarcastic or cutting humor. Sometimes it comes when a decision is made without consulting the spouse or when an expectation is violated. When a person is pinched, the person can do one of four things: (1) let it pass without acknowledgement; (2) say "ouch" and let it pass; (3) let it pass and then retaliate; or (4) talk about it. There is no one correct way to handle every pinch, though retaliation is an unbiblical way to handle anything. Occasional pinches happen in any relationship. What is to be avoided is the continual accumulation of pinches without acknowledgement, followed by a crunch in retaliation.

For many couples, the pinch strikes a responsive chord. They readily identify that they often pinch each other and that they do not acknowledge pinches until they have built up into a crunch. For many couples, long-standing patterns can be broken up merely by reminding each other that they have been pinched.

Use of Family History

Some people do not like the way that their parents interacted. Sometimes you can help them break up harmful patterns of interaction in their own marriages by showing them how they are repeating the patterns of their parents. Ask about the effects of their parents' behavior on the children and on each other. Then ask the person to speculate about the possible effects on their own relationship of doing the very things his or her parents did.

Others like the ways that their parents interacted and try to make their own marriages into copies of their parents' marriage. Spouses often object. Get the person to discuss the differences between his or her spouse and the parent of the same sex as the spouse. Ask about the differences between the person's parents' marriage and the person's own marriage.

In either instance, the parents' marriage can be characterized as governing the person's own marriage inappropriately.

The Card

Fred DiBlasio, who founded and directed Counseling Services of Richmond (Virginia), which operated out of a local church, has created a technique for breaking up hurtful communication patterns.[19] Fred has couples copy 1 Cor 13:4-7 onto an index card:

> Love is patient and kind; love is not jealous or boastful; it is not arrogant or rude. Love does not insist on its own way; it is not irritable or resentful; it does not rejoice at wrong, but rejoices in the right. Love bears all things, believes all things, hopes all things, endures all things.

Couples may be directed to read their cards to each other each morning at breakfast, each night before bed or at any time that one spouse desires to hear it read. In the latter case, the couple is directed to treat the request to hear his card read as a benevolent, loving request rather than as a punitive statement. If the spouse has responded positively to requests throughout the day, Fred has the spouse's partner give the spouse a back or head massage for ten minutes before bed.

Mind reading is assuming that you know what your spouse wants. All couples mind read, both good and poor communicators.[20] Mind reading can be an efficient timesaver or a coercive behavior-control strategy. The tone and context of the mind reading determine its function.

One way to break up old patterns, especially if the couple uses mind reading destructively, is to question mind-reading statements. Ask, "How do you know she wants you to come home directly after work?" Or, "Why do you think she likes to have you initiate lovemaking?" By questioning long-standing assumptions, you sometimes shake the couple's confidence in their knowledge of their spouse's likes and dislikes and make them more receptive to interventions that change their communication.

Questioning Mind Reading

A common impasse can be handled by asking both spouses to identify their dark fantasies.[21] For instance I might say:

What do you think would happen if you did not continually remind Gil of his responsibilities around the house?

What is preventing you from stopping your nagging if you really believe that you "shouldn't" nag? Are you afraid something will happen?

Other impasses might be broken by changing *your own* behavior. For example, if treatment has been totally conjoint and the couple has stopped progressing, try a session with each spouse individually. Often you can suggest that spouses try to exhibit their own understanding of each other's positions without giving any ground on their own positions.

If a session comes to a standstill, change *your* behavior, perhaps drastically. For example, if you have been having a couple talk to each other, launch into a two-minute soliloquy. If the atmosphere is emotionally loaded and tense, shift the topic to some less controversial area. If no one has changed physical positions since the beginning of the hour, direct the couple to move to some different physical arrangement.

Sometimes impasses develop because a spouse harbors questions or criticisms of the treatment you are using. Address the issue head-on:

It seems as though you are reluctant to participate in these exercises. Would you like to share your thoughts about what we are doing in counseling?

Perhaps the couple will complain that the exercises seem "contrived" or "unnatural." Answer that they *are* unnatural—the way a splint is unnatural,

Dealing with Objections and Impasses

although it is necessary to heal a broken leg.

A client might complain that his or her spouse is *merely* following your instructions rather than acting out of love. Answer that your instructions merely make explicit what the spouse wants to do, saying that the spouse is not your slave and does what you suggest only because he or she wants to. Whatever the objection, treat it with seriousness and try to provide a logical answer. If none comes to mind, say:

I know that it doesn't seem like this will have any effect on your marriage, but my experience has shown that it often helps if couples give it a fair chance with an open mind. Let me ask you to continue to work with me and take an attitude that we will wait and see whether this works with you. If not, we will try something else.

One spouse might say, "Why should I continue to pretend that I love him? I don't feel anything for him—neither love nor hate." You might answer:

How do you think you learned to handle pain—by getting numb to all of your feelings?

This might break a deadlock and could channel counseling in a different direction, sidetracking the resistance.

TECHNIQUES FOR BUILDING NEW PATTERNS OF COMMUNICATION

Prepared Programs

Numerous programs have been created and tested that help couples build communication. The counselor can select from programs that offer the training desired. Among the more common programs are the following:

■ *Minnesota Couples Communication Program (MCCP).*[22] This program is primarily concerned with helping couples become aware of the rules that govern their communication and with building communication skills that promote receptivity and self-esteem of the partners. Although the MCCP is generally used within a marriage-enrichment format with groups of couples, it can be adapted easily for individual couples.

■ *Marital Effectiveness Training (MET).*[23] Based on Carl Rogers' nondirective therapy, MET stresses nonjudgmental listening and responding and no-lose negotiation.

■ *Carkhuff's helping skills.*[24] Based on work by Robert Carkhuff in teaching listening and counseling to lay and professional helpers, Pierce's adaptation shows how to apply Carkhuff's principles to deteriorating marriages. The twenty-five hours of training, used in a group format, make the program unwieldy for short-term marriage counseling, but it is adaptable.

■ *Gottman's communication training.*[25] A simple training package has been developed for use by individual couples. Gottman et al., concentrated on five skills: (a) listening and validating; (b) leveling, or sharing true feelings while avoiding harmful communications; (c) editing, or controlling the tendency to argue pointlessly; (d) negotiating agreements; and (e) dealing with hidden agendas.

■ *Jacobson and Margolin's Problem Solving Training (PST).*[26] A manual specifying each step of the training is given in their book. The guidelines are divided into identifying and then solving the problem.

■ *Liberman et al.*[27] Training focuses on becoming aware of how positive communication begets positive communication, and negative communication begets negative communication. The second part of the training trains the couple in how to handle feelings constructively, and it introduces the executive session, which is a formal exercise involving summarizing each message until the couple is sure that they understand the message.

■ *Stuart's five-step model.*[28] Couples are trained in (a) the ability to listen; (b) self-expression; (c) constructive request making; (d) selective, specific and timely feedback; and (e) clarification.

■ *Guerney's Relationship Enhancement (RE).*[29] Communication training involves practice in the apparently simple skills of (a) expressing whatever is important to the expresser; (b) responding, which means helping the expresser achieve a clear statement of his or her experience without letting one's own thoughts, feelings or values interfere with understanding the speaker's message; and (c) requesting a mode change from expresser to responder or vice versa. RE has been found to be surprisingly effective when compared with other communications training programs.[30]

Whatever programs are used, they should fit your style and objectives and your clients' goals. The interventions should be selected because they are consistent with your answers to the questions posed at the beginning of the chapter.

The Marriage Conference

In Wright's book, Raymond Corsini described a technique that promotes understanding between spouses.[31] He stresses that the technique be precisely applied both by counselors and clients to insure maximum results. I will briefly describe the technique but will encourage the counselor who intends to apply it to read the account of the marriage conference in Wright's book and follow it exactly.

First, the couple is told authoritatively that they must follow the procedure without deviation or else they must begin again. If they fail to follow directions after that, they are told that they will be referred to a new counselor.

The couple must schedule four one-hour appointments with each other. The appointments are to have priority over any other activity except a physical emergency. Each person is to arrive promptly at the given place without consulting the other partner. If the partner does not appear or is late, the first partner begins promptly and acts exactly as if the other partner were present. If the other partner arrives late, the first partner should continue with what is being done without acknowledging the arrival of the late spouse.

The wife begins the first and third sessions; the husband begins the second and fourth. A session consists of the initial talker having the floor for precisely thirty minutes. He or she can do whatever is desired—talk or be silent. The listener must listen neutrally, without making verbal or nonverbal acknowledgement of what is said or done. Grimaces, expressions of surprise or disagreement and interruptions of any kind are forbidden. The talker may ask the listener to turn his or her back if desired.

After thirty minutes, the roles are reversed and the same rules are followed for the second thirty minutes. The couple cannot mutually agree to end a session before the full hour has elapsed, regardless of what is said or not said.

Importantly, spouses should not discuss anything that was brought up during the marriage conference except at one of the other marriage conference sessions or during a counseling session. If the couple has difficulty scheduling a session, the counselor can offer to let them use his or her office during the regularly scheduled counseling session—at full fee, of course.

The marriage conference is thought to be effective because it gives more influential power to the counselor, which strengthens him or her for other interventions. It is also thought to give the couple a time in which they can be heard without arguing, since the couple is instructed not to discuss the controversial subjects between marriage conference sessions.

In practice, not every couple is willing to participate in this assignment. Some simply refuse to carry it out correctly or at all. Others complain that it is a worthless use of time. About half, however, seem to benefit from it, and some benefit greatly.

Feelings run high in marriage counseling. Feelings are complex and usually mixed. Ambivalence occurs throughout marriage counseling because troubled marriages are potentially intimate, loving relationships which are marred by pain and hurt. Christians are admonished to speak the truth *in love* in order to build up the body of Christians (Eph 4:15), not just to speak the truth. Christian couples must practice this admonition.

Handling Feelings

Crabb identifies three things that people can do about their feelings: stuff, dump or deal with them.[32] It is just as wrong to stuff feelings inside, shielding one's spouse from the truth, as it is to dump negative feelings on the spouse, showering him or her with hate, hurt and anger.

The counselor must judge the proper amount of expression of feelings to encourage at each point of counseling. There are times when spouses need to know how hurt they each are by their partner's behavior. At other times expression of hurt can sidetrack counseling and undo the gains that have been won over many weeks.

Crabb gives five guidelines for handling anger that I often share with couples.[33]

1. *Be slow to anger.*

2. *Acknowledge anger.* Guard against unbridled expression of anger, but do not pretend anger doesn't exist.

3. *Think through goals.* Usually people become angry when their goals are blocked. Christians should relabel goals that are able to be blocked by spouses as desires rather than needs and then reaffirm their commitment to meet their spouse's needs rather than seek fulfillment of their own.

4. *Assume responsibility for the proper goal.* Determine how to minister to one's spouse.

5. *Express negative feelings if doing so serves a good purpose.* Beware of the tendency to justify oneself. Recall that I usually have couples read Crabb's book as a guide to intimacy. If the couple has read the book, I can simply refer them to the section and read it aloud from my book at my office. If the couple has not read the book, I spend more time explaining each of Crabb's points.

To help control the expression of negative feelings, I often set an agenda with couples about the topics of ensuing counseling sessions. For example, I might say that in the following session we will discuss their disagreements over who will clean the basement and in the session following that, their disagreements over their sexual life.

After we agree on our agenda, I ask the couple not to discuss those issues until we talk about them during counseling. I do this for two reasons. First, it insures that we will have dramatic, memorable sessions together. Second, it also helps the couple be happier between sessions because they both know that they will not be involved in the usual anger-producing arguments.

Couples will often have a "mini-crisis" just prior to a session that promises to be emotional. I try to get the couple to agree to not deal with the crisis, interpreting it as a safe way to avoid dealing with the important issue that they had planned to discuss. I express my understanding that by discussing the emotional issue, they are both taking a large risk because the discussion might not come out exactly to their liking. I offer support and encourage them to be courageous in this matter, as they have been throughout counseling.

During the session, I judge the capacity and need for expression of feeling, probing for additional feeling if I think one spouse is stuffing feelings and interrupting their discussion if the expression of feeling becomes too great or too unkind. If some resolution is reached during the session, the couple must discuss the decision and reflect on how they arrived at the solution. I call their attention to ways they handled their feelings, showing them that they can control their feelings and use them as information rather than as coercive strategies. Often I employ the videotape (or audiotape) if a particularly dramatic event occurred during the session.

Near the end of communication training, I try to solidify the gains the couple has made by giving them a copy of principles of relationship change that Stuart has compiled.[34] Stuart organized the principles into three sections:

☐ 1. Understanding Relationships
☐ 2. Changing Relationships
☐ 3. Understanding and Changing Communication

I generally give couples a copy of the second and third sections. I omit the first section because it does not contribute to the couple's understanding (rather, it is aimed at understanding the philosophy behind behavioral programs). Stuart's principles summarize many ideas that we have worked on throughout counseling.

Stuart's Principles of Relationship Change

SUMMARY

Communication training is so diverse as to be meaningless as a label. Rather, each counselor must make numerous decisions about the style and intent of the training in communication that he or she provides. My preference is to direct couples to talk for a few minutes and then process that communication in detail using videotape or audiotape. I strive to make a few main points each session. Homework is considered very important to insuring that couples actually change their communication patterns.

To help couples change, three types of interventions must be made. The counselor must help couples become aware of the destructive effect of their present communication patterns, then break up the current patterns of destructive behavior and finally create new patterns of communication.

Communication training is understood to be a way to break up and form new patterns, rather than to teach new behaviors. I believe that most people know how they *should* communicate. They just don't communicate well with their spouses. If communication training were primarily a teaching tool, then marriage counselors (who know good communication techniques) would be expected never to have problems with their spouses. Anyone who knows many marriage counselors, knows that this is not true. Counselors know how to communicate within marriage, but many still use poor communication patterns with their own spouses. Rather, communication patterns evolve over time, sometimes in spite of one's knowledge. Only intervention by an outside source seems able to break the patterns. Jesus is an outside source, as are we, his ministers.

Changing Conflict

C OUPLES IN CONFLICT USUALLY GOT THAT WAY OVER TIME BY passing through four stages. Initial differences between spouses were addressed by efforts at *persuasion.* Over time attempts at persuasion were intensified until the power to define the relationship began to be contested. The couple was in fundamental disagreement over who had the power to make decisions and who had the power to say what the solutions were to problems. This second stage involves a disagreement over the *pragmatics* of communication, the effects communications have on the definition of the relationship.

Specific issues seem to trigger fights constantly, and in the third stage the couple begins to use *power strategies* with each other. Strategies might be one-up strategies that use overtly powerful tactics to win arguments or one-down strategies that are played to interfere with the partner's victory or to hurt the partner in retaliation.[1]

The highly visible and emotion-arousing power strategies, when continued long enough, give way to a definition of the problem as being due to the *personalities* of the spouses (stage 4). Core personality issues are blamed as the problem. For example, the problem might be defined as the one spouse's lack of trust and the other's lack of trustworthiness.

The importance of the causes of conflict is almost the reverse of the order in which the causes developed. The causes may be imagined as a tree. *The leaves represent the problem's description in terms of core personality issues.* They are visible to everyone, especially to the couple. Still above ground, but hidden to some extent by the leaves, is the trunk. *The trunk represents the visible and sometimes vicious power strategies that each spouse uses.* Not visible to the couple, nor to casual observers, are the roots. *The roots represent the fundamental disagreement between spouses over relationship definition.*

HOW TO CHANGE CONFLICT

The counselor's job is to uproot the tree of conflict. One way to accomplish the objective is first to cut off the leaves, then to saw the branches off, then to chop the tree down at the ground and finally to dig up the stump, roots and all. A more direct way would be simply to blast the roots while the tree was intact. In counseling, neither of these strategies works very well.

The leaves, core personality issues, are impossible to address *first* because they are inferences from the spouses' behaviors. For example, if trust and trustworthiness are the main issues, they can only be determined by observing a person's behavior.

Because each of these personality constructs is inferred based on a lot of behavior, the couple will rarely stay in counseling long enough for the personality attributes to be changed and for the spouses to acknowledge the changes. If the counselor sets the restructuring of personality traits as the goal of counseling, the counseling is doomed from the start unless the clients agree to very long-term therapy.

On the other hand, the pragmatics of communication (fundamental disagreement about relationship definition) are also difficult to address because they too are inferences made after many interactions and decisions.

In addition, if you point out that the couple is having a power struggle, either (a) they will disagree hotly and insist that they merely are "discussing issues" or (b) your observation will crystallize and harden the power struggle over who can control the relationship into one that is even more difficult to break.[2]

I attempt to work on the three levels simultaneously while avoiding the pitfalls of working explicitly on the first and third levels. The problem is described to the couple as "resolving disagreements," "discussing issues," "solving problems" or "conflict resolution."

If one person tries to define the issue as a personality problem in the spouse, I explain that he or she might be correct but we could never determine whether the spouse had changed his or her personality. If the person persists, I ask, "How would you know that your spouse had become trustworthy (or whatever the problem was)? What exactly would he (or she) have to do to convince you of his (or her) having changed?" If the person answers, that can become a focus of treatment—balanced by a change demanded by the spouse.

Treatment is issue-oriented but is aimed not only at solving the disagreement but also at breaking up old problem-solving patterns and establishing new ones so that the couple can resolve future issues as well. This involves couching your feedback to the couple in terms of whether it contributes to resolution of disagreements. Treatment focuses on inhibiting power strategies and freeing the couple to interact more productively. Feedback about behavior is said to help the couple resolve their differences. Almost all conflict-management programs are structured similarly—de-emphasizing personality difficulties and overt power struggles and emphasizing conflict resolution.

Changing conflict patterns involves the same three components as changing intimacy or communication: (1) helping couples become aware of whatever prevents them from resolving their problems; (2) breaking up old patterns; and (3) building new patterns. Numerous techniques have been developed to accomplish each objective. An example will be given that illustrates a typical session that focuses on conflict management. A discussion of the session will be followed by a brief catalog of additional techniques.

AN EXAMPLE: RUDY AND MAE ROBBINS

Rudy and Mae had been married for thirteen years when they sought counseling. Counseling was precipitated when Marta, their eleven-year-old daughter, entered middle school and began to have problems with her teachers. Three sessions of family therapy convinced me that Marta's difficulties were greatly exascerbated—if not caused—by her worries over whether her parents were going to divorce. They had argued periodically for about seven years, but within the last year, the arguments had become frequent, loud and acrimonious. On several occasions Rudy had stormed out of the house after an argument and Mae had cried for hours. Marta attributed her rebelliousness in school to lack of attention at home. When questioned, she described the state of her parents' marriage. Rudy and Mae admitted that they had considered divorce, and they wondered whether their differences were irreconcilable. I helped them form a plan for how to help Marta through setting new limits appropriate to her new middle school status and through giving her additional attention. Marta as well as Rudy and Mae seemed relieved when I suggested that they might best help Marta through marriage counseling.

Assessment revealed few surprises. Rudy and Mae spent almost no intimate time together. Neither claimed to care much about having sex with each other or with anyone else. Further questioning revealed that they had considered themselves to have a good sexual relationship until about six years ago. They traced the difficulties to the time when Marta entered school and Mae took a job as a school counselor. Rudy blamed the problem on Mae's nightly workload. Mae blamed the problem on Rudy's making demands for sexual behavior that had not been part of their early marriage, specifically demands for oral sex.

Over the years, conflict had spread until they said, "We argue about everything." They often argued about recreation, Mae's involvement in her work, Rudy's "lack of ambition," and Mae's "coldness." Both were involved in church activities. Rudy was a deacon in a large congregation while Mae attended two midweek Bible studies.

We set several goals for counseling: to resolve some of their differences, to decrease the arguments and to increase their intimate time together—

though both stated explicitly that they doubted whether they would ever have any interest in sex again. We agreed on twelve sessions initially.

I observed that Rudy was an emotional person, given to spontaneity and rash statements. Mae was controlled and not often emotionally expressive, though she clearly felt deep emotion and disappointment in her marriage. I attributed their problems as due primarily to conflict, brought on by an unsatisfactory adjustment to two simultaneous life transitions six years ago.

Because recreation was a topic of conflict, I planned to approach that topic first. The first treatment session began with a question about how Rudy's and Mae's weeks had gone. They brought up an argument that had occurred prior to their leaving for work that morning, mentioning that it was not resolved and that each was still angry with the other.

My assessment was that the Robbinses needed to test my ability to handle their conflictual styles before they could trust me with more emotionally loaded issues such as their personality differences or their sexual lives. Because my initial goals were to gain their trust and to help them change their styles of conflict, I discussed their conflict even though I knew it to be transient.

1 Counselor: *So you had an argument this morning. Where were you when the argument started?*

2 Rudy: *Sitting at the kitchen table . . .*

3 Mae: (Interrupting and talking over Rudy) *I spilled my coffee and he gave me "the look." That set us off.*

4 Rudy: *. . . she starts in on me because she* gets frustrated.

5 Counselor: *Hold it. I can only hear one of you at a time. It would be easiest for me if you could re-enact what happened. Then I could see "the look" and tell how things developed. Look, this testing table is the kitchen table.* (Gets up and pulls it into the center of the room.) *Move your chairs up to the table the way they were this morning. I'll move back out of the way. Good. Now, here are some paper cups that can be your coffee cups. Okay? Good. Now what happened?*

6 Mae: *Well, I was reaching for the sweetener . . .*

7 Counselor: *Wait. Don't tell me. Show me. Just pretend that I'm not here.*

8 Mae: (Reaches across and knocks Rudy's cup over with her elbow) *I'm sorry . . .*

9 Rudy: (Jumping back from the table and brushing his lap) *Now look what you've done. You soaked my suit.*

10 Mae: *Wait a minute. That's not what he did. He swore at me.*

11 Rudy: *Yeah, but Dr. Worthington doesn't want us to . . .*

12 Mae: *But it makes me look terrible if you don't because that's part of what I got mad at.*

13 Counselor: *I'm sorry. I apologize. I didn't really make it clear what I wanted. I do want you to act, as nearly as you can remember, the way you did this morning. But I also want you to keep on with the pretending until I stop you, even if the other person does something that you disagree with. After we finish, we will talk about how things might have been different. Ideally, though, you should be thinking about what you did rather than what the other person did. Okay, start again.*

14 Mae: *I'm sorry . . .*

15 Rudy: *Damn! Now look what you've done. You soaked my damn suit. Don't you ever pay attention to what you're doing?*

16 Mae: *I pay attention just as well as you, and I don't appreciate it when you swear at me. Can't you ever control yourself?*

17 Rudy: *You've got your head always up in the clouds somewhere. Now you've made me late for work, 'cause I'll have to change the whole suit.*

18 Mae: *I said I'm sorry. What do you want from me, begging for forgiveness on my knees?*

19 Rudy: *That would be the day!*

20 Mae: *I didn't hear any apology coming from you for swearing at me.*

21 Rudy: *I don't need to apologize. I can talk anyway I want in my own house. If you don't like it, just stick your fingers in your ears.*

22 Mae: *That's unfair.*

23 Rudy: *Tough. I have to change clothes because you soaked me with your space-cadet act. Why don't you go on to work? We can get this ironed out at counseling today.*

24 Mae: *All right. Four o'clock, remember.*

25 Rudy: *Don't tell me to remember. You're the one that forgets things all the time.*

26 Counselor: *Was that the end of it?*

27 Rudy: *Yes. She's always doing things like spilling the coffee. It's the way she is.*

28 Counselor: *So from your point of view she's inattentive and sometimes that inconveniences you. And her too. I guess the thing that I saw in that little vignette was how hard it was for the two of you to determine what you were arguing about. It looked all action-reaction to me, as if someone had choreographed an intricate dance between two people who knew their steps and reacted instinctively.*

29 Mae: *You're right, Dr. Worthington, he's always that way—interrupting and flying off the handle. Also, he didn't really do it exactly right. For instance, his "look" is absolutely obnoxious and provocative.*

30 Counselor: *Suppose we do it again, then, and you can show me how he acts. Let's change things. You pretend to be him and he can pretend to be you.*

31 Rudy: *You mean I get to be the ice queen?*

32 Counselor: *This will give you each a chance to show some of the things that might have been left out of the earlier vignette.*

33 Rudy: (Picks up the coffee cups and rights them) *Let's do it.* (Looks up, rolling his eyes around and, with eyes on the ceiling, finally manages to knock over Mae's coffee cup) *Oh, I am dreadfully sorry* (said with a British accent).

34 Mae: (Glares silently for about thirty seconds, then jumps back so vigorously she knocks over the chair) *Damn!* (She shouts this.) *You knocked over my coffee, you stupid, clumsy space cadet. Can't you ever do anything right?*

35 Rudy: *I'm not that bad. I don't yell and call her names like that.*

36 Mae: *What's the matter? You can dish it out. Can't you take it?*

37 Rudy: *Huh!* (Folds his hands primly in his lap and answers with restraint) *I do pay attention. I don't like it when you swear at me.*

The vignette continued until the end with both Rudy and Mae using exaggerated nonverbal behaviors to caricature each other. At the end of the interaction, I asked what they each thought of their spouses' performance.

38 Rudy: *Well, I thought it was a bit overdrawn, but it was funny too. I wouldn't have thought Mae had it in her to act that uninhibited. I kind of enjoyed it.*

39 Mae: *I enjoyed it too. I admit that I did overdo some of it.*

40 Rudy: *I don't call you all those names.*

41 Mae: *That's right, but that's how it makes me feel.*

42 Counselor: *Mae, do you mean that it hurts when Rudy and you argue?*

43 Mae: *It makes me feel so inadequate, as if I can't do anything right and all of our problems are my fault. So, I strike back to defend myself.*

44 Counselor: *Rudy, how does it feel to know that you have the power to make your wife feel inadequate?*

45 Rudy: *A little like a bully, I guess. But she doesn't act very helpless. She's got a tongue on her too. She never lets me see that anything bothers her. All I see is that nothing seems to affect her.*

46 Counselor: *Mae, it sounds as if you have quite an ability to provoke Rudy too.*

47 Mae: *I don't try to. I can't help it if I don't wear my emotions for everyone to see. I feel them.*

Talk continued for several more minutes about the impact that each was having on the other. Both agreed that they could get to the other person, even though they did not intentionally attempt to make the other person angry. After a while, I summarized.

48 Counselor: *You each try to communicate with the other. I find it hard to believe that either of you wishes to start an argument. You each seem distressed when a fight occurs, regardless of who started it or who might "win" it. I believe that we have a lot of good resources to work with in your marriage. You are both still emotionally involved with each other, still trying to resolve the issues between you, still trying to make things better. It just seems that you are going about things in ways that seem to create pain instead of making things better. You are still responsive to each other too. When you fight, you respond to some of the negative things that are said and done, but at least you are still responding. That encourages me, because it means that if we can get you doing things differently perhaps things will grow progressively more positive instead of negative. What do you think?*

49 Mae: *I'm glad you see some positive in our relationship. I have about lost all hope.*

50 Rudy: *Where do we go from here?*

51 Counselor: *Let's stick with this little incident that happened this morning. Tell me, what do you see in that interaction that you personally did that contributed to the fight instead of to resolving the issue? Rudy, how about you?*

52 Rudy: *Well, if Mae hadn't . . .*

53 Counselor: *Hold it. Mae is going to tell me what she did. I want you to take the hard way and tell me what you did that got things going negatively.*

54 Rudy: *That is tougher. Mae always complains that I stare at her.*

55 Counselor: *Do you think that your stare contributes to a negative interaction?*

56 Rudy: *I guess it does because it bothers her, but I don't do it just to annoy her. I was just thinking. I wasn't staring at all.*

57 Mae: *He was too staring.*

58 Counselor: *Hold it, Mae. This is Rudy's turn. I'll give you the chance to tell about yourself in a minute.*

59 Rudy: *I guess my eyes were staring but I wasn't staring. Does that make any sense?*

60 Counselor: *Let me see if I understand. You were not intentionally trying to provoke Mae with your stare even though you are aware that you looked like you were staring to her.*

61 Rudy: *That's it.*

62 Counselor: *You said that you realize that even though your stare was unintentional, it still was part of what started the argument.*

63 Rudy: *That's right.*

64 Counselor: *Suppose that you knew that it was really important that you not stare like that—unintentionally or intentionally. Could you turn your eyes away?*

65 Rudy: *I guess I could.*

66 Counselor: *Mae, suppose you were to spill coffee on Rudy's lap right now. If he turned his eyes away from you, would you interpret it as his trying hard to avoid a fight?*

67 Mae: *I guess so.*

68 Counselor: *After you apologized for spilling the coffee, could you tell him how much you appreciated his trying to make your relationship better?*

69 Mae: *Yes.*

70 Counselor: *Good. Now Mae, what was one thing that you did that contributed to starting the argument?*

71 Mae: *I guess if I hadn't criticized him for his swearing, things wouldn't have gotten so out of hand. I know he reacts more emotionally than I do, so I guess I should be more tolerant of him.*

72 Counselor: *In fact, during the assessment sessions, you mentioned that that was why you initially were attracted to Rudy—his emotional expression.*

73 Mae: *I know, but it's not the same when he swears at me.*

74 Counselor: *Yet, you see that by criticizing him for swearing, the simple issue of spilled coffee became a battle over what each of you considers to be the other's faults.*

75 Mae: *I know that I could keep from saying anything critical but I would probably still* think *things that are critical.*

76 Counselor: *True. You might think something critical. But you might just as well think something like, "That's my Rudy. Still the same spontaneous guy I married."*

77 Mae: *I guess I could be thinking something like that.*

78 Counselor: *Good. Now, here's what I want you to do. I want you to replay the incident again. One more time. But this time I want you to pretend that you, Rudy, had not stared at Mae and that you, Mae, had not criticized Rudy for swearing. Now I know that this will seem exceedingly dull after the fireworks of earlier, but I want you to go through the motions anyway. That's one thing that is always a concern when a couple that is used to lots of fireworks begins to get their marriage back together: they have to cope with the loss of all that excitement. Are you ready for that trauma?*

79 Rudy: *Gimme that dull, boring love any day.*

Rudy and Mae acted out the incident again without provoking the other. The performance was lackluster and uninspired, but both assured me again that if such a result could be achieved in a spontaneous interaction, they would be satisfied with it.

In the last part of the hour, we established a tentative agenda for issues that we would address in future sessions. We agreed to discuss the differences in recreational preferences during the second intervention session. I knew that both Rudy and Mae were avid readers, so I assigned them to buy and read the entire book *Getting To Yes* before the following session.[3]

This differed from my usual first assignment in that I assigned the entire book rather than the first chapter, and I assigned them to read the book individually rather than read the first chapter aloud together. I avoided the reading-aloud assignment because the couple was more involved in conflict rather than in avoiding intimacy.

By the second session, both had completed reading the book. I reviewed the main thesis of the book and asked for their reactions.

80 Counselor: *Let me summarize briefly. The way I read the book, Fisher and Ury's thesis is that people fail to reach agreement during their disagreements because they stake out positions and then defend the positions. Fisher and Ury recommend that couples identify their interests behind the positions they take. Then, a solution is sought that will satisfy the interests of both spouses without either spouse having to compromise or give in. I guess they might agree with the quote I picked up somewhere from James Russell Lowell, "Compromise makes a good umbrella but a poor roof." What do you think of the general ideas in the book?*

81 Rudy: *I thought it was great! I even used the principles at work once on Thursday to help solve a little dispute between two of the guys I work with.*

82 Mae: *I thought it sounded good in theory, but I wasn't so sure how it would work out in practice. It sounds like it needs a negotiator to make it work well.*

83 Counselor: *I don't know how it will work for you. Frankly, I don't believe there is any quick cure for your relationship unless the Lord miraculously intervenes. But, I have seen this method used by a number of couples, some with conflicts as bad or worse than yours. But we will never know for sure whether it will work for you unless we try it.*

Today, we decided to discuss your differences on how you use your recreational time. Why don't we start by having each of you state what the problem is as you see it.

84 Rudy: *The way I see the problem is that Mae never wants to do anything that is fun. All she wants to do is stay at home and waste time or read. Now I like to read, but I resent using the little time we have together by doing things so self-indulgent. It fits with her whole personality the way I see it. She is just too reserved and emotionally dead.*

85 Mae: *That's not it at all. I am not emotionally dead. The problem is that he's so energetic that he likes to go out and burn those calories off. I like to have some time to myself to think. And mainly, I don't like it when he tries to run my life. I work hard, probably harder than he. When I get off, I want to relax. I don't call running off here and there—boating, bowling, softball— as being relaxing for me. I resent it.*

86 Counselor: *Now you each have stated your perception of the problem in which*

you blame the other person. Rudy, you resent Mae for not spending time with you. Suppose that for just a minute, you stay away from the reasons why you think the problem exists and see if either of you can make a totally neutral and impartial statement of the problem.

87 Mae: *The problem is that we both want our own way and we can't have it.*

88 Counselor: *That's an interesting statement. Fisher and Ury might disagree that you could not have your ways. But put that aside for a while. You identified the problem at a little deeper level than I would like. How about a summary of the issue?*

89 Rudy: *We need to find a way to use our free time without arguing that will still allow us to feel satisfied.*

90 Counselor: *Good! We have a statement of the problem. Do you agree with that statement, Mae?*

91 Mae: *I agree with the problem. I just don't think there is any solution.*

92 Counselor: *Agreeing with the problem is a big first step. This is really the first time I have seen you agree on what the problem is to solve. In all the other discussions you've had, you have each argued totally from your own points of view and not acknowledged a common problem. The second step is to identify your interests. But I want you to do something different. You have been married a long time. You probably know each other very well. I want you to make a list of the interests that your partner has in achieving the position he or she is advocating. Can you do that? Can you make the list so accurate that if I didn't know any better I would say that the spouse had actually made the list?*

Rudy and Mae agreed to make a list of interests for the other. Both lists were well thought out. I asked them to look at the list that the spouse had created and add a few additional interests that might have been omitted. Rudy added two, Mae added three (see Table 6). Each was asked to identify his or her primary interest. Rudy said that his main interest was to be with Mae. Mae said her main consideration was not to feel dominated by Rudy.

93 Counselor: *You have both done an excellent job. I am convinced that you really do understand each other. Until now, you have simply been more concerned with meeting your own needs than with meeting your spouse's— at least for the last few years. That probably has not always been true.*

94 Rudy: *You're right. We used to run around looking for ways to please each*

Table 6
Rudy's and Mae's Interests behind Their Conflict over Use of Recreational Time

Mae's Interests	Rudy's Interests
1. Not to feel dominated	1. To exert physically, preferably if competition is involved
2. To relax	
3. To get enjoyment of reading	2. To relax through doing something that is totally different from office work
4. To be alone	
*5. To avoid physical exertion	3. To socialize, to joke, to laugh
*6. To get respect from Rudy	4. To provide an arena where spontaneity is rewarded
*7. To not argue	
	5. To feel like a man
	*6. To sweat
	*7. To be with Mae

*Added by the person whose interests were being described. Others were written by the person's spouse.

other. Now it seems like we sometimes run around looking for ways to irritate each other.

95 Counselor: *The tough part is whether you can exercise your objectivity and your good problem-solving ability to come up with several ways that both of your interests can be met.*

96 Mae: *Several ways? We can't even come up with one way.*

97 Counselor: *Suppose I said that I would give you a million dollars if you could come up with five ways that had not been thought of before that would satisfy the interests of two hypothetical people. Do you really think that you couldn't do it?*

98 Mae: *Well, I guess I could under those circumstances.*

99 Rudy: *That's a very generous offer, Dr. Worthington. Could we have our million in used hundred-dollar bills?*

100 Counselor: *Yes, but I may have to raise my fees. Look, it's good to laugh about it. Do you think you could think up some good solutions? Remember, just because you think of a solution doesn't commit you to doing it.*

101 Mae: *I think we can do it.*

In fact, the Robbinses could not think of five solutions before the end of the counseling hour; however, they thought of three. One of those solutions was exciting enough to try in the upcoming week. Mae volunteered to plan a picnic during which she would participate in one physical activity of her choosing—with one suggestion from Rudy—if he would set up a hammock and give her one hour of uninterrupted reading time after the activity.

SPECIFIC TECHNIQUES FOR MANAGEMENT OF CONFLICT

Increasing the Couple's Awareness of the Problem

As in all aspects of counseling with couples, the counselor's first objective is to increase the couple's awareness about the extent and consequences of their current behavior should it continue unabated. The assessment sessions should begin to increase awareness. They should conclude with a statement that one goal of counseling is to decrease conflict. However, before the problem can be addressed during the intervention sessions, the counselor must heighten the couple's awareness even further.

In the case of Rudy and Mae, they brought up a conflict early in counseling. Although the conflict was not over one of their usual topics, it had elements of their usual conflict within it. I focused on the conflict that they raised, even though it was not specifically planned prior to the session (action number 1 in the previous transcript). To dramatize the conflict, I had the couple role play the argument (5 and 7). This made the conflict more dramatic than merely recounting the arguments. The role play re-involved the couple in the issue and, in effect, created a new argument that could be immediately used during counseling. Although it was not necessary in this instance, I could have had the couple view the videotaped recording of the in-session argument, which would have heightened their awareness even more.

I initiated the role play by setting the stage—complete with some rudimentary physical props (5). I never said the words "role play." This is important. Many couples bridle at those words and refuse to cooperate with the counselor's directives. Rather, I merely set up the situation and directed the couple to act.

A disagreement soon developed about the ambiguity of my instructions (10-12). I apologized for the confusion and explained my intentions more clearly (13). Such false starts are routine early in conflict management training. Before the couple has become acclimated to role playing their conflicts in front of the counselor, the couple is reluctant to engage in full-scale discussion. They will find one or two reasons to interrupt the role play or not follow the counselor's instructions. This usually provokes the counselor to interrupt the role play.

The couple usually hope to divert the session to the more comfortable *discussion* of conflict rather than *acting out* the conflict. The counselor should consider attempts at diversion as a normal sign of discomfort that any couple has when doing something new, especially when the new action is threatening. The counselor must remain determined to guide the couple into a role play and not be diverted by their defensiveness.

During the role play, the counselor must decide how frequently to interrupt the couple. As mentioned in the previous chapter, I prefer to let the interaction unfold for a while (14-25), rather than interrupt the couple to correct each instance of a harmful communication.

For example, at the end of the role play (26), I had a choice of what to draw the couple's attention to. I chose to overlook Rudy's abusive (15, 21, 31) and accusatory (9, 15, 17, 25) comments and Mae's defensive (16, 18) and accusatory (16) behavior. Accusing them of poor communication would likely make them defensive in future interactions. In the early phases of counseling, it is usually best not to be too zealous at describing flaws in communication. Instead, I commented on how difficult it was for the couple to decide what to argue about, describing the patterns of argument as a well-rehearsed dance (28).

Just as easily I could have commented on the way the couple described minor behaviors as unsolvable personality difficulties or the way the couple skipped from topic to topic without acknowledging that they understood each other's position (semantics of communication) or the way that the couple sidetracked problem solving through excessive meta-communication and thus prevented resolution of the conflict (syntax of communication).

To dramatize the communication even further and to increase the couple's awareness of their behavior patterns, the couple was next directed to reverse roles (30). This can be a tool for sarcasm and ridicule among particularly troubled couples but it usually points out the spouses' perceptions concerning each's behavior and it often increases understanding of the partner by having to argue from his or her perspective.

At the end of the role reversal, I asked each spouse what he or she got from the role reversal (after 37). I particularly asked about their feelings (42, 44, 46) because I was trying in part to increase their motivation for changing their behavior patterns by showing how hurtful the patterns are. Based on my belief that one reason people argue in marriage is that they do not believe they are able to have an impact on each other (effectance), I reflected to each that he or she had the power to affect the other through what was done (44 and 46).

At the end of that discussion, I attributed positive motives to each spouse—that I was sure that neither partner tried to start an argument that he or she knew would be painful—and I reframed their conflict as indicative of continuing emotional involvement (48).

Breaking Up Old Patterns of Conflict

Reframing set the stage for attempting to change the patterns of conflict. In fact, Rudy even asked about the next step (50), which not all couples do. Rather than refer to abstract principles of conflict management or negotiation, I used the incident that had been role played earlier (51). Each spouse identified what he or she did to contribute to the conflict (52-77). I carefully asked each spouse about his or her *own* behavior, rather than the partner's behavior (53 and 70).

Only one item was solicited from each partner, and I wanted each partner to identify something early in the interaction. Identifying numerous problems would distort the focus on trying to change behavior patterns. Identifying a behavior early in the sequence is more likely to change the entire pattern than trying to change a behavior late in the interaction.

Identifying a behavior as contributing to the problem makes it more difficult for the person to willfully do that behavior again because it has been publicly condemned. This helps break up repetitious patterns. Having the spouse rather than the counselor identify the problem contributes to smoother counselor-client relations and less resistance because the client does not feel that the counselor blames him or her.

Breaking up patterns of conflict also depends on having the couple actually behave differently. The couple was directed to replay their interaction, trying to make the one fundamental change that had been identi-

fied (78). Some counselors, especially those who believe that couples behave as they do because they lack adequate knowledge of how to behave,
feel reluctant to have the couple go through the role play a third time. The
pressure on the counselor to change topics is increased by the couple who
does not want to repeat the interaction a third time. Some couples even
object verbally to redoing the role play. The counselor must firmly, but
gently, insist on the repetition, which is crucial to breaking up old patterns
and to readying the couple to engage in new ways to behave.

Before Rudy and Mae replayed the incident without the harmful behaviors, I used a reframing statement intended to motivate Rudy and Mae to
accept less arguing. I characterized conflict without argument as dull in
comparison to their usual style of conflict and described the loss of conflict
as a trauma that needed to be coped with (78). Couples usually affirm that
they will be satisfied with less conflict (79).

The third time that the couple role plays the same argument, they are
usually going to experience little conflict, partly because they are tired of
the conflict and ready to "get on with it." By characterizing their lack of
conflict as due to "improvement," the counselor develops increased confidence that counseling is helping.

Building New Patterns of Conflict Management

The core of the program that I usually use to build new conflict resolution
patterns comes from *Getting To Yes*.[4] I begin by explaining the principles.
If the couple has only begun to read the book, as is usually the case, I
explain the main ideas of the book in more detail than I did with Rudy and
Mae (80), who had read the complete book prior to the counseling session.

The session is structured in terms of resolving a specific issue that the
couple usually argues about. We implicitly or explicitly agree to use the
principles advocated by Fisher and Ury in resolving the issue (83). The first
step is to identify the problem under discussion (83-92). Each partner states
what is thought to be the problem (84 and 85), and the counselor helps the
couple arrive at a working statement of the problem (86-92). Definitions that
involve personalities or power struggles are gently disqualified (87 and 88).
The final statement of the problem should be specific and issue-oriented
(89).

Next, each party's interests are listed. I like to have each person try to list the spouse's interests to increase understanding of each other's perspective (92). Sometimes couples resist because they think that acknowledging that the other person has legitimate interests undercuts their own positions. If both spouses can be induced to list interests of their partners, I consider the prognosis for conflict resolution as good. If they resist, I characterize the task as one that tests (a) their mental fluency; (b) their ability to see both sides of an issue; or (c) their courage. Whether partners can identify the interests of their spouses or not, I let the spouse add to the list.

In the early stages of conflict management, I have the couple try to come up with a solution that satisfies only the primary interests of both partners. I demand that the couple arrive at several solutions, stressing that thinking of possible solutions does not commit the couple to carrying out the solutions (95). If the couple has difficulty thinking of solutions, I might suggest two or three.

Finally, the couple is assigned to try out one of the solutions at home during the week (after 101). It is important that the counselor helps the clients plan the details of how the solution will be put into practice. The counselor treats the solution as only one of many that could have been arrived at. If the solution does not work, it can then be discredited as "not the solution for you," which prevents the couple from questioning the method of conflict resolution just because one solution does not work for them.

OTHER PROGRAMS AND TECHNIQUES

Conflict resolution takes repetition. The same essential method is employed with several issues. Of course, modifications are made in the counselor's behavior during the sessions, but the counselor should choose one method of resolving conflict and stick with it. The couple learns proper methods of conflict resolution quickly—if they did not already know the methods—but it takes a while for them to employ the methods during their discussions at home.

The counselor should be familiar with a number of techniques and programs for helping couples resolve conflict. This increases the counselor's flexibility and helps target the program at the clients.

■ *Jacobson and Margolin's Problem Solving Manual.*[5] This manual is the most explicit and complete manual for helping couples solve problems. It contains twelve guidelines concerning the setting in which problem solving occurs, the spouses' attitudes, the method of identifying the problem and the method of solving the problem. Commentary accompanies each guideline.

■ *Wright's chapter 11, "Helping Couples Resolve Conflict Problems."*[6] This chapter gives nine guidelines adapted from Strong[7] for resolving conflict and seven steps adapted from Margolin[8] for handling anger. The chapter is a clear and succinct reference for those techniques and shares some of Wright's thinking about conflict management.

■ *Chapter 4, "Negotiating Agreements," in Gottman et al.*[9] This chapter leads couples through establishing a family meeting, having a gripe time, setting an agenda and solving problems. It also offers five exercises that couples can use to work through disagreements. Although these exercises can be done without the counselor, they are often usable within counseling too.

■ *Stuart's chapter 10, especially pp. 291-300.*[10] This chapter gives a more theoretical approach to avoiding conflict when possible and containing it when it is unavoidable.

■ *Bach's Fair Fight Training.*[11] This book outlines fifteen steps for arguing without destructive interactions.

During conflict management training, regardless of the program employed by the counselor, other techniques are often useful for helping the couple either become aware of their problems, break up old patterns or build new patterns. For example, Liberman et al. describe the "perfect marriage fantasy."[12] Each spouse writes eight areas in which couples commonly conflict: sex, communication, child rearing, money, leisure and social activities, household responsibilities, jobs and independence. Without discussing them, spouses write descriptions of changes in each area that would make the marriage "perfect." Each spouse then chooses one desire to state aloud. The couple is helped to negotiate changes that help both spouses to fulfill their fantasies. Although this exercise was developed for use in group therapy, it can be adapted and focused toward the specific concerns of individual couples.

Another way to break up recalcitrant patterns of conflict is to prescribe the symptom—block conflict by encouraging it. For example, Joshua and Sandra argued vehemently and often. After a particularly vicious interchange, I said, "It is very helpful when you discuss your differences during the session. It lets me see how you interact with each other. But my presence, I am sure, has some effect on the way that you argue. Is that true?"

"Well," said Joshua, "It's not too different, but I guess we are a little more controlled in here than when we are at home."

I replied, "It would be nice to have an accurate sample of how you argue at home. I've given some thought to how to do that. One way is for you to bring in an audiotape recording of an argument. Do you have an audiotape recorder at home? Good. Where do you usually get into most of your arguments?"

"In the kitchen," said Sandra.

"And in the bedroom," said Joshua.

"Then, choose one of those rooms and put a loaded tape recorder in that room. If you sense an argument starting, one of you just lean down and turn on the recorder. That way, I can get a clear picture of how arguments actually happen at your home. Will you do that this week?"

Most couples will agree to such an assignment, but they usually complain during the following session that they just never had an argument during the week. They are usually quite apologetic about not being able to argue. I stress again the importance of getting an accurate observation of their arguing and reassign the task. If clients comply with the assignment, it can provide good information about the way that they argue at home, but more often, the assignment inhibits arguing, thus breaking up common patterns and giving the couple a respite from the stress of frequent arguments.

SUMMARY

Helping a couple change their established pattern of conflict is difficult because patterns are usually well-rehearsed and automatic. Changing requires patience, creativity and skill from the counselor. The counselor must divert the patterns of blame to attributions of causes of problems that are changeable. By focusing on the issues of disagreement, the counselor must help the couple restructure their power struggles. This is done through guiding the couple into a pattern of conflict resolution that is advocated by neither. By helping the couple use new strategies to resolve their differences, the couple's balance of power can be changed to where less conflict exists.

Furthermore, the couple must make different attributions about the cause of the problems. Usually, spouses will attribute problems to their partner's personality. By governing the conflictual situations so the spouse is seen repeatedly to behave differently than in the past, each partner has his or her attributions undermined. It becomes more difficult to blame the problem on the spouse. The couple begins to blame their former method of conflict for causing the problem and is thus open to trying out new methods of resolving differences.

Changing Hurt, Blame and Sin

E VERY TROUBLED MARRIAGE IS PLAGUED WITH HURT, BLAME AND sin. Those three difficulties not only stand between spouses but also between each person and God. The marriage is more than an earthly mirror of our relationship with God; it affects that relationship (1 Jn 4:20). A counselor who is a Christian is called by God to work toward the reconciliation of spouses with each other and of individuals with God.

Whereas the duty of marriage counseling is restoration of God-ordained marriage, the blessing of marriage counseling is restoration of people with God.

THE PROBLEMS

Hurt occurs in marriage when spouses seem either unwilling or unable to   **Hurt** help meet each other's needs. A spouse seems unwilling to help meet needs when he or she has an affair, intentionally withdraws from the marriage, habitually avoids intimacy or lashes out in hurtful ways. We attribute intentional rejection to the spouse who seems unwilling to meet the needs of his or her partner. A spouse seems not unwilling but unable to help meet needs when he or she develops a psychological problem such as debilitating depression or anxiety or a behavioral problem such as alcohol or drug addiction.

When one's spouse seems unwilling to help meet needs, one feels angry, hurt and righteously indignant. When one's spouse seems unable to help meet needs, one feels compassionate but frustrated and resentful. In either case, both spouses feel a plethora of emotions which surge and ebb as the problem continues.

One key to understanding and helping the troubled couple with their hurt, blame and sin is to understand that hurt occurs because the spouse *seems* unwilling or unable to help meet needs. It is not the unwillingness or inability of a spouse to meet his or her partner's needs that causes difficulties, but it is the meaning the other spouse places on that action. Both spouses, in almost all troubled couples, have chosen to give negative meanings to the actions of their partner. Some cloak their blame in righteous indignation, but even in that case the blame is usually there, smoldering beneath the covering (Mt 7:3-5).

The question often arises whether one spouse is the culprit in a troubled marriage. Usually, that is not a helpful line of thinking to pursue. Even if one spouse simply abandoned the other, sin usually has touched both sides of the relationship. The more productive line of thought is to get each spouse to look to himself or herself and recognize and confess his or her part in the problem. For a spouse to focus on the other person's culpability is counterproductive. It does not reconcile marriages nor does it produce spiritual growth.

However, sometimes one spouse *has* been more hurtful than the other, which makes it difficult for the counselor to avoid forming unequal coalitions. There are times when the counselor must speak the truth in love to a wayward brother or sister. Usually, though, sin is present also in the spouse. The counselor must not be lulled into justifying one spouse who sins privately merely because the other spouse sins more publicly.

In most troubled marriages, spouses forget their partner's needs, thinking only of their own. On the other hand, they blame their spouses for most things that go wrong and are hypervigilant at detecting their spouse's errors.[1] The counselor must reverse the pattern. Get them to focus on their own responsibility for the problems and to think of their spouse's needs. **Blame**

It is natural to blame one's spouse for interactional difficulties. When a couple interacts, they look at, talk to and listen to the spouse. What is more natural than to attribute the cause of problems to the spouse, especially when something goes wrong in the relationship? People naturally justify themselves.

Sins beget sins. If one partner judges the other, judgment will soon be reciprocated. If one rejects the other, he or she should expect rejection. Anger breeds anger, violence stimulates violence, hatred multiplies hatred. The counselor who observes a blatant sin in one spouse should look for its sibling in the other. **Sin**

Sin is the flaw in human nature, and it is clearly and bountifully observed in marriage counseling. We must help people use their new nature, practicing godly behavior with each other until it becomes truly second nature to them.

Sin is insidious. It creeps up on us unaware and poisons our behavior. Counselors must be continually vigilant of the presence of sin in their own lives. As we listen to the woes and foibles of our clients, we can be tempted to pray the publican's prayer, "God, I thank thee that I am not like other men, . . ." (Lk 18:9-14). We must guard ourselves from judging (Mt 7:1), and we must correct our clients with gentleness (Gal 6:1).

SPECIFIC TECHNIQUES FOR CHANGING HURT, BLAME AND SIN

Your goal in dealing with hurt, blame and sin is to move people to see and confess their responsibility in problems and then to understand and meet the needs of the spouse. Telling a person that he or she should do those **Increasing the Couple's Awareness of the Problem** things will almost never result in changed behaviors. The problem cannot be remedied in the abstract, using words like "be responsible for yourself" or "see what you can do to meet your wife's needs."

Rather, you must *show* the person his or her part in the problem. Ask each person what he or she has done to make the problem worse. Ask what he or she could do to make the problem better. Keep the person from focusing on what the spouse has done. Repeat this method with each issue that arises. The pattern of responsibly examining one's own behavior instead of one's spouse's behavior must become habitual. It will not change with one attempt. It requires constant repetition.

When a person verbalizes a need, ask the spouse how he or she could meet the need. Get each person to speculate about the partner's needs. Have each person think about how to meet the partner's needs, and then assign homework that gives the couple practice at meeting each other's needs.

You can show each spouse how to inquire sensitively about the partner by the way that you treat the spouse's partner. Do not assume that the spouses know what you are doing. They may be observing parts of your behavior of which you are not aware. Rather, talk about how you dealt with the needs of the spouse and direct the couple to do what you did. Use the audio and videotape recordings to provide concrete examples of when the couple blame and behave well with each other.

Tape recording the counseling session will often help each person focus on his or her own responsibility in an interaction. Social psychologists have found that putting a mirror in the room with a person helps change the focus of the person to himself or herself.[2] This is called objective self-awareness. The same thing happens when people know that they are being recorded. They focus on their own motives and their own responsibility in interactions more than they do without the observation.

In his "Christian Family" audiotape series, Larry Christenson describes a technique called "empathetic repentance."[3] He suggests that whenever a person catches himself or herself criticizing someone else, the person should consider whether he or she finds the same fault in himself or herself. Empathetic repentance is especially apt in marriages, where sins tend to feed on each other. I will often describe Christenson's idea to couples and have them speculate about how they might be doing the same things of which they are accusing the spouse.

Another way to increase the couple's awareness of their part in their difficulties is to discuss how Christ loved the church. I read Ephesians 5:21-33 aloud to the couple. Sometimes this will result in a discussion of wifely submission, but I usually try to steer the discussion to the main point of the passage, which I believe to be this: whatever position you find yourself in—whether husband or wife, parent or child, slave or master—lay down your life for the other.

I point out, for example, that "husbands [are to] love [their] wives, as Christ loved the church and gave himself up for her" (v. 25). I explain that Christ died for us *before* we were pure (see 1 Jn 4:7-8, 19-21). I then ask the husband how he will show love for his wife before being satisfied with her behavior. His job is to love his wife as Christ did the church, not to worry about whether his wife deserves his love. I also tell wives that they are charged with the same imperative simply because they are Christians. Both spouses are then challenged to find out how the other spouse wants to be shown love and then do it, regardless of what the other spouse does.

Don Danser and I developed a technique for promoting forgiveness between spouses. More recently Fred DiBlasio and I have elaborated on the technique. Generally, two or more sessions are required. The sessions are usually scheduled after the couple has begun to increase their intimacy and practice the rudiments of conflict management. The technique is occasioned when intimacy, communication and conflict management are being hampered by lack of forgiveness between partners.

Breaking Up Old Patterns of Hurt, Blame and Sin

Jack and Marge Simpson had been married for twelve years. They had enjoyed about nine years of happy marriage, but Jack had lost his job three years previously through the failing of the business that employed him. He sought another job within his field but could not find one. Finally, Marge had to return to work to provide for the family. Jack took over management of the household and seemed satisfied to continue in that status. Marge did not enjoy working and resented Jack's inability or unwillingness to get a job. For three years, Jack and Marge had increasingly frequent conflict and hurt. Finally, on the verge of divorce, they sought counseling.

Following are excerpts from the ninth and tenth sessions in which Don Danser, their counselor, dealt with the hurt, blame and sin by promoting forgiveness.[4]

Counselor: *We seem to have made some progress with your marriage for a while, but for the last three sessions I have sensed an impasse. It seems that something is blocking your progress.*

Marge: *I feel it too.*

Counselor: *I think that the basic problem is lack of forgiveness.*

Marge: *I've forgiven him many times. I know that we are to forgive and I try.*

Jack: *Yeah. She sure does that.*

Counselor: *I think that one problem might be in going about forgiveness in a way that is not helpful.*

Marge: *How do you mean?*

Counselor: *Forgiveness is not* just *an act of obedience. In fact, when you just say, "I forgive you," at the same time it says, "I condemn you," because it says, "You have done something that* needs *forgiveness." Do you follow that?*

Marge: (Uncertainly) *I guess . . .*

Jack: (At the same time) *I do! I never really put my finger on it, but I really get mad when she says that she forgives me. I know I shouldn't but it makes me angry anyway.*

Counselor: *That's because forgiveness is meant to follow confession and repentance. Before you try to forgive each other for the hurt and pain you have caused the other, you need to determine what those sources of hurt are.*

Marge: *I can tell him that. I have told him many times.*

Counselor: *Wait a minute, Marge. You are not hearing me accurately. I want you to tell about the things that you* have *done to cause Jack pain and hurt.*

Marge: *Oh.*

Counselor: *In fact, it would take you more time than we have left in this session to be able to do that adequately. So, this week I would like each of you to make a list of all the things you can think of that you are sorry that you have done to your spouse.*

Marge: *Isn't that kind of maudlin, dredging up old hurts?*

Counselor: *It would be if that were the end of it. It certainly would not do good, and would do considerable harm, to dwell on all the things you've done that are wrong. But, for the Christian, that's not the end of it. The Christian can*

bring those hurts under the blood of Jesus and have them taken care of.
Marge: *But I've confessed them to God. Why bring up old sins?*
Counselor: *There are sins that are just between you and God. Those are forgiven and forgotten when they are confessed. But when we sin against God by sinning directly against someone else, it is like squeezing a toothpaste tube. Once the toothpaste is out on your hand, it's a mess. You can try to force it back into the tube, but it never all fits back. You can stick your hand in your pocket and try to cover up the sin, but that just makes your own body messy. In James 5, provision is made for the healing of social sins. That calls for confession to others. That's what you will be doing.*

At the next session, both Jack and Marge brought lists to counseling. After discussing the difficulty that they each had at completing the assignment, Don expressed his pleasure at their courage in carrying out the assignment.

Counselor: *I am really encouraged that you were both willing to put so much effort and thought into this task. I know it is always difficult to admit things that you did that were wrong, but you have carried through marvelously. You have both shown repeatedly how willing you are to make changes. You've taken risks and put a lot of effort into your marriage. That is always encouraging for a counselor to see. You should be proud of yourselves. Now, what I would like for you to do today is to decide who will go first and then for that person to confess whatever he or she wants. It is very important that you confess only what you want. The list of things that you drew up belongs only to you. I will never ask to see it, and I will insist that you never show your spouse, even if you want to. After we finish with the lists, I suggest that we burn them.*

In the same way, the person who hears something confessed should not immediately forgive the spouse. I am going to ask that you take a week to think about it, and next week you each can tell me if you are willing to forgive your spouse for the things that he or she has confessed. Do you understand what I would like you to do today? Good. Who would like to be first?
Jack: *I guess I'll go first. Is that okay, honey?*
Marge: *Sure.*
Jack: *Well . . .*
Counselor: *Wait a minute. Can I ask you to turn your chairs so that you are looking at each other. That might make it easier.*
Jack: (To Marge) *I've given a lot of thought to this during the past week. I*

guess I haven't been much of a bargain to live with for the past few years. I know I've disappointed you by not being more active in finding a new job. I'm sorry. I hope I'll do better in the coming months. I'm going to try. I hope that you'll forgive me for not being considerate of you. I know that you haven't liked to work, but I have been following my own pleasure instead of thinking about what you would like. In fact, it's hard to admit, but I have sometimes even refused to look for work because I knew it would make you angry. I really feel bad about the way I've acted. (Stops, crying.)

Marge: *I don't know what to say* (also crying). *I know I've hurt you too. I didn't really think . .*

The emotion-filled session continued for about thirty minutes. At the end of the time, both Jack and Marge had confessed to knowingly and unknowingly hurting the other repeatedly. All through they had offered forgiveness to each other, in spite of Don's prohibition of forgiving. However, the confession and responses were so authentic that Don did not interrupt Jack and Marge to insist that they hold off on forgiveness until the following week. Finally, the couple began to wind down.

Counselor: *You have both been through the mill today. I am very impressed at your honesty and sincerity during this exercise.*

Jack: *It didn't seem like an exercise. I'm totally drained. I feel as if a great burden has been lifted from my shoulders.*

Marge: *I must admit, I was very skeptical about this all week. I thought that this sounded so, so mechanical. I didn't see how anything good could come from it. I sure was wrong.*

Counselor: *I like to recall an analogy of Larry Christenson's. He talked about how a solid concrete building is constructed. First, a wooden framework is created and is carefully built. Then the steel rods are placed inside for reinforcement. Finally, the concrete is poured and allowed to set. The external framework creates the possibility of an internal work.*

I see what we did as similar to creating a solid basis of forgiveness. The method, which seemed mechanical, is like the external wooden form. The form merely makes it possible for God to pour the concrete of forgiveness into your hearts. The steel bars represent doubts. You each might have doubted the sincerity of the other. But the doubts, when tested and strained, are the very things that strengthen the concrete because they force you to ask questions that you would not have otherwise asked. The concrete is God's forgiveness and the forgiveness of each of you by the other. Now we must wait for the concrete to set and harden.

I expect that you will pull on the reinforcing bars during the upcoming weeks, testing whether the other person is sincere. I believe you will find sincerity. It takes a while for the concrete to set properly. Over the next few weeks, we'll see the building take shape. Once this time is behind you, you will have a new mansion to live in. There will be no need to go back and try to clean the old one.

BUILDING NEW PATTERNS: ACCEPTANCE, NEW BEGINNINGS AND HEALED MEMORIES

Patterns of hurt, blame and sin must be replaced with positive goals. One proper goal for a Christian marriage is to build mutual acceptance. Crabb has described acceptance in his book *The Marriage Builder.*[5] Acceptance is defined as ministering to the spouse without the pressure of "oughts." There are three practical keys to creating an attitude of acceptance in marriage:

Build Acceptance

1. *Minister* to the spouse's needs.

2. *Acknowledge* one's feelings while realizing that feelings need not be acted on just because they are acknowledged.

3. *Forgive* the spouse's debts.

To forgive a debt, a spouse decides not to bring up the debt again and chooses to lay down the desire to punish the partner who caused the injury. Crabb suggests that eschewing the desire for punishment is aided by realizing that needs are sufficiently filled by Jesus and that the spouse cannot block need fulfillment; the spouse can only block "want-fulfillment." This realization strips the spouse's frustrating behavior of its sting.

Although I agree with most of Crabb's thinking, I differ slightly. I *do* believe that spouses are instrumental in meeting each other's needs. They are one of God's legitimate vehicles for meeting needs, as are friends, relatives and others in the church. God will meet our needs through a variety of sources—not just the spouse, though the spouse is usually the primary way God meets our needs. Despite this minor difference with Crabb, I still refer couples to chapter 8 of *The Marriage Builder*[6] to focus their attention on positive goals for their marriage. I discuss the chapter with the couple, and we usually plan specific ways that each spouse can show acceptance to his or her partner. Couples are then assigned to put their plans into effect between sessions.

A Public Burning

Usually, early in counseling, I ask each spouse to list the five biggest complaints he or she has against the partner. I placed the lists in two sealed envelopes that I keep in my file for that couple. If the couple has made substantial progress in counseling, I sometimes will prescribe that the couple have a "public" burning of the unopened envelopes either during a counseling session, just between the two of them, or with others present. This act is symbolic that, by faith, they are giving up their criticisms of the partner. Because the criticisms are to be burned, there is no need to recount their content to each other, to the counselor or to any others in attendance.

Couples are instructed to choose a setting that would be meaningful for them. Some couples invite their friends or family who have been involved with them throughout their struggles, though most do not. Other couples go to a place such as a state park with a beautiful view or a spot by the river that the couple frequented during their dating. Some people choose to have the burning ceremony in their own back yards. Some couples benefit by this kind of ritual, which marks the end of an old era and the beginning of a new one.

The Healing of Memories

After the couple has forgiven each other for past and recent hurts, they sometimes still complain that the memories of those hurts plague them. They say they can forgive but not forget. To help the couple get past that roadblock, I often use an adaptation of Ruth Carter Stapleton's "inner healing."[7] I introduce the idea as follows:

> You say that you cannot forget the past hurts even though you can forgive your spouse for them. I don't think it is possible for us to ever forget such hurts, so I would not let that trouble me if I were you. However, if the hurts still bother you, it might mean that there is a need for further healing. It is like a physical hurt in a way. The top of the hurt can heal, and the hurt is well on the road to full healing, but it can still be tender. Even after a full healing occurs, the scars will remain that can remind us of the hurt.

I have this scar on my shin, where I leaped onto a porch as a boy. Well, I almost leaped onto the porch. Even though the hurt has been healed for thirty or more years, I still see the scar and sometimes even think about the fall that caused the hurt. Of course, it never really bothers me now, and I only think of it maybe once a year or so. But it is part of my past.

But that's not the case here. You say that the hurt is forgiven but still tender. Maybe there is something that can be done about that. God is eternal. He is not constrained by time. The good news of that truth is that he exists in what we call the past as well as the present and future. It would be no trick for him to step into what we know as the past and heal a hurt.

Ruth Carter Stapleton has developed a special kind of prayer in which people afterwards often report a healing of hurtful memories. It involves using your imagination to re-experience a past hurt and bringing the image of Jesus into that situation to promote healing. If you like, we could do that right now.

If the couple agrees, I have them choose a bothersome event. If they are bothered by a more general difficulty, such as a personality characteristic of the spouse, then they tell me of one instance in which they observed the spouse behaving in that way.

After they have described a specific event, they close their eyes and I pray that, as we use the imagination that God has given us, Jesus will, in actuality, enter the clients' lives and produce real changes in their memories and in their lives from the point of that memory onward. I then describe the situation in vivid word pictures, guiding their fantasies. After the hurt is re-experienced, I describe an image of Jesus entering the situation. The imagined results are usually tailored to individual couples, but they include confession, repentance, forgiveness and reconciliation. Most couples become quite involved in the imagery, and I believe that God honors the prayer to make tangible changes in the couple's lives as they become involved in the prayer.

SUMMARY

Hurt, blame and sin are almost always present in a troubled marriage, and thus they must be dealt with in marriage counseling. One of the important parts of counseling with Christian couples is to help them restore both their relationship with each other and their relationship with God. Confession, repentance, forgiveness and acceptance are the tools of the Spirit-guided counselor to help accomplish this restoration.

Promoting Commitment

SUMMARY When the commitment of spouses has eroded as a result of time, stress and mutually hurtful behavior, it is not rebuilt by simple or quick interventions. Rather, commitment must grow, often slowly. It develops as the therapist provides the proper environment to support its growth. Changes in the spouses' behaviors, thoughts and environments must be initiated and, more importantly, sustained. The wise therapist will not take maintenance of change for granted but will seek to consolidate changes deliberately (chapter 15). Further, the therapist will strive to set the couple free of his or her intervention through skillful termination (chapter 16). Often termination with a couple will prompt us to evaluate our own counseling. The final chapter (17) discusses the need for the counselor to examine his or her own commitment—to high-quality counseling and to dependence on Jesus.

15

Consolidating Changes

CHANGES MADE IN COUNSELING WILL NOT AUTOMATICALLY BE maintained. Behavior and the way clients talk about their marriage can both change for a number of ephemeral reasons. The counselor's presence can even be a cause of change. But when counseling is terminated and the counselor is no longer in regular contact with the couple, will the change last? Only if the counselor has helped the couple change the structures of their lives.

Throughout counseling, not just at the end of counseling, the counselor tries to engender long-lasting changes in each spouse's cognitive structures and in the couple's environmental structures. Cognitive structures consist of the couple's (a) understanding of their marriage; (b) expectations about the progress they will experience throughout counseling and about the effort required to maintain changes; (c) goals and plans for the marriage; and (d) attributions. Environmental structures involve the structure of counseling, the practiced patterns of interaction between the spouses and the changes that the couple makes in their home.

This chapter describes ways to consolidate changes in the couple's cognitive and environmental structures. Some techniques are summarized, and some strategies are explained for promoting these changes.

CHANGING COGNITIVE STRUCTURES

Understanding

Although explanations to clients and understanding by clients are essential parts of counseling, marriage counseling is not "insight oriented." Change does not depend on the necessity of client insight. Change depends more often on couples being willing to take risks and try new behaviors.

Cooperation with the counselor's suggestions and directives to make these changes, however, usually depends on the couple understanding what the behavior is expected to accomplish and how. Initiation of change thus depends on understanding.

Maintenance of change also depends on understanding what produced change and why. If the couple is told why a technique worked, the couple is more likely to use the ideas in future situations both to prevent and to remedy problems.

The understanding that you hope the couple has after successfully performing a directive is not necessarily the understanding that helps them perform the behavior initially. The final understanding stresses the personal role of each client in bringing about the change. Prior to a directive, the personal roles of each spouse are not stressed. To the contrary, the *technique* is said to be on trial, not the couple. The task is made as nonthreatening as possible through the rationales used to motivate the couple to try to make changes.

In reality, both the technique *and* the couple are on trial with a directive. Techniques do not work without the personal effort and ability of the clients. Personal efforts to change without using techniques have generally been ineffective for most clients. Your explanations merely call attention to different parts of the total picture for different therapeutic purposes.

By making sure that couples understand what their problems are, how you determined what the problems are, what to do about the problems and why, you help the couple act as their own counselor in the future. Throughout counseling, respect the couple enough to teach them the technology to apply solutions to their problems without your help. In this way, you hope to reduce the likelihood of additional counseling for future problems.

Besides helping couples understand how and why to make changes in their relationship, continually re-educate the couple about what will occur during each stage of counseling. I try to put most of this understanding into the brief paper that I give at the beginning of counseling, "Introduction to Marriage Counseling" (see Figure 10, pp. 117-18). For various reasons— such as failure to read the paper, inability to use written information, forgetting what one reads, and others—you will need to repeat the information throughout counseling. Constant re-education is necessary.

In child rearing, one theory claims that learning is enhanced if information is presented at "the teachable moment." Although the beginning of counseling is a teachable moment for most couples concerning what to expect from counseling, it will not necessarily be the teachable moment for *every* point presented in the paper "Introduction to Marriage Counseling." Be ready with stories, anecdotes, analogies and explanations for the crucial times in counseling when they will be ready for more information. Specific situations and appropriate explanations follow.

1. *The first relapse:* "Remember, most couples have relapses. They go through a surge-euphoria-relapse cycle."

2. *A plateau of little or no change:* "It takes time for a broken bone to heal."

3. *Challenges to your techniques:* "It's like putting your arm in a cast; it feels unnatural, but it lets the bone heal."

4. *Challenges to your ability to help the couple:* "You're right. Changes are due to *your* effort much more than to what I do. I'm just like a hunting guide. . . ."

Most of your re-education and re-inspiration will come in clients' times of discouragement, crisis and success. During those times the couple is hungry to hear words of hope and encouragement, and they will be receptive to them. Although each couple differs from all others, there are topics you will need to repeat often.

1. *Comment on the ways the spouses demonstrate their love for each other.*

2. *Observe their good intentions*—even when the behaviors are sometimes reprehensible. For example, "John, I can see by your constant criticisms of Melinda that you really care about her and want her to live up to her full potential. Do you think the criticisms are achieving your goals effectively?"

3. *Remind them that their success depends on how hard they work and on how willing they are to take risks.*

4. *Remind them of their goals and of how counseling contributes to meeting those goals.*

5. *Remind them of the unevenness of progress in counseling.*

EXPECTATIONS

Expectation of Relapse

Paradoxically, having couples cognizant of the tendency to alternate progress and relapse helps them *avoid* relapse. The couple who is prepared for dips in satisfaction copes with it as a normal part of marriage rather than as a catastrophe.

I help the couple know, using several techniques, that some relapses are likely throughout counseling. One technique is simply to show them the chart of the typical progress of a couple throughout counseling (see Figure 9, p. 108) and to discuss the surge-euphoria-relapse cycle.

A slower way is to assign the couple the homework of making two graphs. Both spouses make a graph of their own spiritual history, their "closeness to the Lord" since birth. Generally, couples construct charts that are characterized by a "conversion euphoria" as well as by peaks and valleys (see Figure 17 for a typical chart). On separate charts, I ask them to graph their marital histories as well.

The charts of their marital and spiritual histories are usually similar. In marriage, there is usually a peak of closeness to the spouse early in the relationship, near the time of marriage. The graph is also characterized by peaks and valleys. Often, transitions—such as births of children—herald increases or decreases in closeness to the spouse. Generally, one difference is that charts of spiritual closeness often end on an "up-tick" while charts of marital closeness don't.

Figure 17
Graphs of One Spouse's Closeness to the Lord and Closeness to His Spouse over His Lifetime

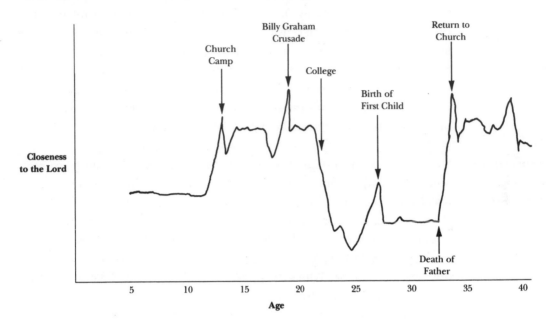

Church
Camp

Billy Graham
Crusade

College

Return to
Church

Birth of
First Child

Closeness
to the Lord

Death
of
Father

Age

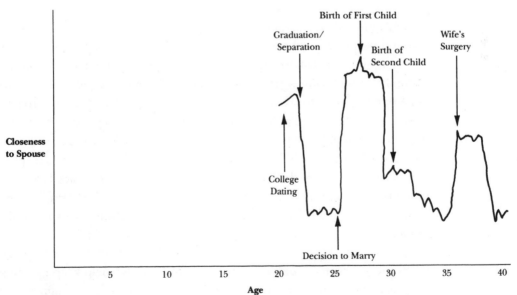

Birth of First Child

Graduation/
Separation

Birth of
Second Child

Wife's
Surgery

Closeness
to Spouse

College
Dating

Decision to Marry

Age

This homework exercise allows me to discuss several important concepts. It directs the couple's attention to their spiritual lives and sometimes shows that they are pulling away from the Lord in the very time of relationship distress when it would be sensible to draw nearer to him. The exercise also allows me to discuss the idea that marriage is God's metaphor for fidelity to him. Marriage is the method God gives us to understand life with him—if we work on our marriage. Thirdly, this exercise demonstrates clearly the fluctuating nature of our interpersonal relationships; thus, it helps combat unreasonable expectations about perfectly blissful marriages.

Expectations of Long-Term Effort

Stuart[1] relates an example that demonstrates clearly some faulty expectations that hamper counseling. He likens marriage harmony to weight control. People often try to handle weight control by exerting great effort over short periods of time while holding expectations of long-term benefit. Strenuous and sometimes dangerous diets abound. Yet, few diets are effective at producing long-term change in weight because they do not change the person's lifestyle. When the person completes the diet, he or she tries to eat less to maintain the weight loss. But before too long, the new has worn off and the person's weight begins to creep up again.

The most effective means of weight control are those that change the person's lifestyle during and after the initial weight loss. For example, behavioral weight control programs are effective because they alter the person's eating habits (where, when and why they eat, etc.) not just the *amount* of food consumed during the diet period. Simultaneously these dieters may commit themselves to a vigorous long-term exercise program involving endurance exercises such as long-distance swimming or jogging.

Similar to weight control, effective changes in marriage depend on a change in the couple's lifestyle. Most married couples who enter counseling expect to exert a great deal of short-term effort that will produce long-term benefits. The counselor must counter those expectations. Sharing Stuart's analogy of marriage counseling to weight control often drives the point home.

Goals

Goals are necessary to guide counseling, but they also help keep marriage on track once counseling is completed. On the termination summary, I identify several goals for the couple to aim at after counseling. This focuses them on achieving the positive and keeps their attention from returning readily to failures.

Systematic changes in the couple's attributions must occur over successful counseling. Couples should move from attributing cause of their problems to each other to accepting personal responsibility for their parts in the problem. This transformation occurs as empathy is built for the other person. Empathy helps the spouse see things from the partner's point of view. Developing each spouse's empathy for the other will help consolidate changes. **Attributions**

Couples should also move from attributing their changes to the counselor or to the techniques of counseling to attributing changes to their own effort and ability. This will help the couple feel they can cope with future problems and will help them resolve future problems rather than look for another counselor.

TECHNIQUES FOR CHANGING ENVIRONMENTAL STRUCTURES

Stuart[2] recommends three ways that the counselor can use counseling sessions to help the couple maintain changes. He suggests using "booster sessions," a six-month "good relationship check-up" and periodic calls from the counselor. **Structure of the Sessions**

Booster sessions have been shown to be helpful for difficult-to-maintain habits. For example, smokers who have quit smoking often schedule sessions with their counselors at future intervals (such as one-month, three-month, six-month and one-year intervals) to "refresh" their memories of the treatments and their motivations for stopping smoking.

Stuart recommends booster sessions with a twist. He suggests that the couple have booster sessions with themselves and not the counselor. He encourages them to set aside one hour each month to discuss the things each has done to maintain a healthy relationship. With his customary thoroughness, he provides evaluation forms for the couple to use to structure their time together.

Although the technique sounds good, I doubt whether many couples actually follow through with it for more than a few months, and I would wager that few use the written evaluation forms without the promise of having to meet the counselor and account for their behavior. Nonetheless, the idea of suggesting that couples take regular times to talk about the relationship is excellent.

Stuart also suggests that couples schedule a good relationship check-up with the counselor approximately six months after counseling ends. He likens this to a well-baby visit. Again, the suggestion has face validity, but in the few cases I have tried this, I have received vague avoidance. Few clients are willing to spend the money for counseling if they feel their relationship is doing well without it.

The third recommendation Stuart makes is that the counselor schedule phone calls at three-month intervals to do a quick check on the couple. This is time-consuming for the counselor; however, enough couples might re-initiate counseling ultimately to pay for the effort. With any substantial case load, this extra time demand on the counselor probably would not be maintained for long.

I probably should not evaluate Stuart's suggestions so negatively, since I have not tried two of them. The suggestions are appealing in principle, but I would like to see empirical evidence about their effectiveness with actual clients. My impression of most clients is that they want to relieve their pain. When their distress is lowered, they minimize their effort and don't want to continue expensive marriage counseling. For this reason, until evidence of effectiveness is presented, I would think that the only suggestion with likely success is the first, which involves the couple, not the counselor.

One additional way to use counseling to help consolidate changes is to lengthen the time between closing sessions. Although the primary reason for doing this is to make termination smoother, a secondary benefit is that the couple is given more time to practice their new behavior patterns while still under the care of the counselor.

Practice New Patterns   Probably the most important environmental structure to which the married person responds is the behavior of his or her spouse. Changed behavioral patterns must be maintained if the couple is to maintain the gains of counseling. The best way to make those new patterns of behavior permanent is to practice them until they are overlearned, automatic.

Robert Zajonc, a social psychologist, found that stressful situations provoke people to perform what he called "the dominant response."[3] The dominant response is the one that is the most practiced. For example, the basketball player practices thousands of free throws so that the dominant response is to make rather than miss the free throws when the game is on. The practice occurs in times of little stress so that the player can perform well under great stress. Yet, basketball players also stage scrimmages and exhibition games. Dominant responses are best learned if they are practiced under conditions that simulate stressful conditions. Both nonstress practice and simulated stress practice helps.

The married couple has one advantage over basketball players. They are under actual stress when they seek counseling, so they learn their new behavior patterns under actual stress conditions. The more they practice while in counseling, the more likely they will cope successfully with future stress. They must continue to practice their good behavior patterns when their marriage is doing well. This will help make good behavior patterns truly the dominant response of their relationship.

Time Schedules

Besides changing their behavior patterns, couples can also rearrange their time schedules. If they see each other only after they both return from a grueling day at work, they can agree to rise one hour earlier and spend the time in a jog or walk together or in devotions or prayer. This new time schedule then constantly reminds them that they are working to maintain an improved relationship.

SUMMARY

Counselors must explicitly strive to promote lasting changes within marriages. The permanent aspects of each spouse's cognitions and environment must be changed.

Clients must understand why change occurs and how to maintain a happy relationship. Further, they must expect ups and downs in their relationship, not becoming discouraged with relapses. Further, maintenance of a happy marriage requires sustained attention to the marriage coupled with a focus on positive goals.

Three aspects of the environment can contribute to permanent changes. First, the structure of counseling can foster long-term maintenance of change. Second, changes in common behavior patterns are also helpful. Finally, changes in time schedules can promote lasting changes in intimacy.

16

Termination

F ROM THE END OF THE ASSESSMENT, COUNSELING POINTS TOWARD termination. In one sense, the goal of counseling *is* termination, for the alliance between couple and counselor is explicitly temporary—even if the couple and counselor interact in other ongoing capacities such as pastor-parishioner, elder-member or casual acquaintances. Counseling is a brief consultation created for the goal of amiable, satisfactory termination.

TASKS OF TERMINATION

Termination is the counselor's last opportunity to strengthen the changes made by the couple. The counselor calls the couple's attention to the differences between their current and past situations.

Strengthen Changes

The work of counseling is over, even though there are usually numerous other issues that could be addressed with profit to the couple. The counselor must avoid the temptation to introduce new goals or interventions. The counselor *almost single-mindedly* pursues the goal of the termination session(s), which is to disengage from a formal counseling relationship.

Illuminate New Directions

Counseling is short term, and not all desired changes can be achieved during counseling. Further improvements in any relationship are always possible. This is certainly true for relationships that were initially troubled enough so that counseling was sought from a professional. One task of termination, then, is to aim the couple toward goals for strengthening their relationship *outside* of counseling. This is commonly done by identifying concrete goals that the couple can work on and writing them on the termination summary that is given to the couple. The final goals are worded so that counseling is not necessary for the couple to achieve them.

In some cases, you might refer the couple to another counselor who specializes in a type of therapy that you prefer not to do. For example, I worked with one couple for eight sessions. The woman complained of persistent depression, and the man complained of lack of career and personal directedness. Both were interested in individual counseling, believing that if they could solve their individual problems, their relationship would improve. I referred them to a wise Christian counselor in Richmond, Carl Rilee, who agreed to work with each individually. At the end of three months, both partners had accomplished much in their personal lives. They briefly resumed marriage counseling, but their assessment of their marriage was correct. Their relationship had stabilized, and they no longer needed marriage counseling.

Dissolve the Counseling Relationship

The third, and main, task of termination is to dissolve the counseling relationship. Final sessions are often characterized by social chit-chat with a reluctance to discuss the dissolving counselor-client relationship. Fear and anxiety over losing the support of the counselor are mixed with pride and confidence that the couple can solve their problems without needing consultation from a professional. One difficulty for the counselor is to quell the fears and anxieties of termination while making it acceptable for the couple to return to the counselor at some later time if that becomes necessary. Too great a reliance on the success of the couple can inhibit them from seeking help in the future. They fear that returning to counseling is an admission of failure.

THE DECISION TO TERMINATE

Premature termination may occur when the clients want to stop counseling before the counselor does. A counselor must realize that he or she might not be the best judge of whether a couple is ready to terminate. Some counselors argue that premature termination means merely that the couple decides to terminate before all of the goals of counseling have been reached. This sounds fine, but my experience is that few couples reach all of the goals precisely as they are set out in the assessment summary. There is a judgment that the couple has "done enough" or that the couple could reach the goals, given enough time. Thus, a premature termination must be understood as a somewhat parochial view, and the counselor must retain his or her humility.

Too Early

Usually when a couple terminates before the counselor believes they are ready, it indicates a failure to establish or maintain a proper therapeutic relationship. In one of my more spectacular failures, I counseled a pastor and his wife. The pastor was committed to the idea that marriage problems were a reflection of spouses' personality problems. In his particular case, he thought the wife had a personality problem. Whenever I discussed the behavior of the couple, the pastor objected and blamed her personality. Rather than argue, I offered explanations, metaphors, examples, analogies—the whole arsenal—to support my treatment. My every attempt to explain met a stone wall.

After about three weeks, I found myself rehearsing arguments with the pastor prior to our sessions. I realized that we were in a power struggle. Attempts to negotiate and reframe treatment failed dismally. The pastor stubbornly prescribed what proper marriage therapy would be. I, of course, maintained the only "sane" position about what "proper therapy" would be. Needless to say, caught in a power struggle, I rapidly had to make a referral to another counselor in town who could take a position that was consonant with the pastor's beliefs.

Going Nowhere

Another time to consider termination is when the couple fails to progress. All couples hit plateaus if they attend counseling for many weeks, but usually the couple eventually can be dislodged from their static position. If the counselor has exhausted his or her repertoire of strategies for stimulating change, this might indicate that some problem is interfering with counseling.

Most likely, the goals of counseling are not accepted by all parties. Either the husband and wife disagree on the final goal of counseling or the counselor and clients disagree. Sometimes one spouse has decided that divorce is inevitable or desirable. That spouse has failed to tell the counselor or the partner. The subtle undermining of therapeutic interventions, though, prevents counseling from progressing.

At other times, the couple has not accepted the goals that the counselor has suggested but has not objected to them openly. This might have occurred despite great skill by the counselor, but more frequently the counselor has not sensitively listened to the subtle objections of the couple or has failed to be persuasive in justifying the goals. One other cause of differing goals is the counselor's attempt to intervene before conducting a thorough assessment.

A second reason that counseling sometimes fails to progress is that the counselor becomes involved in a power struggle with one or both spouses. Power struggles can usually be traced to different expectations about counseling and failure of both parties to give in. Power struggles usually occur over the goals of counseling or the methods of counseling, but sometimes they occur over issues such as differences in the way Scripture is interpreted or differences in the ways that Christianity is talked about.

One pastor was heavily involved in faith healing. Some of his parishioners were from Calvinist backgrounds, and they opposed his practices. One such couple that he counseled quickly dropped out of counseling because they did not want to subject themselves to what they considered "brainwashing," even though the pastor had never mentioned faith healing during the first five weeks of counseling. The power struggle had nothing to do with what went on during counseling, but it was lethal nonetheless.

The third possible reason that counseling might fail to progress is that one or both of the spouses is not revealing a guilty secret. One common secret is the presence of an affair by one spouse. Sometimes Christians are reluctant to admit that they could have been involved in an affair. Both spouses will harbor bitterness and anger over the affair and its aftermath but will be ashamed to reveal it to the counselor.

I, as a counselor, might say:

It seems that counseling is making little progress. It is almost as if something important is responsible for lots of anger in your marriage. I have the feeling that I may be missing some important information somewhere. Is there anything that you can think of that might be inhibiting counseling?

When the past affair is revealed, the couple usually justifies withholding the information, saying that the affair is past and that it has been forgiven. Unfortunately, the *effects* of the affair remained and are all too apparent to the counselor.

Another frequent guilty secret is a past abortion. Sometimes a couple will have disagreed about whether to seek abortion. In some cases, the woman sought abortion without the consent of her husband or obtained an abortion for a premarital pregnancy. Years later, the guilt of the decision or the conflict over the issue will cause mixed feelings to arise between spouses. The couple might be reluctant to discuss the problem in counseling because they perceive the counselor to have values that differ from them, and they fear that counseling will be hampered. Yet, by withholding the information from the counselor, they impede counseling.

Sometimes, despite the use of written assessment reports specifying the approximate length of counseling, the couple and the counselor are reluctant to end their counseling relationship. This is usually because the counselor has become too important to the couple or the couple has become too important to the counselor.

Hesitancy to End

The counselor might become overly important through being too helpful. When counseling seems to revitalize a marriage that previously seemed moribund, the couple often attributes almost miraculous powers to the counselor—despite efforts of the counselor to give credit to God's power and to the couple's initiative and faithfulness. Change might have happened so fast that the couple is unsure whether it will be lasting and are thus careful to maintain ties with the counselor after the need for regular contact is gone.

The counselor might become too important through being too supportive. If the counselor showers love and support on the couple without working to get the couple to support each other, the couple will not want to give up their primary source of caring.

The counselor might also become too important through failing to attribute change to the proper sources—God and the couple. Most counselors want to be important, helpful and supportive. It is a constant pull to bask in credit for producing powerful change in a couple's life. Yet, the counselor must systematically give proper credit for change throughout counseling, not just during termination. If the counselor waits too long to give credit to the couple, they will have a hard time believing that the counselor is sincere.

Though it is hard to admit, there have been times that I did not want to end counseling because I enjoyed meeting with the couple. One young couple sought counseling because of the wife's depression, which was beginning to affect their relationship. We worked primarily on her depression while involving the husband in helping and supporting her. The couple were eager to learn and followed suggestions quickly and enthusiastically. Each week they reported amazing things they were learning about the Lord and about their relationship.

Over the weeks, I looked forward to their visits because I enjoyed seeing them as friends and knew that after counseling we would probably never meet again. I also enjoyed the success and power I felt. After about three months, though, the wife's depression had essentially lifted. I found that I could not bring myself to terminate their counseling and I assiduously avoided even thinking about ending our contact. One week, the woman brought in an article from *Reader's Digest* about depression. She said that the article had revolutionized her life. Her husband agreed and they terminated. I still laugh at God's provision for ending a counseling relationship that had continued too long. I think of it as "The Great *Reader's Digest* Cure."

MAKING TERMINATION HARDER

It is not easy to determine when to terminate, even when the assessment summary has specified a number of intervention sessions. Feelings are usually mixed near the end of counseling. Sometimes love and care for the clients are mixed with fear of turning them loose. Other times frank dislike of the clients is mixed with fear of turning them loose. Just because a counselor has a good working relationship with the clients does not mean that he or she must enjoy counseling with them. I used to feel that I had failed if I did not develop warm feelings for my clients. I have since realized that my feelings will vary with each couple. Counseling interactions are complex. At times the counselor is confidant, punitive parent, loving friend or coolly analytical professional. The various roles create an equal variety of emotions. Feelings are not reliable indicators of the desirability of termination.

Uncertainty and Ambivalence

Nor are "objective" indicators, such as achieving written goals, sure indicators of termination. First, goals are always imprecise, regardless of how carefully worded and specific one tries to make them. Second, specific goals are more easily evaluated but are usually not as complete and as reflective of the clients' evaluation as are general goals. Third, it is hard to determine whether a goal has been reached. Clients can demonstrate knowledge of desirable behaviors and attitudes. They can show that they have the ability to communicate well, to resolve conflict, to have intimacy and to show forgiveness. Yet, the couple might not exhibit stable interaction patterns at home. Counseling exerts subtle—and sometimes not so subtle—pressure for the couple to behave better. The couple may respond more to the demands of counseling than to actual changes in their lives.

Clients' desires for termination are not always good indicators of termination either. Clients' motives are as complex and sometimes inaccessible to consciousness as the counselor's motives. Clients' reasons for termination might have nothing to do with their relationship status. For example, some of my clients have said that financial difficulties, time constraints, conflicts with church activities or even an impending trip to Europe have figured prominently in their wishes to terminate.

Consequently, termination almost always involves uncertainty and ambivalence in both counselor and clients. It is rare indeed for both counselor and client to spontaneously "know" that it is time to terminate.

System Variables

Systems seek stability. Water flows downhill until it reaches stability. A chair falls over when tipped. And husband-wife-counselor triads also become stable systems over time. Stable systems resist change. Water in a basin, when sloshed, returns to the lowest part of the basin. A fallen chair, when lifted slightly, falls back to the ground. A counseling relationship, when threatened with termination, resists the change.

If the counselor suggests that termination is nearing, the couple will sometimes have a mini-crisis that might extend counseling. If the couple arrives at a session and unexpectedly announces that they want to terminate after the session, the counselor will often spend the session systematically directing the couple's attention to the problems that they have not yet fully resolved. Both the couple's and the counselor's behavior are natural parts of established systems. Knowing this, the counselor must use his or her skill and the structure of counseling to help the triad change back into a self-sustaining marital duo.

MAKING TERMINATION EASIER

Attitude

From the initial contact onward, the counselor portrays a consistent attitude toward counseling. The counselor is merely one instrument that God uses, serving as a temporary consultant to a permanent, God-established relationship that was intended to and can solve its own problems. This attitude can be stated verbally throughout counseling and more importantly should be assumed as true.

Assessment Contract

The assessment evaluation, which states the expected time that will be required to complete counseling, is one of the greatest aids to termination. Based on the judgment of the counselor after limited contact with the couple, the agreed upon duration of counseling must be tentatively held, but it usually limits counseling by its nature. As the projected time for termination draws near, the couple's effort often increases. Both problems and solutions are often magnified. Couples that are improving usually spurt ahead during the closing weeks, while couples that are making progress but have many unresolved issues often become more chaotic and conflictual as the deadline draws near.

Throughout counseling the counselor should refer to the time line frequently. Homework might be framed by statements like, "Since we have only ten more sessions to work together, we need to jump right into the thick of the problem." Later sessions might require a beginning statement such as, "Well, after today, we have only three sessions remaining. What would you like to talk about today?" A middle session might include a statement such as, "Counseling is about half over. We only have five sessions remaining. Have you given any thought to what our agenda should include during the last half of our work together?" As a general rule of thumb, I try to refer to the number of sessions remaining one time per session. Each time, the mention is casually worked into a different part of the session.

Faded Contact

If resistance to termination is thought of as a problem in system stability, the solution is to destabilize the system prior to attempting to terminate. Probably the most frequent way to accomplish this is by fading the contact. As the last two or three sessions are approached, they are spaced out. In a twelve-week intervention agreement, for example, the tenth session might be scheduled with a week between the ninth and tenth sessions. The tenth and eleventh sessions might have two weeks between them, and the final two sessions might have a month or six weeks between them.

A second way to end counseling gracefully is to declare a vacation from counseling. Counselor and clients might jointly decide on a vacation or an actual vacation by either client or counselor might be used as an excuse for the couple to try out what they have been practicing without weekly counseling.

A third way to destabilize the system is to tell the clients that they can have one additional session whenever they feel like they need it. Counseling is not officially terminated, but the clients are left with "one in the bank." This might leave some issues unaddressed with the clients, such as not adequately saying good-by, but it can help the clients feel secure while they operate independently of the counselor, which is one of the goals of counseling.

Final Sessions Formal termination usually begins on the next-to-the-final session. For couples that remain in counseling for twenty or more sessions, formal termination might be started one session earlier.

At the end of the session, I say:

Next session is our final time together. At the beginning of counseling, we said that we would determine whether we should continue with counseling at this time. My evaluation is that we probably won't need to extend our time together beyond next session. You might have a different evaluation, though. What I would like for you to do before our next session is to think about, and maybe write down if you want to, where you were when you first began counseling. You should also assess where you see yourselves as a couple now. Finally, you should reflect on what still might be accomplished in your relationship and how you might reach those goals. I will think about those same things and will prepare a summary of my thoughts. Does this sound like something that you two are willing to do before the next session?

During the ensuing week, I prepare a summary of counseling that is tailored for the individual couple. Usually I restate the goals that were listed in the assessment report. I might describe some of the change points of counseling, and I include an assessment of their current status and possible goals that they could achieve on their own. The report is usually laced with attributions to their courage and willingness to work, if that had indeed been the case. The report is formally typed and photocopied so that each spouse can have a copy. An example of a termination report is given in Figure 18.

The final session usually begins with social amenities and sometimes transmutes into pleasant reminiscences of counseling. Near the middle of the session, I ask the couple about their assessment of counseling and how closely they have come to attaining their goals for counseling. After hearing their assessment, I provide photocopies of my final evaluation to each spouse and give them time to read it. They comment on the report and try to resolve any differences in our perceptions of the relationship. I ask about their goals as a couple now that counseling is ending. I then ask whether

Figure 18
Typical Termination Summary

CONFIDENTIAL
James and Lois Sharp

Termination Summary
This statement considers the state of the relationship of the Sharps after having attended counseling for three assessment sessions and ten counseling sessions over a period of four months.

Original Goals
After three weeks of assessment, we agreed to work on:
  1. helping the Sharps build intimacy into a relationship that was then characterized by little time spent together and by frequent bickering and some outright arguments,
  2. reducing the sarcasm and cutting humor employed by both Lois and James,
  3. improving communication through resolving some of the long-standing issues between the Sharps,
  4. improving the time each spent talking about things that are "important."

Modification of Goals
Throughout counseling we agreed to work specifically on some goals in addition to those originally identified. We agreed to work on improving the Sharp's sexual relationship, especially the frequency of their lovemaking, which both found enjoyable but could never seem to find time for. We also focused more intensely on the conflicts over Lois's "compulsive spending."

Summary of Sessions
Although counseling had several ups and downs, overall the Sharps made continual progress on several of the goals. The biggest modifications were in how they allocated time to activities that they both enjoyed. A "truce" was made in which they agreed to set aside one night each week to engage in a mutually pleasant behavior away from the children. They agreed to leave the house on Friday night and not discuss with the boys where they were going. Both were to try to discuss things that were important to them and were to ask each other questions about whatever the spouse was talking about. Both agreed to refrain from intentionally provoking the other. Over all, these nights out proved valuable, and the Sharps agreed to continue the practice for at least three months.

Work on conflict resolution was undertaken, and some progress was noted; however, both agreed to not having the problem licked yet. Sessions were attempted at home in which some of the strategies of *Getting to Yes* were employed. These were discussed in ensuing sessions.

The Sharps reported that when they began their nights out, their sexual relationship improved substantially. Some disagreement still exists over some of the activities that will occur during lovemaking and over the length of their foreplay. Both say that they are willing to compromise, but currently disagreement still exists.

Lois says that she seems better able to control her spending compulsion now that the relationship is more enjoyable.

Recommendations

I recommend that the Sharps discontinue counseling and work toward maintaining their newly attempted intimacy and their new lovemaking routines. In addition, their disagreements should continue to be limited to times that are specifically designated as problem-solving times. Increases in the use of bickering, cutting humor or compulsive spending should (as agreed) be a signal to schedule a problem-solving night within the next seven days so that little disagreements will not poison their relationship again.

Personal Comments

I have enjoyed working with each of you and with you as a married team. You have both been very willing to open yourselves to new things and to try suggestions honestly. I admire the courage with which you have attacked the dissatisfactions in your relationship. You have many strengths as a couple, and I have enjoyed the privilege of getting to know you. I continue to pray that the Lord will bless your marriage and your children.

they can anticipate any future problems that might be troublesome. If some are mentioned, I ask how they might handle them.

Finally, I discuss my feelings about working with them as a couple and share any positive feelings I have about them. Sometimes this prompts them to reciprocate. Usually by that time, the hour is at an end. I mention that it is hard to say good-by. Often we will close the session with prayer by each person, glorifying God for his work in their lives.

SUMMARY

Termination is difficult for clients and counselor because there is often considerable ambivalence in the temporary helping relationship. The counselor, though, must single-mindedly pursue termination, even if clients and counselor *feel* impelled to continue, provided the counselor rationally evaluates the couple as no longer requiring counseling.

17

Commitment of the Counselor

THROUGHOUT THIS BOOK, I HAVE DISCUSSED WAYS TO CONCEPtualize both the marriage and the individual spouses. I have built a plan of assessment and treatment that aims to promote intimacy, enhance communication, reduce conflict, ameliorate hurt, stop blame, curtail sin and rebuild commitment in the spouses. As a counselor, I have the same human needs as my clients: meaning, intimacy, communication, effectance, forgiveness and commitment. In this closing chapter, I would like to discuss our professional commitment as marriage counselors.

COMMITMENT TO CHRISTIAN COUNSELING

Throughout this book, I have tried to present a consistent theory and explication of techniques for counseling troubled Christian married couples. I have avoided the term *Christian counseling* because I believe that there is not one universal way that Christians should counsel. I acknowledge high authority of Scripture as my final rule for faith and practice, and I look to Scripture as God's holy and infallible written Word for guidance. Yet, I do not believe that Scripture prescribes the totality of Christian counseling.

Because of these beliefs, several Christian practices have not been thoroughly discussed as marriage-counseling techniques for use with Christian couples. This is not because I think the practices should be avoided in counseling. Rather, it is because the techniques should be such a part of counseling that they are basic to it. Prayer with and for clients, Scripture study by clients about relevant topics, Scripture exegesis by the counselor, (perhaps) anointing with oil and the use of Scripture for exhortation are as much a part of counseling with Christian couples as are active listening skills, confrontation, clarification and interpretation. I discussed neither class of techniques in detail. The book presupposes that all are within the arsenal of the practicing Christian counselor.

Not every counselor will be comfortable using some of the techniques I have listed. That is fine. We each must develop sensitivity to the leading of the Holy Spirit, who guides us in our work with couples. Not every client can benefit by the use of the techniques either. That's fine too. Jesus tailored his techniques to the needs of the people he ministered to, and we should do the same.

Importantly, whether we use the pastoral practices of historic Christianity within our counseling or whether we merely counsel using love as our attitude and let our behavior be Scripture-consistent, we must place our final reliance not in ourselves or our techniques but in the God of heaven. Jesus is the healer of lives, bodies and marriages. The Holy Spirit is our guide, and he also guides our Christian clients. Let us keep love as our aim and glorify God in our lives. Thus, regardless of our approach to counseling, we must retain a firm commitment to Christian counseling as we understand it.

COMMITMENT TO HIGH-QUALITY COUNSELING

Wouldn't it be nice if all of life were a mountaintop experience? if we never got tired? if we never sighed when we thought of the upcoming hour with a couple who have seemingly made no progress in the last six weeks of counseling? Although I see myself as an encourager, as one who is positive and enthusiastic, I must confess to times when I am in the doldrums. During these times when the breath of the Holy Spirit seems hardly to stir around me, I must, nonetheless, remain committed to giving myself completely to my clients during counseling.

It is tempting merely to go through the motions at times, justifying ourselves by promising to pay more attention next time. It is tempting not to prepare for a session with a couple who seems to resist our every effort to help.

God wants us to be committed to excellence, not only in counseling but in all of life. In Philippians 4:8, Paul writes, ". . . If there is any excellence, if there is anything worthy of praise, think about these things." In Colossians 3:17, he encourages us by saying, "And whatever you do, in word or deed, do everything in the name of the Lord Jesus, giving thanks to God the Father through him." The fact is that Jesus dwells within us and so whatever we do *is* in the name of Jesus. Is there any better reason for being committed to excellence in our counseling? Whether or not we feel like it, we should strive to live out a commitment to the best counseling we can possibly give.

COMMITMENT TO WORKING WITHIN OUR LIMITATIONS

A commitment to excellence in counseling implies that we do not practice outside the limits of our competency. I wish I could handle with competence every marital difficulty that I saw. I simply cannot. My task then is to remain humble in the face of requests for help. I must become aware of my limitations and resist the temptation to counsel a couple merely because they ask, because their problem presents a challenge, because of the money or because of a sense of duty. If their difficulty is beyond my current ability, I must recognize it.

After I become aware of my limitations as a counselor, I must evaluate whether I want to change my limitations. Do I want to develop expertise in the intricacies of sexual therapy or in working with abusive or alcohol-dependent spouses? Am I able to educate myself on the therapy of people with problems with which I have little experience? Further, once I educate myself about the therapeutic treatment of a problem, can I arrange adequate supervision to my therapy as I learn to apply the techniques in practice with actual couples? As Wiley[1] showed in a national study of therapists and supervisors, therapists rarely improved through experience alone. Rather, they generally required supervised counseling experience before they improved.

As you complete the reading of this book, I encourage you to examine yourself seriously to determine your competency at working with married couples. Although a book such as this might have provided you with many techniques to try and with new ways of thinking about couples with problematic marriages, it cannot insure your successful application of the techniques. As a therapist committed to excellence, you must examine your limitations and arrange supervision for instances when you must exceed your experience.

COMMITMENT TO WALK IN JESUS' STEPS

I have just finished reading the classic novel, *In His Steps,* by Charles Sheldon.[2] The book is about the revolutionary changes that took place in a city when the congregation of a large church took up their pastor's challenge to stop before each decision and ask, What would Jesus do in this situation? The people tried to answer this question the way they understood what Jesus would do (without judging others) and tried to act consistently with their answer regardless of the consequences to themselves.

Just before I read *In His Steps,* I reread Charles Malik's book, *A Christian Critique of the University.*[3] Malik was a philosopher trained at Harvard, a former college dean awarded over fifty honorary doctoral degrees and an international diplomat who served as president of the General Assembly of the United Nations. In addition, he presided over four other organizations of the United Nations and was decorated by twelve countries for his efforts at promoting world peace. In 1981, he examined the world university system as a cultural institution by posing the simple question, What would Jesus

Christ think of today's university?

Both of these books have prompted me to ask, What would Jesus Christ think of my counseling? Would he find it motivated by love? Would he find it to be excellent and an honor to his name (by which we Christians are called)? Would he find it sacrificial or self-serving? These are hard questions that we each must ask.

Let us each commit ourselves to walk in his steps so the answer will glorify him and his Father.

APPENDIX:
Current Theories of Marriage Counseling

In this appendix, I will consider five "schools" of marriage counseling: psychoanalytic, systems, behavioral, cognitive and Christian. I will summarize and compare numerous theories within the five schools.

Why am I doing such a masochistic (and some readers will say, sadistic) thing?

☐ Is it is my obsessive personality or my cognitive need for completeness and closure?

☐ Is it the influence of my family of origin and my current family in developing my need to understand and change complex systems?

☐ Is it that since I am in midlife, I like to consider new options?

Each of those three levels of analysis—individual, family and life cycle—might give a good explanation for my behavior. Using each explanation in sequence would be more complete, but you might not have time for such a complete understanding.

Each "school" of marriage counseling uses at least one of these three levels of analysis. Marriage counselors who use only one level are limited. Those who draw haphazardly from all schools to fit momentary purposes soon become confused unless they are guided by some integrative principles.[1]

At the end of this appendix, I identify six needs for an integrated theory of marriage counseling. I summarize and briefly critique current theories of marriage counseling. If you are like most practitioners, you help people competently, using a theory to do so, but you have little knowledge of theories unrelated to yours. If your theory has been developed primarily through practice rather than through study of formal theories, you might be surprised to find the richness of depth you can gain through reading other theories. You will benefit through knowing about the variety of approaches to marriage counseling.

There are a number of things this appendix is *not* intended to accomplish. This appendix is not intended to be an exhaustive summary or critique of all marital therapies, which could be accomplished adequately only in a large text. This appendix likewise is not a summary of *family* therapies. Many well-known family-therapy theorists have written little on marital therapy. For example, Carl Whitaker, Ivan Boszormenyi-Nagy, James Alexander, Robin Skynner, James Framo, Mara Selvini-Palazzoli and others have written excellent theories of family therapy with only incidental reference to marital therapy. I did not include such theories.

Furthermore, this appendix is not an authoritative presentation of each theory. Reviewers of the first draft of this book differed in some of their perceptions of the various theories. Almost universally they called for more summary, comment and critique of some theories. Sometimes they identified different emphases than I did. I readily admit that the practitioner or scholar who is thoroughly ensconced in one tradition of marital therapy might understand the writings of the theorist better than I. Thus, I have tried to footnote liberally within the appendix so that you can find the major writings associated with the theories of most interest to you.

This appendix is not a primer (or brief guide) to some of the main ideas in several of the varieties of marital therapies (as distinct from family therapies). Rather, it is intended to demonstrate that there are many excellent ways to help couples with marital difficulties and to show you the sources of some of the techniques I have recommended throughout the book in the service of promoting my integrative principles (intimacy, communication, conflict redirection, commitment). It is also intended to highlight some of the differences and similarities in theories and to motivate you to read more about the theories that interest you.

Each theory offers explanations for similar issues. First, each theory suggests principles upon which marriage is based. The particular principles that are highlighted are those in which (a) problems arise in troubled marriages and (b) therapists can promote changes. Second, each theory suggests potential solutions for marital difficulties. Third, each theory suggests techniques to accomplish the solutions. Fourth, many theories describe stages through which therapy might progress.

I have organized the appendix according to the relationships among the schools. Psychoanalytic or psychodynamic theories predate family therapies. Many of the theorists who later became family therapists and marriage therapists were trained to employ psychodynamic principles, which shaped many of their views of families and marriages and therapy with families and marriages. I have thus begun with psychoanalytic marital therapy.

Generally, psychoanalysis has emphasized individual psychodynamic functioning; thus, few psychoanalytic marital therapies have been formally proposed. Much of the writing on the marriage from a psychoanalytic perspective has involved either mate selection as a way of meeting individual psychological needs[2] or collusion (unconscious "conspiracy" among couples in their behavior and symptomology that allows them to meet unconscious psychological needs).[3]

I cover systems theories of *marital* therapy next, beginning with Murray Bowen's theory because it draws most heavily on psychodynamic principles. I then discuss the work derived from Bateson's family systems research. The marital therapy derived from that project has emanated from the Mental Research Institute (MRI). Then I discuss Salvador Minuchin's Structural Therapy, which is derived mostly from his work with marital subsystems within family systems. Finally, Jay Haley's strategic therapy is discussed. Haley worked both at the MRI and with Minuchin. Counseling mostly lower socioeconomic-status clients, Haley and later Cloe Madanes, his wife, developed a no-nonsense, directive approach to helping couples and families.

Behavioral marital therapies have also promulgated a straightforward approach to helping couples. Their theory is based largely on experimental observation of couples, the couples' interactions with therapists and social exchange theory.

In recent years, behavioral marriage therapy has considered more cognitive variables. I cover a number of cognitive and cognitive-behavioral approaches to marital therapy, including Clifford Sager, whose roots are again planted in psychodynamic soil.

Finally, Norman Wright has proposed a Christian marital therapy that is based largely on behavioral and cognitive marital therapies, which will be further explored in the later summary.

PSYCHOANALYTIC MARRIAGE THERAPIES

For a number of reasons, psychoanalysts and psychodynamic theorists have not written systematic theories of marriage counseling even though they have written much about the effects of the family on psychological development. Several theorists have written theories that are technically eclectic but use psychodynamic conceptualizations to understand marriage counseling and to guide intervention strategies. Notably, Sager,[5] Ables and Brandsma,[6] Martin,[7] Gurman,[8] Willi,[9] Dicks,[10] Framo[11] and Bannister and Pincus[12] have presented marriage counseling theories that are conceptualized using psychodynamic (either ego psychology/object relations or classical psychoanalytic) conceptualizations.

Summary of Nadelson's Theory[4]

Carol Nadelson[13] presented a compact summary of psychodynamic marriage therapy which will be summarized below as one example of how psychoanalytic conceptualization might be applied to marriage counseling. Some of her thinking is supplemented by work by Christopher Dare.[14]

Problems are seen as due to the developmental history of individuals. While growing up, individuals experience psychological conflicts, some of which remain unresolved. These unconscious conflicts motivate people to resolve, deny or defend against their anxiety through "proper" mate selection. Mates are attracted to each other because they either are similar to parents, are opposite to parents or fill the gaps left by parents in the critical, conflictual areas of growing up. Proper mate selection can lead to fulfillment as an adult when the relationship with the mate allows the person to work through unresolved conflicts. But sometimes partners collude—unconsciously agree—to defend each other from threatening psychological conflicts.

For example, a hysterical woman marries an obsessive man. Both can avoid intimacy, which is hypothesized to be the deficiency in each of their developmental histories. The woman acts emotionally and the man acts intellectually, controlling anxiety through rigid cognitive patterns. The woman drives the man away by continual demands for emotional support, and the man feels justified in not being responsive. They collude to keep a safe, nonintimate distance between them—even though the wife demands (very emotionally) more intimacy. She has selected a mate that she unconsciously knows will not respond intimately to her, and her emotionality insures that her mate will not respond with intimacy.

The goals of psychoanalytic marriage therapy are to solve the marital problems through helping individuals gain insight into the overt and unconscious reasons for their behavior. Dare distinguishes between couples who are motivated mostly by symptom relief (either marital distress or an individual symptom) or by understanding their marriages. He believes all couples have *both* motivations to some degree. He suggests that psychoanalytically informed interpretations and insight play a less central role in the therapy of couples strongly desiring symptom relief than in those desiring deeper understanding of their marriage or themselves. Nonetheless, interpretations and insight are beneficial in all therapy.

Nadelson describes three stages of therapy. In the initial stage, the counselor helps the couple solve some of their interactional problems. Dare suggests that the couple begins either with a discussion of symptoms (if one spouse is symptomatic) or a summary of conspicuous disagreement (if marital tension is the presenting problem). Nadelson recommends a variety of techniques from systems and behavioral marriage therapies to help people straighten out their interactions. Interpretations of transference neuroses—ways people act out their psychodynamic conflicts with each other and with the therapist—are generally infrequent in the initial stage. Dare suggests that usually the couple is induced to talk mostly to each other rather than to the therapist, and the therapist observes and promotes communication between spouses. The therapist attempts to promote symmetry. The conclusion of the initial stage is the conclusion of counseling for many people.

For those who want to explore why they behave as they do, Nadelson recommends a second phase of counseling to achieve insight through interpretations, confrontations and dealing with resistances that arise during counseling. The goals of the second phase are to neutralize and integrate aggressive and libidinal (sexual) needs so that behavior is motivated more in the service of the ego and less by impulse and intrapsychic conflict. Dare suggests that the therapist may explore childhood experiences of one or both partners and help them to understand their past and its employment in their current marriage. Reconstructive interpretations may be offered. There is a need to balance directive and interpretive interpretations.[15]

The third phase of counseling is termination. Once the termination date is set, many conflicts and defenses re-emerge. The therapist helps the couple to identify and work through their anxiety about the impending loss and to review and clarify therapeutic gains.

Gurman, a well-known analyst of family therapies who is inclined toward psychodynamic theories himself,[16] takes issue with some of Nadelson's theorizing.[17] Notably, he believes that therapists must begin from early in the relationship to pursue insight into spouses' unconscious motivations. Interpretations are used prevalently throughout therapy, rather than being concentrated in the second phase.

Critique of Nadelson's Theory

Other criticisms of Nadelson's and other psychodynamic theories are pertinent. Psychodynamic therapists assume that marriages are troubled because individual spouses are troubled. However, there are many marriages that are troubled even though individuals appear psychologically healthy. To the contrary, behavioral and systems therapies usually assume that marriages have characteristics that are separate from the characteristics of the spouses. They might assume that spouses are troubled because the marriage is troubled. Yet, sometimes individuals become troubled while marriages remain untroubled. The truth is that both cases occur.

Gurman argues that most couples terminate marriage counseling in fewer than twenty sessions. They expect short-term problem-solving counseling rather than long-term insight-oriented therapy. Thus, the goals of the psychodynamic marriage counselor must be realistic. He recommends that the therapist aim for: (a) rapid removal or amelioration of the most disabling symptoms; (b) prompt re-establishment of the couple's previous emotional equilibrium; (c) development of the couple's understanding of the current disturbance; and (d) increased coping ability in the future. Personality reconstruction of either spouse (or both) is impossible.

Psychoanalytic marriage therapy is less clearly articulated than any of the other marriage therapies. There are few techniques that are uniquely psychoanalytic, such as interpretation of transference or interpretation of dreams. There has, consequently, been little research on its practice. Generally, therapists who favor psychoanalytic or ego-object theorizing when working with individuals will be comfortable applying the concept to spouses. They might be able to help spouses understand how their past has led to their present difficulties, but the therapist generally will have to rely on techniques from other schools of therapy to induce couples to change. Psychodynamic marriage therapy is best thought of as a way of understanding problems rather than a change-inducing therapy for couples.

MARITAL SYSTEMS THEORIES

Unlike psychodynamic or behavioral approaches to marriage counseling, which are more similar than different, systems theories are so different from each other that sometimes it is difficult to see the similarities. As it is, there are two main approaches to systems theories: Bowen's theory and theories based on general systems theory. General systems theory holds that all parts of a system are mutually interrelated and function with unique rules. Aristotelian logic using linear causality is generally less preferred to "circular causality" or "constructivism" in family systems philosophy. This philosophy has been articulated with force in recent years as a "new epistemology," which has had its critics.[18]

Summary of Bowen's Theory

Bowen's theorizing has roots in both psychodynamic and systems theories. Generally, Bowen sees problematic families as "stuck together emotionally." In early work he called this the "undifferentiated family ego mass."[19] He suggests that two parallel processes exist in humans. First, through evolution, emotional processes are assumed to have developed. These processes are herd processes that bind creatures together for survival. Second, intellectual processes, which are meant to have ascendancy over the primary processes, were thought to have developed. Bowen defines problems as disorders of the emotional system. The solution to these troubles is to assert intellectual control over these primitive emotional disorders.

Some of the ways that the emotional system manifests itself are through triangulation, family projection and multi-generational transmission. Triangulation is the tendency for a third party to be co-opted into any two-person system. The two people form strong pressure for the third person to act out a role that will perpetuate and stabilize the two-person system. Family projections are ways that a family system creates symptomology in a child. Family-of-origin difficulties, unresolved by parents, result in parent-child relations that are either over-involved (either through criticism or smothering) or characterized by emotional cutoff. Psychological or behavioral symptoms of the child maintain the disturbed parent-child relationship and prevent the parents from resolving their family-of-origin issues.

Multi-generational transmission explains how past and current couple dynamics are entangled; spouses repeat the styles of relating that they learned from their parents. The couple must free itself from the pressures exerted from past generations or the marriage is likely to relapse after therapy is ended.

Counselors use their intellectual processes to help marriage partners assert intellectual control over their emotional processes. Counselors use couples' attempts at triangulation to do this. Couples will try (unconsciously) to triangulate the counselor into a role that perpetuates the problems. If the counselor resists these pulls, the marriage will feel counterforces that pull it from its fused state. This helps the partners differentiate from each other and from other family members. Differentiation means that the intellect is governing the emotional system of the couple, or (technically) that the person can distinguish between feeling processes and intellectual processes. The couple understands its behavior well enough to exert conscious ego control over it.

Bowen's behavior during counseling is controlled and intellectual.[20] He calls this "detoxifying" the relationship—getting the poison out of the relationship. He assumes that learning occurs best in an environment of low anxiety, that the most important couple interactions occur outside of therapy (if the therapy is detoxified), and that the effective therapist must be simultaneously detached and involved. Communication generally goes through Bowen. He speaks with one spouse, then with the other. Spouses rarely talk to each other. Sometimes Bowen will "lecture" one or both spouses. He has the couple analyze their feelings rather than act on them. This openly insight-oriented approach often involves more than the couple; Bowen will sometimes invite members of all living generations into counseling sessions. Bowen even advocates therapy groups that involve several couples. However, each couple is dealt with for about a half-hour per session with the other couples observing (but not speaking). Each couple is counseled in turn. Bowen maintains that observing helps couples distance from emotional issues and so they gain understanding even more quickly than when they are being counseled.

Bowen teaches more a theory and a style of operation than he does techniques. His training of therapists parallels his training of couples. It is intellectually oriented, and his ideas are discussed and debated.

One useful technique has been developed from Bowen's thinking by Fogarty, who has identified the emotional pursuer-distancer pattern.[21] One spouse demands intimacy but the other maintains distance. Finally, the pursuer stops pursuing. The distancer then moves closer but is punished by abuse, perhaps hearing, "I don't want intimacy now; where were you when I needed you?" Ultimately, the distancer retaliates with abusive tactics. In its advanced stage, this pattern leaves two emotionally insulated spouses who feel as if they are separated by steel walls. Bowenite counselors[22] break up this emotional pattern by teaching the couples to act opposite to their usual behavior.

A second counseling technique is for the therapist to take "I position" stands. The therapist identifies his or her own position, if it is not in line with the stand of either spouse. This keeps the therapist from being triangulated into the marriage and differentiates the therapist from the couple while keeping him or her in contact with them.

A third technique is explicit teaching by the counselor. Since Bowen wants the couple both to experience and to understand their behavior, the couple is urged to apply Bowen's principles to their emotional functioning. They are taught why they act as they do, which is not unlike the teaching that behavioral counselors do.

Generally, the flow of Bowen's marital therapy is from the marital system to self system to family system to social system.[23] In the beginning of therapy, the therapist attempts to change (deintensify) the emotion in the marital system. The assessment stage of marital therapy, in which the genogram—an elaborate family tree—is developed, helps the couple understand their relationship within the context of their families of origin. The genogram is usually a relatively structured task that is easily controlled by the therapist. In the problem stage of therapy, the therapist proposes that the couple conduct "experiments" with changed relationship behaviors. Throughout the couple's efforts, the therapist focuses their attention on the self system. Spouses are repeatedly stimulated to reflect on their own roles in problems. In the differentiation-of-self stage, which may last for two or more years with biweekly or monthly sessions, the therapist focuses on the self of each spouse in the context of each's family of origin and larger social contexts (for example, church, employment or school).

Critique of Bowen's Theory

Bowen's theory is reminiscent of psychoanalytic theories. It is complex and one of the most complete theories of the marriage and its problems. It is considerably less complex and complete concerning the conduct of marriage therapy, although Guerin and Fogarty have specified rationales and methods for treating specific disorders. But the grand theory of marriage behavior, which is formulated in largely untested and often (by Bowen's own admission) untestable concepts and which draws upon biology (evolution) and general systems theory, makes it useful for understanding marriages. Its comprehensiveness is praised by Gurman,[24] who summarizes:

> While Bowen might take umbrage at the idea, _Bowen theory may be the only currently existing approach to marital therapy that has the potential, in some modified form, of simultaneously (a) operating out of a developmental framework, (b) paying explicit attention (though in different words) to the rules and meta-rules of intimate relationships, and (c) implementing therapeutic change strategies that are readily rather teachable, which center on current observable transactions, and which include a significant didactic-educational component. Stated otherwise, Bowen therapy seems to offer a treatment capable of using some of the best of what psychoanalytic, communications and behavioral therapies have to offer._ (Emphasis his, p. 517)

Bowen's theory is heavily intellectual and seeks to stimulate insight rather than concrete action or emotional functioning, though it is hoped and assumed that successful marital therapy will result in both behavior and emotions that are more satisfactory to the couple than their pretherapy functioning. Bowen keeps tight control of the session through de-emotionalizing it. Philosophically, Bowen's theory is tied to evolutionary theory and to rejection of absolute Truth, which many Christian counselors would find anathema. As with the behavioral approaches, however, it is possible to use Bowen's techniques and style without adopting his philosophy. Unlike the behavioral approaches, which are well-explained technologies, Bowen's therapy describes counseling style more than techniques.

Finally, Bowen's theory has little empirical validation, either of theoretical constructs or of the outcome efficacy.[25] No controlled studies compare Bowen's and other approaches. Thus, the practitioner who adopts Bowen's style wholeheartedly must rely on the testimonials of the practitioners already committed to the approach or on his or her own limited experience.

The Mental Research Institute (MRI) at Palo Alto, California, has applied general systems theory, game theory, cybernetic theory, and epistemology to describe marriage and family therapy. The work began over twenty years ago under the direction of Gregory Bateson.[26] It involved thinkers such as Paul Watzlawick, Jay Haley, James Weakland, Richard Fisch, Don Jackson and, more recently, Carlos Sluzki. Of the systems theorists, the MRI group has most consistently applied general systems theory to their thinking about the family, though they have broadened their thinking to include other theories when it suited their purpose.

Summary of Mental Research Institute Theory

MRI theorists argue that the behavior of a system can be understood without understanding the individual components of the system.[27] This is called the "black box" model. The model is used by such technologies as explosive experts seeking to defuse bombs and cryptographers seeking to understand codes. Essentially, the behavior of the "box"—in this case the marriage—can be understood by understanding the communications between the components (marriage partners) without understanding what makes the components "tick." The inputs to and outputs from each component (spouse) are the data of the marriage. The counselor is thought to be wasting time by seeking to understand the individuals' thoughts, motivations or values. The communication between components can be described in terms of "rules" that predict behavior better than do personality variables.

Communication is any behavior, whether talk or action. Behavior always transmits a message (or messages) from one spouse to the other. Any communication can be analyzed in terms of its syntax, semantics or pragmatics. *Syntax* involves the way information is transmitted. When the counselor is concerned with who speaks more often, how much each spouse speaks and who interrupts whom, the counselor is interested in syntax. Syntax is also an interest in the relationship between important versus "trivial" talk, officially termed *signal versus noise,* or in who talks to whom.

Semantics involves the meaning of what is communicated. When the counselor attempts to help a couple communicate more clearly, or helps each member to understand what the other is saying, the counselor is analyzing semantics. Semantics also involves shared private communication symbols and distinguishes between concordant and confused communication.

Pragmatics refers to the effects of the communication on sender and receiver. Is the communication merely exchange of information or is it a known provocation? How does one spouse respond to a particular type of communication by the other? Does the spouse acknowledge a message or ignore it? Does the spouse qualify the message? In general, the MRI is most interested in the pragmatics of communication.[28] MRI determines which rules govern a relationship's communication. In this way, almost ignoring the semantics and syntax of communication, MRI communication theorists differ from many other communication theorists.

Since all behavior is communication, a symptom is understood as an attempt to solve a problem through behavioral communication. For example, if a wife feels that her husband demands too much housework from her, she might communicate with her husband to try to get him to ease the demands. At first, she might simply ask him to "ease off." He may ascede to her request. But if the couple is locked into a long-standing struggle over who can tell whom what to do, the husband is likely to resist the request, perhaps by ignoring it or even escalating his demands.

The wife might try numerous solutions to the problem. She might nag him about the yard work, trying to establish the implicit contract that *she* will ease off if *he* will. She might whine and plead. She might simply stop doing all housework.

If no solution works to her satisfaction, she might become depressed (a symptom). Her depression sends her husband a different message than he has previously received. It says, "I *want* to do the housework, but I *can't*. My depression won't let me." Because she is "sick," her husband does not continue his demands at his former level. The wife might become chronically depressed, in which she has periodic flareups of depression that worry (and incidentally frustrate) her husband. The depression is a communication strategy in which both spouses participate. Importantly, depression is *not* seen as an intentional strategy but rather as a costly problem that (incidentally) solves other difficulties.

To help the depression, a counselor using the MRI approach would see the couple, not just the woman who is depressed. The counselor will then try to determine the rules (pragmatics) of communication that make it necessary for the wife to behave symptomatically. The counselor would not be satisfied with simply solving the housework issue, for the counselor would suspect that the symptomatic behavior would be repeated around another issue.

Sluzki proposed eighteen discrete rules for the marriage therapist.[29] The rules are stated in an if-then format with a theoretical justification after each. For example, one rule specifies what the counselor should do if the husband (call him *A)* should speak to the counselor about his wife (call her *B)*.

If A speaks to you about B (rather than to B), then:
  (a) keep looking at A rather than B while A speaks;
  and (b) tell A to speak to, not about, B;
  or (c) ask A how he feels about it;

or (d) address a comment about A to B.

Sluzki's rationale for these suggestions is that A is trying to establish a coalition with the counselor by speaking to the counselor about his wife. Avoid the coalition by refusing to look where he is directing your attention (toward B) and by doing something that is not requested by A. Although this type of behavior is done almost instinctively by most marriage counselors, Sluzki gives the theoretical reasons for doing it.

When a counselor is in the room with a couple in conflict, the counselor often feels almost "compelled" to behave in certain ways. Most of the time, following one's feelings with couples can be as treacherous as playing catch with a hand grenade. Couples are adroit at involving you into their usual communication patterns so that you play a supporting role without your consent or understanding. Bowen calls this triangulation; communication therapists call it a coalition; psychoanalytic marriage therapists call it countertransference or becoming involved in the couple's unconscious collusions. Almost every school of therapy recognizes that this frequently happens, leaving the counselor feeling "used" after the couple leaves the office.

Critique of MRI Theory

The MRI theorists have helped counselors understand how these times happen and how to avoid them. They thus offer something valuable to those who read their work. They have clearly specified frequent patterns of behavior in marriage counseling.

However, despite their efficient specification of communication rules in two-person systems, and in three-person systems which include the counselor, their philosophy strongly limits the targets of counseling. The MRI counselor almost inevitably redefines the couple's problem as a communication problem. Furthermore, the counselor has little interest in *what* the couple communicates; the counselor is interested primarily in *how* they communicate. Sometimes couples resent this approach regardless of how skillfully the counselor redefines the problem. Moreover, in actuality, many problems do not seem to be communication problems. There are times when the focus of the counseling is, and probably should be (my value), the individual. Such an approach is precluded by strict adherence to the MRI approach. In addition to these limitations, the MRI approach has surprisingly little research that supports its clinical effectiveness, in spite of its inception in a research project.

Minuchin's theory[30] rests on three assumptions: (1) a person operates within a social context, which interacts with the person; (2) the social context has a structure; (3) the structure can be good or bad. The structure of a marriage is apparent from three observations of the marriage: (1) how the marriage is organized; (2) how transactions are patterned over time; and (3) how the system responds to stress.

Summary of Minuchin's Structural Therapy

Structure depends on organization. For Minuchin, the family is organized into subsystems—for instance, marriage, parent, child and grandparent subsystems. The marriage subsystem is important because (a) it can be clearly delineated as husband and wife; (b) it is the only voluntarily maintained subsystem; and (c) it provides necessary functions to the family (such as adult decision-making). The boundaries, which define who participates in adult functions and how, protect the marriage subsystem from interference in carrying out its functions.

Minuchin believes that a healthy marriage must have clear boundaries that are not so rigid that the husband and wife cannot transact effectively with their children, in-laws, work environments or each other. When boundaries are not clear, they may be either too rigidly separated from other subsystems (disengaged) or too undifferentiated (enmeshed). Practically, this means that when a structural family counselor is assessing the marriage, the counselor will talk with the couple about their relationships with their children (if any), their own parents and other people who are important to them.

Structure of a marriage depends on how transactions are patterned. Like the MRI and Haley (as we shall soon see), Minuchin is more concerned with *how* couples communicate with each other than with *what* they communicate. Minuchin is particularly aware of how the communication fits the context and is alert to the expectations that each spouse has for communication in particular situations. Minuchin discerns the roles revealed by communication patterns. He might find a domineering wife/submissive husband pattern in areas of child rearing but find shared power with finances and sex.

Structure of the marriage depends on how the marriage reacts to stress. Minuchin identifies four sources of stress. Stress might be due to (1) interaction between an individual and forces outside of the family, such as work responsibilities or peer interactions; (2) interactions between the family as a whole and forces outside the family, such as disruption over moving or changing churches; (3) developmental transitions within the family; or (4) idiosyncratic sources, such as natural disasters. More important than the source of stress, however, is the way the marriage adapts to stress, which can lead either to adjustment or rigidity. If problems result from stress, problems may take the form of a stable, unsatisfactory situation or a marital crisis.[31]

Once the structure of the marriage is determined, the counselor attempts to change it. Assessment occurs throughout counseling, not prior to it. Intervention is begun in the first interview. The couple's response to counseling interventions becomes additional assessment information.

The structural counselor is active and dramatic in applying techniques to change the family's structure. Minuchin rules the session with an iron hand. He rarely gives reasons for what he does. Minuchin is not interested in a couple's understanding why they have problems. He is interested in their actions. Watching Minuchin perform is often dizzying. With a clear grasp of what he is looking for, he conducts what often appears to be a chaotic and ill-conceived session in which everyone is active. Understanding his theory, however, makes most of his actions comprehensible.

Perhaps more than any marriage therapist, Minuchin has described techniques to change families and marriages. Minuchin is so vital, energetic and challenging in his personal demeanor that it is no surprise that his techniques are organized around challenge. Minuchin will try to challenge either (a) the structure of the marriage or family; (b) the organization of the marriage or family around the symptom; and (c) the shared conception within the marriage of the causes of the problems. Challenge is generally more necessary when the marriage is in an unsatisfactory stable situation than when a marital crisis exists.[32] This is because challenge unfreezes a "stuck" or stable situation. The therapist is always looking for ways to unlock the stuck adaptive powers of the spouses to free them to act self-sufficiently.

The structure of the marriage can be challenged by making people aware of their spatial positions. For example, if a couple begins to argue and they turn and face each other squarely, Minuchin might suggest that the couple is battling head-to-head and perhaps should face more sideways when they argue. If the couple initially faced sideways when they argued, Minuchin might suggest that the couple was apprehensive about engaging each other directly and should change to face each other head-on when they argue.

Minuchin does not believe that there is only one right way to communicate. Couples develop styles of communication. When a couple is distressed, Minuchin assumes that their structure is rigid due to trying to resolve their problems. So, he tries to change the structure to something different. Anything different. Just so it *is* different! He tries to increase communication flexibility. Changing the spatial positions of the husband and wife in their interactions with each other is a powerful way to dramatize their need to change.

Minuchin might also challenge the structure of the marriage by changing the amount of time that interactions are allowed to go on. Couples establish unconscious signs that signal when interactions are supposed to end. When distress gets too high, one person will break away from the contact. If a third person happens to be present—whether child, friend, grandparent or counselor—that third person often feels pulled to interrupt the couple. Minuchin challenges the structure by teaching counselors to allow certain interactions to go on longer than they otherwise might. Or, destructive interactions are interrupted prior to their usual termination point.

Minuchin might challenge the organization of the marriage around a symptom by using enactments. An enactment is a directive, within the session, that prescribes that the couple behave in a way that they usually behave. The difference between an enactment and the couple's normal behavior is that Minuchin specifies ahead of time just how the couple will behave. This makes the behaviors conscious rather than automatic and often disrupts the normal progression of the pattern. After the couple has followed the enactment for a few minutes, Minuchin will suggest they change their behaviors, often only slightly. Couples will resume their interactions employing the change, which directly challenges how the couple interacts around a symptom.

For example, suppose that the husband withdraws from intimacy with his wife, claiming that he is preoccupied with other demands (work, church, etc.). The wife becomes depressed (a symptom), creating additional demands on the husband. The husband, who feels both sympathetic and angry with his wife, is often "unable" to help her because of his other demands. She becomes angry and accusatory. He withdraws more. After observing this pattern several times in different forms, Minuchin might direct the couple to enact the sequence within the counseling session. Later, he might coach the couple how to interact differently at each point in the cycle.

Minuchin might also challenge the couple's conceptualization of the social reality of their relationship. For example, the couple might share the belief that any arguing means they do not love each other. Minuchin believes in the arbitrariness of social realities, which are subject to easy distortion. Each spouse usually believes that he or she has the true perception of the relationship. When the couple disagrees about what is happening, perceptions often become the battleground to establish authority in the couple. When the couple agrees but still has relationship difficulties, the therapist should reinterpret their perceptions to free the couple to solve their problems creatively. For example, Minuchin might persuade the couple who believed they should never argue that arguing will strengthen their relationship if they can come to some resolution. He will probably not try to persuade them directly but will use a series of techniques that helps the couple conclude that for themselves. The couple might be told to pretend to argue or to speculate on whether two people could ever strengthen their relationship if they resolved a disagreement.

The course of structural therapy with a couple is predictable.[33] Therapy begins with the therapist "joining" with the couple. In joining, the therapist initially accepts the couple's communication and affective styles, creating a bond between therapist and clients. Joining is seen as necessary to empower the therapist for later influence. Early in therapy, each spouse states his or her goals or hopes for therapy. The therapist helps the couple agree on goals that are specific. During assessment the therapist looks for: (a) stressors on the couple; (b) the characteristic pattern of interaction; and (c) responses to the therapist. The therapist formulates a treatment plan, which might be shared with the couple. Generally, each session during the middle of therapy proceeds predictably: homework is reviewed from the previous week, new data and ideas are gathered, enactments are directed and homework is assigned. In termination, change is attributed to the couple's efforts, and significant learning throughout therapy is reviewed with the couple.

Minuchin's is an elegant and comprehensive marriage therapy. He considers each level of the system, from the individual expectations, to the operation of the marriage, to the place of the marriage within the family and, finally, to the couple's place in the family life cycle. His considerations form a unified theory rather than a patchwork theory which merely draws from numerous considerations. The emphasis on the structure of the marriage gives ways to help change the structure. Of all the systems theories, Minuchin's has the most experimental support.[34] Yet, most of the research has not concerned the marriage but has dealt with family therapy of psychosomatic problems. More research is needed on structural marriage therapy.[35]

Critique of Minuchin's Structural Therapy

Minuchin's style of counseling is definitely not for everyone. His flamboyance and daring are often breathtaking, and he uses his quick mind and indomitable personality to direct and sometimes bully clients into changing their behavior. Like Haley's powerful behind-the-scenes directives, and like the behavioral marriage counselors' common-sense reasonableness, Minuchin uses his strengths to affect his clients. He formulated his theory with families of the slums who generally require the direct, action-oriented, flamboyant style that Minuchin is ideally suited for. Not all clients would be equally suited to this approach.

Minuchin's theorizing aggrandizes counseling techniques and gives little attention to the role of the therapist. Todd[36] has described the ideal structural marriage therapist as active, goal-focused and able to conceptualize quickly and accurately. The therapist must also be vigilant to subtle feedback from couples and be willing to change therapeutic hypotheses rapidly. The high activity level required of the therapist suggests that the therapist could easily become too central in therapy, and he or she must remain sensitive to that danger throughout therapy.

Minuchin's philosophizing reflects the modern relativistic world view. He touts "circular causality" and discusses the malleability of social "reality." A Christian must read Minuchin warily, guarding against subtly undermining absolutes and objective reality—which is not to say that the "social reality" is objectively real.

At the same time, Minuchin's detailed explication of techniques makes it easy to use his methods that are compatible with the goals of the Christian marriage counselor. His main thrust is to challenge existing patterns and not to specify how people should interact. He has a positive view of the capabilities of humans.

Jay Haley and Cloe Madanes are a husband and wife who have developed strategic therapy. *Strategic therapy* implies that the therapist acts planfully, using a strategy to provoke couples to change. Like the other systems theories, strategic therapy was primarily a family therapy until recently, when both Haley and Madanes have written more about treatment of the marriage.

Summary of Haley's and Madanes' Theories

Jay Haley is one of the most original thinkers active in marriage and family therapy. Ideas roll off his tongue (and flow from his pen) as quickly as do jokes from Johnny Carson. He has developed theories of change in marriage and family therapy. Most of his work has involved family therapy rather than marriage counseling.[37] Cloe Madanes, too, is an original thinker who has expanded on Haley's work in ways that are distinctly her own.[38] Her two books examine the marriage and provide more sophisticated theorizing about its treatment than most of Haley's writing, which concentrates more on family therapy.

Haley and Madanes write theories of *therapy,* not of the marriage. They never claim to explain how marriage works or ought to work. They are not comparable to Bowen's theory or even to behavioral approaches in the sophistication of their understanding of the marriage. Simply, they contend that a counselor needs to understand how to produce change in a troubled couple, not how an untroubled couple might behave.

Their understanding of how to help couples change is dramatized by directives and paradoxes that leave the reader sometimes scratching the head and looking around in bewilderment for the source of the inspiration. Directives are explained to the reader (but rarely to clients) with such clarity and force of logic that they appear *almost* self-evident. Theirs is the virtuoso performance that makes the observer want to applaud at the end of the case.

Over his twenty-plus years of writing theories of therapy, Haley's ideas have changed considerably. I will summarize some of the principles that characterize his and Madanes' thinking.

In his 1963 book, *Strategies of Psychotherapy,*[39] Haley devotes twenty pages of a thirty-four-page chapter on marriage therapy to the causes of problems in marriage. His main thesis is that problems are due to simultaneous communication of contradictory messages, one overtly and one covertly. The other spouse must disagree because he or she cannot at the same time agree with both levels of the communication.

For example, imagine the Christian woman who attends a weekend retreat on "the Christian wife." The speaker thoroughly discusses the "submissive wife" and makes practical suggestions about how to behave submissively. The woman, armed with solid biblical references and numerous practical suggestions, returns home to her husband and begins to put her plan into effect. For the next month, she is the "perfect" submissive wife. But by the end of the month, the husband is furious.

Why? While on the overt level the wife is submissive, on the covert level she dominates the relationship by defining the couple's behavior without consulting her husband. The husband cannot understand how he can be angry with his "loving" wife, who does whatever he wishes. Yet every time she jumps at his slightest suggestion, he wants to scream.

He begins to demand that they have an egalitarian relationship. The wife argues that such a relationship is not scriptural. If the husband acquiesces, he is resentful and feels the need to exert equal power in some other parts of their relationship. And the fight goes on.

When he demanded an egalitarian relationship, he posed a vicious paradox for the relationship—a paradox that equaled the viciousness of the wife's paradox. He unilaterally demanded that his wife submit to *his* definition of an equal relationship. If she submitted to that definition, though, the relationship would not be egalitarian because one partner defined the relationship. If she were taking her professed submissiveness seriously, she should ascede to her husband's demand. But instead, she asserts her dominance by insisting that she should be submissive. If he were taking his professed desire for an egalitarian relationship seriously, he would not *demand* such a relationship.

Haley devotes the final third of the chapter to marriage *counseling*. He proposes that though the counselor might tell a couple that he or she "wants them to talk and correct the misunderstandings which have arisen, to express their feelings and to gain some insight into their difficulties,"[40] the counselor does not expect those activities to produce change. Rather, change will be provoked by nonrational forces.

For example, the mere presence of the counselor will change the couple's interactions. Also, the counselor will help redefine the relationship through relabeling events. By certain interventions, the counselor may help resolve difficulties over who sets the rules of the relationship. The counselor may give directives to the couple, thus skirting each spouse's tendency to define the relationship paradoxically. The counselor may also direct the couple to behave in the ways that they are *already behaving,* which opens the question of whether the couple or the counselor is in control of the relationship. This sets up the possibility that the couple will defy the counselor by changing their behavior to something happier for the couple.

Madanes picks up the theme that all behavior can be communication and that communication exists on multiple levels.[41] She begins with the idea that a symptom may take the place of another problem. For example, a boy's headache may replace conflict between his parents, for when the boy complains of his headache, his parents stop fighting and rush to see what can be done for the child. In the same way, an entire sequence of behavior can replace another sequence of behavior. For instance in one case, a couple's conflict over the frequency of their sexual intercourse replaced the more threatening conflict over the wife's acceptance of the husband's son by another marriage. Madanes also argues that marital distress is often caused by unequal distribution of benefits to the spouses. (Benefits might be different for each spouse and might appear vastly inequitable to an observer, but if the benefits are *perceived* by the spouses to be equitably distributed, then the couple will be happy.)

Madanes states:

It follows logically from these concepts that when couples or families are having difficulty, all that is necessary to solve the problem is to negotiate a new contract that is more favorable to all involved so that the benefits will be more equally distributed. However, the nature of problems presented to therapy is such that the participants are involved in involuntary, helpless behavior that cannot be changed through reasonable negotiation.[42]

Thus, the counselor uses strategic directives to change the couple's behavior so that benefits can be redistributed. The couple's understanding of the whys of the counselor's directives is not necessary for change. In fact, the client can often be provoked either to comply or resist the counselor by the counselor's explaining or not explaining reasons for directives.

In fact, resisting and avoiding resistance are major parts of strategic marital therapy. Haley loves to tell how Milton Erickson, while a child, laughed at his father who was attempting unsuccessfully to pull a mule into their barn. Erickson's father, angered by his son's impudence, asked if Milton thought he could get the mule into the barn. Milton allowed as how he could. Mr. Erickson stepped aside but Milton, instead of straining against the mule's resistance, stepped behind the mule, tugged on its tail and followed it as it hurried into the barn. In the same way, the strategic marital counselor is admonished not to meet resistance head-on; rather, the resistance is to be accepted and modified so the couple is willing to change.[43]

Critique of Haley's and Madanes' Strategic Therapy

Strategic therapy offers an exciting (and often seemingly magical) theory of therapeutic change. The theorizing is more complete for strategic family therapy than for strategic marriage therapy. The approach focuses attention on communication patterns and power within relationships, but there is even more focus on helping the couple get rid of their presenting complaints—more so than any other marriage therapy. Even the behaviorists do not accept the complaints of the couple with such seriousness as strategic therapists do; they redefine and go beyond the initial complaints.

Another strength of strategic therapy is that it is probably the shortest-term therapy offered. It was developed by working with couples who do not desire insight but merely want the problem taken away and are willing to do whatever it takes if the counselor can help quickly. For such clients, strategic therapy is ideal. More than other marriage therapies, strategic therapy emphasizes the counselor's responsibility to provoke the couple to change, and Haley has described ways to give directives to accomplish what the counselor desires. It is efficient, bold, sometimes brilliant and often risky.

There are some glaring difficulties with this form of counseling, however. It is easily abused by counselors who are not trained by skilled strategic therapy supervisors, yet, because it appeals to our creativity and daring, counselors often try strategic therapy techniques after merely reading about them. While for some therapies this is not a problem, the riskiness of some directives makes this problematic for strategic therapy.

Another limitation of strategic therapy is its restricted focus. Though it discusses relationship rules, communication and behavior sequences, it treats individual personalities and motivations as epiphenomenal (unrelated to therapy) and it ignores both the history of the relationship and the place of the couple in the family life cycle. Other assumptions of the approach are questionable. For example, often it is assumed that if change is induced it will be maintained. Sometimes it is assumed that the couple can handle a similar problem should it arise in the future, even though no attempt was made to teach the couple the principles behind their change.

In addition, the therapy is unsubstantiated by research. No comparative studies have been published. Like most systems theorists, despite the origins of their theories in clinical research, they have failed to interest researchers in investigating their theories. Finally, strategic approaches sometimes employ paradoxical directives in which the counselor suggests or demands a directive that he or she intends (or hopes) for the clients to resist. For example, a counselor might demand that a highly conflictual couple set aside a nightly time and argue—without fail. The counselor generally hopes that the directive will inhibit argument rather than promote it. The difficulty is that couples (especially Christian couples) will not understand the intent of the counselor and thus might label him or her as promoting conflict and divorce. On the other hand, the counselor must self-justify why he or she issues often elaborately explained directives which are contrary to his or her real intentions.

BEHAVIORAL THEORIES

Behavioral approaches to marriage counseling rely on social psychology and social learning theory for their roots. In recent years, some attention has also been given to spouses' cognitions and to individual personality styles.[45] Thus, behavioral approaches are probably poorly named considering the ways they are currently practiced. Jacobson and Holtzworth-Munroe[46] suggest that *social learning-cognitive approaches* more accurately labels current practice. Nonetheless, for historical reasons, I will refer to such approaches as *behavioral* and will summarize techniques from Jacobson and Margolin,[47] Liberman et al.[48] and Stuart.[49]

Summary of Behavioral Approaches[44]

The fundamental premise of behavioral marriage counseling is that in happy marriages, the rewards (reinforcers) outweigh the costs (punishers). It follows that for troubled couples, the balance has shifted to where the costs are greater or nearly greater than the rewards. The counselor, then, should increase the rewards and decrease the costs of the relationship.

Since the major source of both rewards and costs for each spouse is the behavior of the other spouse, the counselor uses his or her influence to promote behavior change that will increase the couple's marital happiness. A number of methods have been developed to increase rewards and decrease costs. Methods are generally similar across therapists.

Generally, the rewards and costs in marriage are influenced by (1) the affective valence for each spouse of the other's behavior (for example, behaviors that are emotionally pleasing or emotionally distressing); and (2) the ways that couples communicate, negotiate differences and solve problems. Since problems are thought to develop and be maintained because couples have difficulties in either or both areas, therapists hope to promote changes in either or both areas to help the troubled couple become happier.

Therapy begins with a thorough assessment that is usually distinct from counseling. In some cases, couples agree to an assessment and then recontract for therapy if they desire it (Jacobson and Margolin), while in other cases, assessment is briefer and is part of counseling (Liberman et al.). Assessment is more or less elaborate with each therapist, usually involving some combination of questionnaires, observation within the interview and perhaps self-monitoring by the spouses.

On the basis of the assessment, a therapy plan involving standardized "modules" or "packages" is offered to the couple. The plan is generally tailored to their needs. Liberman et al. make the fewest allowances for individual needs of couples. Jacobson and Margolin discuss more treatment "packages" than Liberman et al., selecting appropriate packages based on their assessment. Although there is still the flavor of a prepared program, it *appears* individually tailored. Whereas Liberman et al. serve institutional "plate lunches" to couples, Jacobson and Margolin serve the same food, selected by clients cafeteria-style.

Counseling is structured. The counselor generally decides ahead of time what the therapeutic task of each session will be and is not distracted by the small crises that may present themselves each week. Stuart describes the structure of counseling most rigorously of the three, and Liberman et al. adhere to a normal routine also. Each of the counselors would change their plans if large crises arose, but generally, the plan of the counselor is carried out regardless of the clients' daily emotional vicissitudes.

Most techniques increase the spouses' mutual rewards. First, each spouse tries to increase the pleasant things done for the other. These are called *pleases,* based on what each spouse finds subjectively pleasing. The therapist may offer a list of pleases from which couples choose. Couples add their own suggestions so that a truly personal list of pleases can be established. Partners are then shown how to give, accept and ask for pleases from each other. Couples exchange pleases at home between counseling sessions.

A second behavioral technique is Stuart's "caring days," on which couples give large numbers of pleases to each other. Jacobson and Margolin call a variation of this *love days.* Third, Stuart has identified "core symbols" as things symbolizing intimate times. Core symbols are identified and discussed pleasantly, reviving positive feelings through their remembrances.

The strongest part of behavioral treatment programs is communication training, which can be varied in style and content. However, communication training alone is not as good as its combination with increased exchange of pleases.[50] Most behavioral counselors do some form of problem-solving training. Liberman et al. focus more on positive talk, non-verbal communication and emotional communication than do Jacobson and Margolin.

Some techniques decrease the costs in the troubled couple's relationship. All three theories recommend training in conflict management. All therapists try to decrease the couple's coercive interchanges. Stuart overtly addresses the couple's conflicts and power struggles through his "powergram." Using this technique, couples make decisions about who has the authority to make certain decisions.

Some techniques counter couples' resistances. Couples may design and implement behavioral-exchange contracts, in which they exchange pleases (and might specify contingencies for fulfilling and not fulfilling the contracts). There are two types of contracts: quid pro quo contracts and good-faith contracts. Quid pro quo contracts involve agreements like, "I'll do *x*, if you do *y*." This embodies the philosophy that is inherent in much of the behavioral approach—one *gives* in order to *get*. Good-faith contracts are unilateral agreements that specify what one partner agrees to do for the other, regardless of what the other spouse does. These are closer to the philosophical foundations of Christianity, which eschews returning evil for evil or good for good and advocates doing good to others despite what the other does.

Critique of Behavioral Approaches

Behavioral approaches offer many positive features. They clearly specify how to counsel. Techniques are carefully described, and the counselor who works from a behavioral perspective usually knows what is going to happen in each counseling session. Behavioral marriage therapy has been experimentally investigated far more than all other forms of marriage counseling combined.[51] The practitioner can be assured that the counseling will work with most of the couples, though the effects are not necessarily permanent.[52] Probably the main reasons for its clinical effectiveness are (1) its reliance on research findings to modify practice and (2) its simplicity.

As an example of the use of research findings to modify behavioral marriage therapy, consider a recent (1986) summary of the theory by Jacobson and Holtzworth-Munroe.[53] They reviewed research on factors distinguishing distressed and nondistressed couples. From the research comes an increasing importance of (a) perceptions and attributions of causality of each spouse; (b) emotion and awareness of emotion during marital therapy; and (c) the need for follow-up or booster sessions to maintain the gains made in therapy.

Besides its openness to new data as a spur to theory revision, a strength of behavioral marriage therapy is its simplicity. Although the counseling theory is sophisticated in its own right, behavioral marriage counseling focuses on only a few primary causes of marital distress. Thus, treatment is concentrated and can be directed at specific targets and produce measurable changes.

On the other hand, the simplicity of behavioral marriage counseling is also its chief criticism. Of the many criticisms of behavioral marriage therapy that Gurman has levied, most have involved the lack of completeness of the theory.[54] He criticized behavioral marriage counseling as largely ahistorical and not considering the effects of meanings of events, personality needs and motivations, and commitment of the participants.

These criticisms are valid if one assumes that the primary purpose of a theory of therapy is to provide a complete description of why and how change can occur.[55] However, this is generally the purpose of a *research-oriented theory* rather than a *clinical theory*. As a research theory, behavioral marriage therapy is substantially lacking, though it has been vastly more heuristic than its competitors. As a clinical theory, behavioral marriage therapy is powerful, yet with notable deficiencies.

One deficiency is that behavioral marriage counseling does not differentiate treatments according to the phase of the life cycle that couples are in. For example, the communication problems of older couples have been shown to be different than the communication problems of younger couples.[56] For a second, the philosophy that is promoted by behavioral counselors aggrandizes symmetrical relationships and generally promotes role reversibility. For instance, Weiss[57] concludes, ". . . *thus, it would seem that behavioral approaches to marriage are best suited to relationships which already subscribe to more egalitarian than traditional ideological components*" (p. 190, emphasis his).

This is a serious consideration because many (but certainly not all) conservative Christian clients subscribe to somewhat role-oriented, traditional relationships. These couples have been shown through substantial research to be more satisfied with marriage and to have more stable marriages than nonreligious couples.[58] Christian counselors must choose techniques that fit both their clients and their clients' philosophies.

Another philosophical deficiency is that behavioral therapies are overly hedonistic—the fundamental analysis by a spouse is a cost-benefit comparison. Strictly applied, temporal hedonism is antithetical to Christianity. In fact, most critiques of behavioral therapy made by Christians are more objections to radical (Skinnerian) behaviorism than to the techniques and methods of behavioral therapy.[59]

In general, I personally find many behavioral principles useful and consistent with Scripture. As C. S. Lewis observed,[60] people have been created to pursue the reward of ultimate, eternal life; people are indeed hedonistic, though temporal hedonism (hedonism confined to the here and now of the present, seen world) is a perversion of the way we were created. As I have assumed throughout this book, marriage can be a glimpse into our ultimate relationship with God through Jesus.

Thus, we should expect that maximizing benefits relative to costs is an appropriate activity for marriage.

With this (sketchy) justification, I believe the counselor can legitimately encourage the couple to maximize their benefits and minimize their costs within their relationship, *provided* (1) they maintain a perspective that there is more to temporal life than hedonism (such as commitment, altruism and self-sacrifice); and (2) there is more than temporal life to true existence.

COGNITIVE THEORIES

In the spirit of behavioral marital therapy, Donald Baucom and Gregory Lester performed an experimental comparison of:

☐ Behavioral marriage therapy (BMT). This treatment involved twelve weeks of BMT—six weeks of communication and problem-solving training and six weeks of quid pro quo contracting

☐ Cognitive behavioral therapy (CBT). This treatment involved six weeks of cognitive therapy, followed by six weeks of BMT (three weeks each of communication-problem solving and contracting).

☐ A waiting list control group.

Each therapist treated twelve distressed couples—six in BMT and six in CBT. Each of the six sessions of cognitive therapy lasted one and one-half hours.

Session one discussed the tendency for people to oversimplify explanations for problems, especially by blaming and labeling one's spouse. The importance of understanding that problems have many causes and that perceptions may differ was stressed. Session two dealt with overgeneralization and tendencies to make attributions of hopelessness and helplessness, which might lead to depression. Session three focused on tendencies to make attributions to stable or unchangeable factors. Therapists and couples discussed the belief that the partner must change before the spouse will attempt new behaviors.

Session four discussed how extreme expectations for oneself or one's spouse can add to marital problems. Session five identified extreme expectations for the marriage relationship. Session six allowed the couple to integrate learning from previous sessions. One marital problem was discussed in terms of both the attributions of causality and unrealistic expectations covered in the previous five sessions.

Obviously, Baucom and Lester have not articulated an entire theory of therapy; however, they have specified some concrete ways that cognitive elements can be mixed with BMT. Furthermore, they have subjected it to an experimental analysis. They found that the couples who received the cognitive interventions improved

Summary of Baucom and Lester's Cognitive Behavior Theory[61]

Critique of Baucom and Lester's Cognitive Behavior Theory

more on cognitive and behavioral measures than couples on the waiting list. Couples who received BMT alone did not differ in improvement from couples who received the CBT treatment. By the end of treatment, over fifty per cent of the couples defined themselves as nondistressed. These improvements were still found at a follow-up six months later.

Summary of Epstein's Theory

Norman Epstein[62] has outlined cognitive treatments within marriage therapy aimed at three targets. Cognitive techniques can be used to change: (1) couples' unrealistic expectations; (2) faulty attributions of causality; (3) and self-instructions within destructive interactions between spouses.

Unrealistic expectations are prevalent in human existence and certainly exist within the troubled marriage. These exist on both cultural and idiosyncratic levels. Cognitive therapists have developed numerous methods for helping modify people's unrealistic expectations, irrational ideas or marriage contracts. The first step is to help the people become aware of their expectations and of how their expectations are faulty. Ellis[63] does this through rational analysis and logical disputation. Beck[64] and Meichenbaum[65] systematically call the clients' attention to their expectations throughout counseling sessions and then have clients attend to their expectations and self-talk between sessions. Clients often keep journals or count the frequency of certain thoughts.

The second step is to provoke clients to change their thinking. The therapist helps set up situations where clients can test their assumptions and then helps analyze the outcomes in subsequent sessions. One key to successful cognitive modification is that it is done systematically and repetitively throughout counseling; it is not a one-time event. Another key is to plan helpful metacognitions—thoughts about clients' thinking and thoughts about therapy.

Most people have previously tried to modify their thinking and have not succeeded. The reasons for their failure must be addressed explicitly or their doubts will undermine therapy. Ineffective ways to change thoughts include mindless repetition, inconsistency in trying to change their thinking, giving up too easily, instructing themselves *not* to engage in faulty thinking and failing to focus their attention on positive outcomes. Besides helping a couple know what to think, the therapist must help them know *how not* to think.

Attribution difficulties are common in troubled marriages. Generally, people err either by denying any personal responsibility for their marital situation or by taking all of the blame on themselves. The counselor tries to change these attributional patterns.

For example, one couple might interact as if they were involved in World War 3. They fight from the moment they see you enter the waiting room. They criticize each other and deny that they had anything to do with the problem. A second couple might be just as constricted in their behavior. The husband had an affair, while the wife appears to be "an angel." The wife tries not to sound as if she blames the husband for their difficulties, but it is clear that she holds him totally responsible. The husband accepts the blame and feels guilty. Rigid attributions of blame and guilt lock them into a destructive marriage.

In the first case, the counselor might try to help each partner accept more responsibility for his or her own behavior. In the second case, the counselor might try to help both partners see that the woman also had some responsibility for the marriage difficulties—which is not to excuse the man. The counselor will help change attributions through challenging the couple's shared conceptualization, setting up situations in which each partner must confront his or her own responsibility, or reframing a problem as a strength, such as when the therapist says that a couple's repeated arguing is not bad because it indicates that the couple is still very intensely involved with each other.

Self-instructions can be used to help control harmful interactions. For example, a couple that fights frequently can be taught to delay their argumentation through anger management strategies. They can warn themselves when arguments are likely and can use self-instruction to cope with the provocations before they initiate an argument. The therapist usually teaches the clients to recognize the cues to the emotions or behaviors that the couple wants to avoid. Once the couple can reliably recognize the cues, they are taught to instruct themselves to control their behavior and emotion.

Generally, the strategies that Epstein outlines have been shown, through experiments and through use in clinical settings, to help people gain control of their behavior and their emotions. They should be applicable to the marriage. In individual therapy, however, therapy is completely organized around these cognitive techniques. Usually, a nonsystematic effort at changing thoughts will not succeed. Thus, these techniques should be used only when the counselor wants to make cognitive change a major goal of counseling. Otherwise, the use of the cognitive strategies will merely dilute the power of the counseling. **Critique of Epstein's Theory**

On the other hand, cognitive therapy with couples can be powerful because both partners are present during training. The counselor can set up an enactment—to use Minuchin's term—and then, after it is complete, have the couple discuss the thoughts they had during the enactment. This can be especially powerful when videotape or audiotape recordings are made and reviewed.

Epstein's theorizing would suggest that techniques from cognitive therapy with individuals can be used in marriages. Besides the study by Baucom and Lester, which used only part of Epstein's suggested interventions, there have been no empirical investigations of Epstein's ideas. They thus remain interesting but unproven as a legitimate theory of marital therapy.

Summary of Sager's Theory

Sager[66] is eclectic regarding counseling techniques. He draws heavily on psychoanalytic thinking (which, in a way, brings us in a circle, having begun with psychoanalytic approaches), but he openly recommends techniques from all schools of counseling. He uses some behavioral and some systems techniques. The mainstay of his theorizing involves the belief that people develop expectations about marriage and that violations of those expectations produce anger and bitterness. Sager labels these expectations *contracts*.

He identifies two types of contracts: individual and interactional contracts. An individual contract is a set of expectations by the individual. These expectations can be summarized on a form that Sager asks spouses to complete. They list expectations that are conscious. Some individual expectations are not accessible to awareness and are heavily defended against psychologically. One task of the marriage counselor is to uncover the hidden expectations and help the individuals negotiate realistic expectations.

The second type of contract is the interactional contract. Motivated by their conscious and unconscious expectations, couples collude to meet their healthy and neurotic needs. They evolve a set of interactional patterns with unconsciously agreed-upon "rules" for meeting their needs, which comprise the interactional contract. People generally are less aware of their interactional contracts than they are of their individual contracts.

Sager's main assumption is that if expectations become explicit, agreement can be negotiated. Therapy begins with talk of the couple's difficulties. Talk is expected to relieve the immediate pressures. Sager next introduces the idea of contracts. He uses interviews and a lengthy questionnaire to assess the individual and interactional contracts of the couple. Sager identifies points of congruence (shared expectations), complementarity (different but nonconflictual expectations) and conflict, and he makes them explicit to the couple. Sager also identifies the typical behavior patterns of the couple.

Each spouse is typed as a parental, childlike, rational, companionate, parallel, equal or romantic partner. Based on the combination of husband and wife, Sager formulates hypotheses about their marriage behavior, which are tested during counseling.

In one or two areas of conflict, compromise solutions are proposed by the counselor and negotiated by the spouses. Generally, the solution satisfies neither spouse but meets their basic needs. Clear goals are set and the couple tries to implement this compromise in their daily interactions. When couples resist the compromise, the counselor interprets the resistance in light of intrapsychic factors and motivations. Successful counseling is built around achieving a single workable contract and creating the mechanisms for it to work in the couple's life.

Critique of Sager's Theory

Sager's counseling is based largely on psychodynamic principles. Sager strives to make the unconscious become conscious, assuming that only an outside party (the counselor) can discover some of the couple's contracts. He concentrates on accomplishing only a few tasks in counseling and exerts most effort in trying to defeat the couple's resistances. Conceptualization of the problem is more emphasized than is treatment.

His methods appeal to counselors who value rational approaches to counseling. He often acts as a mediator of disputes, tracking the content of arguments and offering creative solutions acceptable to both marriage partners. He relies more on resolving specific areas of conflict than on training the couple in how to communicate differently.

Philosophically, Sager's rational approach will probably be objectionable to fewer Christian counselors than most marriage therapists' theories. Sager's emphasis on cognition fits well with the rational approach of many professionals trained in theology. Counselors will be more polarized about his heavy reliance on psychodynamic methods and assumptions.

Sager's typology about spouses' behavior within the marriage is intriguing to read. I recognized many of the patterns he described; however, his typology is too unwieldy for easy use and not specific enough to provide detailed information about behavior. Dealing exclusively with assessment, it is not tied specifically to treatment goals or methods.

My main concern with Sager's theorizing is that it will not be effective with couples who have severely disturbed marriages. For years I tried to act as a mediator in marriage disputes but was effective only about half of the time. Couples often know that their expectations differ, but still stubbornly pursue their ends. Haley argues that making a power struggle explicit, as is recommended by Sager, will simply fortify the power struggle and make it more difficult to change.

Sager's theory has little research that supports it. Even Sager has done little to investigate the effectiveness of his theorizing. His notion of marriage contracts—individual and interactional—are useful as techniques to help negotiate agreement, but we must conclude that they remain questionable as a comprehensive theory of marriage counseling.

CHRISTIAN, COGNITIVE AND BEHAVIORAL THEORY

Norman Wright has written what he calls "a biblical, behavioral, cognitive approach" to marital counseling.[67] His is the best text currently available for teaching some of the practicalities of marriage counseling from a Christian slant. Wright is eclectic in his choice of techniques of marriage counseling, drawing most freely from behavioral theorists but also including ideas from cognitive theories (expectations and needs), behaviorists and Rogerian therapists (semantics and syntax of communication, which are more heavily stressed than pragmatics) and even some

Summary of Wright's Marital Counseling Theory

techniques from Gestalt and psychoanalytic therapists.

Wright has aimed his book at ministers who wish to counsel couples in ways that are Scripture-consistent. He draws on several Christian writers who have written about counseling in general (such as Gary Collins), Christian marriages or marriage counseling. Wright is clearly attentive to scriptural principles and writes one chapter about scriptural principles in counseling and another portion of a chapter that adduces evidence from Scripture that supports a positive behavioral approach to counseling. Many of the frequent examples that Wright uses to illustrate counseling concern Christians.

Wright conceptualizes marriage problems as due largely to problems in four areas: (a) unmet needs and unrealistic expectations; (b) lack of positive behavioral reciprocity; (c) poor conflict resolution strategies of the spouses; and (d) negative communication. Techniques are chosen from the various schools of marriage counseling to help couples change.

The general flavor of the counseling is behavioral, including formal assessment sessions and a relatively structured approach to counseling. Once intervention is begun, the emphasis is shared between behavioral techniques, such as Stuart's "caring days," or marriage contracts (called covenant therapy by Wright) and communication approaches that analyze semantics and syntax. Wright has couples talk to each other in his presence. Occasionally he will talk to one spouse (in the presence of the other). He helps couples understand how they can communicate better. The cognitive and biblical emphasis mentioned in the subtitle of his book appear more in the instructions to the counselor than in the sessions with clients.

Critique of Wright's Marital Counseling

Wright summarizes numerous techniques for marriage counseling that might be used by ministers. He illustrates many techniques with conversations between counselors and clients or between husband and wife, which makes his book valuable for ideas about technique.

Most of his emphasis on Christianity is implicit rather than explicit. Rather than theorize about the nature of the individuals who marry, or about the nature of the marriage, or about the nature of the problems that might arise in the Christian marriage, Wright has been content to use the behavioral framework and add techniques from a variety of schools that might accomplish his objectives. The book is useful, and the techniques are screened to eliminate those that promote behavior not in line with Christian values. However, the book does not put forth a distinctively Christian *theory* of marriage counseling.

Wright considers individuals within a marriage as responsible adults. He writes one chapter about changes that occur across the family life cycle, though once that chapter is complete, no further mention is made of those concepts.

SUMMARY

After reviewing these different approaches to marital therapy, I am struck with their similarities and by the number of aspects of marital therapy that need to be addressed by a comprehensive clinical theory that is easily usable by Christian counselors. My impression of the theories is that they split a common pie of marriage into different-shaped pieces. The picture of the troubled marital relationship is relatively constant. It is characterized by difficulties in intimacy, communication problems (not enough positively valenced communication and too much negatively valenced communication), unresolved and increasingly hurtful conflict, waning or nonexistent commitment to the relationship, and absorption in the troubled relationship so that the partners are often drawn away from their spiritual roots. Various theories emphasize different troubles.

All therapies try to solve problems through meeting with couples. All therapies believe that there are deep causes for the troubles, though ideas of what the causes are differ depending on the theory. All therapists agree that clients must be treated with respect and honor and that it is generally dangerous for their marriages if the counselor cannot control the interactions of the couple. Generally, most therapies believe that counseling will take some substantial time and will require regular attention if the couple is to use the counseling productively. The therapist is seen as an active participant with the couples in helping solve their problems. All therapists agree that it is best to operate from some well-thought-out theoretical perspective as opposed to merely going by momentary reactions to the couple.

Despite the helpfulness of adhering to a theory, no theory is perfect. There are at least six distinct weaknesses in existing theories:

1. An integrated theory of the marriage is needed—one that considers individuals as well as marriages and that puts the marriage within the framework of the life cycle.

2. An integrated theory of marital therapy, based on such a theory of the marriage, is needed.

3. More attention needs to be given distinctly Christian ideas in the theory.

4. The theory needs to be compact so that it can be used clinically.

5. The theoretical underpinnings of the theory need to be rich enough to stimulate research.

6. Techniques need clear exposition which shows how and when to use them in marital therapy.

Obviously, I hope that the present book addresses these needs in a useful way. The theory I describe is largely influenced by cognitive-behavioral, structural and strategic therapies. Christians of other theoretical persuasions need to offer other theories also for the practitioners who find other theoretical views more compatible with their beliefs.

NOTES

Chapter 1: The Need for Marriage Counseling by and for Christians

[1]Andrew J. Cherlin, *Marriage, Divorce, Remarriage* (Cambridge, Mass.: Harvard University Press, 1981).

[2]Ibid.

[3]Ibid.

[4]L. F. Henze and J. W. Hudson, "Personal and Family Characteristics of Non-cohabiting and Cohabiting College Students," *Journal of Marriage and the Family* 36 (1974):722-6; E. D. Macklin, "Heterosexual Cohabitation Among Unmarried College Students," *The Family Coordinator* 21 (1972):463-72.

[5]Graham Spanier, "Married and Unmarried Cohabitation in the United States: 1980," *Journal of Marriage and the Family* 45 (1983):277-88.

[6]J. F. Lyness, "Happily Ever After? Following-up Living Together Couples," *Alternative Lifestyles* 1 (1) (1978):55-70; D. J. Peterman, "Does Living Together Before Marriage Make for a Better Marriage?" *Medical Aspects of Human Sexuality* 9 (1975):39-41; Michael D. Newcomb and P. M. Bentler, "Cohabitation Before Marriage: A Comparison of Married Couples Who Did and Did Not Cohabit," *Alternative Lifestyles* 3 (1980):65-85; also see Everett L. Worthington, Jr., *Counseling for Unplanned Pregnancy and Infertility* (Waco, Tex.: Word, 1987) in which research studies prior to 1987 are tabulated.

[7]See Cyril J. Barber, "Marriage, Divorce, and Remarriage: A Review of the Relevant Religious Literature, 1973-1983," *Journal of Psychology and Theology* 12 (1984):170-7 for a review of four Christian positions on divorce and remarriage.

[8]Worthington, *Counseling for Unplanned Pregnancy and Infertility;* in the present text I will use *counseling, therapy* and *psychotherapy* interchangeably.

[9]Alan S. Gurman and David P. Kniskern, "Family Therapy Outcome Research: Knowns and Unknowns," in *Handbook of Family Therapy,* ed. Alan S. Gurman and David P. Kniskern (N.Y.: Brunner/Mazel, 1981).

[10]J. D. Arnold and C. Schick, "Counseling by Clergy: A Review of Empirical Research," *Journal of Pastoral Care* 14 (1979):76-101.

[11]G. Gurin, J. Veroff and S. Feld, *Americans' View of Mental Health* (N.Y.: Basic Books, 1960); Gurman and Kniskern, "Family Therapy Outcome Research."

[12]Jay Haley, *Problem Solving Therapy* (San Francisco: Jossey-Bass, 1976).

[13]Everett L. Worthington, Jr., "Religious Counseling: A Review of Published Empirical Research," *Journal of Counseling and Development* 64 (1986):421-31.

[14]Everett L. Worthington, Jr., *When Someone Asks for Help: A Practical Guide for Counseling* (Downers Grove, Ill.: InterVarsity Press, 1982).

[15]C. S. Lewis, *Mere Christianity* (N.Y.: Macmillan, 1946).

Chapter 2: Individuals and Their Coupling

[1]C. S. Lewis, letter, in Sheldon Vanauken, *A Severe Mercy* (N.Y.: Bantam, 1977), p. 90.

[2]See Genesis 3:15, 18-24.

[3]I have written about this previously in Everett L. Worthington, Jr., *Counseling for Unplanned Pregnancy and Infertility* (Waco, Tex.: Word, 1987). Many authors, beginning with the author of Genesis, have identified love and work as fundamental human needs.

[4]This model of the individual was presented more fully in Everett L. Worthington, Jr., *When Someone Asks for Help.*

[5]William Lederer and Don D. Jackson, *Mirages of Marriage* (N.Y.: W. W. Norton and Co., 1968).

[6]Derek Prince, *The Marriage Covenant* (Ft. Lauderdale: Derek Prince Ministries, 1978); John Stott, *Marriage and Divorce* (Downers Grove, Ill.: InterVarsity Press, 1985).

[7]Barber, "Marriage, Divorce, and Remarriage."

[8]Prince, *The Marriage Covenant.*

[9]Paul Evdokimov, *The Sacrament of Love* (Crestwood, N.Y.: St. Vladimir's Seminary Press, 1985).

[10]Richard B. Stuart, *Helping Couples Change: A Social Learning Approach to Marital Therapy* (N.Y.: Guilford, 1980).

[11]Ibid.

[12]Lawrence O. Clayton, "The Impact upon Child-Rearing Attitudes of Parental Views of the Nature of Humankind," *Journal of Psychology and Christianity* 4, no. 3 (1985):49-55; Norval D. Glenn, "A Note on Estimating the Strength of Influences for Religious Endogamy," *Journal of Marriage and the Family* 46 (1984):725-7; Tim B. Heaton, "Religious Homogamy and Marital Satisfaction Reconsidered," *Journal of Marriage and the Family* 46 (1984):729-33; Bruce Hunsberger, "Parent-University Student Agreement on Religious and Nonreligious Issues," *Journal for the Scientific Study of Religion* 24 (1985):314-20; Patrick H. McNamara, "Conservative Christian Families and Their Worldviews: Are the Critics Correct? A Preliminary Report" (Paper presented at the meeting of the Pacific Sociological Association, Albuquerque, New Mexico, 1985).

[13]Everett L. Worthington, Jr., "Understanding the Values of Religious Clients: A Model and Its Application to Counseling," *Journal of Counseling Psychology* 35 (1988):166-74.

[14]Lederer and Jackson, *Mirages of Marriage.*

[15]David Olson, Hamilton I. McCubbin, Howard Barnes, Andrea Larsen, Marla Muxen and Marc Wilson, *Families: What Makes Them Work* (Beverly Hills: Sage, 1983); also for a review see Everett L. Worthington, Jr., and Beverley G. Buston, "The Marriage Relationship During the Transition to Parenthood: A Review and a Model," *Journal of Family Issues* 7 (1986):443-73.

[16]Stuart, *Helping Couples Change.*

[17]Olson, McCubbin et al., *Families.*

[18]L. A. Peplau and D. Perlman, eds., *Loneliness: A Sourcebook of Current Theory, Research and Therapy* (N.Y.: John Wiley and Sons, 1982).

[19]John Gottman, *Empirical Investigations of Marriage* (N.Y.: Academic Press, 1979).

[20]William J. Doherty, "Cognitive Processes in Intimate Conflict: I. Extending Attribution Theory," *American Journal of Family Therapy* 9, no. 1 (1981):3-13.

[21]Ibid.

[22]See Stuart, *Helping Couples Change,* for a review.

[23]Ibid.

[24]Olson, McCubbin et al., *Families.*

Chapter 3: Principles of Marriage within the Family

[1]L. Von Bertalanffy, *General Systems Theory* (N.Y.: George Braziller, 1968).

[2]Jay Haley, *Leaving Home: The Therapy of Disturbed Young People* (N.Y.: McGraw-Hill, 1981).

[3]Prince, *The Marriage Covenant.*

[4]C. S. Lewis, *The Four Loves* (N.Y.: Harcourt Brace Jovanovich, 1960).

[5]Vanauken, *A Severe Mercy.*

[6]Erich Fromm, *The Art of Loving* (N.Y.: Bantam Books, 1956).

[7]There have been many fine writings on love. One of the best recent treatments has been Robert J. Sternberg, "A Triangular Theory of Love," *Psychological Bulletin* 93 (1986):119-35. Sternberg argues that love has three components: intimacy, passion and decision/commitment. He explains differences in relationships as being due to different balances among the components. For example, infatuated love is high on passion in the absence of intimacy and decision/commitment; romantic love combines passion and intimacy but lacks decision/commitment; companionate love combines intimacy and decision/commitment but lacks passion; and consummate love embodies all three components.

[8]Larry Christenson, *The Christian Family* (Minneapolis: Bethany Fellowship, 1970); Larry Christenson and Nordis Christenson, *The Christian Couple* (Minneapolis: Bethany House, 1977); Haley, *Problem Solving Therapy;* Salvador Minuchin, *Families and Family Therapy* (Cambridge, Mass.: Harvard University Press, 1974).

[9]Paul Evdokimov, *The Sacrament of Love.*

[10]Carol Gilligan, "In a Different Voice: Women's Conceptions of Self and Morality," *Harvard Educational Review* 47 (1977):481-517.

[11]For a discussion of the aims of marriage, see Paul Evdokimov, *The Sacrament of Love.*

[12]Cole Barton and James F. Alexander, "Functional Family Therapy," in *Handbook of Family Therapy,* ed. Gurman and Kniskern.

[13]Michael Argyle and Adrian Furnham, "Sources of Satisfaction and Conflict in Long-term Relationships," *Journal of Marriage and the Family* 45 (1983):481-93.

[14]Barton and Alexander, "Functional Family Therapy."

[15]This table is adapted and expanded from Barton and Alexander, "Functional Family Therapy."

[16]Haley, *Problem Solving Therapy.*

[17]Cloe Madanes, *Strategic Family Therapy* (San Francisco: Jossey-Bass, 1982).

[18]C. S. Lewis, *The Problem of Pain* (N.Y.: Macmillan, 1962), p. 93.

[19]Worthington, *When Someone Asks for Help;* Everett L. Worthington, Jr., *How to Help the Hurting* (Downers Grove, Ill.: InterVarsity Press, 1985).

[20]Christopher W. Camplair, Arnold L. Stolberg and Everett L. Worthington, Jr., "The Roles of Family, Friends, Clergy, and Other Professionals in Decisions about Child Custody after Divorce," *Journal of Pastoral Care* 41 (1987):259-68; Haley, *Problem Solving Therapy.*

[21]Gottman, *Empirical Investigations of Marriage.*

[22]Neil S. Jacobson, "Behavioral Marriage Therapy," in *Handbook of Family Therapy,* ed. Gurman and Kniskern.

[23]Peter Steinglass, "The Conceptualization of Marriage from a Systems Theory Perspective,"

in *Marriage and Marital Therapy: Psychoanalytic, Behavioral and Systems Theory Perspectives*, ed. Thomas J. Paolino and Barbara S. McCrady (N.Y.: Brunner/Mazel, 1978).

[24]Ibid.

[25]Everett L. Worthington, Jr., "Treatment of Families During Life Transitions: Matching Treatment to Family Response," *Family Process* 26 (1987):295-308.

Chapter 4: The Marriage throughout the Family Life Cycle

[1]R. W. White, "Motivation Reconsidered: The Concept of Competence," *Psychological Review* 66 (1959):297-333.

[2]Sigmund Freud, *Introductory Lectures on Psychoanalysis*, trans. James Strachey (N.Y.: W. W. Norton and Co., 1966; originally published 1917).

[3]Erik Erikson, *Childhood and Society*, 2nd ed. (N.Y.: W. W. Norton and Co., 1963).

[4]Jean Piaget, *Adaptation and Intelligence: Organic Selection and Phenocopy* (Chicago: University of Chicago Press, 1980).

[5]Lawrence Kohlberg, "Stage and Sequence: The Cognitive-Developmental Approach to Socialization," in *Handbook of Socialization: Theory and Research*, ed. D. A. Goslin (Boston: Houghton Mifflin, 1969).

[6]Evelyn M. Duvall, *Family Development*, 4th ed. (Philadelphia: J. P. Lippincott, 1971).

[7]Gail Sheehy, *Passages: Predictable Crises of Adult Life* (N.Y.: Dutton, 1976).

[8]Both stage and transition theories are needed to explain life. In the same way, theories that focus on both content and process are needed to explain counseling. I have described some of the dangers of concentrating on processes to the exclusion of content in a paper "The Impact of Psychology's Philosophy of Continual Change on Evangelical Christianity," *Journal of the American Scientific Affiliation* 36 (1984):3-8.

[9]Duvall, *Family Development*.

[10]Olson, McCubbin et al., *Families*.

[11]Joan Aldous, *Family Careers: Developmental Change in Families* (N.Y.: Wiley, 1978).

[12]Olson, McCubbin et al., *Families*.

[13]Gayla Margolin, "Behavior Exchange in Happy and Unhappy Marriages: A Family Cycle Perspective," *Behavior Therapy* 12 (1981):329-43.

[14]Olson, McCubbin et al., *Families*.

[15]I explain this model of response to transitions in more detail in two recent papers, "Treatment of Families During Life Transition," and Everett L. Worthington, Jr., and Beverley G. Buston, "The Marriage Relationship During the Transition to Parenthood."

[16]Dennis A. Bagarozzi and Paul Rauen, "Premarital Counseling: Appraisal and Status," *American Journal of Family Therapy* 9, no. 3 (1981):13-30.

[17]Luciano L'Abate, "Skills Training Programs for Couples and Families," in *Handbook of Family Therapy*, ed. Gurman and Kniskern.

[18]Spanier, "Married and Unmarried Cohabitation in the United States."

[19]Haley, *Strategies of Psychotherapy*.

[20]Everett L. Worthington, Jr., "A Preliminary Study of Guerin's Stages of Marital Conflict" (unpublished paper, Virginia Commonwealth University, 1985).

[21]John Gottman, C. Notarius, J. Gonso and H. Markman, *A Couple's Guide to Communication* (Champaign, Ill.: Research Press, 1976); Robert L. Weiss, "The Conceptualization of Marriage from a Behavioral Perspective," in *Marriage and Marital Therapy*, ed. Paolino and McCrady.

[22]Cherlin, *Marriage, Divorce, and Remarriage*.

[23]Olson, McCubbin et al., *Families*.

[24]For a review of theories and research and an application of my theorizing to the birth of

a first child, see Everett L. Worthington, Jr., and Beverley G. Buston, "The Marriage Relationship During the Transition to Parenthood."

[25]One author has called this "rattle fatigue," Linda Lewis Griffin, *Rattle Fatigue* (San Luis Obispo, Calif.: Impact, 1986).

[26]Cherlin, *Marriage, Divorce, and Remarriage.*

[27]Bill Cosby, *Fatherhood* (Garden City, N.Y.: Doubleday, 1986).

[28]Cherlin, *Marriage, Divorce, and Remarriage.*

[29]Olson et al., *Families.*

[30]Haley, *Leaving Home.*

[31]Haley, *Problem Solving Therapy.*

[32]Elizabeth A. Hill and Lorraine T. Dorfman, "Reaction of Housewives to the Retirement of Their Husbands," *Family Relations* 31 (1982):195-200.

[33]William H. Quinn, "Personal and Family Adjustment in Later Life," *Journal of Marriage and the Family* 45 (1983):57-73.

[34]Worthington, "Treatment of Families During Life Transitions."

Chapter 5: Overview of Counseling: Assessment, Intervention and Termination

[1]Gurman and Kniskern, "Family Therapy Outcome Research." This research finding has been questioned recently: Richard A. Wells and Vincent J. Gianetti, "Individual Marital Therapy: A Critical Reappraisal," *Family Process* 25 (1986):43-51; Alan S. Gurman and David P. Kniskern, "Commentary: Individual Marital Therapy—Have Reports of Your Death Been Somewhat Exaggerated?" *Family Process* 25 (1986):51-62; Richard A. Wells and Vincent J. Gianetti, "Rejoinder: Whither Marital Therapy?" *Family Process* 25 (1986):62-65.

[2]For a review, see Stuart, *Helping Couples Change*, pp. 139-148. There is other research that suggests that people continue to benefit through twenty counseling sessions. See Kenneth J. Howard, S. Mark Kopta, Merton S. Krause and David E. Orlinsky, "The Dose-Effect Relationship in Psychotherapy," *American Psychologist* 41 (1986):159-64.

[3]R. J. Bent, D. G. Putnam, D. J. Kiesler and S. Nowicki, "Expectancies and Characteristics of Outpatient Clinics Applying for Services at a Community Mental Health Facility," *Journal of Consulting and Clinical Psychology* 43 (1975):280; Gurman and Kniskern, "Family Therapy Outcome Research"; R. B. Slaney, "Therapist and Client Perceptions of Alternative Roles for the Facilitative Conditions," *Journal of Consulting and Clinical Psychology* 46 (1978):1146-7.

[4]Sigmund Freud, " 'Wild' Psychoanalysis," *Standard Edition* (London: Hogarth Press, 1957), 11:221-7.

[5]Gurman and Kniskern, "Family Therapy Outcome Research."

[6]For a review see Gurman and Kniskern, "Family Therapy Outcome Research."

[7]Worthington, *When Someone Asks for Help.*

Chapter 6: Joining the Marriage

[1]Everett L. Worthington, Jr., "Compliance with Therapeutic Homework Directives," *Journal of Counseling Psychology* 33 (1986):124-130; Glen A. Martin and Everett L. Worthington, Jr., "Behavioral Homework," in *Progress in Behavior Modification*, vol. 13, ed. M. Hersen, R. M. Eisler and P. M. Miller (N.Y.: Academic Press, 1982).

[2]Note that other counselors give such information although the content varies substantially from counselor to counselor. Liberman, E. G. Wheeler, L. A. J. M. deVisser, J. Kuehnel and T. Kuehnel, *Handbook of Marital Therapy: A Positive Approach to Helping Troubled Relationships* (N.Y.: Plenum Press, 1980), gives a short description of counseling (pp. 3-6 of client's workbook); Stuart, *Helping Couples Change*, provides a treatment contract (p. 170) and describes

an audiotape he uses. Norman Wright, in *Marital Counseling: A Biblical, Behavioral, Cognitive Approach* (N.Y.: Harper and Row, 1981), uses a warning about confidentiality during his assessment battery (p. 79).

[3]Frederick H. Kanfer, "Self-Management Methods," in *Helping People Change*, 2nd ed., ed. Fredrick H. Kanfer and Arnold P. Goldstein (N.Y.: Pergamon Press, 1980); Charles A. Kiesler, *The Psychology of Commitment: Experiments Linking Behavior to Belief* (N.Y.: Academic Press, 1971).

[4]Haley, *Problem Solving Therapy*.

[5]Steinglass, "The Conceptualization of Marriage from a Systems Theory Perspective."

[6]Haley, *Problem Solving Therapy*.

Chapter 7: Assessing the Marriage

[1]Stuart, *Helping Couples Change*, pp. 61-66; see also Neil S. Jacobson and Gayla Margolin, *Marital Therapy: Strategies Based on Social Learning and Behavior Exchange Principles* (N.Y.: Brunner/Mazel, 1979), pp. 69-72.

[2]These three ways of analyzing and understanding communication are elaborated in the appendix of this book under the section "Mental Research Institute Theory," which is one form of Marital Systems Theory.

[3]Richard B. Stuart, *Couple's Precounseling Inventory* (Champaign, Ill.: Research Press, 1983).

[4]Mark T. Schaefer and David H. Olson, "Assessing Intimacy: The PAIR Inventory," *Journal of Marital and Family Therapy* 7 (1981):47-60.

[5]Jacobson and Margolin, *Marital Therapy*, p. 90.

[6]Liberman et al., *Handbook of Marital Therapy*, p. 29.

[7]Ibid., pp. 33-34.

[8]H. J. Locke and K. M. Wallace, "Short Marital Adjustment and Prediction Tests: Their Reliability and Validity," *Marriage and Family Living* 21 (1959):251-55.

[9]Graham B. Spanier, "Measuring Dyadic Adjustment: New Scales for Assessing the Quality of Marriage and Similar Dyads," *Journal of Marriage and the Family* 38 (1976):15-28.

[10]Stuart, *Couple's Precounseling Inventory*.

[11]C. F. Sharpley and D. G. Cross, "A Psychometric Evaluation of the Spanier Dyadic Adjustment Scale," *Journal of Marriage and the Family* 44 (1982):739-41.

[12]Schaefer and Olson, *PAIR*.

[13]The appendix has a more detailed summary of Jay Haley's theory, which he outlines in *Strategies of Psychotherapy* (N.Y.: Grune and Stratton, 1963).

[14]Gurman and Kniskern, "Family Therapy Outcome Research."

[15]Haley, *Problem Solving Therapy*.

[16]Pauline Boss, "The Marital Relationship: Boundaries and Ambiguities," in *Stress and the Family, Vol. I: Coping with Normal Transitions*, ed. Hamilton McCubbin and Charles R. Figley (N.Y.: Brunner/Mazel, 1983).

[17]See Stuart, *Helping Couples Change*, pp. 194-6, and Jacobson and Margolin, *Marital Therapy*, pp. 158-61, for reviews.

[18]Gottman, *Empirical Investigations of Marriage*.

[19]Stuart, *Couple's Precounseling Inventory*.

[20]Olson, McCubbin et al., *Families*.

[21]Philip J. Guerin, Jr., "The Stages of Marital Conflict," *The Family* 10 (1982):15-26.

[22]Worthington, "Preliminary Study of Guerin's Stages."

[23]H. L. Rausch, W. A. Barry, R. K. Hertel, and M. A. Swain, *Communication, Conflict and Marriage* (San Francisco: Jossey-Bass, 1974).

[24]For several other examples, see Stuart, *Helping Couples Change*, pp. 287-90.

[25]Gurman and Kniskern, "Family Therapy Outcome Research."

[26]Charles A Kiesler, *The Psychology of Commitment: Experiments Linking Behavior to Belief* (N.Y.: Academic Press, 1971).

[27]Robert L. Weiss and M. Cerreto, "Marital Status Inventory" (unpublished manuscript, University of Oregon, 1975).

[28]James C. Coyne, "Strategic Marital Therapy for Depression," in *Clinical Handbook of Marital Therapy*, ed. Neil S. Jacobson and Alan S. Gurman (N.Y.: Guilford, 1986).

[29]Coyne, "Strategic Marital Therapy for Depression"; Steven R. H. Beach and K. Daniel O'Leary, "The Treatment of Depression Occurring in the Context of Marital Discord," *Behavior Therapy* 17 (1986):43-49; Neil S. Jacobson, "Marital Therapy and the Cognitive Behavioral Treatment of Depression," *Behavior Therapist* 7 (1984):143-7.

[30]Aaron T. Beck, A. John Rush, Brian F. Shaw and Gary Emery, *Cognitive Therapy of Depression* (N.Y.: Guilford, 1979).

[31]By attending individual counseling, the depressed spouse establishes an unwitting alliance with the other therapist that makes later marriage counseling more difficult.

[32]Haley, *Problem Solving Therapy* and *Leaving Home.*

[33]P. Guerin, "The Stages of Marital Conflict."

Chapter 8: Setting Goals

[1]Haley, *Problem Solving Therapy.*

[2]Cloe Madanes, *Behind the One-Way Mirror: Advances in the Practice of Strategic Therapy* (San Francisco: Jossey-Bass, 1984).

[3]M. B. Parloff, "The Narcissism of Small Differences—and Some Big Ones," *International Journal of Group Psychotherapy* 26 (1976):311-19.

[4]Alan S. Gurman, "Contemporary Marital Therapies: A Critique and Comparative Analysis of Psychoanalytic, Behavioral and Systems Theory Approaches," in *Marriage and Marital Therapy,* ed. Thomas J. Paolino, Jr., and Barbara S. McCrady (N.Y.: Brunner/Mazel, 1978), pp. 543, 545.

[5]Luke 16:10; 19:17.

[6]Jacobson and Margolin, *Marital Therapy.*

Chapter 9: Conducting Assessment and Feedback Sessions

[1]Suzanne Gascoyne Dougherty and Everett L. Worthington, Jr., "Preferences of Conservative and Moderate Christians for Four Christian Counselors' Treatment Plans for a Troubled Client," *Journal of Psychology and Theology* 10 (1982):346-54; Everett L. Worthington, Jr., and Suzanne Gascoyne, "Preferences of Christians and Non-Christians for Five Christian Counselors' Treatment Plans: A Partial Replication and Extension," *Journal of Psychology and Theology* 13 (1985):29-41.

[2]Mark T. Schaefer and David H. Olson, "Assessing Intimacy."

[3]Stuart, *Couple's Precounseling Inventory.*

Part 4: Changing Troubled Marriages

[1]Salvador Minuchin and H. Charles Fishman, *Techniques of Family Therapy* (Cambridge, Mass.: Harvard University Press, 1981).

Chapter 10: Promoting Change through Counseling

[1]Haley, *Problem Solving Therapy.*

[2]S. Duval and R. A. Wicklund, *A Theory of Objective Self-Awareness* (N.Y.: Academic Press, 1972).

Chapter 11: Changing Intimacy

[1]Lawrence Crabb, Jr., *The Marriage Builder* (Grand Rapids, Mich.: Zondervan, 1982).

[2]A. Y. Napier, "The Marriage of Families: Cross-generational Complementarity," *Family Process* 10 (1971):373-95; Carl A. Whitaker, "A Family Therapist Looks at Marital Therapy," in *Couples in Conflict: New Directions in Marital Therapy,* ed. Alan S. Gurman and D. G. Rice (N.Y.: Jason Aronson, 1975).

[3]Minuchin and Fishman, *Techniques of Family Therapy.*

[4]P. Guerin, "The Stages of Marital Conflict."

[5]Carlfred B. Broderick, *The Therapeutic Triangle* (Beverly Hills, Calif.: Sage, 1983).

[6]Napier, "The Marriage of Families"; Whitaker, "A Family Therapist Looks at Marital Therapy."

[7]Katherine B. Guerin, "Engaging the Emotional Distancer in Family Therapy," *The Family* 11 (1983):13-17.

[8]P. Guerin, "The Stages of Marital Conflict."

[9]Jacobson and Margolin, *Marital Therapy,* pp. 319-26.

[10]Roger Fisher and William Ury, *Getting To Yes: Negotiating Agreement Without Giving In* (N.Y.: Penguin, 1981).

[11]For a thorough discussion of reading aloud, see Sam Hamburg, "Reading Aloud as a First Homework Task in Marital Therapy," *Journal of Marital and Family Therapy* 9 (1983):81-87.

[12]Broderick, *The Therapeutic Triangle.*

[13]K. Guerin, "Engaging the Emotional Distancer in Family Therapy."

[14]Liberman et al., *Handbook of Marital Therapy.*

[15]Stuart, *Helping Couples Change,* pp. 197-207.

[16]Jacobson and Margolin, *Marital Therapy,* pp. 165-6.

[17]Gottman et al., *A Couple's Guide to Communication,* pp. 189-200.

[18]Ibid., pp. 152-4, 201-15.

[19]Fredrick A. DiBlasio, "The Royal Family Exercise: A Technique for Restructuring Family Interaction," *Journal of Marital and Family Therapy* 12 (1986): 195-7.

[20]Liberman et al., *Handbook of Marital Therapy,* pp. 75-81.

[21]Gottman et al., *A Couple's Guide to Communication,* pp. 145-6.

[22]Liberman et al., *Handbook of Marital Therapy,* pp. 83-86.

[23]Gottman et al., *A Couple's Guide to Communication.*

[24]See Frieda M. Stuart and D. Corydon Hammond, "Sex Therapy," in Stuart, *Helping Couples Change,* pp. 301-66.

[25]B. L. Greene, *A Clinical Approach to Marital Problems* (Springfield, Ill.: Charles C. Thomas, 1970).

[26]E. Frank, C. Anderson, and D. Rubenstein, "Frequency of Sexual Dysfunction in 'Normal' Couples," *New England Journal of Medicine* 299 (1978):111-5.

[27]J. S. Annon, *Behavioral Treatment of Sexual Problems* (N.Y.: Harper and Row, 1976).

[28]William H. Masters and Virginia E. Johnson, *Human Sexual Inadequacy* (Boston: Little, Brown and Co., 1970).

[29]Broderick, *The Therapeutic Triangle.*

[30]Jay Haley, *Ordeal Therapy* (San Francisco: Jossey-Bass, 1984).

Chapter 12: Changing Communication

[1]Jacobson and Margolin, *Marital Therapy;* Liberman et al., *Handbook of Marital Therapy;* Stuart, *Helping Couples Change.*

[2]Gottman, *Empirical Investigations of Marriage;* Gottman et al., *A Couple's Guide to Communication.*

[3]Virginia Satir, *Conjoint Family Therapy* (Palo Alto, Calif.: Science and Behavioral Books, 1967); Carlos E. Sluzki, "Marital Therapy from a Systems Theory Perspective," in *Marriage and Marital Therapy*, ed. Paolino and McCrady; Paul Watzlawick, Janet Bevelas and Don D. Jackson, *Pragmatics of Human Communication* (N.Y.: W. W. Norton and Co., 1967).

[4]Clifford J. Sager, *Marriage Contracts and Couple Therapy: Hidden Forces in Intimate Relationships* (N.Y.: Brunner/Mazel, 1976).

[5]Carol C. Nadelson, "Marital Therapy from a Psychoanalytic Perspective," in *Marriage and Marital Therapy*, ed. Paolino and McCrady.

[6]John W. Drakeford, *Games Husbands and Wives Play* (Nashville: Broadman Press, 1970).

[7]Haley, *Ordeal Therapy.*

[8]Broderick, *The Therapeutic Triangle.*

[9]Crabb, *The Marriage Builder.*

[10]Gottman, *Empirical Investigations of Marriage.*

[11]D. E. Kanouse and L. R. Hanson, *Negativity in Evaluations* (Morristown, N. J.: General Learning Press, 1972); G. Levinger and D. J. Senn, "Disclosure of Feelings in Marriage," *Merrill-Palmer Quarterly of Behavior and Development* 13 (1967):237-49; Gayla Margolin and Robert L. Weiss, "Comparative Evaluation of Therapeutic Components Associated with Behavioral Marital Treatment," *Journal of Consulting and Clinical Psychology* 46 (1978):1476-86: D. H. Sprenkle and David Olson, "Circumplex Model of Marital Systems: An Empirical Study of Clinic and Non-clinic Couples," *Journal of Marriage and Family Counseling* 4 (1978):59-74.

[12]For a review see Stuart, *Helping Couples Change*, pp. 216-21.

[13]Haley, *Problem Solving Therapy;* Murray Bowen, *Family Therapy in Clinical Practice* (N.Y.: Jason Aronson, 1978); Whitaker, "A Family Therapist Looks at Marital Therapy"; Satir, *Conjoint Family Therapy;* Leslie Greenberg and Susan Johnson, "Emotionally Focused Couples Therapy," in *Clinical Handbook*, ed. Jacobson and Gurman.

[14]Stuart, *Helping Couples Change*, pp. 266-71.

[15]Broderick, *The Therapeutic Triangle*, pp. 131-4.

[16]Ibid., p. 131.

[17]William James, *Psychology* (N.Y.: Fawcett, 1963, originally published 1892).

[18]John J. Sherwood and John C. Glidewell, "Planned Renegotiation: A Norm-Setting OD Intervention," in *Contemporary Organizational Development: Approaches and Interventions*, ed. Warner Burke (Washington, D.C.: NTL Learning Resources Corporation, 1972).

[19]Fred DiBlasio is now on the social work faculty at the University of Maryland, Baltimore.

[20]Gottman, *Empirical Investigations of Marriage.*

[21]Broderick, *The Therapeutic Triangle.*

[22]S. Miller, E. W. Nunnally and D. B. Wackman, *Alive and Aware: Improving Communication in Relationships* (Minneapolis: Interpersonal Communications Program, 1975).

[23]Thomas Gordon, *PET in Action: Inside PET Families, New Problems, Insights, and Solutions* (N.Y.: Nyden Books, 1976).

[24]R. M. Pierce, "Training in Interpersonal Communication Skills with Partners of Deteriorated Marriages," *The Family Coordinator* 22 (1973):223-7.

[25]Gottman et al., *A Couple's Guide to Communication.*

[26]Jacobson and Margolin, *Marital Therapy*, pp. 215-51.

[27]Liberman et al., *Handbook of Marital Therapy.*

[28]Stuart, *Helping Couples Change*, pp. 216-21.

[29]Bernard G. Guerney, Jr., *Relationship Enhancement* (San Francisco: Jossey-Bass, 1977).

[30]Edward R. Ross, Stanley B. Baker and Bernard G. Guerney, Jr., "Effectiveness of Relationship Enhancement Therapy Versus Therapist's Preferred Therapy" *American Journal of Family Therapy* 13, no. 1 (1985):11-21.

[31]Raymond J. Corsini, "The Marriage Conference," in Wright, *Marital Counseling,* pp. 337-51.

[32]Crabb, *The Marriage Builder.*

[33]Ibid., p. 76.

[34]Stuart, *Helping Couples Change,* pp. 370-71.

Chapter 13: Changing Conflict

[1]Claude Steiner, *Scripts People Live: Transactional Analysis of Life Scripts* (N.Y.: Bantam, 1975).

[2]Haley, *Problem Solving Therapy.*

[3]Fisher and Ury, *Getting To Yes.*

[4]Ibid.

[5]Jacobson and Margolin, *Marital Therapy,* pp. 215-51.

[6]Wright, *Marital Counseling,* pp. 247-84.

[7]John Strong, "A Marital Conflict Resolution Model Redefining Conflict to Achieve Intimacy," *Journal of Marriage and Family Counseling* (1975):269-76.

[8]Gayla Margolin, "Conjoint Marital Therapy to Enhance Anger Management and Reduce Spouse Abuse," *American Journal of Family Therapy* 7, no. 2 (1979):13-23.

[9]Gottman et al., *A Couple's Guide to Communication,* pp. 61-81.

[10]Stuart, *Helping Couples Change,* pp. 291-300.

[11]G. Bach and P. Wyden, *The Intimate Enemy: How To Fight Fair in Love and Marriage* (N.Y.: William Morrow and Co., 1969).

[12]Liberman et al., *Handbook of Marital Therapy,* pp. 81-83.

Chapter 14: Changing Hurt, Blame and Sin

[1]A substantial minority of couples collude to show a different pattern of blame—one spouse is identified as the scapegoat and the other as the angel. For most couples showing this pattern, blame is not as clearly one-sided as they present.

[2]S. Duval and R. A. Wicklund, *A Theory of Objective Self-Awareness* (N.Y.: Academic Press, 1972).

[3]Larry Christenson, "The Christian Family" (audiotape series).

[4]This transcript is actually my creation. Don worked with the couple under my supervision, but we did not save the tapes of the session. Thus, much of the session consists of ways that I have since used this intervention.

[5]Crabb, *The Marriage Builder.*

[6]Ibid., pp. 123-43.

[7]Ruth Carter Stapleton, *The Gift of Inner Healing* (Waco, Tex.: Word, 1976).

Chapter 15: Consolidating Changes

[1]Stuart, *Helping Couples Change,* p. 374.

[2]Ibid., pp. 374-6.

[3]Robert B. Zajonc, "Social Facilitation," *Science* 149 (July 16, 1965):269-74.

Chapter 17: Commitment of the Counselor

[1]Mary O'Leary Wiley, "Developmental Counseling Supervision: Person-Environment Congruency, Satisfaction, and Learning" (Paper presented at the annual meeting of the American Psychological Association, Washington, D.C., August, 1982).

[2]Charles Sheldon, *In His Steps* (Westwood, N.J.: Barbour, 1985).

[3]Charles Hibib Malik, *A Christian Critique of the University* (Downers Grove, Ill.: InterVarsity Press, 1981).

Appendix

[1]Jay L. Lebow, "Developing a Personal Integration in Family Therapy: Principles for Model Construction and Practice," *Journal of Marital and Family Therapy* 13 (1987):1-14.

[2]Hendrika Vande Kemp, "Mate Selection and Marriage: A Psychodynamic Family-Oriented Course," *Teaching of Psychology* 12 (1985):161-4; D. Klimek, *Beneath Mate Selection and Marriage: The Unconscious Motives in Human Pairing* (N.Y.: Van Nostrand Reinhold, 1979); William W. Meissner, "The Conceptualization of Marriage and Family Dynamics from a Psychoanalytic Perspective," in *Marriage and Marital Therapy,* ed. Paolino and McCrady.

[3]Jurg Willi, *Couples in Collusion* (N.Y.: Aronson, 1982); Jurg Willi, "The Concept of Collusion: A Combined Systemic-Psychodynamic Approach to Marital Therapy," *Family Process* 23 (1984):177-85; Jurg Willi, *Dynamics of Couple's Therapy* (N.Y.: Aronson, 1984).

[4]Carol C. Nadelson, "Marital Therapy from a Psychoanalytic Perspective," in *Marriage and Marital Therapy,* ed. Paolino and McCrady.

[5]Clifford J. Sager, *Marriage Contracts and Couple Therapy.*

[6]B. Ables and J. Brandsma, *Therapy for Couples* (San Francisco: Jossey-Bass, 1977).

[7]P. Martin, *A Marital Therapy Manual* (N.Y.: Brunner/Mazel, 1976).

[8]Gurman, "Contemporary Marital Therapies."

[9]Willi, *Couples in Collusion* and *Dynamics of Couple's Therapy.*

[10]H. V. Dicks, *Marital Tensions* (London: Routledge and Kegan Paul, 1967).

[11]James F. Framo, *Explorations in Marital and Family Therapy* (N.Y: Springer, 1982).

[12]K. Bannister and L. Pincus, *Shared Phantasy in Marital Problems: Therapy in Four-Person Relationship* (London: Tavistock Institute of Human Relations, 1965).

[13]Carol C. Nadelson, "Marital Therapy from a Psychoanalytic Perspective," in *Marriage and Marital Therapy,* ed. Paolino and McCrady.

[14]Christopher Dare, "Psychoanalytic Marital Therapy," in *Clinical Handbook,* ed. Jacobson and Gurman.

[15]Alan S. Gurman, "Integrative Marital Therapy: Toward the Development of an Interpersonal Approach," in *Forms of Brief Therapy,* ed. S. Budman (N.Y.: Guilford, 1981).

[16]Alan S. Gurman, "The Therapist's Personal Experience in Working with Divorcing Couples," *American Journal of Family Therapy* 11 (1983):75-79.

[17]Gurman, "Contemporary Marital Therapies."

[18]Papers advocating a new epistemology include Paul F. Dell, "Beyond Homeostasis: Toward a Concept of Coherence," *Family Process* 21 (1982):21-41; Paul F. Dell "In Search of Truth: On the Way to Clinical Epistemology," *Family Process* 21 (1982):407-14; Paul F. Dell, "Family Theory and the Epistemology of Humberto Maturana," in *The International Book of Family Therapy,* ed. Florence W. Kaslow (N.Y.: Brunner/Mazel, 1982); Alan S. Gurman, "Family Therapy Research and the 'New Epistemology,'" *Journal of Marital and Family Therapy* 9 (1983):227-34; Brad P. Keeney, *Aesthetics of Change* (N.Y.: Guilford, 1983). Some papers have been critical, such as J. C. Coyne, "A Brief Introduction to Epistobabble," *Family Therapy Networker* 6 (1982):27-28; J. C. Coyne, B. Denner, and D. C. Ransom, "Undressing the Fashionable Mind," *Family Process* 21 (1982):391-96; Paul F. Dell, "In Defense of 'Lineal Causality,'" *Family Process* 25 (1986):513-22.

[19]Murray Bowen, "The Use of Family Theory in Clinical Practice," *Comprehensive Psychiatry* 7 (1966):345-74; Murray Bowen, "Theory in the Practice of Psychotherapy," in *Family Therapy: Theory and Practice,* ed. Philip J. Guerin, Jr., (N.Y.: Gardner Press, 1976); Murray Bowen, "A Family Concept of Schizophrenia," in *The Etiology of Schizophrenia,* ed. Don D. Jackson (N.Y.: Basic Books, 1960); Murray Bowen, *Family Therapy in Clinical Practice* (N.Y.: Jason Aronson, 1978); Norman L. and Betty Byfield Paul, *A Marital Puzzle* (N.Y.: W. W. Norton and Co., 1975).

[20]Robert C. Aylmer, "Bowen Family Systems Marital Therapy," *Clinical Handbook,* ed. Jacobson

and Gurman.

21Thomas Fogarty, "The Distancer and the Pursuer," *The Family* 7 (1979):11-16.

22P. Guerin, "The Stages of Marital Conflict"; Katherine B. Guerin, "Engaging the Emotional Distancer in Family Therapy," *The Family* 11 (1983):13-17.

23Aylmer, "Bowen Therapy," pp. 117, 125.

24Gurman, "Contemporary Marital Therapies," p. 517.

25Even advocates such as Robert C. Aylmer, "Bowen Family Systems Marital Therapy," in *Clinical Handbook,* ed. Jacobson and Gurman, pp. 107-48, admit that research support is sparse. Some outcome research has been reported by Thomas Fogarty, "Emotional Climate in the Family and Therapy," in *The Best of the Family, 1973-1978* (New Rochelle, N.Y.: Center for Family Learning, 1979); S. Burden and J. Gilbert, "Stage III Marital Conflict," *The Family* 10 (1982):27-39.

26Gregory Bateson, *Steps to an Ecology of the Mind* (N.Y.: Ballantine, 1972).

27Paul Watzlawick, J. Weakland and R. Fisch, *Change: Principles of Problem Formation and Problem Resolution* (N.Y.: W. W. Norton and Co., 1974).

28Paul Watzlawick, Janet Bevelas and Don D. Jackson, *Pragmatics of Human Communication* (N.Y.: W. W. Norton and Co., 1967).

29Carlos E. Sluzki, "Marital Therapy from a Systems Theory Perspective," in *Marriage and Marital Therapy,* ed. Paolino and McCrady.

30Salvador Minuchin, *Families and Family Therapy* (Cambridge, Mass.: Harvard University Press, 1974); S. Minuchin, B. L. Rosman and L. Baker, *Psychosomatic Families: Anorexia Nervosa in Context* (Cambridge, Mass.: Harvard University Press, 1978); Minuchin and Fishman, *Techniques of Family Therapy.*

31Thomas C. Todd, "Structural-Strategic Marital Therapy," in Jacobson and Gurman, *Clinical Handbook,* pp. 72-74.

32Todd, "Structural-Strategic Marital Therapy"; Thomas C. Todd, "Strategic Approaches to Marital Stuckness," *Journal of Marital and Family Therapy* 10 (1984):373-9.

33Todd, "Structural-Strategic Marital Therapy," pp. 76-81.

34Harry Aponte and John M. VanDeusen, "Structural Family Therapy," in *Handbook of Family Therapy,* ed. Gurman and Kniskern.

35Todd, "Structural-Strategic Marital Therapy," pp. 101-3.

36Ibid., pp. 91-95.

37Jay Haley, *Strategies of Psychotherapy;* Jay Haley, *Problem Solving Therapy;* Jay Haley, *Leaving Home.*

38Cloe Madanes, *Strategic Family Therapy;* Cloe Madanes, *Behind the One-Way Mirror.*

39Haley, *Strategies of Psychotherapy.*

40Madanes, *Strategic Family Therapy,* p. 137.

41Madanes, *Strategic Family Therapy* and *Behind the One-Way Mirror.*

42Madanes, *Strategic Family Therapy,* pp. 32-33.

43Thomas C. Todd, "Structural-Strategic Marital Therapy." Also see Todd, "Strategic Approaches to Marital Stuckness."

44Jacobson and Margolin, *Marital Therapy,* Liberman et. al., *Handbook of Marital Therapy;* Stuart, *Helping Couples Change.*

45Neil S. Jacobson and Amy Holtzworth-Munroe, "Marital Therapy: A Social Learning-Cognitive Perspective," in *Clinical Handbook,* ed. Jacobson and Gurman.

46Jacobson and Holtzworth-Munroe, "Marital Therapy: A Social Learning-Cognitive Perspective," p. 29.

47Jacobson and Margolin, *Marital Therapy.*

48Liberman, et al., *Handbook of Marital Therapy.*

[49]Stuart, *Helping Couples Change.*

[50]Neil S. Jacobson and William C. Follette, "Clinical Significance of Improvement Resulting from Two Behavioral Marital Therapy Components," *Behavior Therapy* 16 (1985):249-62.

[51]Jacobson and Holtzworth-Munroe, "Marital Therapy: A Social Learning-Cognitive Perspective," p. 59.

[52]Donald H. Baucom and Jeffery A. Hoffman, "The Effectiveness of Marital Therapy: Current Status and Application to the Clinical Setting," in *Clinical Handbook,* ed. Jacobson and Gurman, pp. 597-608.

[53]Jacobson and Holtzworth-Munroe, "Marital Therapy: A Social Learning-Cognitive Perspective."

[54]Alan S. Gurman, "Contemporary Marital Therapies."

[55]Note that Gurman's criticisms are less true today than they were in 1978 (when he made them) because the therapy has changed toward more complexity in the ensuing years.

[56]Robert L. Weiss, "The Conceptualization of Marriage from a Behavioral Perspective."

[57]Ibid., p. 190.

[58]Erik E. Filsinger and Margaret R. Wilson, "Religiosity, Socioeconomic Rewards, and Family Development: Predictors of Marital Adjustment," *Journal of Marriage and the Family* 46 (1984):663-70; Richard A. Hunt and Morton B. King, "Religiosity and Marriage," *Journal for the Scientific Study of Religion* 17 (1978):399-406.

[59]Rodger K. Bufford, "On the Possibility of Integration: Response to McKeown's Characterization of Behavioral Psychology as Myth," *Journal of Psychology and Theology* 9 (1981):21-25; Rodger K. Bufford, "Behavioral Views of Punishment: A Critique," *Journal of the American Scientific Affiliation* 34 (1982):135-44; Bruce McKeown, "Myth and Its Denial in a Secular Age: The Case of Behaviorist Psychology," *Journal of Psychology and Theology* 9 (1981):12-20.

[60]C. S. Lewis, "The Weight of Glory," in *The Weight of Glory and Other Addresses* (Grand Rapids, Mich.: Eerdmans, 1949).

[61]Donald H. Baucom and Gregory W. Lester, "The Usefulness of Cognitive Restructuring as an Adjunct to Behavioral Marital Therapy," *Behavior Therapy* 7 (1986):385-403.

[62]Norman Epstein, "Cognitive Therapy with Couples," *American Journal of Family Therapy* 10 (1982):5-16.

[63]Albert Ellis, *Reason and Emotion in Psychotherapy* (N.Y.: Lyle Stuart, 1962).

[64]Aaron T. Beck, *Cognitive Therapy and the Emotional Disorders* (N.Y.: International Universities Press, 1976).

[65]Donald Meichenbaum, *Cognitive-Behavior Modification: An Integrative Approach* (N.Y.: Plenum, 1977).

[66]Sager, *Marriage Contracts and Couple Therapy.*

[67]Wright, *Marital Counseling.*

[68]Baucom and Lester, "Cognitive Restructuring."

Subject Index

adolescence, adolescent, teen *35, 53, 64, 67, 68, 69, 77-81, 83, 89, 176, 183, 184, 268*

alcoholism *53, 146, 147, 161, 162, 183, 184, 185, 189, 211, 288, 325*

analogies *116, 303, 306, 313*

argue, argument *225, 228, 239, 251, 313, 321;* alternatives to *219;* children, displacement onto, impact upon *81, 268;* communication techniques used poorly in *139, 143, 145, 146, 184, 247, 259, 265, 283, 341, 342;* counselor's assessment of, *272, 273, 276;* effectance problems, due to *91, 148, 280;* emotional intensity of *179;* engagement, during *177;* frequency of *177;* habitual behavior pattern *45, 148, 269;* methods of *347, 353, 355;* as motivation for seeking help *97;* over rule-making *54;* over sexual dissatisfaction *134, 235;* relatives' impact upon *180;* resistance to counselor's ideas, limits, goals *135, 140, 159, 167, 168, 246, 261, 262;* role play of during counseling sessions *235, 249, 269, 271, 278, 281;* stages defined *149, 150;* taping of *113, 128, 129, 191, 244, 278, 284*

assess, assessment *93, 117, 311, 312, 313;* characteristics of, objectives in *29, 45, 59, 87, 91, 125-64, 173, 216, 278;* clients' reaction to *105, 108;* of counseling by couple *320;* counselor's own personality traits, and *214;* counselor's report, effect on *113, 118, 174, 175, 176;* in goal setting *166, 168-69, 171, 172, 175, 185, 217, 323, 348;* intervention during *314;* and positive joining *114, 124;* session guidelines *94, 95, 100, 101, 103, 187-95, 200, 205, 348;* as stage of marriage counseling *104, 105, 108, 109, 113, 118, 119, 120, 122, 125-64, 173, 174, 177, 179, 180, 183, 185, 186, 187-95, 199, 236, 245, 246, 268, 274, 321, 336, 340, 342, 348, 354, 355, 356*

attributions of causality *43, 44, 126, 153, 177, 233, 254, 269,* *284, 285, 288, 289, 301, 307, 315, 316, 320, 342, 349, 351, 352, 353*

audiotape *128-29, 140, 191, 202, 244, 262, 263, 284, 290, 353*

authority *49, 126, 159, 162, 185, 342, 349*

behavior *31, 58, 71, 92, 116;* affected by environmental events, structures, transitions *30, 45, 46, 127, 137, 179, 200, 205, 308;* affecting relationships *55, 106, 123, 135, 211, 261, 278, 279, 281, 290, 297, 299, 308, 348;* agreement upon, in marriage *75;* approaches to marriage therapy *334, 336, 337, 338, 339, 345, 346, 347, 348, 349, 350, 351, 352, 353, 354, 355, 356;* blaming for *44, 126, 184, 206, 290, 353;* "caring days" *348;* cognitive-behavioral theory *208;* cognitive events, changing cognitive structures *29, 302;* communication, poor, influence upon *138, 153, 279, 338;* communication training *349;* counselor's, in positive joining, influencing *114, 248, 257, 282, 304, 317, 339, 345;* defined by alcohol/drug problems, AA techniques *161, 288;* defined by family of origin *74, 256, 334;* distracting forms of *96, 97;* and effectance *54;* evidence of problems *128;* insight into through role-reversal, role play, structural feedback *203, 249, 281;* monitoring *130;* patterns, building new *117, 201, 204, 206, 226, 229, 237, 245, 253, 254, 266, 267, 280, 290, 291, 299, 301, 309, 332;* therapy principles consistence with Scripture *350;* understanding context of *29, 113, 203, 204, 332;* value of homework in affecting *204, 205, 245, 248*

behavioral marriage therapy *10, 19, 77, 170, 239, 329, 331, 332, 333, 334, 336, 337, 343, 344, 347-51, 354, 355, 356*

behavioral monitoring *130, 348*

bitterness *56, 91, 102, 152, 153, 154, 162, 164, 214, 253, 315, 354*

blame *20, 26, 28, 44, 49, 55, 56, 58, 94, 102, 112, 120, 125, 126,* *127, 128, 146, 152-53, 164, 165, 167, 184, 189, 194, 197, 200, 201, 208, 216, 231, 276, 280, 284, 285, 287-98, 323, 351, 352, 353*

booster sessions *307, 349*

boundaries *134-35, 137, 164, 171, 212, 214, 340*

career, work, job *30, 33, 61, 63-66, 75, 77, 78, 79, 80, 82, 86, 88, 97, 132, 133, 134, 143, 144, 158, 210, 211, 212, 213, 220, 221, 223, 224, 257, 270, 283, 291, 294, 309, 312, 336, 340, 342*

caring days *226, 348, 356*

case studies, illustrations, assessing intimacy (John and Mo) *132-34;* the assessment session *188-94;* children caught in crossfire *80-81;* complementing behaviors—intimacy vs. distancing *211;* the compromise (George and Susan) *246-47;* distancer-pursuer (Roy and Sally) *220-21;* effects of counselor's bad assumptions on therapy *100-101;* engaging the emotional distancer *214;* expectations of counselor *100;* finding creative solutions (Maria and Carlos) *219;* goal-setting to reduce conflict *169;* grandparents and grandchild vs. parent *83-84;* husband unaware of difficulties (Tim and Sue) *177-80;* inattention to the client *248;* intimacy through shared housework (John and Marie) *224;* little intimacy (Ray and Cheryl) *180-82;* marriage vs. dating relationships *73;* metaphors in therapy (Danny and Elizabeth) *252;* negative communication patterns (James and Hedda) *142, 147;* overinvolved couple (Laura and Rob) *223-24;* reframing conflict (Dick and Jeannie) *220;* the reluctant spouse *118-23;* roles in communication (Judy and Stan) *136;* severe conflict (Win and Betty) *183-85;* too much communication (David and Margaret) *139-40*

challenge *107, 109, 141, 168, 174, 228, 291, 303, 325, 326, 341, 342, 343, 353*

change *130, 164, 197, 209, 214, 287;* areas and theory of *199-*

Author Index